Dialogue as a Means
of Collective Communication

Dialogue as a Means of Collective Communication

Edited by

Bela Banathy

Late of Saybrook Graduate School and Research Center
San Francisco, California and
International Systems Institute
Carmel, California

and

Patrick M. Jenlink

Stephen F. Austin State University
Nacogdoches, Texas and
International Systems Institute
Carmel, California

Kluwer Academic / Plenum Publishers
New York, Boston, Dordrecht, London, Moscow

ISBN 0-306-48689-X
eISBN 0-306-48690-3

©2005 Kluwer Academic / Plenum Publishers, New York
233 Spring Street, New York, New York 10013

http://www.wkap.nl/

10 9 8 7 6 5 4 3 2 1

A C.I.P. record for this book is available from the Library of Congress

Memoriam—Bela H. Banathy

Originally, this compendium began as a conversation between Bela and myself, and was shaped by our belief that dialogue offered a means for humankind to collectively work together toward a future society that was more civil, and hopefully more concerned with its own evolution. Bela and I visited, frequently, about the importance of dialogue as a collective means of communication that would enable a transcendence of existing social systems, a means of communicative action that would animate a self-guided evolution of humankind through the creation of new systems. We hoped that our species, *Homo Sapien Sapien*, would overcome its destructive capabilities and foster new creative possibilities for the future generations of humankind that would follow.

Unfortunately, Bela was not to see the compendium in its completed form. On September 4, 2003 Bela passed away, leaving the world a better place for his presence, and our lives richer for having known him.

Bela found inspiration in the works of William Blake (1991), in particular the illuminated work *Jerusalem: The Emancipation of the Great Albion*. It is from this work that I quote the following passage, in memory of Bela. I believe it illuminates his life and his work as a systems scholar and practitioner (Blake, pl. 10, l. 20):

> I must create a system,
> Or be enslaved by another Man's;
> I will not Reason and Compare,
> My business is to Create.

Bela's life was one of creating. He was a source of great energy in the ebb and flow of humanity. Bela was a systems scholar and practitioner concerned with creating systems that would make the world a better place for humankind. Bela's life was lived with purpose, and his legacy of systems knowledge and ideals serve to guide the work ahead for all of us that care for the future of humankind. He was my teacher, my mentor, and above all else, he was my friend. He will be missed.

Patrick M. Jenlink
April, 2004

Dedication

In Remembrance of David Bohm
and
In Service of the Next Generations Concerned for the Future

.

Preface

We are, as a social species–*Homo Sapien Sapien*–communicative by nature. Communication presupposes community, which in turn means a communion of consciousness of the persons in the community. That we are also sentient beings places within our reach the capability to be equally creative and destructive, whether through discourse or social action. In our evolution as a species we have demonstrated our capacity for terrible acts of destruction—the most horrible of nightmares. September 11, 2001 stands as an example of such nightmares. Yet, as a species, we have demonstrated our capacity to come together in times of great tragedy as a community—to communicate in such ways as to create solutions and foster new hopes for the future.

When we consider, in relation to being a species characterized as communicative and sentient, that we are also an extremely diverse species, we are filled with great potentials.

The fact that we display great diversity–that we are different culturally, linguistically, ethnically, politically–figures largely into our potential for creative actions, and holds promise for present and future generations to overcome the destructive nature of our species that all-to-often marks our evolutionary history. The realization of our potentialities as a species, rests in no small measure, in our capacity for cultural creativity and in our capacity to achieve new levels of consciousness.

David Bohm, theoretical physicists, and Martin Buber, religious and social philosopher, stand as prominent figures who understood that evolving consciousness and creating culture resides in our capacity to foster and sustain dialogue—genuine dialogue concerned with the generative and creative capacity of our species. Genuine dialogue is a turning *together* in conversation, to create a social space–a *betweenness*–in which personal opinions and ideologies are suspended and wherein persons conjoin in community to search for new meaning and understanding,

It is in the recognition that our species is ultimately responsible for its future that we also recognize the necessity for fostering genuine dialogue if we are to embrace our responsibilities in the global society and for our future. It is incumbent of us to create conditions favorable for dialogue, for us to understand each other, for social justice, equity, and tolerance to become markers that define our species. That such genuine dialogue is possible–for each person to stand where the other is standing–will require much of our species.

In this Compendium, the contributing authors set forth their ideas, experiences, and perspectives as the path of a *learning journey*—a journey of new meaning, of new understanding, and of becoming self-aware of dialogue as culture creating and consciousness evolving.

The Compendium is organized by five themes. *Section I* examines foundational perspectives of conversation. This examination helps to create a foundation for a deeper study of the emergent and salient aspects of conversation in relation to social creativity and the evolution of human consciousness. Authors examine dialogue from philosophical, cultural, spiritual, and historical perspectives. *Sections II-IV* examine the philosophical and theoretical perspectives as well as methodological ideas related to conversation. These writings also explore different modalities of conversation and the application of design conversation within and across various types of design settings and human experiences. Also examined is the importance of capacity building for engaging in conversation, as well as providing insight into how to build capacity and develop the capability of the human system for conversation. In *Section V* the editors reflectively examine the contributions to the book and present their own thoughts on the next steps in the evolutionary relationship of conversation, human systems, and systems design.

Contents

SECTION III: MODALITIES OF CONVERSATION

SECTION IV: PRACTICAL APPLICATIONS OF CONVERSATION

INTRODUCTION

Chapter 1

DIALOGUE
Conversation as Culture Creating and
Consciousness Evolving

PATRICK M. JENLINK*[#] and BELA H. BANATHY[#]**
Stephen F. Austin State University*, International Systems Institute[#],
Saybrook Graduate School and Research Center**

1.   INTRODUCTION

In this opening chapter, first, we review the purpose of this Compendium and provide an overview of the *learning journey* presented by the editors and authors. The chapter is presented in two parts. *Part I* begins with an exploration of the meaning of dialogue. Then, we examine the relationship of conversation to culture creating and consciousness evolving within society. Dialogue is introduced as a form of conversation that enables our species to connect within and across cultures, forming and sustaining communities through intersubjectivity and cultural creativity. The chapter will examine why dialogue is important as well as how dialogue may be used to create a collective evolutionary consciousness essential to designing our own future. *Part II* overviews how the compendium is framed into five themes, which present a reflective context for exploring dialogue conversation.

2.   AN OVERVIEW OF THE LEARNING JOURNEY

A two-pronged *purpose* has guided the development of this Compendium. Our first purpose was to introduce the learner to dialogue conversation as the means of collective communication for which we must be both students and consumers as members of a changing, global society. The second purpose of the book was to demonstrate–and develop an appreciation for–the empowering and liberating quality of conversation as a medium and means of communication for cultural creativity and societal change. The Compendium offers a rich set of perspectives and experiences

Dialogue as a Means of Collective Communication, Edited by Banathy and Jenlink
Kluwer Academic/Plenum Publishers, New York 2005

related to dialogue as a culture creating and consciousness evolving means of collective communication.

The path of the *learning journey* begins by exploring historical perspectives of dialogue as means of collective conversation. This exploration sets in place a foundation for grounding the examination of the emergent and developing characteristics of disciplined conversation. In the main body of the text, we explore the philosophical and theoretical perspectives that are sources of methodological ideas and practices of dialogue. We examine different modalities of applications in a variety of settings, and provide examples of dialogue events. We also provide ideas and programs that serve capacity building that enable individuals, groups, and communities to initiate, engage in, and guide the disciplined inquiry of dialogue.

In *Part One*, we explore the meaning of dialogue and its role in culture creating and consciousness evolving. First, we examine the meaning of dialogue, exploring the etymological roots and historical origins. Then we explore dialogue as a method and means of collective communication in the larger context of culture and society. In *Part Two*, we provide an overview of the five organizing themes for the Compendium, and briefly examine author contributions that set the path for our *learning journey* towards dialogue as a collective means of communication.

PART ONE: DIALOGUE AS CULTURE CREATING AND CONSCIOUSNESS EVOLVING

In this *Part*, first, we explore the etymology of dialogue. Then we explore dialogue as a genuine, relational means of collective communication. Dialogue as cultural creating and consciousness evolving is then examined in relation to transforming society. Two figures are prominent to our work with dialogue, David Bohm, theoretical physicists, and Martin Buber, religious and social philosopher. While other individuals have helped to shape our understandings of dialogue, Bohm and Buber are at the forefront of our thinking.

3.   THE MEANING OF DIALOGUE

Dialogue is a culturally and historically specific way of social discourse accomplished through the use of language and verbal transactions. It suggests community, mutuality, and authenticity–an egalitarian relationship. So understood, dialogue provides a meeting ground, *communitas*, and manifests itself in a variety of spontaneous and ritual modes of discourse in which nature and structure meet (Turner, 1969, p. 140). In this section we examine the meaning and nature of dialogue.

3.1   Etymological Meaning of Dialogue

Etymologically, dialogue means a speech across, between, though two or more people. Dialogue comes from the Greek *dialogos*. *Dia* is a preposition that means "through," "between," "across," "by," and "of." *Dia* does not mean two, as in two separate entities; rather, *dia* suggests a "passing through" as in diagnosis "thoroughly" or "completely." Logos comes from *legein*, "to speak" Crapanzano (1990, p. 276). Logos means "the word," or more specifically, the "meaning of the word," created by "passing through," as in the use of language as a symbolic tool and conversation as a medium. As Onians (1951) points out, *logos* may also mean thought as well as speech–thought that is conceived individually or collectively, and/or expressed materially. Consequently, dialogue is a sharing through language as a cultural symbolic tool and conversation as a medium for sharing.

The picture or image that this derivation suggests is a "stream of meaning" flowing among and through us and between us. Etymologically, dialogue connotes a flow of meaning through two or more individuals as a collective, and out of which may emerge new understandings (Bohm, 1996, p. 6).

3.2   Dialogue as Collective Communication

Dialogue may be transformative or generative in nature, as well as strategic. That is, it may be seen as transformative in relation to the creative actions of individuals through collective communication, the sharing of thought and knowledge of individuals as the generative materials to transform existing beliefs as well as create new innovations and cultural artifacts. It may also be seen as strategic or positional in relation to implementing an innovation or introducing new thoughts and knowledge into a cultural setting. In collective communication, as Bohm (1998) explains, the basic idea is to suspend opinions as well as judgement of what others share, trying to understand.

3.3   Dialogue as Relational

Dialogue is not something we do or use; it is a relation that we create and sustain by conjoint agreement and through shared discourse. As a relation, dialogue is characterized by inclusion and a reciprocal sharing, such that the individual's become one in and with each other. Gadamer (1976) is instructive in understanding the nature of dialogical relations:

> when one enters into a dialogue with another person and then is carried further by the dialogue, it is no longer the will of the individual person, holding itself back or exposing itself, that is determinative. Rather, the law of the subject-matter is at issue in

the dialogue and elicits statement and counter-statement. And in the end plays them into each other....We say that we 'conduct' a conversation, but the more fundamental a conversation is, the less its conduct lies within the will of either partner....Rather, it is more correct to say that we fall into conversation, or event that we become involved in it. (Gadamer, H-G, 1976, p. 66)

A dialogical relation will show itself in authentic discourse, but is not composed of this entirely or only. Shared silence as well as shared speech forms the relation that connects individuals through dialogue. Once created, the dialogical relation continues, even when the individuals are separated by space or distance, "as the continual potential presence of the one to the other, as an unexpressed intercourse" (Buber, 1965, p. 97). The fundamental tension underlying a dialogical relation is that participants need to be similar enough to share in genuine communication, but different enough to make it worthwhile (Burbules & Rice, 1991).

3.4   Dialogue as Genuine Discourse

Dialogue, wherein each individual conjoins with the others to share through conversation, suspending personal opinions and judgements to listen deeply, "derives its genuineness only from the consciousness of the element of inclusion" (Buber, 1965, p. 97). In this expression of genuine dialogue, each participant regards the "other" as the person he is, becoming aware of the "other" and that s/he is different from the person. In such relation through dialogue, one accepts the "other" setting aside the need to sway by opinion or judge the "other" so as to form a reciprocal relation that is genuine on both an individual and collective level. Buber explains,

> There is genuine dialogue–no matter whether spoken or silent–where each of the participants really has in mind the other or others in their present and particular being and turns to them with the intention of establishing a living mutual relation between himself and them. (1965, p. 19)

The genuineness of dialogic discourse resides in creating and sustaining a "living mutual relation" that enables all participants to share a common space, a community of creative possibilities. Fostering genuine dialogue requires that participants create what Buber (19988, 1992) referred to as the interhuman–a social sphere in which person meets person. Bohm (1998) suggests that one of the first steps toward dialogue is for people to engage in dialogue together, without trying to solve any problem" (Bohm, 1998, p. 117). If we are to be genuine in our dialogue, we must first come together and create a social sphere, without concern for outside problems. In the next section, we examine dialogue as culture creating, identifying what is problematic in culture and the conditions necessary to cultural creativity.

4. DIALOGUE AS CULTURE CREATING

Dialogue, as a connection between the subjective individual consciousness and the socially institutionalized structure of society, offers the opportunity to understand the influence of existing cultures and the differences that distinguish one culture from another, and a people in one culture from the people of other cultures. Equally important, dialogue offers the possibility of creating new cultures across differences, using difference as the very energy that fires social and cultural creativity.

4.1 Dialogue and Culture–Implicate Order

Implicate order, or the enfoldment of everything into everything, explains Bohm (1998) in his book *On Creativity*, means that everything is internally related. Applying this metaphor to culture, there are patterns of values, beliefs, and assumptions implicate within cultures, patterns enfolded one into another. Equally important, enfolded into a single pattern is the whole, such that, like a hologram, the whole image–in our case cultural image–is enfolded into specific elements or patterns. As such, within culture is language or symbol systems that enable individuals to communicate within and across communities of difference, and which transmit the implicate order of a culture.

Dialogue begins with the belief that there is implicate individual wholeness that can be made explicate (Bohm, 1996). Dialogue consists of meaning that requires a shared "field" of experience and attention. Dialogue, as a medium for making the implicate order explicate, is conceived "as part of the process of the coming into being of meaning" (Gadamer, 1982, p. 147). Unfolding that which had been enfolded in culture and the individual consciousness of members of a culture begins with sharing meaning through discourse.

4.2 Dialogue and Cultural Creativity

When conducted dialogically, the direct relation between person and person within society fosters social creativity and it can "generate frameworks of common discourse between different, often disparate, sectors of society" (Buber, 1992, p. 16).

Understanding the nature of intersubjectivity in the human experience, and its relation to cultural creativity–the conditions necessary to social and cultural creativity–for Buber (1992), centers on authentic intersubjective social relations. He believed that these conditions exist to some extent in all cultures but that their fullest development and fulfillment rarely occurred. One might interpret Buber's interest in dialogue as a concern for how to mediate the problematic nature of culture that, for him, made cultural creativity a rare experience.

The problematics of human creativity in general, and cultural creativity in particular, can be found in Buber's (1992) ideas on the essence of culture. He conceived of culture as constructed around several poles, around several contradictions, from which he signaled out four basic components of duality or polarity in culture:

a)...There are two aspects of culture: creativity and tradition. On the one hand, all cultural life is based on personal creative production. Culture derives its vitality from the plethora of creativity, and when in any culture the flow of innovation ceases, its power is annulled, since that culture lacks any power if it does not have the power of innovation, the power of constant renewal: or self-renewal. But on the other hand, none of these productions succeeds in developing a social character; that is to say, does not become an integral part of that culture, unless it enters into the process of give and take; if is does not become material which can conveniently be passed on and be joined to all productions created throughout the generations to become something paradoxical: a form of generality. There are two basic sides to culture: revolution and conservatism, i.e., initiative and routine existence. Each one alone has great historical value, but only the two together have cultural value.

b) ...Cultural activity is characterized by a basic duality. First of all it gives to life itself form and permanence, restriction, and elaboration, molds people's behavior, raises the standard of their association and develops social relationships through selection and concentration. Secondly, it creates over and above life, or at least beyond it, a world of matter in the same way as nature is a world of matter, a world of beings independent of each other, like creatures of nature which are bound to each other by invisible bonds: this is the second world, the unique world of mankind...

c) there are two basic elements related to the crystallization of culture: the development of form and the development of awareness. Both of them, form and awareness, exist within man's experience as a matter of potential. Form grows, as it were, of its own volition...but awareness can also grow, as it were, within us on its own, but it remains within us and does not wish to leave us....

d) every culture that is in a state of full development tends to produce a number of cultural types and areas which are totally independent, each of which has its own domain and immutable laws, that is, it has a tendency to pluralism of spiritual spheres...(The Face of Man, pp. 383-386; in Hebrew). (Eisenstadt, 1992, pp. 9-10)

While Buber believed that the tensions giving rise to the problematics of cultural creativity were necessary, he also believed that the central characteristic of situations conducive to creativity is the existence of dialogue, a communicative openness. For Buber, dialogue was both an intersubjective relation between an individual and others, and between an individual and God. It is in these intersubjective relations that the development or "crystallization of a common discourse could occur, and it...is essential for holding a society together, for meeting conditions conducive to cultural creativity and for counteracting the possible stagnative or destructive forces that are endemic in any society" (Eisenstadt, 1992, p. 11).

5. DIALOGUE AS CONSCIOUSNESS EVOLVING

David Bohm (1998) explains that the basic idea of dialogue is to be able to communicate while suspending personal opinions, not trying to convince the "other" but simply trying to understand. This is an important step to understanding how consciousness evolves through discourse. The realization on the part of each person that s/he has a perspective–the evolution of perspectival consciousness. The evolution of conscious awareness of perspective, through dialogue, begins with all individuals' capacity to "perceive all the meanings of everybody together....That will create a new frame of mind in which there is a common consciousness....a kind of implicate order, where each one enfolds the whole consciousness" (Bohm, 1998, p. 118).

5.1 Consciousness as Implicate Order

David Bohm, in his book *Wholeness and the Implicate Order* (1995), is helpful in understanding consciousness as implicate order, an enfoldment of thought, perspective, worldview. An individual's consciousness is an enfoldment of many thoughts and perspectives over time, creating implicate patterns or relationships. Not dissimilarly, a collective or societal consciousness such as that represented in a particular culture or people may also be understood as being implicate order. When one individual's thought or perspective is enfolded on that of another person's, then patterns of thought or perspective become enfolded into the cultural fabric. Implicate in these patterns are the values, beliefs, and assumptions of individuals within the culture, and likewise these patterns are implicate in each individual.

Language, as an artifact of a culture and its people, is an enfoldment of symbols and meanings that create an implicate order. Meaning enfolded in the words and structure of language creates implicate patterns of meaning through the use of language to generate thought and action. As individuals engage in communicative relationships, the meaning implicate in language is unfolded in the social or cultural groups through the discursive interactions. As meaning unfolds through communication, the implicate nature of meaning is made explicit, creating opportunity for the participants to generate common meaning through sharing. Such sharing moves from the individual consciousness level to a collective consciousness level. Thus, as Bohm and Peat (1987) note, "there is an internal relationship of human beings to each other, and to society as a whole" (p. 185). What is seen in society–the explicate order–on one level is seen as enfoldment inseparably within the consciousness of each individual member in the society. Therein, implicate order "is the *content* of the culture, which extends into the consciousness of each person" (p. 185). Consciousness as implicate order, is made explicit by engaging in the unfolding of what individuals, culture, and society has enfolded. Making the implicate explicit requires a evolving of consciousness–a dialogic consciousness.

5.2   Dialogic Consciousness

Dialogic consciousness refers to a "way of being in the world, that is characterized by what Schachtel (1959) calls "allocentric" knowing…a way of knowing that is concerned with both *the totality of the act of interest* and with the "participation of the total person" (of the knower) (p. 225). It requires an attitude of profound openness and receptivity–a trust relation. It involves, Schachtel (p. 181) explains, a temporary eclipse of all the individual's egocentric thoughts and strivings, of all preoccupations with self, and self-esteem. For Bohm (1996, 1998), this is the suspension of personal opinion and desire to judge the opinion of the "other." For Buber (1992), this is the creation of an authentic intersubjective relation made possible by genuine dialogue.

Dialogic consciousness is where one is turned toward other (human or nonhuman) "*without* being in need of it" or wanting to appropriate it to achieve something. The latter would point to preoccupations with self that antedate the experience of "I" as separate from the world and block full perception of other (p. 177). Such participatory consciousness is possible through genuine dialogue wherein the participants yield to the will of the "mutual living relation," and create a shared collective consciousness.

The importance of dialogic consciousness to culture creativity rests in genuine dialogue that gives way to cultural creativity. Importantly, evolving to a level of dialogic consciousness means recognizing that differences within and across cultures are implicate in the individual consciousness of each participant. It also means recognizing that differences translate into thought, which "may establish distinctions," but the distance "*between* those distinctions–between people" is mediated by dialogic consciousness (Bohm, 1996, p. 89). As Burbules and Rice (1991), explain, "if dialogue across difference is to succeed, sensitivity is required to the various kinds of diversity one may encounter" (p. 407).

5.3 Dialogic Consciousness and Differences

At the present there are great differences that define society, and many of these appear non-negotiable. Differences in perspective–Buber's dualisms–contribute to the problematic nature of culture and therein limit the potential for cultural creativity. Likewise, differences concern the evolving of consciousness understood as necessary to cultural creativity. It is important to understand that when these differences are enfolded in society–then dialogue may run "up against deep linguistic, cultural, or paradigmatic uncommensurabilities" (Burbles & Rice, 1991, p. 408).

Differences are not necessarily always problematic, rather it is in the differences that Buber (1992) believed that the creative tensions necessary to cultural creativity resided, in part. Respecting difference as a defining aspect of *genuineness* also enables the participants to recognize

> the constructed world-view and subjectivity of the persons who enter a dialogical relation; thus difference (or its absence) cannot always be inferred or assumed from the outside. (Burbules & Rice, 1991, p. 407)

Where difference in thought, perspective, beliefs, values, and assumptions are enfolded at a number levels in society, what "may not be apparent to, or salient for others, may be paramount in the minds of the individuals at hand" (Burbules & Rice, 1991, p. 407). Dialogue–evolving to dialogic consciousness–offers a path to establishing intersubjectivity and a "mutual living relation." Genuine dialogue is recognized and enables participants to create "a degree of understanding across (unresolved) differences" (p. 409). Recognizing this carries those engaged in the communicative act

> beyond the conception of dialogue as a single, convergent method aimed toward Truth. Dialogue can also serve the purpose of creating partial understandings, if not agreement, across differences. Complex understanding and total incomprehensibility are not the only two alternatives—indeed, both of these are quite rare. (Burbules & Rice, 1991, p. 409)

Importantly, dialogue does not eliminate differences, rather through dialogue, participants create a consciousness of differences that can sustain differences within a larger social compact of toleration and respect. Genuine dialogue enables the evolution from individual consciousness, to a level of conscious awareness of differences, to a level of dialogic consciousness.

In *Part Two*, we provide an overview of the six themes that set the organizing structure for the Compendium. Then, briefly, we examine the central premise of author contributions that shape the organizing themes.

PART TWO: ORGANIZING THEMES OF COMPENDIUM

6.   FIVE ORGANIZING THEMES

The Compendium is organized by five themes. Section I, *Foundational Perspectives of Conversation*, opens with *Chapter 2* by Lee Nichol, in which the author revisits the work of David Bohm, exploring the idea of *wholeness regained*. Drawing from David Bohm's early work with dialogue, Nichol guides the reader to an understanding of how certain essential features of dialogue have been marginalized, resulting in popular conceptions of dialogue that often lead to frustration and confusion when implemented. In *Chapter 3*, Maurice Friedman explores through a philosophical lens the work of Martin Buber and Mikhail Bakhtin, drawing out the *dialogic stances* that defines the views of Buber and Bakhtin who are considered two of the most important contributors to dialogue. Contributing the philosophical exploration of dialogue, in *Chapter 4* Ionna Tsivacou is concerned with "well-being" in the context of social systems. Her examination of *human well-being* brings into consideration dialogue as a form of conversation necessary to addressing the concerns for *well-being* in social systems.

In *Chapter 5*, Danny Martin introduces the reader to dialogue and spirituality, exploring the art of being human in a changing world. Martin examines dialogue through a spiritual dimension that sees dialogue as fundamentally a way of relating to the world that has implications for human society at all levels.   Maureen O'Hara and John K. Wood, in Chapter 6, bring a humanistic perspective to bear on dialogue and the building of group consciousness. Examining the transformative potential of dialogue the authors use person-centered approaches as a context within in which the relationship between individual and group consciousness. Martin Friedman concludes this section with a personal philosophical reflection on the centrality of Martin Buber's dialogue in his own studies on dialogue. In *Chapter 7* Friedman delves into the nature of dialogue, I-Thou relations, individuation, and confirmation as defining elements of not only Buber's work with dialogue, but importantly as defining elements of the authors own understanding of dialogue.

Section II, *Perspectives of Dialogue Conversation*, opens with *Chapter 8* by Mario Cayer, in which the author delineates five dimensions of dialogue aligned with the practical application of Bohm's dialogue. In *Chapter 9*, Matthew Shapiro examines the notion of *Universal Demosophia* in relation to facilitating global conversations. Concerned with democratic practice, Shapiro delves into the importance of dialogue in accessing the "wisdom of the people," fostering a more democratic approach to conversation. Maurice Friedman examines the importance of "becoming aware" in *Chapter 10*, focusing on a dialogical approach to consciousness. In *Chapter 11*, Alexander Sidorkin takes the reader into the setting of the school, examining conversation as a means of analysis for understanding the school as a complex social system. Linda Ellinor, in *Chapter 12*, revisits David Bohm's notion of dialogue, guiding the reader on a exploration of the philosophical roots that guided the theoretical physicists work to make connections between quantum physics and the meaning of dialogue. In *Chapter 13*, Alexander Sidorkin brings Mikhail Bakhtin's idea of *carnival* to play in examining dialogue.

Raymond A. Horn, Jr. opens Section III, *Modalities of Conversation*, with *Chapter 14* as he examines the meaning of *post-formal conversation*. First examining postmodern though, he then situates his thoughts on post-formal discourse in relation to contemporary perspectives of conversation. In *Chapter 15*, Karen Norum guides the reader through an exploration of *future search conversation* and the work of Marvin Weisbord. In *Chapter 16*, Glenna Gerard brings dialogue conversation and *improvisation* together as she considers the importance of developing capability for effective conversations. Kathia Laszlo and Alexander Laszlo conclude this section with *Chapter 17*, in which they examine the methodology of thriving conversation and the conditions necessary to c0-creating connections and meaning within learning communities.

Section IV, *Practical Applications of Conversation*, introduces the reader to practical applications of conversation, and opens with *Chapter 18* by Judith Bach, in which the author shares her experiences with a community round table conversation and the notion of *self-organizing conversation*. In *Chapter 19*, Diane Gayeski and Gordon Rowland take the reader into corporate setting and examine conversation with respect to representative communication behaviors and shifting those behaviors to enhance performance. Closing this section is Kathryn Kinnucan-Welsch and Patrick M. Jenlink who present a case study in *Chapter 20*, in which they examine the use of conversation to create professional learning communities. The authors focus on dialogue and its importance in creating discourse communities.

In Section V, *Reflections on Searching Together for the Future*, editors Bela H. Banathy and Patrick M. Jenlink offer reflect thoughts in *Chapter 21* on the learning journey presented in the Compendium. The editors direct their reflections on the evolution of *Homo Sapien Sapien* as a species, and the evolution of conscious awareness.

7. CLOSING THOUGHTS

We are, as a social species, communicative by nature. That we are also sentient beings places within our reach the capacity to be equally creative and destructive, whether through discourse or social action. When we consider, in relation to being a communicative species as well as sentient beings, that we are by nature extremely diverse, we are filled with great potentials, potentials waiting to be unfolded through genuine dialogue. Whether we choose, as sentient beings, to be creative or destructive, is a consequence of our choices in matters of communicative action within our cultures and societies.

The fact that we display great diversity–that there are differences–figures largely into the potential for either creative or destructive actions. Always present is the question of how we shape our actions through conversation, which in turn shape our future. The realization of our potentialities as a species, rests in no small measure, in our capacity for cultural creativity and in our capacity to achieve new levels of consciousness.

REFERENCES

Banathy, B.H., and Jenlink, P., 2002. *Dialogue as a Means of Collective Communication.* Kluwer Academic/Plenum Publishers, New York.

Bohm, D., and Peat, D., 1987. *Science, Order, Creativity.* Bantam Books, New York.

Bohm, D., 1995. *Wholeness and the Implicate Order.* New York: Routledge.

Bohm D., 1996. *On Dialogue.* Routledge, New York.

Buber, M., 1965. *Between Man and Man.* Collier Books, New York.

Buber, M., 1988. *The Knowledge of Man: Selected essays.* Humanities Press International, Atlantic Highlands, NJ.

Buber, M., 1992. *On Intersubjectivity and Cultural Creativity.* The University of Chicago Press, Chicago, IL.

Burbules, N. C., and Rice, S., 1991. Dialogue across differences: Continuing the conversation. *Harvard Education Review*, 61, 393-416.

Crapanazno, V., 1990. On Dialogue. In T. Maranhão (Ed.), *The Interpretation of Dialogue* (pp. 269-291). The University of Chicago Press, Chicago, IL.

Combs, A., 1996. *The Radiance of Being: Complexity, Chaos, and The Evolution of Consciousness.* Paragon House, St. Paul, MN.

Eisenstadt, S.N., 1992. Introduction. In M. Buber, *On intersubjectivity and cultural creativity.* The University of Chicago Press, Chicago, IL, pp. 1-23.

Gadamer, H-G., 1976. *Philosophical Hermeneutics.* Berkeley, CA: University of California Press.

Gadamer, H-G., 1982. *Truth and Method.* Crossroads, New York.

Onians, R.B., 1951. *The Origins of European Thought About the Body, the Mind, the Soul, the World, Time Fate.* Cambridge University Press, Cambridge, UK.

Schachtel, E. G., 1959. *Metamorphosis: On the Development of Affect, Perception, Attention and Memory.* Basic Books, New York.

Turner, V., 1969. *The Ritual Process.* Cornell University Press, Ithaca, NY.

SECTION I

HISTORICAL AND CULTURAL
PERSPECTIVES OF CONVERSATION

Chapter 2
WHOLENESS REGAINED
Revisiting Bohm's Dialogue

LEE NICHOL
Free lance writer and editor, Albuquerque, New Mexico

1. INTRODUCTION

Beginning in 1985, David Bohm put forward a series of propositions regarding a new vision for contemporary dialogue. This vision received considerable attention throughout the United States, Canada, and Europe. Dozens, if not hundreds of formal and informal groups sprang up, inquiring into Bohm's model of dialogue. Numerous internet sites and chat rooms emerged as complements to "flesh and blood" dialogue groups. Bohm's inquiry into dialogue was also widely embraced by various organizational development and management communities.

But despite such widespread interest in Bohm's vision, the sustainability of dialogue seems to have been erratic, even meager. In part, this may be due to the natural cycling of fads, which are notoriously hot and cold. Partly as well, this lack of sustainability may arise from the commercialization of dialogue, in which the training of facilitators takes precedence over sustained immersion in the activity of dialogue itself. And partly, the lack of sustainability may arise from an incomplete understanding of dialogue itself, as proposed by Bohm.

This chapter will focus on the last of these prospects, examining the manner in which certain essential features of dialogue have been marginalized, resulting in a popular conception of dialogue that often leads to frustration and confusion when implemented. By way of this examination, I hope to take at least a few small steps toward restoring these essential features to their rightful place in Bohm's scheme. It will perhaps become clear that Bohm was not particularly interested in finding novel ways to arrange our cultural and conversational furniture. Rather, his interest was in the possibility of a radically new state of mind, a concrete alteration that penetrates the core of a person's experience and has the potential to communicate itself directly in a group setting.

Dialogue as a Means of Collective Communication, Edited by Banathy and Jenlink
Kluwer Academic/Plenum Publishers, New York 2005

2.   DIALOGUE IN CONTEXT

Shortly before his death in 1992, David Bohm made a curious remark regarding the vagaries of dialogue. The conversation had to do with why dialogue groups struggled so much, why many people felt discouraged with the process after serious and sustained attempts to exploit its potential. "I think people are not doing enough work on their own, apart from the dialogue groups," Bohm offered.[1] This observation seems paradoxical, not least because dialogue is by general definition a collaborative process, and by Bohm's definition one which seeks to move beyond a sense of strict individualism and open into a domain of collective, participatory fellowship. The notion of working "on one's own" would seem to circumvent the very essence of dialogue itself.

We can begin to unravel this paradox by recognizing that Bohm's work in dialogue derives from a larger context of inquiry that had captured his imagination for decades. In tracing the origins of Bohm's ideas on dialogue, we find that virtually all of his published material on this topic was excerpted from meetings and seminars in which dialogue was an outgrowth of more fundamental issues regarding the nature of consciousness and experience *per se*. In most of these seminars an examination of the ego, and the ego's compulsive insistence on stabilizing its perceived territory, played a central role. Bohm claims that the ramifications of the ego process–both individual and collective–are at the root of human fragmentation and suffering.

In these seminars, participants moved through days of in-depth exploration of the ego process. Sometimes woven into these days, and sometimes at the very end of them, Bohm would put forward the rough outlines of his current thoughts on dialogue, inquiring into "the flow of meaning," "impersonal fellowship," and "suspension of assumptions." In this way would transition the groups from an emphasis on the individualistic aspects of ego to an emphasis on these same issues as they might appear in a group context.[2] At the heart of his dialogue proposal was the prospect that awareness of the movement of ego, willingly engaged in by a number of people simultaneously, might quicken insights into the ego process that could take much longer if approached only on an individual basis.

After a few years of these meetings, Bohm's thoughts on dialogue were collected in a small self-published booklet, *On Dialogue*. Intended primarily for distribution to those on the mailing lists of the "Bohm seminars," this booklet sold a surprising 20,000 copies.[3] While covering many of the central features of dialogue, the booklet nonetheless contained relatively little overt emphasis on the nature of the ego. This was in part due to the fact that its initial target audience was already familiar with this territory, either through having attended meetings with Bohm or through having read transcripts of those meetings.

Effectively, then, a "shorthand" version of dialogue–a pithy but incomplete extraction–found its way into mainstream culture. The incomplete version of dialogue disseminated in this way has been amplified in recent years, primarily through the publication of several mass-market "how-to" books which put forward variants of Bohm's dialogue themes. Taken together, Bohm's original booklet and these secondary materials have more or less defined the field of dialogue for an entire generation of enthusiasts.

This contextual gap between "shorthand" dialogue and Bohm's larger themes helps to clarify his suggestion that "people need to do more work on their own." Bohm was likely signaling the need to reintegrate the shorthand dialogue vision with its origin–that is, a keen and sustained awareness of the movement of the ego in daily life. Working outside the dialogue setting, and bringing the fruit of that inquiry back into the group, might provide the missing element that could bring dialogue to its full potential.

3. THREE ASPECTS OF WHOLENESS

In attempting to re-establish the wholeness of Bohm's vision, we will examine three areas that are often absent from popular presentations of dialogue. Though hardly exhaustive, this short list–*the self-image, the body,* and *meaning*–will perhaps give some indication of the richness of inquiry that is available to those interested in the full scope of Bohm's inquiry. As outlined here, these three areas are explored as they might look if a person were to work "on their own." How this exploration might look in the context of a dialogue group is a fascinating topic, perhaps one to be pursued in a later essay.

3.1 The Self-Image

The first area is *self-image*, or *ego*. As it will be discussed here, ego is not necessarily a chest-beating, get-out-of-my-way-I'm-the-best-in-the-world mentality. Rather, basic ego, or self-image, is simply the sense that wherever I go, whatever I do, whatever I think, there is a portable "me" that is always there–the very one who goes, does, and thinks. This sense of "me" as an essential and indispensable interior entity seems to form the basis for our existence in the world; all aspects of experience are felt to flow from it, and refer back to it.

Coexistent with this sense of "me" is an enormous cache of values, views, assumptions, aspirations, struggles, desires, and fears, any one of which may act as the vanguard for the entire ego structure. In Bohm's view, this content of the self-image is identical with our image of "the world"–any value or assumption that is experienced internally has an external correlate, usually perceived as "how things are." If I see the driver in the lane next to me as bumbling and incompetent, this would be reflected inwardly by a tacit image of myself as a skillful and responsive driver. These two apparently different images are actually as inseparable from one another as one side of a brick is from the other side. Bohm's term for this mutually dependent structuring was "self-world view." In the remainder of this essay we will thus use the terms ego, self-image, and self-world view interchangeably.

In contemporary Western civilization, examination of the self-image is predominantly oriented toward some version of ego-modification. From this perspective, the basic structure and value of the ego is taken for granted, the operative question being whether or not my ego is in satisfactory condition. If it is not in satisfactory condition, I will follow some kind of methodology for bringing it more in line with how I want it to be. If my ego desires to perceive itself as slim, fit, and sexually attractive, I will diet, exercise, or perhaps have some reconstructive surgery. If the ego desires to perceive itself as powerful and lordly, it will perhaps go through the machinations of establishing a business venture with many employees and a visible impact on society. If the ego desires to perceive itself as spiritual in nature, it may learn how to meditate and bask in the glow of its newfound spirituality.

It is of course possible that any of these activities can be undertaken from a benign or practical standpoint, rather than from strictly ego-driven purposes. I might exercise for sheer physical exuberance. I might start a business out of necessity or simple interest. I might learn to meditate out of a genuine inspiration to achieve clarity and understanding. But more often than not, our motivations and goals are infused with the potent tinge of basic ego, like the cartoon character Snoopy: "Here's the up-and-coming entrepreneur, well on her way to impressive accomplishments and a daunting reputation," or equally, "Here's the down-on-his-luck jilted lover, taking solace in well-warranted existential angst." Whatever your scenario of the day, there is no great mystery in this aspect of our experience. We all know what this ego is and how it operates; we all know we "have" one, and we all know everyone else "has" one.

From a Bohmian perspective, our deepest, unarticulated assumptions about this ego process are called into question. But unlike many other lines of contemporary discourse, Bohm's approach is distinctly *not* a process of reformulating or redirecting the ego, shuffling and substituting one image for another in endless succession. Nor is this questioning an intellectual pastime intended to discuss some novel, *avant-garde* theory of the ego. Finally, it is most certainly not a game of "Gotcha!" in which the inevitable display of ego-structures is seized upon as a dialogical prize.

In what way, then, does Bohm ask us to question the ego? To begin with, he suggests that we loosen our assumption that the ego is *a real thing.* He proposes that the self-image may be a kind of imaginary display, a fantasy character used to give coherence to the massive amount of stimulation that floods us every second. He often referred to the ego as a "thought god," analogous to the "rain gods" we sometimes find in various ancient or aboriginal cultures. By this he meant that peoples such as the ancient Greeks seemed to have looked for a simple way of explaining the vicissitudes of rain, thunder, and lightning, and came to the conclusion that there was an entity–a rain god–who was behind the scenes, causing weather to happen. Similarly, in the midst of the constant flow of thoughts and impressions that make up our consciousness, we yearn for continuity and coherence, and thus project an image of "me"–a thought god behind the scenes, causing thought to happen. This attribution, of course, is not spontaneously invented anew with every person. We receive ample help from our social environment when we are very young, learning unconsciously how to construct this sense of inner entity and invest it with meaning.

But what if the self-image is really only "there" when we look for it (continuously), think about it (compulsively), remember it (reflexively)? What if the feeling of "me" is a *product* of the flow of thoughts, rather than the *source* of them?

In most of the literature available on dialogue, Bohm uses the term "assumptions" to signify the activity by which the ego navigates the world.. He of course recognizes that from a commonsense, practical perspective we need to have certain working assumptions. We must assume that our car is likely to start when we go to work in the morning; we must assume that our circle of friends and relations is at least somewhat reliable and stable. But navigating the physical and social world via *practical* assumptions is not what causes most of the confusion and difficulty in our lives. It is, rather, our assumptions about *who we really are*, and *how the world should be in relation to us*, that cause us.

However, the shorthand language of contemporary dialogue discourse tends to leave intact the most basic assumption of all–the assumption of the solidity and primacy of the ego. In marginalizing sustained and pointed questioning of the ego *per se*, the current dialogue discourse leaves open a stance in which one may question all manner of one's own assumptions, and the assumptions of others, but rarely if ever question the basic existence or seeming solidity of the ego itself.

We could think of this version of questioning assumptions as *serial-horizontal*. In this approach we question assumptions in a perpetual sequence, as though we were driving along a flat desert highway, "questioning" each new item that appears through the windshield. This process is indeed central to the practice of dialogue, and is by any measure a valuable and enlightening exercise. But our minds tend to be organized in such fashion that the loosening of one strongly held assumption will eventually be followed by the strengthening of another one, or the re-emergence of the old one in a new guise. We can go on this way for years, perhaps a lifetime, examining the topical features of the ongoing parade of assumptions that passes through our consciousness. All the while, the ego–the "mother of all assumptions"–remains conveniently shielded from scrutiny by tacitly positioning itself as *the one who is examining the serial assumptions*.

But if we sense that this approach could indeed go on endlessly without really revealing the core of our problems, then we may be inspired to explore an alternative. Amply provided in Bohm's larger body of work is a complementary approach to assumptions, one which is holistic rather than serial, vertical in addition to horizontal. This *holistic-vertical* questioning of assumptions is more akin to an archaeological dig, in which we stay with one assumption in a sustained way, ferreting out its generic structure, rather than simply surveying its topically salient features.

In a serial approach, I might examine my ingrained prejudice against very fat people who live in trailer parks. If I am persistent and sincere, I might gain insight into the causes and limitations of this prejudice, and thus free myself to a lesser or greater extent from this prejudice. Next week, I might examine my assumptions about the motives and intentions of CEOs of multinational corporations. Through this examination, I will perhaps uncover various fallacies, and arrive at a less restrictive view of such individuals.

In a holistic approach, I may well engage in exactly these serial processes, but with one additional, and crucial, hypothesis: Each particular prejudice or assumption I examine in sequence is but a temporary display–an advertisement, if you will–a of a deeper generating source: the sense of ego itself. From this perspective, to ignore my deep assumptions about the existence and veracity of the ego, in favor of examining its display *du jour*, is very likely to result in an endless recycling of modified assumptions. But if I am willing to see the particular assumptions/displays as flags indicating the more generic patterning of the ego, it may be possible to enter into a genuinely new order of insight. In addition to questioning the assumption, we are now questioning the questioner.

3.2   The Body

In exploring the terrain of the self-image, it is all too easy to slip into a highly abstract and intellectualized version of our experience. As suggested in the previous section, being "aware" of assumptions can become a repetitive habit like any other, a closed intellectual loop that never proceeds significantly beyond the surface of experience. As a complement to the initial emphasis on "thinking through" the nature of the self-world view and its assumptive process, Bohm proposes that we use *the body* as a source of immediate, concrete feedback for our inquiry. While this emphasis on the body is fairly apparent in Bohm's source material on dialogue, the secondary literature has tended to minimize or altogether eliminate this aspect of the dialogue process. In this section we will review in some detail why Bohm sees the body as an indispensable component in deepening our understanding of both ego and dialogue.

The most immediate way we can utilize the body–both in and out of the dialogue process–is to recognize the body as a highly sensitive and accurate display for disturbances to the self-image. To do this, Bohm suggests that we expand our attention–usually focused on our mental reactions arising from provocations to the ego–to include the physiological correlates of these reactions. These correlates are not mysteriously hidden away; they are readily apparent if we are open to seeing them. Consider, for example, that one of my core values–women have the right to choose whether to abort a fetus–is vehemently challenged. In addition to my likely *thoughts* about the challenger ("This person is venal and reactionary...he is only concerned about imposing his views on others...at the very least he is misguided and ignorant"), I will also have a cluster of physical signs of disturbance. My heart may begin to beat faster. My adrenaline may begin to surge. My jaw may subtly clench. My posture may rigidify.

In normal social intercourse, we may (a) ignore these physiological signals through force of habit (b) bulldoze our way past them in order to find a new zone of equilibrium (c) take them as implicit proof of the rightness of our position. In all such cases we tend to fall into the default mode of *thinking* our way forward–we marshall an array of intellectual arguments and justifications for why our view is right and good, and why the challenger's view is wrong and bad.

However, in such a scenario there is always a phase in which both aspects–the physiological manifestations and the internal verbal cogitation–are simultaneously present. Bohm's suggestion is that at this very point, we experiment with diminishing our reliance on the "thinking habit," and allow the physiological correlates to come more clearly into felt awareness. This in no sense means suppressing the thoughts, but something more like a figure-ground reversal, in which our typical structure of our awareness–with thoughts far more dominant than our physiology–is reversed, with the physiological responses now coming to the foreground.

There are a number of reasons Bohm suggests experimenting with this figure-ground reversal, and a comprehensive assessment of them all is well beyond the scope of this essay. But two points in particular warrant scrutiny. First, there is the "truthfulness" aspect of the body. Honest attention to the signals in the body will often give a very different picture of what is happening in our experience than the ego would like to imagine. If someone has said something that has hurt or offended us deeply, we have a lifetime of practice at acting outwardly as if this hurt did not occur. And once this process of obscuration is set in motion, we often go so far as to deny–even to ourselves–that we are hurt. But close, sustained attention to the body, alert to signals like those mentioned above, makes it difficult to maintain the habit of obscuring the actual nature of our experience. One effect of giving attention to the body, thus, is to bring our conscious awareness more closely in line with what is actually occurring.

Second, as we attempt to read the information of the body, and move toward closer alignment between what is actually happening and what we would like to think is happening, we will inevitably encounter a certain degree of conflict. This conflict is directly attributable to physiological information that is contrary to my self-image. My body tells me that the attitudes and words of a person I am in interaction with frighten and threaten me. But the self-image says, "This is absurd. I shouldn't be threatened by this person or their views. I can't be weak or vulnerable. I must find a way to regain my solid ground."

It is exactly the structure of this experience, and its many variations (which include the seemingly opposite experience of gratified self-validation), that can lead us to the edge of the generic self-world view and open the possibility of an entirely new way of relating to ourselves and others. For in such moments we have a vividly clear display of the inner mechanism by which the ego sustains itself and its fixed views of the world.

On the one hand we have the body and all that it is signifying: uncomfortable impulses, uninvited surges of energy, uncharitable thoughts and images, all swirling and mixing in a dynamic that is, at least inwardly, out of control. On the other hand there is the apparently stable and unchanging "internal watcher," the one who notices these bodily signals and either approves or disapproves of them, directing or redirecting energy until some satisfactory equilibrium is found (this "watcher," not coincidentally, is identical with the "questioner" we visited earlier). In trying to clarify the nature of what is happening in such moments, our first task is simply to be distinctly aware of these two processes: the movement of energy and impulses, and the sense of an internal entity who is watching these.

We are now in a position to notice a subtle but palpable oscillation of neurophysiological energy that occurs when the "observer" attempts to categorize, judge, alter, redirect, validate, or suppress the display in the body. With a bit of persistence, it becomes increasingly natural and easy to tune in to this oscillation. It is sensed as a kind of "extra" or "added" impulse, often in conflict with that of the initial bodily responses. One variation of this would be the case of self-justification or validation, where the bodily display would be "sanctioned " by the watcher–in which case the added impulse would likely be one of pleasure rather than conflict. But in either case the relevant factor is the reflexive emergence of the "extra" impulse, not whether it is conflictual or pleasurable.

Once we acquire some familiarity with this dynamic, we can experiment with what happens if we do not sanction the impulse to categorize or act upon what is displayed in the body. We may instead simply be aware of the whole of what is going on: the initial thinking habit, the initial physiological correlates, and the emergence of a watcher which injects an additional level of discernable energy. In this case, "being aware" arises from all our faculties–cognitive, physiological, and affective. We both "see" and "feel" the simultaneous presence of thoughts, feelings, and the watcher, *but without trusting and following the impulsive interjections of the watcher*.

In this way we arrive at a radically new orientation. Normally in the course of daily life, we follow the dictates of one of two masters. Either we follow our random thoughts and urges, or we follow the implicit dictates of the inner watcher, which monitors the random thoughts and urges, judging and directing them in one way or other. But now we are *watching the watcher*, as well as all else that is happening. This particular awareness is not a disembodied, bird's-eye, "objective" view, such as occurs in many kinds of introspective analysis; nor is it the perspective of a so-called "neutral watcher," which is usually nothing more than a shift in positioning of the ego. To the contrary, this awareness is *completely within* all that is occurring. It is alert to all cognitive, physiological, and affective movements, yet curiously, it also partakes of these movements, and is in some essential sense grounded in them. Rather than awareness from the "outside looking in," this is more akin to awareness from the "inside looking out."

The novel, even strange aspect of this approach is the implication that we are capable of conscious awareness that does not in any fundamental way depend upon the ego. In large part this seems strange because our culture does not recognize or assign value to awareness that is decoupled from the ego, much less provide tools and support for its development. In fact, quite the opposite is more often the case. We are trained from a very early age to (a) produce this inner distinction between observer and observed, in which the ego is felt to be the vital living source of all thought and awareness (b) assume the validity of this structure so thoroughly that it passes out of conscious awareness (c) invest total trust in its efficacy. But in our current inquiry, this deep cultural conditioning is turned on its head: awareness is now seen as primary; thoughts flow from awareness; and the ego, far from being a "real thing," is merely a reflexive display resulting from ingrained thought patterns.

Interestingly enough, we have ample everyday evidence for awareness that is decoupled from the self-world view. Moments of shocking beauty in the natural world, intense sexual communion, deep immersion in work or sport–all of these indicate a momentary loss of self in which we are nonetheless intensely aware. But these moments are fortuitous, and are all too easily romanticized or compartmentalized. When approached in this manner, such awareness is made into an object of desire by the ego, which invariably resurfaces and reflects longingly upon these moments. In this way an ironic cycle of confusion is engendered, in which the absence of the ego is desired by the ego.

Here however, we are suggesting that this same heightened awareness can be accessed in the midst of our most mundane and taxing moments. Bohm's perspective allows us to *utilize the generic appearance of the ego itself* as a means of prompting awareness. By using the body to bring to light the oscillation between the watcher/ego and neurophysiological energy structures, we need no longer look to "special moments" for an opportunity to prompt basic awareness. In the act of watching the watcher, awareness is fully present, at least momentarily.

Further, we can now see a new relationship between serial and holistic suspension of assumptions. It becomes increasingly clear that the watcher and the assumption *are one and the same structure*–they are both products of thinking. When the watcher is thus no longer given privileged status as a central entity, but is apprehended by awareness in the same way that any other assumption would be, the distinction between serial suspension and holistic suspension collapses. Every serial observation becomes a holistic observation; the observation of each superficial assumption gives access to the entire generic movement of the ego process, rather than to some isolated fragment of this process.

From this inclusive Bohmian perspective, we thus find that the body is the gateway to a remarkable wealth of unexpected information. Clearly, if we marginalize and downplay the significance of the body, we lose access to this information. But new information, in and of itself, can be meaningless. What then are we to make of this new information? What, if anything, does it have to tell us?

3.3   Meaning

"A change of meaning is a change of being." Increasingly in his latter years, Bohm was fond of broaching and contemplating this statement. It is an enigmatic statement, not least because the words *meaning* and *being* are notoriously difficult to define. If asked to define them, we may come up short for a verbal definition, yet still have an intuitive sense that we know what they mean, a kind of feeling for what they actually refer to in our experience. At the very least, "meaning" seems to suggest something of value or significance–people, places, events, or ideas that are in some way important in our lives. And at the very least, "being" seems to point to our actual existence, our sense of presence and vitality.

In following through Bohm's proposal that our self-image is inseparable from our view of the world, and that this mutually arising "self-world view" is the operant basis of our experience, we now come to a pivotal question: If the demands of the self-world view can dissipate, even if only in short bursts, what are the implications for our meanings and our being?

Bohm has suggested one possibility–that rather than clinging to fragmentation, isolation, and territoriality, we might begin to discern a *participatory* universe, one in which conceptual boundaries and sharp definitions are tools for use in the moment, rather than serving as crystallized identity structures. Perhaps in such a participatory universe, communion and fellowship are natural features of the topography. Perhaps in such a universe, intrinsic human warmth–currently locked down or carefully channeled in so many of us–is common currency, part of the shared meaning of nature and society.

If Bohm is even partly right when he claims that the mind-body continuum is concretely related to the deepest orders of the universe,[4] then a *change of meaning* may open us to these orders, bringing us face to face with new aspects of *being* that are only vaguely intimated by our current world view. It is up to each individual to then ask: Do I want to live the rest of my life playing out yet another variation of contemporary values? Am I willing to test the boundaries of my self-world view, in order to glimpse a larger, perhaps very different universe? Am I willing to take risks for the possibility of new understanding, knowing there can be no money-back guarantee?

Such questions lie at the heart of Bohmian dialogue–not as fad or theory, but as the deepest promptings of our humanity. To the extent that questions of this order are ignored in favor of technique, it is perhaps inevitable that Bohm's vision of dialogue will degenerate into the algorithms of the workshop and seminar circuit. But if such questions can be revisited and revitalized, then this vision may still find good soil and contribute to a new and radical creativity.

NOTES

[1] Personal communication.

[2] For a representative documentation of such a seminar, see Bohm, D., *Thought as a System*, Routledge, London, 1994.

[3] This booklet has subsequently been revised, extended, and incorporated into a more comprehensive volume of the same name. See Bohm, D., *On Dialogue*, Routledge, London, 1996.

[4] See Bohm, D., *Unfolding Meaning*, Routledge, London, 1985; and *The Essential David Bohm*, Routledge, London, 2002.

Chapter 3

MARTIN BUBER AND MIKHAIL BAKHTIN
The Dialogue of Voices and the Word That is Spoken

MAURICE FRIEDMAN
Professor Emeritus, Sand Diego State University

1. INTRODUCTION

Martin Buber and Mikhail Bakhtin are two individuals who figure
prominently in the evolution of dialogue. The philosophical threads that
connect the two individual perspectives of dialogue are examined through a
dialogue of voices.

2. MARTIN BUBER

In his classic work *I and Thou* Martin Buber (1958) distinguishes between
the "I-Thou" relationship which is direct, mutual, present, and open, and
the "I-It," or subject-object, relation in which one relates to the other only
indirectly and nonmutually, knowing and using the other. What is
essential is not what goes on within the minds of the partners in a
relationship but what happens *between* them. For this reason, Buber is
unalterably opposed to that psychologism which wishes to remove the
reality of relationship into the separate psyches of the participants. "The
inmost growth of the self does not take place, as people like to suppose
today," writes Buber, "through our relationship to ourselves, but through
being made present by the other and knowing that we are made present by
him" (Buber, 1988, p. 61).
Being made present, as a person is the heart of what Buber calls
confirmation. Confirmation is interhuman, but it is not simply social or
interpersonal. Unless one is confirmed in one's uniqueness as the person
one can become, one is only seemingly confirmed. The confirmation of
the other must include an actual experiencing of the other side of the
relationship so that one can imagine quite concretely what another is

Dialogue as a Means of Collective Communication, Edited by Banathy and Jenlink
Kluwer Academic/Plenum Publishers, New York 2005

feeling, thinking, perceiving, and knowing. This "inclusion," or "imagining the real" does not abolish the basic distance between oneself and the other. It is rather a bold swinging over into the life of the person one confronts, through which alone I can make her present in her wholeness, unity, and uniqueness.

This experiencing of the other side is essential to the distinction which Buber makes between "dialogue," in which I open myself to the otherness of the person I meet, and "monologue," in which, even when I converse with her at length, I allow her to exist only as a content of my experience. Wherever one lets the other exist only as part of oneself, "dialogue becomes a fiction, the mysterious intercourse between two human worlds only a game, and in the rejection of the real life confronting him the essence of all reality begins to disintegrate" (Buber 1985, p. 24).

3.   MIKHAIL BAKHTIN

In an interview quoted in the *New York Review of Books* the great Soviet literary critic and philosopher of the human sciences Mikhail Bakhtin said that he thought of Buber as "the greatest philosopher of the twentieth century, and perhaps in this philosophically puny century, perhaps the sole philosopher on the scene."

> Bakhtin then went on to explain that while Nicholas Berdyaev, Lev Shestov, and Jean–Paul Sartre are all excellent examples of thinkers, there is a difference between them and philosophers. "But Buber is a philosopher. And I am very much indebted to him. In particular for the idea of dialogue. Of course, this is obvious to anyone who reads Buber.[1]

Bakhtin already read Buber when he was in the gymnasium in Vilnius and Odessa. It is not surprising that Bakhtin uses Buber's terminology and shares his emphases, for Bakhtin was deeply influenced by Buber. The relation between Buber and Bakhtin is much greater, in fact, than has been recognized in any of the literature on Bakhtin that I know.[2] What is most important here is the fact that Bakhtin rings true as a thoroughly dialogical thinker.

> For Bakhtin, the voice of the person is inseparable from the dialogue between I and Thou. What became explicit in the philosophy of Martin Buber two generations later was already implicit in the thought of Dostoevsky as Bakhtin expounds it. Dostoevsky's dialogical logic is in turn based upon a dialogical anthropology and a dialogical ontology: 'A single person, remaining alone with himself, cannot make ends meet even in the deepest and most intimate spheres of his own spiritual life, he cannot manage without *another* consciousness. One person can never find complete

fullness in himself alone.' The reason for this is that personality means neither Descartes' solipsistic I nor an object but *another subject*: 'The depiction of personality requires...*addressivity* to a *thou.*' (Bakhtin 1984, pp. 299, 99f., 177, 300)

A character's self–consciousness in Dostoevsky is thoroughly dialogized: in its every aspect it is turned outward, intensely addressing itself, another, a third person. Outside this living addressivity toward itself and toward the other it does not exist, even for itself. In this sense it could be said that the person in Dostoevsky is the *subject of an address*. One cannot talk about him; one can only address oneself to him. Those "depths of the human soul," whose representation Dostoevsky considered the main task of his realism "in a higher sense," are revealed only in an intense act of address....At the center of Dostoevsky's artistic world must lie dialogue, and dialogue not as a means but as an end in itself...in dialogue a person not only shows himself outwardly, but he becomes for the first time that which he is...not only for others but for himself as well. To be means to communicate dialogically....Two voices is the minimum for life, the minimum for existence (Bakhtin 1984, p. 281 f.).

For Bakhtin, like Buber, the person does not dwell within himself but on the boundary; for his self–consciousness is constituted by his relationship to a *Thou*. The loss of the self comes from separation, dissociation, and enclosure within the self. Absolute death is the state of being unheard, unrecognized, unremembered. Martin Buber says in strikingly similar fashion that abandonment is a foretaste of death, and abandonment is not just being left alone but being unheard as the unique person that one is, being "unconfirmed." Confirmation, as we have seen above, depends upon one person's concretely imagining what is really happening to and in the other.

To Bakhtin the achievement of self–consciousness and the most important human acts arise out of the relation to a "Thou." "Life is dialogical by its very nature. To live means to engage in dialogue, to question, to listen, to answer, to agree." In exact parallel to Buber's contrast between I–Thou and I–It, dialogue and monologue, Bakhtin defines "monologism" as the denial of the existence outside oneself of "another *I* with equal rights *(thou)*." Authentic human life can only be verbally expressed in *"open–ended dialogue"* in which one participates wholly and throughout one's whole life. Entering into dialogue with an integral voice, the person "participates in it not only with his thoughts, but with his fate and with his entire individuality" (Bakhtin 1984, p. 292 f.).

For Bakhtin personality only reveals itself freely dialogically (as a *Thou* for an *I*). To be a person is to be the subject of an address. "To be means to communicate dialogically." The communion of the I with the "other" takes place directly in genuine community. outside of all social forms and conditioning (Bakhtin 1984, pp. 251 f., 280). Bakhtin also shares Buber's emphasis upon the alternation of distancing and entering relation as the heart of genuine dialogue:

The author speaks not *about* a character, but *with* him....as another point of view. Only through such an inner dialogic orientation can my discourse find itself in intimate contact with someone else's discourse, and yet at the same time not fuse with it, not swallow it up, not dissolve in itself the other's power to mean....To preserve distance in the presence of an intense semantic bond is no simple matter. But distance is an integral part of the author's design, for it alone guarantees genuine objectivity in the representation of a character (Bakhtin 1984, p. 63 f.).

Bakhtin attributes to Dostoevsky precisely that encompassing awareness of the other side of the relationship without losing one's own that Martin Buber calls "inclusion," or "imagining the real": "Dostoevsky had the seeming capacity to *visualize directly someone else's psyche*" (Bakhtin 1984, pp. 18, 36). Inclusion, or imagining the real, does not mean at any point that one gives up the ground of one's own concreteness, ceases to see through one's own eyes, or loses one's own "touchstone of reality."

Bakhtin distinguishes in *every* creative act between a first stage of empathy or identification and a reverse movement whereby the novelist returns to his own position. "Aesthetic activity begins properly only when one returns within oneself at one's place, outside of the one suffering, and when one gives form and completion to the material of identification." In close consonance with this Bakhtin sees "all events that are creatively productive, innovative, unique and irreversible" as presupposing the relationship of two consciousnesses that do not fuse" (Bakhtin 1984 quoted in Todorov 1984, pp. 96 f., 99).

4.   A DIALOGUE OF VOICES

One of the most surprising resemblances between Buber and Bakthin, that is the correlation between Buber's concept of the "eternal Thou" and Bakhtin's "superaddressee." To Buber the "eternal Thou" is met every time an "I" goes out to meet a finite "Thou," whether that be an animal or tree, a fellow human being, or a work of art. As Buber puts it in *I and Thou*, the parallel lines of relation meet in the "Eternal Thou." Although Bakhtin was by all accounts a religious Orthodox Christian, he did not, to my knowledge bring God into his literary theories--with the partial exception of his superaddressee. To Bakhtin dialogue was not really a duet but a trio, the third person being "the particular image in which they model the belief they will be understood, a belief that is the *a priori* of all speech."

...in addition to {the immediate addressee] the author of the utterance with a greater or lesser awareness,, presupposes a higher *superaddressee* (third) whose absolutely just responsive understanding is presumed, either in some metaphysical distance or in distant historical time....In various ages and with various understandings of the world, this superaddressee and his ideally true responsive understanding assume various ideological expressions (God, absolute truth, the court of dispassionate human conscience, the people, the court of history, science, and so forth). (Bakhtin 1986, p. 126)

In his introduction to *Speech Genres* Michael Holquist comments on the above paragraph with a trenchant statement that brings Bakhtin even closer to Buber's "eternal Thou" in whom one cannot believe as in a knowledge proposition but only trust in unreserved dialogical relationship:

If there is something like a God concept in Bakhtin, it is surely the superaddressee, for without faith that we will be understood somehow, sometime, by somebody, we would not speak at all. Of if we did, it would be babbling. And babble, as Dostoevsky shows in his short story "Bobok" is the language of the dead. (Bakhtin 1986, p. xviii)

To Bakhtin every word is directed to an answer and cannot escape the profound influence of the answering word that it anticipates" (Bakhtin 1981, p. 279 f.; see also Bakhtin, 1986, p. 161). Like Buber in his essay by that title in *The Knowledge of Man*, Bakhtin finds the significance of language in "the word that is spoken."

The word, the living word, inseparably linked with dialogic communion, by its very nature wants to be heard and answered. By its very dialogic nature it presupposes an ultimate dialogic instancing. To receive the word, to be heard. The impermissibility of *second–hand* resolution. My word remains in the continuing dialogue, where it will be *heard, answered and reinterpreted. (Bakhtin 1984, p. 300)

For Bakhtin the person departs, having spoken his word, but the word itself remains in the open–ended dialogue. The authentic sphere where language lives is dialogic interaction. "The entire life of language, in any area of its use (in everyday life, in business, scholarship, art, and so forth), is permeated with dialogic relationships. A dialogic reaction personifies every utterance to which it responds" (Bakhtin 1984, p.183 f.).

To Buber, however, in contrast to Bakhtin, it is poetry rather than the novel that witnesses to the "word that is spoken":

Were there no more genuine dialogue, there would also be no more poetry....The present continuance of language] wins its life ever anew in true relation, in the spokenness of the word. Genuine dialogue witnesses to it, and poetry witnesses to it. For the poem is spokenness, spokenness to the Thou, wherever this partner might be....Poetry...imparts to us a truth which cannot come to words in any other manner than just in this one, in the manner of this form. Therefore, every paraphrase of a poem robs it of its truth. (Buber 1988, pp. 101, 108)

Buber insists that "the mystery of the coming–to–be of language and that of the coming–to–be of man are one." "There is no 'word' that is not spoken; the only being of a word resides in its being spoken," Buber states. "Every attempt to understand the present continuance of a language as accessible detached from the context of its actual speakers, must lead us astray," writes Buber in "The Word That Is Spoken." It is from the spoken word, from human dialogue that language draws its ontological power. Language derives from and contributes to the sphere of "the between," the I–Thou relationship. Language is a "system of tensions" deriving from the fruitful ambiguity of the word in its different uses by different speakers. In "The Word That Is Spoken" Buber finds the struggle for shared meaning essential to humanity: "It is the communal nature of the logos as at once 'word' and 'meaning' which makes man man, and it is this which proclaims itself from of old in the communalizing of the spoken word that again and again comes into being" (Buber 1988, "The Word That Is Spoken").

The written word is never, for Buber, just a monument to past dialogue. It calls out for dialogue with the other, the Thou to whom it is spoken. In responding to the address of the literary work, the reader and interpreter lifts the written words anew "into the sphere of the living word" as a result of which the literary work "wins its life ever anew." This does not mean staying enclosed within the dialogue between reader and text but bringing one's interpretation into dialogue with others in that "common logos" and "communal speaking" which Buber points to in "What Is Common to All" (*The Knowledge of Man*).

In "The Word That Is Spoken" Buber distinguishes between faithful truth in relation to the reality that was once perceived and is now expressed, in relation to the person who is addressed and whom the speaker makes present to himself, and in relation to the factual existence of the speaker in all its hidden structure. This human truth opens itself to one just in one's existence as this concrete person, who answers with faithfulness for the word that is spoken by one. "The truth of language must prove itself in the person's existence" (Buber 1988, p. 110).

Bakhtin speaks of a hidden dialogue or a hidden dialogicality, which expresses and reflects the anticipation of a rejoinder or at least the sideways glance to where another speaker stands. "In Dostoevsky's world there is...no word about an object, no secondhand referential word--there is only the word as address, the word dialogically contacting another word, a word about a word addressed to a word." The dialogical word wants to be heard and answered (Bakhtin 1984, pp. 197, 199, 237, 300). Contextual meaning has a responsive nature. One of Bakhtin's most frequently used words is "addressivity" (Bakhtin 1986, pp. 92-95, 145).

Like Buber, Bakhtin always sees speech as a present reality, as wedded to the event, which leads him to see the world itself as an event. He expresses this concept through the phrase "speech tact," which is determined by the aggregate of all the social relationships of the speakers, their ideological horizons, and, finally, the concrete situation of the conversation" "Each individual event is a link in the chain of speech communication" (Bakhtin 1985, p. 85; Bakhtin 1986, pp. 162 f., 92-96).

The chief characteristic of Dostoevsky's novels, according to Bakhtin's seminal book *Problems of Dostoevsky's Poetics*, is "a plurality of independent and unmerged voices and consciousnesses, a genuine polyphony of fully valid voices." The consciousness of a character is not turned into an object but is given as *someone else's* consciousness. The word of the character about himself and his world is as fully weighted as that of the author. "It is not subordinated to the character's objectified image as merely one of his characteristics, nor does it serve as a mouthpiece for the author's voice."

This extraordinary independence of the character's voice alongside the author's and that of the other characters constitutes a fundamentally new novelistic genre–the polyphonic novel–one which Bakhtin felt after Dostoevsky burst upon world literature. "Dostoevsky's novel is dialogic." Its wholeness is constructed from the interaction of several independent consciousness which do not become an object (Buber would say an "It") for other characters but remain a Thou which cannot be absorbed into other consciousness. There are no non-participant third persons, either in the point of view of the author or that of the reader, who must be, like the author, a participant in the overall dialogue of the novel. There is no place here for a "monologically all–encompassing consciousness."

Thus in contrast to those who make of the isolated consciousness their "touchstone of reality," to use my phrase, in Dostoevsky consciousness is always found in intense dialogic relationship with another consciousness. It is important not to mistake this for "a meeting of true minds" for such disembodied mental interaction really characterizes dialectic. Ivan Karamazov and Rubashov in Arthur Koestler's *Darkness at Noon* are excellent examples of this, as are the dialectical and intellectual conversations of Settembrini and Naptha in Thomas Mann's *Magic Mountain.*

A powerful proof of Bakhtin's thoroughly dialogical stance is the radical distinction which he, like Buber and myself, makes between dialogue and dialectic. Dialectic is close to the psychologism which both Buber and Bakhtin reject because it removes events which take place between persons into the intrapsychic. Dialectic is also close to what both Buber and Bakhtin call monologue in which the word that arose in dialogue is neutralized and depersonalized in monological consciousness. Truth is not born from dialectic in the head of an individual person but "between people collectively searching for truth, in the process of their dialogic interaction." "Dialectics is the abstract product of dialogue" (Bakhtin 1984, p. 293). "Take a dialogue and remove the voices,...carve out abstract concepts and judgments from living words and responses, cram everything into one abstract consciousness--and that's how you get dialectics." This does not mean that dialectics is always bad or evil. Like Buber's "I-It" it is evil only when it blocks the return to "I-Thou." "Dialectics was born of dialogue," writes Bakhtin, "so as to return again to dialogue on a higher level (a dialogue of *personalities*)" (Bakhtin 1984, pp. 9 f., 12 f., 25 f., 30, 10, 104, 291-293; Bakhtin 1986, pp. 147, 162).

Bakhtin like Buber was concerned with methodology for the human sciences, and like Buber too he found that methodology in the dialogical. The tendency of by far the largest and most dominant methodologies in most human sciences today is to begin with dialectic and to examine dialogue as part of that dialectic. Putting this in Buber's terminology, it means that the mutual knowing of the I-Thou relationship is subsumed under the subject-object knowledge of the I-It relation. A radical reversal of this perspective would not mean any rejection of dialectic, which remains essential to the whole human enterprise of connected through from one generation to another. What is does mean is a shift in emphasis toward understanding dialogue as the source of knowing and dialectic as an elaboration of that source. "The 'corrective' office of reasoning is incontestable," wrote Buber, "and it can be summoned at any moment to set right an 'error' in my sense perception—more precisely its incongruity with what is common to my fellow men." In the I-It relation what is received in the I-Thou is elaborated and broken up. Here errors are possible that can be corrected through directly establishing and comparing what is past and passive in the minds of others. "But it [reason] cannot replace the smallest perception of something particular and unique with its gigantic structure of general concepts, cannot by means of it contend in the grasping of what here and now confronts me" (Buber 1964, p. 53 f.). In *Martin Buber and the Human Sciences*, a book of which I was editor-in-chief, there are twenty-six essays on philosophy and religion; the written and the spoken word: hermeneutics, aesthetics and literature; economics, politics, and history; and dialogical psychotherapy and contextual (intergenerational) family therapy (Friedman 1996). Taken together these essays offer a powerful witness to the importance of Martin Buber's dialogical approach to the human sciences.

Most of what Bakhtin has to say about methodology in the human sciences is found in his essay "The Problem of the Text." There he relates thinking in the human science to

> a special kind of dialogue: the complex interrelations between the text (the object of study and reflection) and the created, framing context (questioning, refuting, and so forth) in which the scholar's cognizing and evaluating thought takes place. This is the meeting of two texts—of the ready-made and the reactive text being

created—and, consequently, of two subjects and two authors. (Bakhtin, 1986, p. 106 f.)

To Bakhtin everything linguistic is only a means to the end of the extralinguistic, dialogic aspects of the utterance. *Explanation* entails only one consciousness, but understanding, *comprehension* entails two consciousnesses, dialogue. Images, language-styles in a work, have a *dialogical relation* that cannot be reduced either to the purely logical (even if dialectical) or the purely linguistic (compositional-syntactic). Even utterances from various eras have a dialogic relationship if they are juxtaposed. Bakhtin feels that in probing understanding as dialogue we are approaching the frontier of the philosophy of language and of thinking in the human sciences in general. "Linguistics studies only the relationships among elements within the language system, not the relationships among utterances and not the relations of utterances to reality and to the speaker (author). Bakhtin believes that the monologism of thinking in the human sciences could be overcome if we recognized that "dialogic boundaries intersect the entire field of human thought." The word, or in general any sign is interindividual because it is a voice addressing another voice, a Thou. "Everything that is said, expressed, is located outside the 'soul' of the speaker and does not belong only to him." To Bakhtin dialogic relations are always present even among profoundly monologic speech works. Understanding being dialogical, the criterion of *depth* of understanding is "one of the highest criteria for cognition in the human sciences" (Bakhtin 1986, pp. 109, 111, 115-122, 125-127).

One of Bakhtin's last short essays is entitled "Toward a Methodology for the Human Sciences." While the limit of precision in the natural sciences is identity, in the human sciences precision means surmounting the otherness of the other without transforming him or her into purely one's own. Bakhtin conceives of a "great time" of infinite and unfinalized dialogue in which no meaning dies. "I hear voices in everything," Bakhtin exclaims, "and dialogic relations among them."

At any moment in the development of the dialogue there are immense, boundless masses of forgotten contextual meanings, but at certain moments of the dialogue's subsequent development along the way they are recalled and invigorated in renewed form (in a new context). Nothing is absolutely dead: every meaning will have its homecoming festival. (Bakhtin 1986, p. 169 f.)

The summit of the meeting between Buber and Bakhtin is their Poetics of Dialogue.[3] Bakhtin's clearest presentation of the Poetics of Dialogue is found in his book *Problems of Dostoevsky's Poetics*. We do not see Dostoevsky's hero but hear him, according to Bakhtin, for he is not an objectified image but a *pure voice*. Only he can reveal himself in a free act of self–conscious discourse, for he can only be revealed as a Thou and not in the externalizing secondhand definition of an It. Dostoevsky's discourse about his characters is about *someone actually present* who hears the author and is capable of answering him. (Bakhtin 1984, pp. 53, 58, italics in original)

Thus the new artistic position of the author with regard to the hero in Dostoevsky's polyphonic novel is a fully realized and thoroughly consistent dialogic position, one that affirms the independence, internal freedom, unfinalizability, and indeterminacy of the hero.

> For the author the hero is not "he" and not "I" but a fully valid "thou," that is another and other autonomous "I" ("thou art"). The hero is the subject of a deeply serious, *real* dialogic mode of address... And this..."great dialogue" of the novel as a whole takes place not in the past, but right now, that is, in the *real present* of the creative process. (Bakhtin 1984, p. 63, italics in original)

Even the ideas that Dostoevsky presents in his characters are not part of an authorial surplus of meaning but of the profound dialogic nature of human thought. So far from lying in one person's isolated, individual consciousness, the idea begins to live and human thought becomes genuine only when it enters into genuine dialogical relationship with the ideas of *others*, ideas embodied in someone else's voice. The idea does not reside in a person's head but in dialogic communion *between* consciousnesses. Therefore, it "is a *live event*, played out at the point of dialogic meeting" and, like the word with which it is dialogically united, wants to be heard, understood, and "answered" by other voices. (Bakhtin 1984, p. 37 f.)

It would be a mistake, therefore, to regard Dostoevsky's novels as "novels of ideas," as has been so often done. Dostoevsky did not think up ideas the way philosophers do. He *heard* them as they entered reality itself, including the "latent, unuttered future word," as "The Legend of the Grand Inquisitor" in *The Brothers Karamazov* so marvelously exemplifies. "Dostoevsky possessed an extraordinary gift for hearing the dialogue of his epoch," writes Bakhtin, or, more precisely, for hearing his epoch as a great dialogue, for detecting in it not only individual voices, but precisely and predominantly the *dialogic relationship* among voices, their dialogic *interaction* (Bakhtin 1984, p. 90).

Dostoevsky's creative stance, Bakhtin points out, does not imply that in him all positions are equally valid, as if the author passively surrendered his own viewpoint and truth.

> Rather it is a case of an entirely new and specific interrelation between his truth and the truth of someone else. The author is profoundly *active*, but his action takes on a specific *dialogic* character....Dostoevsky frequently interrupts the other's voice but he does not cover it up, he never finishes it from the "self," that is from an alien consciousness (his own). (Bakhtin 1984 quoted in Todorov 1984, p. 36)

The author is the participant, but he is also the organizer of the dialogue. It is the author who holds the reins between the ideal dialogue of the word and the actual dialogue of reality. To Bakhtin Dostoevsky's authorial surplus was love, confession, and forgiveness. "Everything essential is dissolved in dialogue," Bakhtin concludes, "positioned face to face" (Bakhtin 1984, pp. 296-299).

NOTES

[1] Mariya Kaganskaya, "Shutovskoi Kohaarovod," *Sintaksis* 12 (1984): p. 141. Quoted in Joseph Frank, "The Voices of Mikhail Bakhtin," *The New York Review of Books*, No. 16 (October 23, 1986), p. 56.
[2] This holds even for Nina Perlina, who wrote the only article on the two that exists in English. Like most other Bakhtin critics she has very little understanding of Buber.
[3] As is shown in some fullness in the "Hermeneutical Appendix; Toward a Poetics of Dialogue" in my book *The Affirming Flame: A Poetics of Meaning* (Amherst, New York: Prometheus Books, 1999, pp. 209-231). This appendix also discusses my own poetics of dialogue and in more condensed form that of Walter Stein, Walter Ong, Robert Detweiler, Paul Celan, Steven Kepnes, and Tsvetan Todorov.

REFERENCES

Bakhtin, M., 1981. *The Dialogic Imagination: Four Essays.* (M. Holquist, ed., trans. by C. Emerson and M. Holquist). Slavic Series, No. 1. University of Texas Press: Austin, TX.
Bakhtin, M., 1984. *Problems of Dostoevsky's poetics.* (C. Emerson, ed. & trans., Introduction by W.C. Booth, *Theory and History of Literature*, Vol. 8, University of Minnesota Press: Minneapolis.
Bakhtin, M., and Medvedev, P.N., 1985. *Formal Method in Literary Scholarship: A Critical Introduction to Sociological Poetics.* (Foreword by W. Godzich, trans. by A.J. Wehrle). Harvard University Press: Cambridge, Mass.
Bakhtin, M., 1986. *Speech Genres & Other Late Essays.* (C. Emerson and M. Holquist, eds., trans. by V.W. McGee). University of Texas Press: Austin, TX.
Buber, M., 1964, in Sydney & Beatrice Rome, eds., Philosophical Interrogations. New York, Holt, Rinehart, & Winston. Buber section conducted & edited & Buber's answers translated by Maurice S. Friedman, Ch. II - Theory of Knowledge.
Buber, M., 1985. *Between Man and Man.* (Introduction by Maurice Friedman, trans. by Ronald Gregor Smith. Macmillan: New York.
Buber, M., 1988. *The knowledge of Man: A Philosophy of the Interhuman*, ed. with an Introductory Essay (Chap. l) by Maurice Friedman, Atlantic Highlands, NJ: Humanities Press International, 1988, now distributed by Prometheus Books, Amherst, New York), "The Word That Is Spoken," & What Is Common to All," both trans. by Maurice Friedman.
Friedman, M., 1996., (editor-in-chief). *Martin Buber and the Human Sciences.* State University of New York Press: Albany, New York.
Friedman, M. 1999. *The affirming flame: A poetics of Meaning*, Amherst, "Hermeneutical Appendix: Toward a Poetics of Dialogue," Prometheus Books, New York, pp. 209-231.
Todorov, T. 1984. *Mikhail Bakhtin: The dialogical principle*, trans. by Wlad Godzich, *Theory and History of Literature*, Vol. 13. University of Minnesota Press: Minneapolis, MN, p. 106.

Chapter 4

DESIGNING COMMUNITIES OF IDEAS FOR THE WELL-BEING

IOANNA TSIVACOU
Department of Communication and Mass Media, Panteion University, 136 Sygrou Avenue, Athens, 17671, Greece

1.   INTRODUCTION

After the repudiation of "grand narratives"[1] our era remained without absolute truths to found value judgments and defend the supremacy of the human subject. Particularly in the middle of the past century, we became witnesses of a rejection of the autonomous rational subject and his replacement by a "docile subject" (Foucault, 1966). Later, we followed the full deconstruction of the subject and the rise of an entity unstable and indefinite, linguistically constructed by diverse meanings and interpretations (Derrida, 1976; Lacan, 1977).

Nevertheless, at the end of the 20th century, due to the universalization of communication and to the formation of a global society, the human being came back to the center of the philosophical and political thought. The notion of "*objective*" emancipation, on which the narration of socialism has been founded, is now almost abandoned.[2] Social research gave up the attempts to highlight the phenomenon of objective emancipation as well as to overthrow the causes of its emergence. The common belief of the weakness of the human being to confront the power of information technology and of the new organization of work has turned the interest of social philosophy and sciences to a kind of "subjective alienation. Today, research attention is rather focused on the transformation of the self and its identity under the new conditions. Philosophers and social scientists investigating social pathologies, debate on the question of autonomy or authenticity as the new human ideals, propounding the new validity claims that accompany them.

It should be noted that autonomy is regarded as the main normative judgment, of universal validity, since it is based on the belief that it consists the essential quality of the internal core of human beings, namely of the self. Therefore, the self has been raised as the trustee of any normativity. The proposal for a moral, social context, compatible with the anthropological normative core, suggests justice as the supreme value and the guardian of social order. Of course, the obtaining of social order does not necessarily entail a situation of human well-being.

The ideal of authenticity is connected with that of self-realization or self-fulfillment, as it suggests that a self knows its inward inclinations and desires to bring them in presence. Otherwise, self-realization is accomplished and leads a human being to well-being if it has been conceived not as an internal psychological situation, but as the moral development of a self that pursues its authenticity.

The debate concerning the two notions is old and has its roots in the Europe of 17th and 18th centuries, in the writings of Hume, Kant, and Rousseau. In 19th century the same debate, revolved around the nature of the human being and the moral values, which must govern his/her life. Liberalists, such as Locke, Condorcet, and Stuart Mill found themselves face to face with socialists and romantics. In our years, we have a revival of the same debate. Liberalists of different nuances (from Habermas to Rawls, from Milton Friedman to Robert Nozick), cross swords with the followers of the republican thought and the defenders of tradition and community (as McIntyre, Sandel, Walzer, Taylor, Etzioni, Gutmann, and others).

The recent debate rotates in the pathologies of politics and state, and particularly in those that touch principles responsible for the integration of contemporary, functionally differentiated societies. Liberalists claim that integration is likely to be succeeded through a centralization of the state administration and a decentralization of market's regulations. On the contrary, communitarians see it as a result of social solidarity obtained by the means of a political-ethical discourse. Communitarians, arguing about ethical discourse, conceptualize it as a process developed in a public sphere–the community–between participants of shared value orientations.

Both perspectives, as Selznick (1996, p. 112) writes, "are usefully understood as polar contrasts, that is, as quite different and even incompatible ways of relating oneself to others." Both, in order to found their argument, discuss about a self that possesses an essential core. On the one hand, liberalists following Kantian tradition, adopt the notion of autonomy, and look for an internal normative context, that is, an autonomous self, which could be viewed as the source of any validity regarding the evaluative criteria of social pathologies. On the other hand, communitarians seek a community of values, which is, according to their opinion, the most suitable to provide the necessary validity claims for evaluating human self-fulfillment. Thus, communitarians appear to be the defenders of *Lebensphilosophie* (as it emerges through the works of Nietzsce, Bergson or Simmel), claiming that the internal psychic core consists of the substantial, innate inclinations and needs of the individual.

In summary, liberalists and communitarians hold the intersubjective constitution of subjectivity. They both deny the argument of an existentialist subjectivity and share the idea of a self communicatively constituted. However, the autonomy thesis is more connected with the problem of social order, since it emphasizes the universality of the moral law. On the other hand, the authenticity thesis is more related to the human well-being since it emphasizes particularity instead of universality.

For the realization of well-being the notion of community acquires a crucial importance. It is used by communitarians to denote a social place of common understanding and deciding together, as well as a place most suitable for the development of the values of caring, individual recognition and substantive justice. Due to these qualities, communities are represented in communitarian thinking as the loci that allow a human self to retrieve or to be symmetrical with the essential core of him/herself and so, reach his/her well-being. However, nobody can be sure that actual communities possess the aforementioned qualities. If this is not completely sure, then it should be defined under which conditions values of caring and substantive justice, together with a common understanding, could be created. Subsequently, the investigation of design's possibilities to contribute to the realization of a similar social locus, becomes a fact of great importance.

Nevertheless a similar investigation raises some epistemological problems. Considering that design is an activity guided by the principles of systems thinking, to examine it, as a promoter of well-being should be compatible with systems perspective and not with that of *Lebensphilosophie*. The latter, especially as communitarian thinking understands it, focuses on a kind of *affective* and *traditional* type of action (according to Weber categorizations), therefore it connects well-being with this kind of action. On the contrary, a systems design by its nature as a disciplined inquiry is rather similar to the Weberian categorization of *purposive-rational* action.[3] If this is true, the present analysis should be focused on the possibilities of a *purposive-rational action*, such as design, to lead participants of a discursive context to their self-realization or self-fulfillment. In case that it is not possible, some ideas regarding the transformation of design in order to satisfy the previously mentioned prerequisite will be discussed.

In the following section I am trying to investigate well-being in a systems perspective. I am interested in *human well-being* and not in *well-being of organizations* already studied by known scholars of design (Churchman, 1989). I continue arguing about contemporary social conditions in which the human being is obliged to live, and which impede seriously the realization of well-being. Immediately afterwards the opportunities allowed by these social conditions or, differently, the "openings" of the social systems for a social transformation, and consequently the chances for a situation of well-being, are outlined. Finally, a new conceptualization of design, able to modify it to a useful means for the realization of these chances, is commented.

2.   THE NOTION OF WELL-BEING

A serious approach to the notion of human well-being should be started from its roots, that is, its Aristotelian origin. According to Aristotle (1992/1993), the highest state of well-being is the reaching of *eudaimonia*. *Eudaimonia* is a mental situation of happiness, achieved by the good (*agathos*) man, when he reaches the absolute good or goodness. He refers to the free citizen of the ancient *polis* (city-state), and even more, to an individual completely released from the poverty and the need for material resources. The *eudaimon* (happiest man), according to Aristotle, is the wise citizen who has the opportunity to speculate theoretically, fulfilling by this activity the true destination (*telos*) of man, that is, the full cultivation of his mind.

Nevertheless, Aristotle does not devalue *eudaimonia* derived from the accomplishment of moral projects motivated and executed by the combination of other bodily and psychic energies, even if he considers this kind of *eudaimonia* inferior in comparison with the *eudaimonia* of contemplation. In any case, a situation of happiness is achieved through the cultivation and exercise of virtues. This is the reason that well-being is connected only with the life of the moral man–the *agathos*–and moral action is the only one that contributes to the well-being of a person.

In this frame of reference, virtues emerge as the focus of the interest of social (*political* according to the Aristotelian terminology) practices. *Eudaimonia*, in spite of its subjective character and its designation as a mental situation, is not a psychological feeling. It is a result of human behavior regulated by virtues. Virtues are habits (*hexis* in the Greek language), not simply attitudes, nor dispositions, as Western thought usually misinterprets them, confusing them with the concept of values. These habits, are established by education, conduct human beings to a mental situation generative of enjoyment and happiness.

The Aristotelian man is imprisoned in moral obligations that society imposes on him. At the same time, he is a being who follows the *telos* that is dictated by the finest of his attributes–his/her mind. It is a *telos* with the strength of the physical law, but, in order to be accomplished, the law of the city-state must accompany it. This teleology of a non- deterministic character, as it does not set boundaries to human will, is the necessary condition that renders effective the pursuit of virtues and, through them, of well-being.

Later, the virtues of the Christian world, which have substituted for those of the ancient one, have also concurred with a non-deterministic *telos*. A *telos*, which had been dictated by a divine order and had suggested a suitable behavior for the accomplishment of well-being. The arising question is, how can well-being be attained, if any *telos* has disappeared from the horizon of modern man? Is it any more possible Aristotelian and Christian virtues to serve as guides for well-being when the spirit of uncertainty and relativism has overrun contemporary thought? In other words, if good has lost its intrinsic validity and become context dependent, defined by atemporal and asocial forces, how is it possible to be used as a steady orientation of human relations?

The ideal of well-being promoted by the great projects of modernity is responsible for the orientation of the individualized man to consumerism and emotivism (MacIntyre, 1984); that is, to ideologies opposed to living harmoniously in a social community. Pleasure, as an emotional experience, which is mainly actualized in the field of consumption, is the principle of the new hedonism, so well described by known cultural theorists (Bauman, 1996; Campbell, 1987). The continuous demand of aesthetic pleasure and emotion has led to the self-adoration of the ego, that is, to the shaping of a narcissist personality (Lasch, 1979). However, a similar personality is usually accompanied by a fragmented and individualized self (Bellah et.. al., 1985; Sennet, 1977), a self completely disconnected from the other.

Living in the modern world of the uncertainty and relativism, philosophical and sociological thinking–either of a liberalist or a communitarian perspective–in order to realize well-being, search to re-find the linkages between the ego and the other. If the *ego-other* relationship is developed into open, without frontiers societies, it is governed by universal principles; if it is generated into closed communities, it is formed by the traditional and shared values of them. In any case, the study of this relationship also includes those social conditions that allow democratic forms of discourse to define the evaluative criteria as well as the legitimation authorities regarding decisions. Probably contemporary thinking denies teleology, but surely it looks for an ethical aim in the well-being "with and for others in just institutions" (Ricoeur, 1984, p. 180).

The subject of the "other" is crucial for the contemporary thinking. Not only philosophers, but also neurobiologists insist on the importance of the other for the shaping of a self-identity. Varela for example, and his coauthors, argue "the so-called self occurs only in relation to the other.... because self is always codependent with other" (Varela et. al., 1991, p. 246). The self cannot be generated neither acquire an identity without entering an internal dialogue with the other. Internalizing the other's distinctions (attitudes, thoughts and expectations) the ego proceeds to its own distinctions, answering internally to the *generalized other*. (Mead, 1964, 1967). "Ego" and "other" are exchangeable distinctions, which produce a reiterate process or loop of self-reference. This loop constitutes the self and also offers the ground for the shaping of self-identity (Tsivacou, 2000).

In short, the notion of well-being defended by this essay is based on the construction through social action of an authentic, reflective self who founds its authenticity intersubjectively. The socially constructed self is authentic not when it is able to realize its factual uniqueness, but when it realizes his self-reference with an ego open to the other. In other words, *ego–other* relationship is not a relationship of observing and manipulating, but a relationship full of sentiments of caring, respect, recognition and substantive justice for the other. In this perspective, the individual well-being is not the alignment of one's idea of good with some normative standpoint, but one, which inspires the conduct of an individual for the benefit of his/her community and at the same time for the promotion of his/her self-knowledge.

If dialogue is the means for the meeting of the ego with the other, the places of social *acting*, that is, modern institutions, are surely the point of this meeting. Consequently, if modern institutions are in a position to create conditions of authentic dialogue and promote relationships of reciprocity and shared concern between *ego-other*, they are likely to be viewed as places for the reaching of well-being. Nevertheless, in our era, social *acting*, as it is mediated by technology, is subjugated to an instrumental rationality. The result is the replacing of values by technocratic media of communication, and consequently the disappearance of those terms which guarantee well-being. In the next chapter the inhibitors that instrumentality stands out against well-being are delineated.

3.   INSTRUMENTAL ACTION AND DESIGN

3.1   The Instrumentality of Action

Instrumentality has emerged during the new years as the main quality of *acting*. The term "instrumentality" usually means the transformation of entities (material or social), considered in oldest periods of time as final ends of action, to means for the advancement of action. This transformation is the cause for a deep change in the human understanding and interest concerning action. The events of action are replaced by *acting*, the final end by a process. Otherwise, human aims and goals have been substituted by a self-organizing and self-producing process of becoming that is, *acting*.

Let us compare action with the ancient notions of *poiesis* and *praxis*[4] (Aristotle, 1992/1993). This comparison will make explicit the impact of instrumentality on the understanding of action. *Poiesis*, at least according to Aristotle, leads to the production of a thing which already exists in the mind of the producer. Therefore, it could be conceived as a process or a means directed toward the accomplishment of a pre-existing human intention. *Praxis* could be conceptualized as a totality of activities that contain a final end. In sum, *praxis* intends to improve the living conditions of the community. For example, politics is a *praxis*, since its final end is the maintaining of the social order of a given community. Strategy is also a *praxis*, because it is intended to gain the obstacles of the war and thus to defend a community from its enemies. The same is economics, the duty of which is the increase of the communal wealth, etc. (Aristotle, 1992/1993: 1140a, 1140b). In any case, either as *poiesis* or as *praxis*, action is a sequence of independent events distinguished by the fact that in each of them the final end is present.

The deep change in the meaning of action is due to the different understanding of time. The old time, as it is well known, was based on circularity, and the new one, established during Modernity, is grounded on linearity. The meaning of progress has been inaugurated by this change with very serious effects on the organization and direction of human societies. However, this alteration could not be realized if previously a redefinition of human action and institutionalized practices would not happen. This redefinition has been achieved because the social meaning that accompanied the new technologies (such as navigation, typography, industrial machinery, etc.) was not only enriched by new notions, but also because it contributed to the creation of a new *imaginary*, as Castoriadis (1978) would say. In order to design and manipulate reality, the need for a new social imaginary emerged. The duty for the simplification of the emerging complexity, and consequently of the construction of a new conceptualization of the world, have been raised as the main endeavor of the new institutions. A complexity which, on the one hand, corresponded to the real world, and on the other hand, owed its increase to the new understanding and, of course, to the novel action that this understanding stimulated.

The division of labor and specialization that were established during industrialism annulled the independence of any event, suspending it from the next. Now action is not a succession of events, but a series of events anchored on the chain of time. The unwinding (or the unraveling, disentangling) of the chain, unfolds the events, thus the chain of time is important and not the events. Due to its importance, the unwinding of chain cannot conceal any surprise, therefore, it should be typified; it should be transformed into a pre-given structure of expectation (Luhmann, 1995, p. 289). In short, the unity of action should be confirmed a priori in its trajectory and not a posteriori in the completed events.

If expectations are possible distinctions from the horizon of meaning, that is, future communicative distinctions, then any structure of expectation is a surplus of communication at the disposal of a given community. In the frame of this analysis, the line of time, operating as a structure of communication, grasps the events, entangling them in the linkages of the chain. In this way, it transfers from the future to the present expressed and understandable information, that is, expectations.

Thus, communication is identified with time and it emerges as a tissue, in which any kind of action is unfolded. According to the kind of the communicative distinctions, action is engaged to be structured in a different chain of time. The result is the functionally differentiation of society in social systems, each of which accomplishes a diverse kind of action (Alexander & Colomy, 1989; Luhmann, 1989, 1995). Social systems are self-referential processes that use communication for producing communication.

The communicative self-referentiality is stimulated by some symbolic categories of meaning, codified in simple forms, that is, *communication media*.[5] Because the latter are able to assimilate the differences and restore symmetries in an asymmetrical world, they have been raised to the status of general media of equivalence of values. Namely, the values of every social system are homogenized and standardized through their subjugation to a general medium of equivalence (Tsivacou, 1996). That means, *communication media* not only manage the mechanism of systems' selectivity, but, as substitute of values, they also regulate the selectivity of human consciousness.

It should also be noted that modern, functionally differentiated social systems are not homogenous. Other forms of *acting* are emerged spontaneously in them, stimulated by self-referential codes opposed to the respective ones of social systems. The opposed codes operate as the negation of the official ones and thus, lead to the emergence of social movements, such as of emancipation, women's, ecology, youth, religion, or colored minorities.

The intensification of the difference, otherwise the resonance of the difference in the social system results in the following: (a) If the system is in transition, then *difference* (that is, social movement) re-enters in the social system and, by influencing its code of selectivity, promotes transition. (b) If the system is powerful, then its code absorbs the *difference* and it is reconstructed. In the last case, not only the generating forces of the social movement are cancelled, but also the velocity and the quality of the system communication are rather improved.

The functional differentiation of society intensifies the velocity of communication, because under its influence, each social system, looking for its survival, increases through the mechanism of self-reference the extension of communication. Communication rightly has been regarded as the constitutive element of modern society, because it is the only one able to coexist with or to follow the perpetual flow of time. Walking together with the ceaseless tempest of time, and glorifying velocity, communication unifies spaces, transforming parallel activities-events into spacio-temporal continuities.

The dominance of *acting,* that is, the change of action in a series of communicative acts, is responsible for the detachment of an event from its ends, and consequently for the appearance of instrumentality. Nobody is any more interested in the final product of his/her work, than only for the phase of production that he/she must perform. The decline of the final end reveals the "needs" of any phase of *acting.* "Need" means the forwarding of a given activity in a way that the next activity will be prepared and facilitated. Thus, need could be viewed as a problem, the solution of which leads to the next problem, and so forth. Consequently, any activity is transformed in a means for the promotion of a materially and mentally invisible and untouched action. Into this social and intellectual framework, instrumentality emerges as the dominant quality of *acting.*

In the post-modern world, instrumentality is continuously extended transforming little by little *acting* to a network of mental representations without duration and final aim. Some years ago, the instrumental activities of an industrial firm or of a state bureaucracy were coordinated by conceptual, de-materialized models, such as the accounting system or the system of planning. Today that information technology is responsible for the course of action, not only instrumental activities are designed in accordance with abstract models, but also the formal codification of information technology impregnates all organizational texture. Organizational activities have been converted to instrumental packages, the language of which promotes rationalization. The impact of this effect is the decoupling of all organizational features (such as tasks, roles, rites and procedures) from their individual properties and their modification to impersonal, decontextualized terms.

The consciousness of the actor is influenced on the one hand, by the *communication media*, as already mentioned, and on the other hand, by information technology. As Robert Bellah and his coauthors (1985) say, "the world comes to us in pieces, in fragments, lacking any overall pattern" (p. 277). Consciousness is now obliged to run behind the new rhythms of motion, absorbing abstract codes instead of personal relations. Being aware of its limitation concerning the velocity of information (Bickerton, 1990), as well as its incapacity to deal with an information overload (Warfield, 1994), consciousness ends to be disturbed and perplexed. The problem of *double contingency* that Parsons first delineated now becomes more acute. *Double contingency* is a term invented by Parsons in order to declare, "Ego's gratifications are contingent on his selection among available alternatives. But in turn, alter's reaction will be contingent on ego's selection and will result from a complementary selection on alter's part" (Parsons and Shils, 1951, p. 16). Otherwise, it is a situation equally uncertain and contingent for both participants in interaction, which makes interaction indeterminate.

In the past, the participants trying to solve the problem of *double contingency* were assisted by some cultural tools, such as the common norms or values, shared symbols and manners, which worked as stabilized modes of interaction. Today, the differentiation in social systems and the multiplicity of *communication media*, the velocity of time and the impersonal character of communication, promote the loosening of moral and symbolic ties between participants leading to an uncontrolled relativism. Relativism facilitates communication but annuls a moral context, which is necessary for the development of feelings of caring for the other or of substantive and not formal justice. In short, it does not permit the development of a human self with a steady identity, and thus able to realize his/her well-being.

Nevertheless, there is an exception. This is the case of social movements, produced by *acting* in the modern social systems. Due to their voluntary and moral binding with these movements, humans shape them as the communities of ideas in which the effects of *double contingency* could be decreased if not deleted. In this kind of communities a final end is again discovered, as the common understanding of goodness inspires it. Moreover, these communities, due to their critical stance toward system rationality, at least the first period of their operating, condemn instrumentality and announce the principles of a new conceptualization of justice.

Just below, we argue more extensively on these communities. In the meantime, we should examine if it is possible, in the framework of the dominant system rationality, methodological tools which promote dialogue, such as design methodologies, to operate as diminutioners of instrumentality. Without doubt design and design methodologies are governed by the principles of dialogue and participation. The question is if theory and practice of design that usually deal with the accommodation of the double contingency's problem, operate on behalf of social systems. If yes, they surely are limited to serve the trajectory of the action, that is, the trajectory of communication and thus, the demands of time. If they are not necessarily connected with systems rationality, they perhaps dispose such qualities to decrease instrumentality. In this last case, they may create into the domain of dialogue these conditions which restore, even provisionally, the necessary for the well-being terms. A possible answer to this question is the theme of the next section.

3.2   The Instrumentality of Social Designing

Design in general and social systems design in particular (which is the subject of this section) aims at the mastering of *acting*, the settlement of its unforeseen contingencies in accordance to the coordinates of time, hence at the control of expectations. Design is in the service of communication, attempting to set aside the organizational obstacles that restrain its victorious marching. Even if these obstacles are referred to objectives or goals, or to methods and processes, in any case the subject of design is the capture of the indefinite, unpredictable and unanticipated element of *acting*. By capturing this element, design makes *acting* compatible with the chain of time, and consequently with the expectations constitutive of it.

As design is usually connected with a *purposive-rational* action, it does not include final ends, therefore it could be characterized as a *meta-function* of instrumental rather dimension. The mission of this *meta-function* is to organize and promote methodologies of problem solving for fuzzy situations emerged during the different phases of *acting*. Thus, a system of ideas, namely a cognitive scheme such as design, handles the conceptualizations of the actual world, attempting at their settlement. In this way, design is a social construction, which is in the service of other social constructions, such as the social systems and their organizations.

In Modernity, representation does not try any more to copy the world accurately as it did during the Middle Ages (Foucault, 1966). Rather it filters the things of the world, and thus reduces the whole world in some filtered and thus immaterial and abstracted things. In this way representation becomes able to measure, classify, divide and manipulate the world. If, now, we accept that design is, as Van Gigh (1991) argues, the modeling of representations, and consequently the portrayal of abstraction, then it should be considered as the height of modernity.

Design attempts to describe a problem situation. By accepting that any description is not an object of reality, but a subjective observation, it is obvious that the partiality of any description is recognized. Therefore, if design likes to have a nearest to reality description of the situation, then it should pursue as many descriptions as possible. However, an exact understanding of reality cannot be equal with the sum of descriptions. Various descriptions include contradictions and repetitions, and consequently, the image produced by them is likely to be confused and incomprehensible. Therefore, it is necessary a process of selection to be preceded, during which some descriptions as distinctive visions of the situation will be selected in common. To define this process, Van Gigh (1991, p. 235) adopts the notion of "generalizing abstraction" used by Langer in order to signalize the selecting of the common features of several descriptions emerged in the discursive domain. Van Gigh reminds us that abstraction is a mental process strictly connected with that of symbolism, and characterizes the first phase of social designing. This is the reason that this phase of design is here called as "first order abstraction". During this phase some of the produced representations about the world are selected creating a global representation of the problem situation.

The second phase of design is the modeling of global representation derived from the process of first order abstraction. This phase of modeling is here called "second order abstraction". Typifying the already abstracted problem situation in graphic forms, second order abstraction proceeds to a sequence of concepts logically interconnected, aiming at an immediate and holistic grasping of reality. For this grasping, design models try to use simultaneously elements of analytic and symbolic thought. As it is well known, the symbolic elements, by addressing feelings, transcend the boundaries of things, capturing their hidden and unexpressed totality. However, the power of the symbolic forms of design, due to their simplistic and discursive character, is so week that it is unable to irritate the imaginary and affective elements of the human mind. On the contrary, analytic thought is able to motivate new ideas and thus, to promote creativity. The created analytically meaning included in the conceptual models, is the product of a cognitive process, which by revealing causes and interrelations, produces reasonable propositions.

Due to the predominance of analytic thought over symbolic, design does not grasp the emotional core of "discourse".[6] This core, underlying the rationalist element of the discourse, nestles in the *unsaid* element of interaction. The word «*unsaid*» characterizes the part of meaning, which is rather inferred than explicitly pronounced. While manifested meaning uses the sequential and indexical structure of the proposition, the *unsaid* becomes available only through the passive voice of feelings, namely, of the face and body expressions. Avoiding the whole universe of discourse, design remains in the boundaries of instrumentality.

Design methodology, as it is applied to functional social systems, results in a process of objectification and rationalization of the participants' worldviews. These worldviews are separated from the enunciator and as independent and autonomous elements of a self-referential process, contribute to the generation of new observations, more complicated and also more abstracted. Thus design, instead of binding system observations, ends to multiply them, and in this way to increase organizational complexity. This is a serious reason for characterizing design as a promoted phase of instrumental thought.

Despite the efforts of designers to emphasize the moral element of design, and in spite of their insistence to view design rather as a means of moral transformation than simply as a tool for problem solving,[7] I would say that design methodologies, in practice, fail to come out of instrumental perspective. I do not also ignore the preference of designers to a hermeneutic rather than to an instrumental approach. However, as most applications are in the service of organizational rationality, that is, of instrumentality, design methodologies are subjected to the rationality of modern *acting*, distorting in praxis the theoretical principles of hermeneutics. The results of this distortion enter the structural models, that is, the conceptual articulations, in which meaning is already deposited, and result to restrict meaning instead of liberating it.

Design methodologies did not pay the appropriate attention to their basic advantage, that is, oral language. For most of them language is a communicative tool and not a source of meaning constitutive of the world. For example, John Warfield (1994) in his theory of *Generic Design* attempts to deal with the problem of language from a rather technical side. Leaving aside the origin of language, he looks for an accurate language, which cannot be a prose but a graphically integrated language system. This endeavor leads him to the structuring of a really effective methodology, that is, *Interactive Management*, which, however, cannot escape from the constraints of instrumentality. The reason is that by grasping and stabilizing meaning in articulated models, *Interactive Management* investigates only the meaning that emerges during the interactive process, without being able to elaborate the latent sides of meaning, that is, the *unsaid*.

Even one of the most developed issues of *Interactive Management*, and one of the most effective design methodologies, the *Cogniscope Systems Approach*, which Christakis (1999) and his fellows apply, does not exhaust all design possibilities to deal with the plurality of language games. *Cogniscope* recognizes communicative distinctions as the ontological elements of action, and tries hard to substitute the core of the communicative distinctions, that is, their persuasion by power to the power of persuasion (Christakis, 1998). However, in *Cogniscope* also, any enunciation is regarded rather as an utterance, the ultimate end of which is to be crystallized in a structural conceptual model. By using an oral language a priori subjected to the needs of the conceptual models, some essential "nuances" or "traces" of the spoken language are lost. Such traces viewed as *differences* of meaning, are hidden in the *unsaid* part of it, and thus, they fail to be illuminated.

Of course, many design theorists have investigated diverse issues of meaning or a pre-understanding produced by collective *acting*. But since the self and its identity are of no interest to instrumental thinking, the speakable part of a design methodology focuses rather on the function of the communicative process than on the personality and subjectivity of the speaker. In this way, methodology handles the speaker as a simple commissioner of the language games, leaving free the rational element of discourse to subjugate the non-rational one. In short, methodology keeps away from its course whatever springs from the affected part of the self, and specifically whatever characterizes the ego standing in front of the other. Methodologies give priority to utterances, to communicative distinctions, and not to the persons who enunciate them. Thus, communication as a process regulative of the social systems' selections becomes more important than human consciousness.

Each time that methodologies proceed to the investigation of human intentions, their aim is the accommodation and the harmonization of these intentions with the demands of the social systems. Human ends enter methodologies to such an extent that they enlighten the «need» of an activity, or of a phase of *acting*. The occupation of methodologies with human ends is limited to the settlement of fuzzy situations created by the structural couplings of humans with social systems. The further investigation of human intentions has been left to psychology. However, the latter deals with the intentions from the moment that a pathological situation is generated, and not when they cause the withdrawal of well-being from the life of a human being.

Another problem not decisively solved by design methodologies is that of validity claims and legitimation. Even *Critical System Thinking* (Flood & Jackson, 1991), which is aligned with Habermas teaching, does not face the problem of validity and legitimation according to Habermas theory. The latter promotes a social reform based on a pragmatic and intersubjective understanding of rationality. He claims that any communicative act makes a claim to validity based on truth and moral rightness. This claim is bound by universal standards; therefore dialogue is possible because it is founded on the common acceptance of these universal standards.

Design methodologies in general, and critical methodologies in particular, neither investigate these standards, as it seems, nor accept them as a common ground of the pursued consensus. On the contrary, consensus itself is the common ground on which the truth of any declarative utterance is evaluated; given that, legitimation springs from the linguistic practices and the effectiveness that *acting* promotes. Moreover, concerning the untroubled unfolding of different judgments, critical methodologies are rather worried of any power derived from oppressive authorities than of the untruthfulness and incorrectness of judgments themselves. Therefore, they hold that judgments are likely to by better uttered in a methodological context of equality than of expertise. In short, what is endangered in design is the principle of jurisdiction, as Lyotard (1988, p. 74) would say.

The pursuing of equality and consequently of elimination of power instead of jurisdiction based on expertise, compels design methodologies in general to apply the "principle of toleration" regarding the deeper values on which the worldviews of the participants are anchored. Designers, by adopting the principle of toleration, are aligned with liberalists according to whom "it is left to citizens individually to resolve questions of religion, philosophy, and morals, in accordance with the views that freely affirm" (Rawls, 1987, p. 15). Of course, as it will be further commented in this essay, methodologies, while not arguing about the subject of jurisdiction, have silently internalized the jurisdiction of science as an absolute authority. We should not forget that design is a scientific construction, even if its principles are not exclusively founded on scientific axioms.

The acceptance of toleration as a principle of design results in the introduction of moral relativism in design methodologies even in the critical ones that declare self-reflection and emancipation. Relativism, in regard to values, while enhancing human freedom and autonomy, does not lead to authenticity and hence to steady identities; consequently, the ideal of a common good is very difficult to coexist with this perspective. Nevertheless, there is a critical methodology, that of *Critical Heuristics of Social Planning*, of Werner Ulrich (1983), which tries to avoid relativism. By accepting the intersubjective building of reason, and trying to avoid the risks of relativism, *Critical Heuristics* raises emancipation as the absolute principle, that is, a principle of Pure Reason (as Kant defines it). Thus, emancipation is proposed as the a priori value for the definition of the validity claims. However, as the categories of Pure Reason are set a priori, while the content of emancipation is clarified only a posteriori, during methodological process, *Critical Heuristics* cannot also solve the contradiction between Pure Reason and Social Rationality.

Not only their relativistic approach, but also their subject-centered reason impels design methodologies to avoid discussions on common good and matters of public policy. Without being able to lead participants to a common understanding about the good, design methodologies do not help participants to shape value judgments for a critical estimation of a state of life. Nevertheless, the lack in value judgments does not help methodologies to build a conversational domain, in which the claims to good or evil could be raised at the same moment with those of a procedural right. In other words, in design methodologies justice is superior to goodness. This fact results to the non-building of an epistemological approach related to human subjectivity and well-being, with one exception: the methodology that Fuenmayor, Lopez-Garay, and others developed in the University of Los Andes in Venezuela, which they called *Interpretive Systemology*.

Fuenmayor argues that a methodology aiming at a consensus is of interest only if it operates as a learning process (Fuenmayor, 1991). Learning in

Interpretive Systemology is not a way of gaining knowledge for a regulative and manipulated aim, but an itinerary for the approaching of the other. By uncovering through interpretive thinking other contexts of meaning, human consciousness has an opportunity to come out from its self-reference and to understand the other. The problem is, as Fuenmayor confesses, the weakness of any design methodology to be compatible with the dominant rationality of the contemporary high-technological society.

Before ending this section, lets pay attention to the fact that design methodologies have been constituted in the decade of 80s, when social as well philosophical and sociological demands for human emancipation from power was to the fore. In this social frame of analysis design theorists and especially critical systems thinkers were impressively aware of the connection between self-reflection and subjective emancipation. But they could not speculate about well-being and authenticity since these ones were not issues of their time. Only today, after the changes that occurred in human theory and practice, that of authenticity and well-being has supplemented the interest in power and autonomy.

Surely a similar supplement, such as that referred above, has not yet been noticed in design and respective methodologies. The fact that methodologies are in the service of organizational rationality is perhaps the cause of this delay as well as of the observed contradictions concerning morality between design theory and practice. Organizational rationality gives priority to rational persuasion instead of interhuman understanding. This is not something peculiar, if we take into consideration that methodologies have their origin in the discipline of *Operational Research* and its attempts to face complex and pluralist situations in typical organizations.

In sum, the pursuit of modeling as well as the satisfaction of the organizational demands impel to the following: (a) The neglecting of the *unsaid* meaning. In this way they grasp only the part of meaning explicitly appeared in the declarative utterances. (b) The conceiving of the other as a participant of the discourse rather, than as a human being who suffers in common with me, or who partakes of my happiness or misfortune. This is due to the fact that methodologies do not enlighten the self as a social entity constructed by the incessant interaction between the ego and the other. This disregarding reduces the other to a social role, in spite of the attempts of methodologies, through abstraction, to release participants from the load of their role.

Nevertheless, the instrumental perspective of systems methodologies is due neither to the nature of design, nor to the inherent properties of the methodologies. As it is already mentioned, it is due to the field of design applications. If we apply design to social contexts such as those of social movements, maybe it could contribute sufficiently to the forming of steady identities. Through oral language, methodologies imply the *unsaid* and the *undesigned*, therefore are potentially suitable for the unfolding of understanding among conscious entities.

During a process of design, actors enunciate their personal experiences. In this way, actors have the opportunity to reveal their existence in the world or, better, their stance in front of the other. This act of revealing potentially can force human beings to deviate from the flow of time, otherwise from the course of *acting* and to stand in the world, asking themselves "who am I?" Answering this question, individuals reconstitute their morality, allowing their personal values to enter organizational place. As long as a genuine conversation endures, individual consciousness excavates the layers of experiences; it stops making distinctions and it proceeds to a self-reflection and a self-opening toward the others. Of course, this is a short opportunity offered to consciousness by momentary cracks of time, when methodologies gather time around the present. Surely, this is an advantage of design methodologies rarely expressed and specifically in applications no related to organizational rationality.

Design is a deontological approach as, on the one hand, it is concerned with what it ought to be (Banathy, 1996; Banathy, 1997; Simon, 1981) and, on the other hand, it deals with intellectual activities able to transform existing situations into desired ones. If the desired situation is the realization of the human well-being, then the social context which allows the implementation of a non-instrumental design must firstly be investigated; In continuity, how design methodologies should be slightly modified will be examined, so that some inherent properties of them could be unfolded.

4. APPROACHING COMMUNITIES

4.1 The Present Day Discussion

Communities arise as the social context in which goodness and human well-being could be pursued. Therefore, in this section we proceed to a larger unfolding of the idea of "community" which is already mentioned in the *Introduction*. Starting from the debate between liberalists and communitarians we repeat that these two theoretical perspectives define morality and, of course, self and identity, differently. Liberalism conceptualizes human subject as a self-interested, rational calculator, tied basically with the other by contractual terms. Communitarianism sees it as a human being born and constructed into a network of human interactions taking place in social institutions. In these institutions, human beings found bounds on mutuality and solidarity and not on abstract ideas.

The decay of the national state is accompanied by the demolition of any mediation between individuality and social values, reducing the former to become a prey of uncontrolled and inexorable interests. At the same time, community appears to be the favorable social context for the securing of these mediations that help individuality to reach the wholeness of the world.

Communitarians hold that community provides normative notions, which operate as a medium of meaning for the communication of its members. This position at first sight does not differ importantly from that of liberalists, who also argue about some normative categories of meaning universally and a priori given. The only difference is that communitarians, instead of attributing these notions to some universal anthropological characteristics, see community as the origin of them and individuals as their a posteriori possessors.

Cultivating traditional values, the members of a community develop an ideal good through which the person of the other fixes the limits of the world. In contrast to liberalists (Rawls, 1971), who defend the priority of the right over the good, communitarians give rise to the good, claiming that each person must be treated as an end in itself and never as a means. In their critique against liberalism, communitarians debate about the liberalist self as a deontological one, individualized in advance and not shaped in relations with others (Sandel, 1982).

Communitarians have brought the linking between self-identity and the good to the fore; however, intense argumentation regarding the content of good has developed among them. The reason for this argumentation in the interior of the communitarian circle is due to the dual approaching of good. On the one hand, good implies generality and impersonality, since it must give each actor a neutral, moral ground for understanding, or a horizon of moral meaning, in which every one could find his/her personal, ethical conduct.[8] On the other hand, taking into consideration the plurality of the personal attitudes toward the "good", it has been accepted that these attitudes should not be opposed to the abstract image of good generally shared by the community's members. Otherwise, the abstract conceptualization of the "good" should not contradict the morality of the community. The last phrase does not mean the subjection of individuality to the community, but the need for a social context into which individuals may avoid the abstractness of any universal procedure regarding the definition of duty. Also, it means that through a discursive forging of shared visions of the "good", a public sphere of ideas is likely to be shaped which will counterweight the privacy promoted by modern life.

It is evident that communitarians found an interesting discourse in regard to the human, affective needs and the idea of the absolute good. However, they are not so convincing for the possibility of modern societies to promote the communitarian ideal of solidarity and concern for the other. In contemporaneous communities this solidarity and concern are usually reserved for their members, creating in this way insecure and narrow-minded people, unable to face the challenges of our era.

The reason for this discord between theory and practice perhaps is due to the fact that communitarian thinking does not proceed to a sociological analysis of contemporary society. Contrary to the past theories of community (I remind Töennies and his known distinction between *gemeinschaft* and *gesellscaft*, as well as the sociological studies carried out particularly between 1920 and 1950) current communitarian research looks into political and not sociological aspects of contemporary communities. The most known communitarians investigate community as a place that produces a sense of belonging or rather as a normative force, than as a part of a functionally differentiated society. However, it would be not only interesting but also useful for communitarian thinking sociology to deal again with the subject of community.

According to the argument of this essay, contemporary society is not composed of communities but of functional social systems. It is true that in these systems an observer could distinguish groups of people or communities involved in activities neither similar to the leading ones of the social systems, nor opposed to them. I mention the voluntary organizations of civil society, such as athletic or charitable associations. Usually communities of this kind are activated in a social system, which produces social goods no commercialized, such as the system of religion, of family, art and science, health and social welfare. Nevertheless, it is also true that organizations of civic society, despite their intentions, rarely succeed in avoiding the self-referential code of the social system and its dominant rationality.

In their majority modern communities, such as the described above, do not dispose some predominant features of social structure. They are rather social settings operating into the boundaries of social systems and they would be better regarded as places of repose from the plurality of communicative distinctions. Their members are usually activated in practices complementary to the main ones of social systems, but instead of being oriented by a *purposive-rational* or *value-rational action*, they are rather driven by an emotivist perspective (MacIntyre, 1984), which cannot conduct them to self-reflection and self-fulfillment and consequently to well-being.

Emotivism, as we already referred, derived from the great projects of Modernity and goes in parallel with individualism and the privatization of the modern individual (Sennet, 1977). The latter, prisoner of a culture that accentuates personal feelings and emotions, is more interested in persons that enter his/her private place and belong to his/her social environment than in outsiders in his/her community or foreigners. The outsider is the impersonal other who becomes familiar and subject of concern and affection only from the moment that the mass media bring him/her closer revealing his/her personal adventures. This kind of emotional interest disappears as soon as mass media display another personal history, which substitutes the previous one.

In short, one observes not a true caring for the other, but a sentimental pleasure that an individual feels following the fate of the unfortunate other. The fact of emotion is more important than the unhappy events and the moved individual is more attracted by his/her psychological situation than by the causes of the other's misfortune. This kind of narcissistic behavior as Lasch (1979) argues, is not a selfish one, but a behavior characterized by the fear of binding commitments or of giving attention to the needs of the other. As the fundamental trait of narcissism is self-love, then it is understood that feelings of caring and genuine altruism cannot be developed in the psyche of the modern individual.

If the narcissistic individual is the member of the modern communities, then, where can we find social contexts with features such as those described by communitarians?

4.2 "Anti-structural" Communities

I wonder if the only communities in correspondence to communitarian ideas are those activated in the social movements. These communities function as "anti-structures" (Turner, 1995) in a well-structured functional system. Due to their atypical form, they can operate as the alter ego of power and instrumental action. A community of this type is not a permanent system, but a spontaneous scheme that operates as a critique regarding the unequal, power-bounded relations.

The anti-structural communities of the social movements are temporal, historical events that after a short period of function fall into the norms of structure giving their position to legal institutions. As long as they function, they could liken to the public space described by Taylor (1996), that is, an extra-political place of discussion, which does not obey the exercise of power.

Turner (1995) describing an authentic community says that it breaks in "through the interstices of structure, in liminality; at the edges of structure, in marginality; and from beneath structure, in inferiority" (p. 128). Replacing the word "structure" with the word "systems rationality", we can transfer the thought of Turner in our model of the functionally differentiated social systems, and argue about authentic communities, which operate in the frame of social systems, under the impulse of a code contradictory to the leading one of the systemic self-reference. Hippies' communities are according to Turner good examples of such «anti-structures» in modern Western society. Other examples are those of the feminist, ecological, colored minorities and homosexual movements.

These communities emerge spontaneously from social movements and claim the cancellation of the dominant structural arrangement and hierarchical order. Therefore, they are characterized by a revolutionary spirit and temporality. Due to this temporality, if communities do not create immediately strong fluctuations and consequently radical changes in the social systems, they soon stop functioning as revolutionary agents and fall into the situation of structure. However, as long as they operate as «anti-structures», they create a novel public sphere, which impels modern individuals to come out from their privacy. This public sphere could be seen as Taylor (1996) argues, "as being outside power. It is supposed to be listened to by power, but it is not itself an exercise of power" (p. 191).

The members of an authentic community could really develop a genuine concern for the other, because the community teaches them the staring at the good. Moreover, as these communities are established as the denial of structure, that is, *anti-structures*, they cancel the constitutive features of structure such as roles, procedures and tasks. By annulling structure, they invalidate also instrumentality, and thus, they unhook consciousness from the chain of time allowing its integration with the world. A liberated consciousness develops a self-reflective and self-fulfilled subjectivity, that is, a self with a steady identity, able to come to a relationship full of friendship and solidarity for the other.

Within the context of communities of social movements design methodologies operate as propulsive means of well-being. The reason is that methodologies adjusted to a communal context, do not need to surpass the weaknesses that an instrumental approach dictates to them. The community itself provides a priori the necessary means, which an actual methodological process, as it has already been noted, does not dispose.

4.3   Communities in the Economic System

It has also been commented that a functional social system permits a group of people to operate with goals complementary to its own rather, than an authentic community to emerge. The best that one can hope to be established in a social system is the temporary rise of a "community of ideas". As Fowler (1996) argues, a "community of ideas" is established when some human beings decide together "conversing with, and respecting each other in a setting which is as equal as possible" (p. 89). However, even in the case of a community of ideas, there are not a priori conditions for the building of a self-reflective personality. These conditions are even more rare and difficult to be met in the economic system, in general, and in the representative organizations of this system, in particular. The reason is that profit organizations such as business firms are the kingdom of instrumentality therefore communities of ideas are difficult to make their appearance in a similar context.

Below, I intend to investigate if and under what premises it is possible to build at least a community of ideas in the economic system and in parallel with the typical for profit organization.

Modern firms are embedded in *purposive-rational* action, that is, in space and time of instrumentality. Therefore, the possibility of creating in this place a participatory community of ideas is a priori undermined. For building a community of this kind, communal action should renounce its instrumental character. It should be anchored on a chain of time different from that of the communicative distinctions. Otherwise, action should be based on the personal relationships of interaction, and not on the impersonal relations of communication. Only thus, on the one hand action is not subjugated to its self-production, but obeys the community's purposes, and on the other hand, the community's members, aiming at communal ideals, espouse them as their supreme good.

An action based on interaction, that is, a non-instrumental action cannot produce goods that become commodities. The mission of a non-instrumental action, as MacIntyre claims, is the development of practices oriented to the production of "internal goods", that is, goods produced not for the market but for the welfare of the community.[9] Extending the argument of MacIntyre, I would say that "internal goods" satisfy not only the needs of the participants in the practices but also of the affected by these practices. Such practices coincide with the respective ones of the social movements, when the latter continue to be critical, that is, located on the boundaries of social systems, just before adopting the rationality of the structure.

Modern firms surely do not produce internal goods. In their case the old practices as well as the accompanying virtues are lost. The labor process encourages the alignment of consciousness with the prevailing *communication media,* and the human intentions for wealth and power supersede the caring for the other. Knowing this situation, communitarians do not ground their theory on the workplace of the modern for profit organizations.

Neither communitarian thinking or organization theory has developed an approach for linking self-identity and morality with workplace. It is true that during the last decades some studies referred to self-identity and business ethics (du Gay, 1996, 2000; Parker, 1998). Nevertheless, most of them continue to face the human existence as a valued asset, a source of competitive advantage due to its high quality performance, intelligence and adaptability. The organization theory, sometimes before and sometimes behind practice, in order to reinforce business internal consistency, flexibility and quality, proposes new managerial methods more suitable for the new entrepreneurial needs. The extensive use of communication systems, team-working with flexible job design, innovative training and learning, involvement in decision making with responsibility, performance appraisal with tight links to contingent pay, etc., are known examples of such methods. All of them reveal that modern organizations continue to face employees as a means to an end, reducing them to the position of the other resources they use for maximal return.

If communities of ideas are founded on a genuine dialogue, then surely, in the modern workplace, this possibility of a genuine dialogue is a priori undermined. Action as it is previously analyzed, does not so much leave limits to dialogue as to decision taking. The velocity of the communicative distinctions continuously increases not only due to the competition produced by diminishing resources but, mainly, due to innovations. As the phases of *acting* are ends by themselves, they lead to continuously shifting goals, and in this way they compel employees to accept the intensification of work, and adopt an inauthentic behavior. Moreover, it is very difficult for the employees of the modern workplace to divest of their roles and the power that they imply, entering with their whole personality a genuine dialogue.

It is obvious that modern employees cannot institutionalize a community into which a self-identity steadily oriented to the absolute good and well-being will be constituted. As organized work does not aim at the production of internal goods, the development of ideals of participation and genuine dialogue are rather ineffective. The time also disposed by modern employees is not enough for participating in the communities of ideas outside their workplace. In short, the public spheres of dialogue such as the communities of ideas are today available only to persons disconnected from circuits of work (such as young or aged individuals). The organizations of "civil society" are mainly composed of inactive or unoccupied individuals, situated on the edge of social systems.

5.   DESIGNING COMMUNITARIAN DISCURSIVE AREAS

The previous analysis drove us to the conclusion that methodologies are compatible with the social context of their implementation. If they are applied to anti-structural contexts, such as those of social movements, they could contribute to the promotion of communal aims, and also to the self-reflection of the community's members leading them to a situation of well-being. On the contrary, if they are applied to social systems, then systems rationality will also be adopted by design. Many problems arise in this last case, and could be summarized in the following question: under which conditions design methodologies could be able to exploit their inherent advantages and overcome the constraints of instrumentality. Otherwise, is it effective design methodologies to be transformed themselves to "anti-structures" in the framework of social systems?

In the next section I am attempting to examine the possibilities of designing in a functional system a discursive area where not only space but also time will be in suspension. This is not a utopian plan, since a similar discursive place where the main subject of argument was human well-being, has already been realized. I mention the Athenian Academy and Lyceum, where Plato and Aristotle inaugurated a discourse on Morality, Ethics and Well-being.

5.1   The Ancient Discursive Place

The answers of contemporary philosophy and sociology regarding well-being are greatly connected with democracy. The realization of well-being needs a context of dialogue where equal opportunities for decision making and taking are effective. In the ancient *polis*, and especially in the Athenian democracy, dialogue had been raised as the most important means of the public life at the end of the Persian war. The difference of the discursive process between contemporary world and Athens, which makes the latter a classical model of democracy, is that "the discussions outside this body (the official public sphere of the ancient *polis*) prepare for the action ultimately taken by the same people within it" (Taylor, 1996, p. 191). That means people responsible for the emergence of power supervised political power. This is the reason that the ethical life of citizens was the criterion for their competence in politics.

Ending 4th century B.C., Greek democracy is in decline. It was then, that traditional public spheres, and of course political thought and action developed in them, began to lose their value orientation, and a need for their substitution emerged. Thus, while academic schools were places of philosophical discourse, they had been transformed to loci for the re-building the old citizenship, through reason's search for truth, friendship and well-being.

Many studies concerning Greek philosophy have paid attention to the fact that well-being for ancient Greeks is not only a subject of inquiry, but also a way of living. For a long period of time, Greeks have tried to realize well-being in their schools of teaching, such as Academia, Lyceum, Stoic school, Epicures garden, etc. Especially at the end of the 4th B.C. century, Academia first and Lyceum later, were viewed not only as abstracted places of teaching, but also as social places where, far from material conditions, theoretical modes of existence took place at the level of discourse. The soul and mind of students, following the rules of arguments, were governed by reason, and in this way, the reconciliation between politics, absolute good and well being was pursued.

In the old academic schools teaching was developed on the one hand, on contemplative activities and cultivation of virtues and, on the other hand, on gymnastics, that is, on exercises of the body. Each school had its own rules for the regulation of the whole discursive process. The inner organization of the academic activities allowed students the distraction from the actual life of *polis* and their metaphorical transfer to a space where goodness and virtues could be contemplated.

Analyzing the creation of a dramatic space in the *Republic* of Plato, Adi Ophir (1991) develops a similar point commenting on the ideas of Plato about the philosopher-king (6th book, paragraphs 484c-486):

He (Plato) opened within the city yet outside it, a new possibility of action for Greek men. He opened for them a new space within which to move, a new space in which to exercise their (transformed) manhood, to go after their (sublimated) desires, to face their (now partial) finitude, to strive for a (new type) of excellence, and to imprint their (displaced) will and power, molding anew the organization of the space, molding it for others to follow and remember them. Their will to power is to be displaced from the city onto discourse and is to direct them in the pursuit of more knowledge not more power. The will to knowledge would lead them–already within the discursive space–from the particular to the universal, and from the universal to the whole. (p. 128)

I would like to entrust methodologies of design with a similar role. Otherwise, to examine if design, operating into the functionally differentiated societies in general, and into the workplace of the modern firm in particular, could establish a permanent learning process such as that created in the ancient schools. This learning process, as it would be institutionalized in actual workplaces, could be viewed as an *anti-workplace*. It could be regarded as space and time in suspension regarding the tasks and duties of the working life. Operating outside the flow of modern *acting*, the designed anti-workplace is likely to create a temporal frame in which the affective and rational stance of the ego toward the other would be reconciled with instrumentality.

5.2   Discursive Areas in the Modern Workplace.

Our problem as designers is to see how it is possible to maintain the atypical form of communities of ideas and the beneficial outcome derived from their function into a structured social system, especially into the economic one. If dialogue is the constitutive element of communities, firstly, we should examine the attributes of a similar dialogue.

It is not enough dialogue to achieve the conditions of an ideal, transcendental situation by satisfying some basic rules of argumentation, such as truthfulness and equality of participants. Neither it is sufficient everybody to participate in dialogue and in decision-making. The terms of truthfulness, equality and participation are indispensable terms of any dialogue evolved in a public sphere. It is not also enough that during dialogue participants "understand themselves as belonging to a community which shares some common purposes and recognizes its members as sharing in these purposes" (Taylor, 1996, p. 204). More than all that, dialogue should be structured in a way that participants understand what a stable and healthy identity means. To obtain it, a discursive reflection on the common good is required. A dialogue inspired by a shared vision of good shapes steady identities, capable of entering discursive processes propulsive of self-reflection and self-realization. In sum, a similar dialogue makes human consciousness able to face the inhibitors that social systems raise up against it.

In this discursive community participants would be mutually encouraged to develop self-confidence and to be recognized as human beings of shared purposes and modes of life. They would generate a heightened sense for their capacity to come out from the rationality of the *communication media* and, surpass the problem of *double contingency*. In short, this community would create in the heart of instrumentality and technical rationality an area devoted to human understanding.

Design methodologies have a lot in common as well as important differences with the discursive processes of the ancient philosophical schools. Their similarities and differences are summarized as below:

Similarities: (a) Displacement of the actors' attention from the actual to the purely contemplative realm. This displacement does not mean the forgetting of the actual, but a transition of thought to pure contemplative forms, of which the object is exactly the actual. In short, both consider contemplative realm as a time of suspension in the course of everyday business. (b) Installation through dialogue of a permanent learning process. (c) Constitution of a shared understanding. d) Investigation of alternative solutions. (e) Implementation of a generative and strategic dialogue.

Differences: (a) The purposes of dialogue–Ancient schools aimed at the creation of a spiritual community and the reaching of well-being. Design methodologies do not include any concrete aim, but they embrace the purposes of the participants. (b) The form of dialogue–In the ancient schools dialogue is unstructured, while in systems methodologies dialogue is structured in order to be grasped by systems models. (c) The duration of dialogue–In ancient schools dialogue was continuously repeated, while in modern firms it is usually a short-term event. (d) The kind of commitment–Systems methodologies promote the commitment to an action, while the ancient dialogue tried to build new self-identities through wisdom and ethics. (e) The role of the teacher versus the role of the facilitator–In ancient schools, the teacher conducted the process of teaching and he was competent to deal with the said or the uttered propositions. In methodologies there is no teacher, but only a facilitator or director of the process. The jurisdiction of methodologies does not belong to any expert, but only to the group of participants. (f) The sense of time–Ancient schools of thought run their activities at the same time with the rest of the political activities. The society as totality had a unified sense of cyclic time. Today we have the same phenomenon. Design follows the time of social systems but, as already noted, our era has a linear conceptualization of time, leading to infinity.

The above differences are mainly differences of culture and it is obvious that their cancellation, even if it would be desirable, would be difficult to be obtained. However their suggestion is useful, because it shows the conditions under which communities of ideas could be developed within social systems. The difference teaches us that an attempt for bridging the two discursive domains obliges systems methodologies to investigate the presumptions of constructing through a methodological process a teleological social system, that is, a community out of the ordinary stream of business. An ethical or healthy community as Nelson (1989) names it, should not be the locus of purposeful activities motivated by instrumental rationality, but a locus of common self-understanding. Moreover, it should be a place where time will lose its linear direction.

The building of a similar community presupposes the clarification of the notion of good because only a shared understanding of good leads to feelings of caring and proximity. Making participants aware of the common good, methodology pulls them out of "fragmentation". The latter emerges in an individualist society, "when people come to see themselves more and more individualistically or, otherwise put, as less and less bound to their fellow citizens in common projects and allegiances" (Taylor, 1996, p. 211).

Seeing good as "a fuzzy situation", participants will approach it without oversimplifications. Guided by reason, and using simultaneously their creativity and empathy, participants will be encouraged to articulate their deepest experiences, to devise alternatives of good and well-being, to form patterns, to synthesize their opinions, and finally to model their desired, ideal situation. This last prerequisite differentiates design activity from a therapy group process, which addresses only new ways of understanding.

Nevertheless, ancient communities, such as those of the ancient schools, while instructing us the appropriate *telos*, they cannot do the same to the methodological process. This is due to the fact that the process is the materialization of time and time is the main cause of difference between the two cultures. How the two flows of time, the one of communities and the other of social systems, could coexist? If both times are real, how could they cooperate and work in parallel without social disturbances?

There is a form of discourse able to change the historical time, and this is *narration*. The narrative time is the only one that establishes a sense of the present; let's say of a narrative *Now* (Chatman, 1978). If design institutionalizes in the social systems an *anti-structure* that recalls *Now*, then the linearity of time is canceled and with it instrumentality; consciousness, beyond the anxiety of time, reintegrates life with the whole world.

5.3   Design and Narrative Time

Narration always evolves in the present. The narrated events are developing now, despite the fact that their history concerns the past or the future. Namely, the historical time, that is, the time in which the story happens, is annulled and the narrated action, through selected narrative forms, is concentrated on the present; thus, a closed circuit of time is created.

On the contrary, in design designers and participants conceptualize time linearly, because the beginning of time is in the past and its end in the future. As it is already commented, this is the time of instrumentality. Nevertheless, an alternative solution could be found. Thus, the atemporalization of design process, otherwise, the transformation of the linear direction of time to a cyclic one would be fulfilled.

If we view design process as a narration, according to which conceptual models will be regarded as events of the story's composition, then, following Ricoeur (1990), we could say that the alternative solution is the act of *repetition.* By *repetition,* we mean the existential probing deeply into plot, in a way that human consciousness is situated in an atemporal or ahistorical time, that is, into *remembrance.* Remembrance, as Ricoeur (1990) claims, is not the evolving of the episodic time, but the movement that brings us back to the horizon of the potentialities that narration recollects.

In design narration has a dialogic form. Using all linguistic games,[10] the participants of dialogue could have the opportunity to deconstruct or to proceed to a genealogical inquiry of their everyday work and life experience, to recollect by narrating the instants of their life, and thus, to recycle time. In so doing, a genuine hearing and talking are created and thus, participants, sharing their vision of good, proceed to a self-reflecting on their proper working conditions and life styles.

In sum, design process, before reaching expectations, should help participants, on the one hand, to traverse all the phases of reflection regarding goodness and, on the other hand, to reveal their personal stance in front of the world. By returning to the past through the narrating of their experiences and through the hearing of the others' experiences, the participants of a design methodology maybe comprehend "what Ithaca means" as the Greek poet Kavafis suggests writing about the return of Ulysses.

NOTES

[1] The term «grand narratives», according to the meaning that Lyotard attributed to it, contains on the one hand, the big theories, which deal with the development of the human spirit, and on the other hand, the practical or political discourse referred on human emancipation (J. F. Lyotard, 1988).

[2] The distinguishing of two kinds of emancipation—objective and subjective—derives from the writings of Karl Marx. According to Marx, "objective" emancipation is referred to the capitalist conditions of production, in which labor is objectified in merchandises exchanged in the market. The result is that labor, as it is embodied in material goods, stands in front of the worker as something adversary, not belonging to him. In "subjective" alienation the impact of the work under capitalism on the psychological situation of the worker is analyzed (T. B. Bottomore and M. Rubel, 1961, p. 169).

[3] As Weber (1964, p. 115) describes it, this is a type of action which is oriented to "a system of discrete individual ends (zweckrational), that is, through expectations as to the behavior of the objects in the external situation and of other human individuals, making use of these expectations as "conditions" or "means" for the successful attainment of the actor's own rationality chosen ends".

[4] "Poiesis" is a word derived from the Greek verb *poiein* that means constructing or producing. "Praxis" is similar to the notion of practice, as Alasdair MacIntyre interprets it. The latter understands practice as "any coherent and complex form of socially established cooperative human activity through which goods internal to that form of activity are realized in the course of trying to achieve those standards of excellence which are appropriate to, and partially definitive of, that form of activity... " (MacIntyre, 1984, P.187).

[5] These symbolic categories of meaning have first been analyzed by Parsons (Parsons and Shils, 1951) as meaningful categories for the steering of the subsystems of society. Later, Habermas

(1984) uses the same media, called *steering media*, such as money and power, in order to explain the social differentiation and function between systemic and life world. Finally, Luhmann (1989, 1995) applies the same media, called *symbolically generalized communication media*, not only as means for promoting or for explaining the differentiation of society in social systems. He also considers them as means of conditioning a system's selection of communication, that is, as a code for the self-reference of the social system.

[6] Here "discourse" is used to refer to human interaction; that is, to production and interpretation of dialogic forms between speaker and addressee.

[7] I mention the works of C.W. Churchman (1971, 1982), G. Vickers (1981), I. Mitroff and H. Linstone (1993), W. Ulrich (1983), B. H. Banathy (1996), and others.

[8] This division of good between moral/generalized and ethical/particularized has been inspired by the Habermas (1994) distinction between moral and ethical discourses. According to Habermas, ethical discourse is referred to the norms of actions, which contribute to our self-understanding, while moral discourse submits our norms of action to a universalization test in which the results of our actions are judged according to the degree of their generalization. A generalized conceptualization of good, that is, good in its abstractedness, is usually conceptualized either as happiness or pleasure (see utilitarian good), either as an achievement of humans' inherent mental potentialities (see Aristotelian well-being), or as love for the other (see Christian good).

[9] According to MacIntyre, *external goods* are those "that when achieved they are always some individuals' property and possession.". On the contrary, *internal goods* are those "that their achievement is a good for the whole community who participate in the practice" (1984, p. 190-191).

[10] Wittgenstein in Philosophical Investigation used the term "linguistic games" firstly. This term has been again used by Lyotard in *Post-modern Condition*. Here, it is used according to the meaning given to it by Lyotard.

REFERENCES

Alexander, J., and Colomy, P. (eds.), 1989. *Differentiation Theory: Problems and Prospects*, Columbia University Press, New York.

Aristotle, 1992/1993. *Nicomachean Ethics*, Kaktos Publisher, Athens, Greece.

Banathy, B.H., 1996. *Designing Social Systems in a Changing World*, Plenum, N.Y.

Banathy, B. A., 1997. Information, evolution and change, *Systems Practice*, 10: 759–784.

Bateson, G., 1972. *Steps to an Ecology of Mind*, Ballantine, N.Y.

Bauman, Z. (1996). *Postmodern Ethics*, Blackwell, Oxford.

Bellah, R., et al., 1985. *Habits of the Heart: Individualism and Commitment in American Life*, Berkeley, CA.

Bickerton, D., 1990. *Language and Species*. University of Chicago Press, Chicago.

Bottomore, T. B., and Rubel, M., 1961. *Karl Marx. Selected Writing in Sociology and Social Philosophy*, v. I, Watts and Co, London.

Campbell, C., 1987. *The Romantic Ethic and the Spirit of Modern Consumerism*, Mac Millan, Oxford.

Castoriadis, C., 1978. *The Imaginary Institution of Society* (Greek edition), Rappas Publications, Athens, Greece.

Chatman, S., 1978. *Story and Discourse, Narrative Structure in Fiction and Film*, Cornell University Press.

Christakis, A.N., 1998. Book review of B. Banathy, Designing Social Systems in a Changing World, *Systems Research and Behavioral Science*, 15/1: 71–74.

Christakis, A.N., and Dye, K.M., 1999. Collaboration through communicative action: Resolving the systems dilemma through the cogniscope, *Systems: Journal of Transdisciplinary Systems Sciences*, 4/1.

Churchman, W.C., 1971. *The Design of Inquiring Systems*, Basic Books, N.Y.

Churchman, W.C., 1982. *Thought and Wisdom*, Intersystems, Salinas, CA.

Churchman, W.C. (ed.), 1989. *The Well-being of Organizations*, Intersystems, Salinas, CA.

Derrida, J., 1976. *Of Grammatology*, John Hopkins University Press, Baltimore.

du Gay, P., 1996. *Consumption and Identity at Work*, Sage, London.

Du Gay, P., 2000. *In Praise of Bureaucracy*, Sage, London.

Etzioni, A., (ed.), 1995. *New Communitarian Thinking*, University Press of Virginia, Virginia.

Flood, R., and Jackson, M. C., (eds.), 1991. *Critical Systems Thinking*, Wiley, N.Y.

Foucault, M., 1966. *Les Mots et les Choses. Une Archeologie des Sciences Humaines*, Editions Gallimard, Paris.

Fowler, R.B., 1996. Community: Reflections on definition, in A. Etzioni (ed.), *New Communitarian Thinking*, University Press of Virginia, Virginia.

Fuenmayor, R., 1991. Between systems thinking and systems practice, in R. Flood and M. C. Jackson (eds.), *Critical Systems Thinking*, Wiley, New York.

Habermas, J., 1984. *Theory of Communicative Action*, Beakon Press, Boston, MA.

Habermas, J., 1994. *Between Facts and Norms. Towards a Discourse Theory of Law and Democracy*, Polity Press, Oxford.

Lacan, J., 1977. *Ecrits*, W.W. Norton, N.Y.

Lasch, C., 1979. *Culture of Narcissism*, W. W. Norton, New York.

Luhmann, N., 1989. *Ecological Communication*, The University of Chicago Press, Chicago.

Luhmann, N., 1995. *Social Systems*, Stanford University Press, Stanford, CA.

Lyotard, J–F., 1988. *Postmodern Condition*, (Greek edition), Gnossi Publications, Athens, Greece.

MacIntyre, A., 1984. *After Virtue*, University of Notre Dame Press, Notre Dame, Southbend, Indiana.

Mead, G.H., 1964. *Selected Writings*, The University of Chicago Press, Chicago.

Mead, G.H., 1967. *Mind, Self, and Society*, The University of Chicago Press, Chicago.

Mitroff, I., and Linstone, H., 1993). *The Unbounded Mind*, Oxford University Press, New York.

Nelson, H., 1989. Unnatural states of health in natural organizations, in W. C. Churchman (ed.), *The Well-being of Organizations*, Intersystems, Salinas, CA.

Ophir, A., 1991. *Plato's Invisible Cities: Discourse and Power in the Republic*, Barnes and Noble, Savage, MD.

Parker, M., 1998. *Ethics and Organizations*, Sage, London.

Parsons, T., and Shils, E., 1951). *Toward a General Theory of Action*, Cambridge University Press, Cambridge.

Rawls, J., 1971. *A Theory of Justice*, Cambridge University Press, Cambridge, Mass.

Rawls, J., 1987. The Idea of an Overlapping Consensus, *Oxford Journal of Legal studies*, 7.

Ricoeur, P., 1990. *Narrative Time*, (Greek edition), Kardamitsas Publisher, Athens, Greece.

Ricoeur, P., 1994. *Oneself as Another*, The University of Chicago Press, Chicago.

Sandel, M., 1982. *Liberalism and the Limits of Justice*, Cambridge University Press, Cambridge, Mass.

Selznick, P., 1996. Personhood and moral obligation, in A. Sennet, R., 1977. *The Fall of Public Man*, Knopf, New York.

Simon, H.A., 1981. *The Sciences of the Artificial*, The MIT Press, Cambridge, Mass.

Taylor, C., 1996. Liberal politics and the public Sphere, in A. Etzioni (ed.), *New Communitarian Thinking*, University Press of Virginia, Virginia.

Tsivacou, I., 1996. Function of meaning and me-mifferentiation of the labor process for agents's identity, in G. Palmer and S. Clegg (eds.), *Constituting Management, Markets, Meanings, and Identities*, de Gruyter, Berlin.

Tsivacou, I., 2000. *The Itinerary of the Self in the Modern Work Place*, (Greek edition), Themelion Publications, Athens, Greece.

Turner, V., 1995. *The Ritual Process*, Aldine de Gruyter, New York.

Ulrich, W., 1983. *Critical Heuristics of Social Planning*, Haupt, Berne.

Van Gigch, J., 1991. *System Design Modeling and Metamodeling*, Plenum Press, New York.

Varela, F., Thompson, E., and Rosch, E., 1991. *The Embodied Mind*, The MIT Press,

Tsivacou Ioanna

Cambridge, Mass.

Warfield, J. N., 1994. *A Science of Generic Design: Managing Complexity through Systems Design,* Iowa State University, Ames, Iowa.

Weber, M., 1964. *Social and Economic Organization,* Free Press, New York.

Chapter 5

DIALOGUE AND SPIRITUALITY
The Art of Being Human in a Changing World

DANNY MARTIN
Cross River Connections, Cross River, New York

1. INTRODUCTION

The revival of spirituality suggests that something essential is not being addressed adequately in our society today. The roots of this revival are two-fold: One concerns our unprecedented situation of human capacity and impact (technology, resources) and the (related) problems (environmental degradation, social inequity) that it brings in its wake. The other concerns our lack of a foundational story–a functional cosmology–that would enable us to understand what is happening: who we are and where we fit in the grand scheme of things. Spirituality has to do with making sense of our world and knowing how to live creatively in it.

A related aspect of our situation is that the institutions that direct and express our lives–politics, health, law, education, and religion–are no longer adequate to the challenges we face in modern society. They are no longer able to help us sufficiently in the various aspects of living that they represent. These institutions require radical redesign in order to fulfill their stated purposes in a world that has changed enormously since the time they were first developed. Spirituality also has to do with institutions and structures in that it inspires them with vision and purpose.

Dialogue is not only a technology for redesign or for organizational change management, though it is that too. It is however more fundamentally a way of relating to the world that has implications for human society at all levels. Dialogue, therefore, may be seen as related to spirituality, perhaps even a form of spirituality.

The intention here is to explore aspects of dialogue and relate them to spirituality and spiritual practices. For example, the attitude of openness and the skill of listening constitute the kind of attention that prayer speaks of. In this way it is hoped to show how dialogue can enrich spirituality with its disciplines for living more creatively, while spirituality can offer a context and vision to dialogue that enables it to come to full maturity as a continuous encounter with reality (God) however understood and defined.

2.   THE POWER OF CONVERSATION

Both dialogue and spirituality are kinds of conversations. The former is generally understood as happening with others (people, animals, things), while the latter is normally viewed as an encounter with the deeper aspects of life– with God, however defined. The two are related, perhaps as levels of the same conversation.

Conversation is about connecting with life through others. The word has its roots in the Latin word 'con-vertere' which means to 'turn with.' It has the sense of working with life: with other human beings, certainly, but also with other things.

> To work with things in the indescribable
> relationship is not too hard for us...
> – Rilke

The word 'conversion' which has the same root adds a dimension of change or development. When we work <u>with</u> life, things change: we see things differently, we understand better what is going on; we co-create as we participate in the emergence of new meaning. When we converse, life happens, the world unfolds.

My experience of good conversation has included moments of breakthrough, sometimes out of painful impasses. At such times only the skillful reflection of a friend or counselor could enable me to see things in a new way that allowed for unanticipated resolution. More often this conversation has involved a gradual building of relationship over time, with now and then a glimpse of the unexpected. Always, however, at its best, conversation like this is about discovery and becoming, a creative process, even in its more casual forms. Interestingly, the word 'gossip' is a shortened form of 'God speaks.'

There has been also the sometimes heady experience of working with a partner or on a great team. In this case, it is as if the intensity of the interaction is heightened by the focus, allowing insights to flow more steadily. Athletes speak of being in the 'zone' to describe something that can happen whenever two or more are gathered for a common purpose. Skill added to this intention can bring the collaboration to ever-new heights.

Of course, there were the conversations around the fire or in the pub which have a measure of both of the above. Here casual conversation is taken to new places. In some cultures, like my own Irish world, it is a true process of re-creation to spend a couple of hours in what can only be described as an art form where normal exchange is enriched with story and sometimes spiced with song. Conversation, at its best, is often experienced as something quite playful.

> May what I do flow from me like a river,
> No forcing and no holding back,
> The way it is with children...
> – Rilke

Finally, there has been what at first glance appears to be the direct opposite: the silent, in the sense of wordless, conversation of meditation. To sit with others (whether distant or immediately present) in silence with the intention and focus that meditation requires is to participate in the unfolding of life in a way that is perhaps even richer than the exchange of words. Here, the flow is less cluttered with the baggage that talk can bring and the exchange less contrived because one is deliberately focused on making space for truth. Conversation like this is joining forces to allow life to happen, to enable the unknown, the not-yet, to find form.

> I believe in all that has never yet been spoken;
> I want to free what waits within me,
> So that what no one has dared to dream of
> May for once spring clear without my contrivance...
> – Rilke

When we add to this exchange the challenge of diversity–cultural, religious, gender, age, etc.–the possibilities are even greater. The insight that it is important to love our enemies comes not from a moralizing place but from the awareness that it is the holding together of differences that creates new possibilities, whether in human intercourse or the symbiosis of less complex organisms.

In all of these conversation experiences it has struck me that I was participating in something more than the sharing of information. In time I came to realize that I found–discovered, experienced, realized–my truest self in good conversation. In fact even my private reflections were related to these conversations, either as preface or postscript. In meditation I might distill the insight but the work had been done in earlier conversation. I concluded that good–in the sense of skilled–conversation could be a tool of the spiritual process. On further reflection it seemed that every personal encounter/conversation (with nature, for example) was actually a potential spiritual experience, especially if the encounter was enhanced with skills and other supports. When I began to work in a formal way with dialogue as a tool for fostering creative interaction in groups and organizations it became clear to me that here was a body of knowledge and practices that could actually make conversation a spiritual tool. The conclusion appeared to be that dialogue and spirituality are deeply connected; that dialogue is a practice or discipline (perhaps even the essential practice) of spirituality while spirituality offers a context or at least a vision for any true dialogue.

The purpose of these reflections is to explore the connections between dialogue and spirituality. I will do this by defining the two terms and then making what I see are the connections. I will conclude by exploring some aspects of a Dialogue-Spirituality and its applications. But, before that, let me offer a context for these reflections.

3.   A CONTEXT

The following attempt at describing a context uses what I trust is a helpful mix of philosophy, theology and science. I offer it with the 'caveat' that, while it is clearly not possible to describe reality, this realization has never stopped us from trying. It would seem that the desire to have meaning, even if it is the meaning we ourselves create, is essential to the human condition.

3.1   Levels of Reality

I propose three levels of reality: the Virtual, the Quantum, and the Material. By the Virtual I refer to the world of mystery, the unknown or perhaps, more accurately, the not-yet. It is the source of life where all potential lies and all possibility exists. It might be defined as a reservoir of energy that feeds all things, the ground of being itself, the life force that drives the universe.

The Quantum level of reality is the world of relationships: patterns of interaction beneath the surface of things that suggest probability, which is how physicists would define objects–"patterns of probability." One example of these patterns of probability is the relationship of electrons that circle a nucleus and which constitute–are the foundation for–an atom. Atoms, which we tend to think of as the building blocks of things, are, in fact, mostly space (possibility) where particles relate in patterns (probability) that allow the atoms to exist.

The Material, finally, is the world of things that are, therefore, the manifestations of invisible energy–the Virtual–which are born out of multiple, changing relationships–the Quantum. The word 'exist' comes from the Latin 'ex-stare' which means to stand out. Existence is the web of relationships that allows the Virtual to stand out in the form of things. It is the continuous change going on in these relationships that constitutes growth and development, and life and death thereby.

At the heart of the Virtual is the impulse of differentiation. This creative force that has been described more poetically as (holy) longing, pervades all relationships and all things. It is the underpinning 'isness' of life that makes each thing unique–different. It is the energy of life that impels the process of unfolding, evolving, becoming.

At the heart of the Quantum is the capacity to relate that comes from an essential 'interiority' or intelligibility. This interiority is the foundation of the autonomy and dignity of all forms of life. The capacity to relate constitutes all things. We speak of the soul of a person or a place or an object when we want to articulate its essence which lies beneath appearances. All things are energized by the creative force of the universe and shaped by relationships. All forms of life, in other words, serve the unfolding of the Virtual by giving expression to it through the relationships that constitute their existence: bodies, the world of plants and animals, the things we construct, etc. In human beings this process has produced not only our particular physical form but also our self-reflective consciousness. Human beings are holy longing come to consciousness. Human beings serve the unfolding of life by bringing the Virtual to self awareness through our relationships.

At the heart of the Material–the world of objects–is 'communion': all things are drawn toward everything else. This applies at every level of existence, from stars to flowers, and from gravity to sex. Things grow and develop through the impulse to relate. The unfolding of the universe takes place through the coming together of (different) things in a communion that does not deny the interiority of any individual. This is how life in all its forms is born.

In a sense, the myriad forms of life 'celebrate,' just by being alive, the source that enlivens them and the quantum relationships that shapes them in their unfolding. In doing so, they call the Virtual into being. This is the purpose of all things. It is why birds sing and plants bloom, it is why the mountains tower and the waters flow, and it is why human beings are aware of what's going on around them.

All things together in the web of existence manifest the mystery of the Virtual more completely than any single form of life. While it is tempting to think of ourselves as the peak of the evolutionary process and the ultimate refinement of the unfolding energy of life, it is more accurate to see ourselves as the bearers of a great gift that everything has conspired to create and that therefore belongs to all things. Self-reflective consciousness is not simply the possession of human beings, but is, more accurately, the consciousness of all life–all things, all souls, all relationships–because all things have contributed to its development. We come from the stardust that formed the earth and created the plants and the animals. Through my eyes the stars now look back at themselves in wonder. The stars come to themselves in a new way in my self-reflective relationships. Where two or three are gathered in loving relationship, the stars shine more brightly in the communion that also enriches the lives of the participants in the relationship:

> You filled him as he called you into being....
> – Rilke

These ideas are shaped by the findings of modern science which describe reality to us as vast space filled with potential (the Virtual): a Quantum world of relationships that underpins all things. Life emerges, the scientists tell us, as a chord that explodes out of separate notes held together into something that had no reality before the relationship, and has no reality when the relationship ceases. All things are like chords in the music of the spheres: inspired/moved/initiated by the infinite potential of the Virtual, shaped, formed and held in being by the underpinning relationships of the Quantum, and returning to the Virtual whence they came to become part of yet other chords–the material process of life and death. The universe unfolds through relationships–multiple, messy relationships–that bring together all things in creative symbiosis. Life is less the survival of the fittest than the flourishing of those that fit together. The basic impulses of cosmogenesis–differentiation, interiority and communion–together constitute the unfolding of life.

To participate creatively with life means then to understand how things are related. If we are to impact anything we will only do so by focusing on the quantum level of relationships that hold the thing in existence. In this sense, all true encounters happen at the quantum level, just as all true change happens when the underpinning relationships that determine a situation are explored.

3.2 A New Story

There is a second aspect of our context that impacts in more immediate ways and that is the times we live in. These are times of unprecedented problems as well as great potential, times when old forms–ideas, institutions, and structures–have become inadequate to the new challenges we face. The challenges catalyze us into action, but how we act is related to how we understand reality. Cultural historian and environmentalist, Thomas Berry (1999) speaks of the Story that makes sense of the world for us. He is referring to a 'functional cosmology.' Cosmology is our founding story, our story of origins and our source of intelligibility and value. Cosmology is what enables us to make sense of things, of change and challenges, of sickness and death. The fundamental problem, says Berry (1999), is that our old cosmology is no longer adequate to the world we find ourselves in today. Our old assumptions about the origins and directions of life have been discarded. The findings of science have caused us to dismiss many beliefs about how the world works, and with them the systems we have built around these beliefs. Religion can no longer speak of a God in a physical heaven. Jurisprudence can no longer claim inalienable rights for humans only. Education cannot simply teach children to exploit the earth. And business can no longer think only in terms of a material 'bottom line.' The Old Story of life is finished. The soul of human society–the web of our relationships–has been changed.

The problem is that a New Story has not yet been fully developed in the sense that the findings of science which do indeed offer a framework for a functional cosmology have not yet been adequately translated into mythical or theological or ethical or educational or commercial terms. Efforts have certainly been made in this direction in all of these areas, including, for example, the development of an Earth Charter that articulates foundational principles for a New Story, but much more has to be done to draw out the implications. For this we will need what British social historian, Theodore Zeldin, calls 'a new conversation' (2000). The New Story has to be told at every level. We need the poets and artists to capture its spirit and develop the mythical dimension. The various institutions will then redefine themselves accordingly. The religions will recreate their symbology, education will prepare our children for a different world, and so on. For this, however, we need multiple, cross-sectoral conversations. We need, in fact, a comprehensive approach that can inspire and direct our efforts which are nothing less than redefining what it means to be human in a new world.

4. DEFINING SPIRITUALITY

These concepts reflect the wisdom of the great spiritual traditions that predate religion, which is only one of the mediators of spirituality. In fact, religion, which has contributed substantially to the spiritual journey, has often also undermined spirituality for reasons that had more to do with fear and control which are the roots of the patriarchal impulse that has dominated religion for

5000 years. Spirituality, on the other hand, has much deeper roots, stretching back 70,000 years to the first glimmers of consciousness.

Spirituality would describe the three levels of reality as God/Mystery, the Soul, and the World. Most of the major religions (with the exception of Islam) describe the mystery of cosmogenesis in similar trinitarian forms such as Father, Son and Spirit, or Creator, Destroyer, and Redeemer.

We suggested that poets and artists must capture the spirit of the New Story of the unfolding universe and develop the foundational myth needed to underpin our thinking and actions. The implication is that spirituality is not confined to human beings but more accurately describes the process of life itself: the journey of the Virtual into existence through relationship. Spirituality is the story of God-becoming-world through the soul. We might define spirituality, therefore, as the journey of life as it unfolds into and out of form after form, becoming itself through multiple, messy relationships. Spirituality is the process of all things which instinctively follow the impulses that drive them.

For most things this happens naturally–spontaneously, as it were–only in human beings does a complication arise:

> Each thing ---
> each stone, blossom, child --
> is held in place.
> Only we, in our arrogance,
> push out beyond what we each belong to
> for some empty freedom...
> – Rilke

In human beings who are blessed (and cursed) with self-awareness, there is a certain deliberateness or choice about this process and the possibility, therefore, of confusion and distortion. The self-awareness which adds infinite potential to the unfolding of the world also presents what one might call the 'challenge of separateness' to the bearers of this ambivalent gift. I am not referring here to the fact of difference and uniqueness that is ideally the cause of richer possibility, but the illusion of 'apart-ness' (what Rilke describes as 'empty freedom') that is born out of the distortions of self-reflection. It is this illusion of separateness that is fear's first cause and is at the root of the power struggles, exploitation and destruction that create suffering as the attempt to protect ourselves against the infinite spaces that threaten, it would appear, to annihilate us.

> If we surrendered
> to earth's intelligence

we would rise uprooted, like trees.
Instead we entangle ourselves
in knots of our own making
and struggle, lonely and confused.
                                    – Rilke

In the face of this challenge we need help to enable us to participate creatively in the unfolding world, for it does not come easily to us to 'surrender to earth's intelligence.'

I would suggest then that spirituality for us is essentially the art of being truly human and the practice of living creatively in the world. As we noted, while other creatures are programmed genetically to know how to live in the world, we have to figure it out for ourselves in a sense, throughout the course of our lives. We are genetically programmed to adapt, to learn, and to act accordingly. This is the source of our cultures–our many ways of being in the world. These cultures have been responses to particular circumstances that have now changed: from the local to the global, for example, and from the simple to the more complex. We need a new culture that addresses these changed circumstances. What that means effectively is the application of spirituality as the art of being human in the world today to the redefinition of our role in the web of life and the redesign of our institutions to reflect this understanding.

One way of approaching this task might be to ask, when am I most truly myself? The implication is that we already know who we are and what it means to be human, though the distractions and cares of everyday life, and by extension the values and attitudes of our modern culture, cause us to forget or ignore this. The reason we know is that we are indeed woven into the fabric of life and are shaped by 'earth's intelligence.' Being human then means living as a part of the web of life. It means recognizing, for example, that our aspirations are essentially to be in harmony with the mystery (the Virtual/God) that underpins our existence. It involves seeing that our purpose is to live in interdependent communion with all things (the Quantum/Soul). And it includes appreciating that our particular contribution (the Material) to the world is the gift of awareness that we bring to the process. However, in the face of the distortions that dog us–the 'knots of our own making'– spirituality first has to do with liberating ourselves from the illusion of being separate and fostering a deeper awareness of how we are in fact connected to the world.

This awareness includes the fundamental intuition that life is ultimately meaningful and good. The intuition is universal; it is confined neither to religion nor to any one culture. It is a knowledge imprinted on every human heart as it were. This intuition is the foundation of the spiritual journey which at its most basic is the intention to live deliberately, as Thoreau put it: to cooperate with life and to participate in its unfolding. It is articulated variously in the world of religion as the desire to have meaning in one's life, to experience the presence of God, however named or not named, and to have the support of God in our quest for peace and creativity. It is to become one with the mystery of life.

For this intention to be realized, however, certain basic conditions must be created and fostered. These include an essential openness to life, both the people we meet and the things we encounter ('surrendering to earth's intelligence..'). Such conditions do not occur automatically, of course, but require the application of disciplines to reinforce intention. The disciplines are intended to foster the ability to be truly present in a way that would allow us to experience the depths of the things we encounter. They include also study to deepen our understanding of this experience within the larger context of the world we inhabit, reflection to draw out the (moral) implications for us as part of this web of life, and decision and action to complete (and continue) the process. These disciplines constitute nothing less than continuous personal (and public) transformation at the most fundamental level.

From this we might extrapolate a method for the spiritual journey: Level one is **experience**, the immediate encounter with life in whatever form that reveals a glimpse of the Virtual–the god, the energy, the beauty that is the source of its being–and of the quantum relationships–the souls–that underpin its material forms. Level two is **understanding** what this experience means in the larger context of existing knowledge. Others have experienced life at this level and they have much to teach us. Level three involves **reflection** on the (moral) implications of this experience-now-understood for my life. Level four, finally, is **decision that leads to action** that is based on the conclusions of the previous levels. This method is how human beings participate in the unfolding of life. It is how the Virtual becomes incarnate through us and how morality translates into justice in the worlds we create. It is, moreover, a continuous process whereby each decision/action leads to a new experience that starts a new cycle toward deeper understanding and more creative reflection.

Prayer, which perhaps more than anything else characterizes the spiritual process, is really the application of Thoreau's 'deliberateness.' It implies a quality of presence that can heighten experience, deepen our understanding, refine our reflections and enrich our actions. In the Christian world, there is the axiom: 'age quod agis' ('do what you are doing') that reflects the better known concept of 'mindfulness' of the Buddhist experience. Prayer as this quality of presence is the essential discipline of spirituality. From this perspective we can understand how spirituality and life can be the same thing as indigenous cultures believe and how some traditions can teach that 'to work–to do anything in fact–is to pray.' The difference is in the quality of presence and attention. Prayer reflects a spirituality that is understood as being deeply and creatively present in the world.

Ritual, another essentially spiritual activity, is a way of celebrating the meaning of life: not in the sense that life is thereby understood, rather in the sense that this is a way of deliberately joining with a mystery that we are part of. Human beings, the ultimate symbolic creatures, have always celebrated the larger realities within which they exist: Like the rhythms of the seasons or the return of the sun after winter. Ritual, in the context we have described, would celebrate the New Story with its particular canon of saints and martyrs: the supernova who sacrificed themselves to become the building blocks of the planets; the oceans that provided our first home; the bacteria who took up residence in the new hosts that evolved into our bodies, etc.

All of these are ways in which we can learn to participate in the great spiritual unfolding of life. In us, the stages of the process begin with simple survival. This is the case in both personal development and human evolution. A second stage is when we experience a sense of some control over life. In time this translates into an experience of peace with the world I share. Later stages include the development of intuitive wisdom and a more conscious co-creative relationship with things. The highest stages of our spiritual journey take us to the awareness of unity with God. One can see these stages not only in individuals but also in cultures. The stages of the journey have determined the kind of god worshipped and the kind of society created. For example, a person or people at the stage of survival will worship a distant, fearful god and create a hierarchical society with one or a very few powerful figures holding control over the masses who are without power. The stages represent the spiritual journey of the human form of the universe. The journey is our own personal process but it is also our way of participating in and contributing to the work of life: what Thomas Berry (1999) calls 'the Great Work.' What is implied in the process is the ongoing transformation of human and planetary life

This work, however, cannot be done in a vacuum or without support, whether in the vast reaches of the galaxies or in the more humble surroundings of a human life. Change (transformation) is enabled by appropriate parallel changes in one's environment: changes that will support the new understanding and convictions. The various methods of recovery and healing–12 Step programs, etc. –all highlight the same conclusion: we cannot change alone. Nothing happens in isolation, rather relationship is the fundamental component of all growth and development.

Spirituality then is nothing less than the ongoing process of universal unfolding through the awakening, understanding, reflecting, deciding, and acting that happens in our relationships. In concrete terms it is the continuous process of redesign of all forms of life–planets, mountains, organisms, human lives, social structures, institutions–to reflect and support these changing relationships.

Modern science describes the world as a seamless web that holds all life in a common process of interacting forms, all of them different, and all of them reflecting in their unique way the energy that created them: A unity-in-diversity. The uniqueness of human life is its self-reflective capacity. In human beings the unfolding universe becomes self-aware. Being truly human, therefore, means being aware on behalf of the world that shapes us and gives us life. It is co-creating with the universe, the way all things do. It means interacting with others–people and things–in an increasingly conscious/aware way: being present to them, understanding them, holding their uniqueness, and allowing life to unfold through this interaction. In practical terms, this might translate into the protection of the environment, or the preservation of cultures, or the promotion of justice.

Spirituality is the art of interacting with the world in a way that is conscious, intentional, and skillfully creative. It is Zeldin's (2000) 'new conversation' for redesigning our world and redefining our place in it.

5.   DEFINING DIALOGUE

The word dialogue comes from two Greek words: 'logos' which refers to 'meaning,' 'knowledge,' 'word'; and 'dia' which means 'through.' Dialogue is essentially participating in the unfolding of meaning. It is a creative interaction that allows–enables–new insights and unexpected ideas to emerge from the encounter. When we say that a relationship or a team is more than the sum of its parts we are referring to dialogue.

Today dialogue has lost this richer sense and is understood (or misunderstood) to mean simply talk of any kind. However, for many societies in the past, dialogue was regarded as a special form of exchange. For the Greeks, the word 'logos' actually referred to ultimate meaning. The early Christians, writing their gospels in Greek, used the word 'logos' to define the creative word of God: 'In the beginning was the Word (logos) and the Word was God.' is the opening phrase in the Gospel of John. Dialogue was understood, therefore, to be a sacred act, a co-creative process with God. In fact, most early societies used dialogue as the means to define themselves. Indigenous peoples in North America sat in a 'talking circle' to make important decisions about the tribe. In tribal society in general, the individual is defined by the group. In this sense a person comes to know him/herself through dialogue.

Dialogue has actually taken many creative forms in order to achieve a variety of goals. The Salons of the Renaissance brought dialogue to new levels of elegance. The Quakers used 'silent' dialogue as a form of prayer. The '12 Step' movement of sharing and support has proved effective as a way of recovery from addiction. Today, the emphasis in many of our institutions is on collaboration and partnership as the most effective way of addressing complex issues. Social commentator, Daniel Yankelovich (1999), says that as the world becomes increasingly complex, and the potential for misunderstanding each other even more than we already do increases with this complexity, we will need something more than ordinary conversation if we are to live in harmony with each other. Thomas Berry (1999) would add that this harmony would have to include not only the human but also the natural world in what he calls 'mutually enhancing human-earth relations, if we are actually to survive in the future. It is time now for a new conversation that is deliberate, intentional, and skillful; that will take place between individuals and among communities, across sectors, across gender, race and creed; and even across species. I suggest we use the word 'Dialogue' for this conversation, that we capitalize it as a proper noun to emphasize the deliberateness implied and the skills that must be (re)learned.

David Bohm, the English scientist who was known as the Father of Quantum Physics,' brought his interest in the interaction of quantum particles to the way people interact. In conversational experiments with Indian philosopher Krishnamurti, Bohm concluded that it is possible to foster collective thinking by which he meant, individuals thinking together without losing their individuality. The image of a flock of birds in flight, moving as one without destroying the reality of the individual birds, captures the idea. The poet Rilke describes the process as holding differences together in a creative tension:

> I am the rest between two notes
> Which are somehow always in discord
> Because death's note wants to climb over.
> But in the dark interval, reconciled,
> The stay there trembling and the song goes on, beautiful.
> – Rilke

Dialogue uses the differences between things to create something new.

After Bohm's death the organizational development world became interested in Dialogue as a way of addressing the challenges of organizations in a more creative way. In recent years, we at Cross River Connections have attempted to apply Dialogue to community health through partnership building.

Dialogue, we are suggesting then, is not simply discussion, which focuses on analysis, reduction, comparison, contrast, and conclusions based on already existing criteria. The word 'discussion' has its roots in the word to 'cut in two.' It is of course a very useful process for measuring and comparing and concluding. But Dialogue is about getting beyond differences to something new.

Nor is Dialogue the same as debate which comes from the Latin to 'beat down' (de-battere). Debate, we might argue, is appropriate in certain circumstances but it tends to produce winners and losers with little new knowledge produced from the process. Dialogue offers a way in which every participant wins because every participant is creating the outcome.

The story of the five blind men who are asked to describe an elephant has become something of a classic example of Dialogue in action. One man 'sees' the elephant as a tree, another as a wall, a third as a rope, etc. When you ask the question, which of the blind men is right, the first answer tends to be, 'all of them are right.' But then immediately comes the realization that, of course, none of them is right in the sense of having a complete picture of the elephant. How the blind men need to interact in order for the elephant to emerge is a description of the skills and values of Dialogue. As Rilke highlighted in his poem, it is, in fact, the differences between the perspectives that will allow a more complete picture to emerge. Provided, that is, that the differences are held in a creative tension, that each opinion is understood and honored without necessarily being agreed to. I deliberately said 'a more complete picture' to emphasize that the unfolding of meaning is never finished, that the process is infinite, that truth is a proleptic concept.

Dialogue consists of a combination of attitudes and skills that will allow this to happen: attitudes like a willingness to be influenced, and skills like the capacity to listen deeply. Underpinning both attitudes and skills, however, is intention. The intention in Dialogue is not to win or force a position but to work toward greater truth through deepened understanding. Yankelovich (1999) speaks of three essential conditions that enable Dialogue to happen: these are openness, empathy, and equality. When these are in operation, Dialogue is happening. We have all known this experience in various ways, whether on a good team or in a great exchange. We know when Dialogue is happening, for we feel enriched, even energized, by the encounter. By the same token we also know when it is not happening for we feel enervated, even abused by the exchange.

Dialogue focuses on the underpinning and usually unconscious (tacit) assumptions that shape our thinking and behavior. To change a situation we need to change the thinking that created it. In order to change what we think we need to change how we think. Dialogue is about thinking together; thinking with others in order to come to shared understanding. When this occurs all sorts of things can happen: people see things in new ways; they relate to the world differently; they participate in the emergence of new insights that are owned by all the participants in the conversation.

5.1 The Prison of Perception

We live in a world of constant interaction. The encounters we have with others–people, things, places, ideas–are the foundation of our lives. They are the means of our survival: the things we eat and wear, the fundamental tasks we perform. They are the way we learn: the information we take in, the ideas we generate. They are the food of our soul: the love we receive, the meaning we discover, the hope that arises in us. Through our exchanges we co-create with the forces that energize and ground all things. This theory is more often honored in the breach. Our interactions are seldom ideal and they are often less than creative.

The basic reason for this is that many of our interactions are what we might call "petrified relationships." By this I mean that the way we interact with others becomes stuck in a groove, the way the gramophone needle used to get stuck in the grooves of the old records, continuing to play the same tune over and over until something nudged the needle forward. In other words, we tend to develop habits of interaction–ways of relating–that produce the same kind of results over and over. In time, we come to assume that this is the way of things: this is how life is, this is what relationships are like, this is what you can expect from people, and so on. If nothing ever nudges us forward, we will continue to relate to life in this way, deepening the groove we are in with every encounter, and reinforcing thereby our convictions about reality.

One definition of madness is 'doing the same thing over and over and expecting different results.' It is clear that we are all touched by this madness. Could it be otherwise? Could things be different? Better? Lots of things–the advertising world, the ideas we read about, the memories of childhood, the hopes that lie deep in the heart, the promises of religion–suggest to us that they could. So we tell ourselves, 'tomorrow will be better,' and we make promises. But. like the New Year resolutions that don't last beyond January 3, we soon break our promises and find ourselves back in the same old place. Only this time, our expectations have been lessened, our hopes somewhat dimmed; we have become a little more skeptical, a little less trusting. Of course, we can see quite clearly why this happens: we have not nudged the needle forward. Which means that we have not broken the habit, not managed to break out of the groove. We see that this is because the groove has come to feel like the right way, the natural thing to do. It is certainly the way of least resistance, whereas attempting to do things differently creates real challenges. So how to move forward effectively?

The first step is to understand what is happening: what is preventing us from moving forward and doing things in a way that would produce new and better results. The first thing we notice when we begin this process is that it is hard–perhaps impossible–to do this alone. It's as if we were trapped in a cage without knowing where the bars were. Or it is like looking out at the world through glass walls and not realizing that the glass is actually there; not knowing, in other words, that we are actually behind such a wall. We might call this state of things, "a prison of perception" which suggests a situation or condition perhaps that is made up biases, prejudices, attitudes, etc. that shapes the way we even experience things in the first place: the data we select, for example, or the meaning we add to that data, and so on. It also begins to sound like an impossible task to break out of this prison. After all there is no one without biases or attitudes, while it is impossible to have 'immaculate perception' since we are all blessed with a certain 'givenness' that inevitably shapes our perspective: our gender, race, age, health, etc.

However, it is possible to break out of this prison in a way that will allow us to interact with the world in more creative ways. But to do this we have to understand what we are dealing with: what is this prison made of?

We spoke earlier of how scientists describe objects–like atoms–as "patterns of probability." In the case of atoms they are referring specifically to the relationships of the electrons that whiz around the central nucleus. It is the patterns of these relationships that constitute the material atoms. In our case, our essential identity is like the nucleus while the assumptions (values, beliefs, etc.) that we have inherited and ratified for ourselves, are like the electrons. It is the patterns of the relationships (between the assumptions) that constitute our identity and our sense of reality at any given moment or in any given encounter with the world. The problem is that our assumptions get frozen into particular patterns, either because these patterns have been handed down to us by our parents and/or because further experience has reinforced this particular form or bias. With our assumptions thus frozen, the "patterns of probability" become "patterns of certainty" and these patterns becomes then the lens through which we look out at the world. In time, we forget that there is a lens between us and the world, in much the same way as we forget we are wearing contact lenses (until they begin to cause us problems, which is another part of the story).

So, this prison of perception consists of frozen assumptions–deeply rooted, often inherited values and beliefs that shape attitudes and are defended with emotion (our famous 'buttons' that people push)–that constitute the pattern of probability which is our sense of identity and our perspective. The prison determines how I encounter the world. American poet, William Stafford (1993) captures the idea:

> If you don't know the kind of person I am
> and I don't know the kind of person you are
> a pattern that others made may prevail in the
> world
> and following the wrong god home we may miss
> our star.

The poem, however, also suggests a way out of the prison: understanding one another. This actually means much more than it at first seems for how will I ever be able to understand you except from my perspective and through the lens of my prison? And how will you ever be able to get what I'm about? Unless, that is, I am able to tell you; which means, unless we can create the conditions whereby we can begin an exchange that will allow us to get beyond the normal reactions that constitute most exchanges. Stafford (1993) underlines this aspect of the challenge:

> For there is many a small betrayal in the mind,
> a shrug that let the fragile sequence break
> sending with shouts the horrible errors of
> childhood
> storming out to play through the broken dike.

How often have we found ourselves in this situation? We are moving along quite well in a conversation when something gets triggered and there is a change: a reaction, followed by a counter-reaction, and the exchange escalates until we find ourselves arguing with more emotion than we can understand. It's as if we were re-living old exchanges, with parents or teachers.

So, how can this new kind of exchange begin? To return for a moment to the analogy of the needle stuck in the groove of the record, the process is begun with a nudge, in this case what I have called a "cosmic nudge" when life breaks in as it were. We have all experienced this in many forms: A friend dies, a job is lost, a diagnosis of illness comes, and we feel like our world is falling apart. What is falling apart, in fact, is the world we have participated in creating: the prison of perception that constitutes our identity. When this happens we find ourselves saying things like, 'now I know what's important,' or 'from now on I will...' It's as if the light of truth had shone for a brief moment into our prison and we realized what was going on. This 'cosmic nudge' is the first step toward breaking out of our prison and learning how to relate differently with life. Dialogue begins with a gift. In fact, the gift is available all the time, in any moment. However, it takes the nudge of a special moment to wake us up. It would seem that life conspires to make this happen, breaking down the walls of the prison we insist on shoring up again and again. Life itself, then is the essential Dialogue; we participate in its mysterious process. The more consciously we can do so, the richer our lives will be.

The purpose of the 'cosmic nudge' is to unsettle us long enough to ask ourselves fundamental questions about the reality we clearly create, at least partly, for ourselves. The opportunity does not last that long and the crack will quickly mend itself unless we force it a little wider with some gentle probing. Dialogue is about such probing. In theory it is something we can do alone but it is clearly more effective to do it with others who are also, like you, looking for a little more truth.

It starts by creating a safe space that consists of good intentions, positive attitudes, appropriate skills, and, over time and experience, a certain facility. Such a space provides a 'container' that can hold the many differences together. Can allow them to interact, even get quite heated, until something new begins to be born of the exchange.

5.2   Dialogue and the New Story

Dialogue is a form of storytelling that allows a collective story (the New Story?) to emerge. Stories are the way we imagine who we want to be. It is the form people have used for discovering how to live in new circumstances. If we can imagine something it becomes possible to create it. The loss of imagination is one of the signs of chronic depression. Sometimes a culture can be depressed. If we are to redesign our society to address the new challenges we face the 'new conversation' that Zeldin (2000) spoke of will be a form of storytelling. The disciplines of Dialogue release the individual and the collective imagination by making space for what wants to happen, for the story that wants to be told. Often when we are in conversation or at a serious meeting we can feel as if there is something trying to find expression. Usually, however, the many blocks that prevent us hearing or even being open to each other prevent this from happening. Dialogue frees the collective imagination.

Dialogue, of course, is not confined to words but can happen through many non-verbal forms. We mentioned earlier the 'silent Dialogues' of the Quakers. Theater can be Dialogue, as can music or dance. All of these are the ways we tell our stories. Ritual from the perspective of Dialogue is storytelling acted out. It has been the glue that binds cultures together. In the Dialogue of ritual, a group imagines together who it is; it comes to shared agreement out of a process of open, empathic interaction.

Like spirituality, Dialogue has its own stages of development. Most often we interact in ways that reflect the fragmentation that characterizes the world we have helped create. In this world where the individual is dominant and competition is the driving force, there is little collaboration. People tend not to listen to one another so there is not a lot of mutual understanding. Instead we act out of the mental models we have developed out of our inherited assumptions and values: models of what things mean and how people are supposed to be. At this level there is little creativity. However, once the intention to act differently is engaged, a process is begun that can lead to the building of trust and the development of new attitudes and values that can be the foundation for a different way of being together. When we do this we create a 'container' from these new attitudes and values within which we can begin to interact more positively. When we add skills like listening and inquiry, the dynamic can change almost immediately. As we stay with the disciplines of these practices, we can reach deeper and richer stages of encounter. In time, we learn to build together out of a shared consciousness, transcending our differences however wide to participate in the emergence of new meaning that belongs to all of us. Finally, we reach a place where we become totally present to each other in an experience of unity that continues to allow–even enrich–our differences.

In terms of the 'field of activity' within which Dialogue operates we can see parallels with the levels of reality we described earlier. For David Bohm (1995), the collective intelligence fostered by Dialogue was the way we give form to the Implicate Order, which was his term for the Virtual or the driving force of the universe. Dialogue is how we interact with the 'unknown'. True creativity is always working with the unknown to draw new forms of life from its infinite source. This happens when usually tacit assumptions are revealed and explored to allow a deeper understanding of each other's perspectives. When these perspectives are able to be held together in a tension that does not lessen the value of any one, something happens that can be described, as Yankelovich (1999) does, as 'magic.' Like the miracle of a mind awakened to a new awareness, there is the sense of surprise; even delight at something that feels like it was there all the time, simply waiting to be noticed. All 'eureka moments' are like that. When they happen through Dialogue (sometimes the Dialogue is with something non-human but the same process applies) the insight is collectively owned. Agreement is spontaneous, therefore, and genuine, unlike the agreements of compromise or manipulation. These levels of activity parallel the dynamics of cosmogenesis whereby the Virtual becomes material through the quantum/soul level relationships that hold it in existence. When Dialogue explores a person or a thing at the level of the relationships that underpin its existence (soul) and holds this soul together with the soul of another a new relationship (soul) happens that is the essence of a new reality–an idea, a symbol. Sometimes, there are no words to express the new reality, and silence is the only possible response. But it is a silence full of life and meaning.

> Out beyond ideas of wrongdoing and rightdoing,
> there is a field. I'll meet you there.
>
> When the soul lies down in that grass,
> the world is too full to talk about.
> Ideas, language, even the phrase *each other*
> doesn't make any sense.
> – Rumi

Dialogue, at its best, therefore, is deliberate, creative, skillful interaction in the 'field' of the unknown, at the level of assumptions that are usually unconscious, or at least seldom adverted to. As we come to understand each other at this level (it is clearly a process with levels of capacity and stages of realization) new things happen: insights, agreements; new kinds of awareness and connection.

Finally, when Dialogue happens, the participants themselves are also transformed. This happens because one's opinion or position has been laid open and explored at the underpinning level that constitutes its existence and juxtaposed with another that has is similarly open. When this happens–insofar as this happens–these foundational, inner relationships are also transformed by the attention thus brought to bear on them. In Dialogue things happen at all the levels of reality: First, something new is born as an idea, a relationship or a song out of the interaction of different things (positions, opinions, sounds) held together without judgment. Secondly the things themselves that have been opened for examination at the level of the relationships that constitute their existence are also thereby changed. And thirdly, the Virtual that is the source of all–the things, the relationships and the interaction between them–is changed in the sense of being made manifest as a new material form. This is why a good conversation is so energizing: life has unfolded into existence, touching all in its becoming.

6. A DIALOGUE SPIRITUALITY

As I mentioned above, for earlier peoples, Dialogue was a sacred act whereby human beings deliberately work with life to create new forms. In fact, most indigenous peoples did not distinguish between the spiritual and the material as our modern culture tends to do. Many had no name for religion but instead saw their essential purpose as a dialogue with life. For them Dialogue was their Spirituality.

> My words are tied in one
> With the great mountains,
> With the great rocks,
> With the great trees
> In one with my body
> And my heart.
> — Yokuts Indian Prayer

Here, then, we are resurrecting an ancient awareness, an innate knowledge that has been lost, a victim of our struggle to integrate the consciousness that has caused us to 'push out beyond what we each belong to.' The advent of Dialogue in its new form offers us the opportunity to recover an ancient truth about living in the world. The art of Dialogue can enable us to practice our Spirituality in practical and relevant ways and to address the challenges that face us today with new skills and resources.

It is in this sense I believe that Dialogue offers a new perspective on Spirituality as a co-creative way of being in the world, while Spirituality highlights the larger vision and goals of the art of Dialogue. Once again, the poet Rilke:

> Take your practiced powers and stretch them out
> Until they span the chasm between two
> Contradictions – for the god
> Wants to know himself in you.

The purpose of Dialogue, like the purpose of Spirituality, is to enable new life to emerge in the form of understanding, insight, and action. The ability, implies the poet, is innate but needs expanding in order to be able to hold together differences–'contradictions'–that we have made ourselves and enshrined in our cultures (rich and poor, black and white, male and female). The process is a divine work of creativity that brings the unknown–the Virtual, 'the god'–into being.

Let me reflect on what I will call a Dialogue-Spirituality by bringing together some suggested conclusions from the two fields that I have paralleled here. First, some conceptual notions and then some thoughts on practice.

1.   Dialogue-Spirituality is a way of being in the world that is aware of the larger context (an interconnected web of life). This awareness includes an understanding of the purpose of human existence as serving the whole

(rather than simply the species). Life, as Vietnamese writer Thich Nhat Hanh says is 'inter-being' and not separate individual existences. We <u>are</u> each other in an essential way. Such a conviction gives new meaning to the 'golden rule that characterizes many religions: love your neighbor as yourself. It now appears that my neighbor actually <u>is</u> myself.

2. Dialogue-Spirituality is committed to the purposes implied here: the benefit of all life. The intention of this spirituality, therefore, is the good of the whole through the release, as it were, of more (deeper) truth, more creative outcomes.

In terms of practice:

- Dialogue-Spirituality fosters an openness to life. It promotes values of respect, curiosity, and patience. It encourages the suspension of judgment and it strives for justice which it understands as right relations.
- Dialogue-Spirituality focuses on the development of attention and presence through the practice of (all the levels of) listening, and the skill of balancing inquiry and advocacy for the deeper exploration of assumptions.
- Dialogue-Spirituality directs its attention toward deepened understanding of the beliefs and assumptions behind positions and opinions. Dialogue begins with mutual understanding and continues through the holding of differences together in a creative tension. This 'allows' shared understanding to emerge in the form of insights, agreements: glimpses of the deeper dimensions of truth, reflections of the unknown foundations of life. It is in this way that growth occurs, development happens, truth emerges, and meaning unfolds.
- Dialogue-Spirituality reframes challenges and problems in a way that allows them to be resolved more creatively with outcomes that are rich and sustainable. (Because relationships are enhanced in the process as well as results being achieved.)

In summary, Dialogue-Spirituality offers an enhanced way of being in the world today that, enables humans to play their appropriate role as co-creators, fosters the enhancement of all forms of life, and participates in the emergence of meaning and the unfolding of truth.

7. FIGURES

a. Intention = **Differentiation**
- Humans are the earth-conscious-of-itself: The intention of Life (and humans) is toward a richer, fuller life

b. Attention = **Interiority**
- All life is 'alive' and demands respectful attention.

c. Creativity = **Communion**
- Life happens through multiple messy relationships: this is the process of creative interaction at work.

Figure 1. Basic Elements of a Dialogue-Spirituality that reflect the Principles of the New Story

New Cosmology		Spirituality		Dialogue
Virtual	=	God	=	Unknown
Quantum	=	Soul	=	Tacit assumptions
Material	=	Visible/manifest	=	Decision/action

Figure 2. The Fields of Activity

Spirituality		Dialogue
Survival	=	Instability/fragmentation
Some control	=	Creating a 'container'
Inner peace	=	Inquiry/listening skills
Intuitive	=	Deeper listening/inquiry
Co-creative	=	Presence, learning to build together
Visionary	=	Transcending, participating in emergence meaning
Unitive	=	Oneness, total presence

Figure 3. Stages of Development

8.   DIALOGUE-SPIRITUALITY IN ACTION

Dialogue-Spirituality is a liberation movement that goes to the deepest roots of systems and structures and actions by addressing the thinking that creates them. It provides a method that is equally applicable to an individual and a culture.

In this process of liberation the universe offers us the initiating grace. Step one of a Dialogue-Spirituality is this gift of life. Spirituality, we said, is not just about humans but is more accurately the unfolding of life itself. A Dialogue-Spirituality begins with the impulse of the universe toward new possibility. It is the universe-in-us that is continuously talking the first step. It is not we who have to make it up or start the process. In fact, our first responsibility is to notice. And when we do so it is because life has finally caught our attention. Dialogue-Spirituality begins (and ends) with the Virtual. Our role is always to respond. What is asked of us initially is intention: what do you want? How do you want your world to be?

However, when this finally happens–when we take notice of the 'cosmic nudge' and respond with intention–it is not a permanent state that is thereby achieved. Again, as we noted earlier, even when the gramophone needle has been nudged forward, it can easily slip back into the familiar groove. In the same way, we too fall back so easily on old habits, even when we have had the light of a 'cosmic nudge' shine on our situation. So intention has to be reinforced with new, positive attitudes, like *openness*–a willingness to be influenced–and *empathy*–I have compassion for you and your situation–and *equality*–I respect who you are as well as the validity of your position. These are, as we noted earlier, the basic conditions for Dialogue, that allow a new kind of exchange to occur. The second response in this Dialogue-Spirituality, therefore, is to foster the attitudes that will allow these essential conditions to occur.

It becomes clear that the Dialogue is working in two ways: the more obvious way concerns how we relate in a proactive way with the things we encounter. The less obvious but perhaps more important way concerns how we respond to the ways that life addresses us. To repeat, Dialogue-Spirituality is what is happening in the unfolding of the universe. In us this involves a breaking open and a freeing from the 'knots of our own making' that prevent us from participating in this process and the development of forgotten or unlearned capacities to relate creatively with life.

Attitudes, however, need to be nurtured or they will change into something else as the old habits kick in again. Attitudes are nurtured by skills, such as listening and inquiry that can help us explore each other's assumptions. In this way we can come to understand each other. Then follows the skill of building together whereby shared understanding can grow and shared agreements emerge. It is these agreements that are the foundation of a new relationship where all kinds of things are possible. Welsh poet, D.H. Lawrence's poem *Escape* describes the experience of new possibility:

> When we get out of the glass bottles of our ego,
> and when we escape like squirrels turning in the
> cages of our personality
> and get into the forests again,
> we shall shiver with cold and fright
> but things will happen to us
> so that we don't know ourselves.
>
> Cool, unlying life will rush in,
> and passion will make our bodies taut with power...

What he is describing is the flow of life happening whereby the Virtual comes into existence through relationships that are open and fluid. In spiritual terms, God is born in the world through the creative interactions of souls. In this kind of relationship, we hardly know ourselves because we have dropped the old identities and now stand naked, as it were, before life (shivering with cold and fright). But things happen because we are not blocking the flow of 'cool, unlying life.' When we relate to the world like this, everything is possible.

8.1   The Stages of the Process

This is the fundamental spiritual practice: to participate in the unfolding of life/meaning; to give birth to God by relating creatively. This applies to every encounter, and at every stage of the process. Earlier we described the spiritual method as one that begins with **experience** and moves through **understanding** and **reflection** to **decision and action** in a continuous, deepening way. At each of these stages the emphasis is somewhat different in terms of Dialogue-Spirituality practices.

At the stage of experience, the emphasis is on presence, whereby the soul–the essential identity of the person–relates to life through prayer/meditation. Prayer as this quality of presence is the essential discipline of spirituality. In prayer, soul speaks to soul–deep speaks to deep–as one meets another at a level beneath normal (prejudiced, polite) exchange. A Spirituality, enriched by Dialogue, enables a person to be more fully present because intention is clear, attitudes of openness and empathy and respect are brought to the encounter, and skills of listening heighten the experience.

These practices clearly enrich this aspect of spirituality that focuses on connecting with God in the things of one's life. The capacity to be present in this way removes the obstacles that normally block or obscure any true meeting. It enables one to get beyond the usual (learned) reaction to situations which is one of screening data and allowing in only that which reinforces already existing assumptions and beliefs. The simple practices of Dialogue can bring this aspect of Spirituality to new depths.

Ritual which we have described as a way of deliberately joining with the mystery that we are part of is another aspect of this level of experience. When we connect with the movements of life we remember in a sense who we are. This fundamental spiritual activity is also enhanced by Dialogue which enables us to connect with another (person, place, time) at ever-deepening levels. The new rituals we suggested earlier–to celebrate our connections to the stars and the oceans, etc. –require the skills of Dialogue to help us get past our learned manipulations and our jaded materialism to a playfulness and a lightness of spirit that our world sorely needs. Ritual is sacred/serious play for there is nothing more serious or sacred than play. It is how our children learn how to be in the world.

> May what I do flow from me like a river,
> No forcing and no holding back,
> The way it is with children...

Experience is soul-level work. Experience is where I encounter the world in my own unique way. It is this experience that catalyzes the human process and impels it forward. It is experience that is the ground of learning. Without this fundamental dimension, the process of development is incomplete: one receives information on the word of another; one borrows someone else's concepts; experience in this case is second-hand and therefore cannot have the same force as one's own first-hand encounter. While it is true that one can never encounter the world in a vacuum (there is no 'immaculate perception') and while it is always the case that every experience comes in forms that we have inherited from others (words, concepts, at least), nonetheless, through the practices suggested by a Dialogue-Spirituality, we are able to be more aware of the forms that carry our experience in a way that allows the uniqueness of our own encounter to come through. By realizing that I carry within me a certain structure or hardware with which I encounter the world–a certain 'givenness'–I can create a space for the uniqueness of my particular experience to exist. The more aware I am of the many levels of my encounter, the more space there can be for what is mine to stand out ('exist').

In terms of growth, experience is comparable to religious conversion where one meets life/god in an immediate or unmediated way. However, experience does not remain simply at the level of the unmediated. Perhaps, as we are saying, it never was truly unmediated. In any case, in the process of encountering life, experience continues as it were into a second stage of understanding whereby we attempt to make sense of what has just occurred. Understanding is mind-level work. At this level we explore our experience and search among the 'givenness' for ways to make sense of it. In formal spirituality we study the experiences of others, for example, in order to situate our own experience: to measure and compare it, to analyze and evaluate. The practices of a Dialogue-Spirituality would also enrich this stage of the process: the attitude of openness, certainly, would be important, but also the skill of inquiry that is heightened by awareness of one's internal reactions. One might suggest that such awareness allows for deeper perception, and may even be an essential tool for any comprehensive understanding. True understanding happens when assumptions are encountered, explored and loosened, as it were. When I am reading a book and find myself reacting to an idea it is because my assumptions have been triggered. The capacity to pursue this reaction, to follow it to its assumption-roots, allows something new to enter the mix of underpinning relationships and thereby reshape the understanding I hold.

In terms of human transformation, understanding of this kind relates to intellectual conversion. However, the process does not stop here either but continues into the realm of reflection which is a kind of inner Dialogue whereby I make sense of this experience-now-understood in terms of what it means for me and my life. Reflection of this sort is heart-level work for there is an emotional quality to this stage of the process where I am drawing conclusions and forming beliefs that will become values which I will hold and defend in the future. We realize just how much emotion gets attached to the conclusions of this stage when someone questions our values or beliefs, however indirectly. Then we find ourselves bristling with defensiveness: 'our buttons (of belief/value) have been pushed,' we say. Dialogue-Spirituality practices, like the capacity to hold the tension of differences or listen to what is trying to be said (a sensitivity we all have to greater and lesser extents) can enable us to reach richer conclusions about what is right and wrong, or what is appropriate in a particular situation. In terms of transformation, reflection of this kind relates to moral conversion.

The final stage of the process is the stage of decision and action. Here we translate what we have concluded to be right into appropriate decisions for action. Action is clearly body-level work in the sense that it is in concrete form that this process of life-encountered is incarnated in new ways. Dialogue brings participants to shared agreements through shared understanding that is born out of the explorations we have described. The decisions made are really affirmations of this shared understanding. From this rich collective field new, often unexpected things emerge as ideas for action. Dialogue does not directly address a problem but creates the shared understanding about an issue that allows it to be reframed, seen differently, and perhaps, thereby, to be resolved in ways not anticipated.

In terms of a Dialogue-Spirituality, it is here that moral conversion becomes justice, that intellectual conversion impacts the structures of our lives, and that religious conversion changes the world. The Virtual, met in the soul (received through experience, situated through understanding, and integrated through reflection), is finally manifested in the material through decision and action. It is the energy of the experience that carries the process through to concrete resolution; the more powerful the encounter, the stronger the impulse to manifestation. A Dialogue-Spirituality allows more life to unfold in the world, more god to be born in the world, by enriching each stage of the human process. A Dialogue-Spirituality increases the possibilities of justice in the world by deepening each stage of the human process that translates the love of God into life.

Finally, the process is continuous and epigenetic, one level building on the previous. And, the process is endless, we can say, in a universe whose unfolding exceeds the parameters of any understanding. If Spirituality is the miracle of this unfolding in all its forms, then Dialogue-Spirituality can be understood as the 'deliberate' participation in the process that humans have the privilege to choose.

8.2   Redesigning Society

The first level of a Dialogue-Spirituality is personal transformation that allows life to flow through us or, as we have described it above, to allow the Virtual/God to be born in the world. The second level flows from the first as the redesign of the structures we create as extensions of our intentions in the various aspects of our lives: commerce, education, health, religion, etc. The context of this work is a society where institutions are no longer adequate to the challenges that change has brought and require redesign in order to fulfill their original and essential purpose.

One example I am involved in is the redesign of Public Health to reflect more accurately the shift in understanding that has taken place in that field. The emphasis here has moved from a service-delivery approach to a convening-enabling one that requires new skills, new policies and new structures: a radical redesign process. Essential to this process are not only the skills of Dialogue but the more radical method of a Dialogue-Spirituality. In the conversations that are the foundation of this process people are learning to meet each other at new levels of understanding that go beyond the functional. This is because of the growing realization that something more than simply changing policies or structures from above is required. More important has been the genuine interaction of all the participants–the traditional recipients as well as the traditional deliverers–to address problems that neither group can address by itself. This level of interaction goes to places not normally associated with organizational redesign: the exploration of old mental models that groups and individuals hold about each other, the development of a sense of interconnectedness, the building of shared vision, and the emergence of collectively owned outcomes. While there is no explicit reference to spirituality in the process, it is clear that what is happening is indeed a Dialogue-Spirituality process. Participants will often comment on the unanticipated results of transformed relationships and personal renewal that appear to have come directly from the functional activity of redesign.

A Dialogue-Spirituality enables us to reach deeper and more creative places together. When the work of 'unblocking' the flow of creative energy has been done, the work of directing this flow toward our institutions is enriched a hundred fold. The 'new conversation' that Theodore Zeldin (2000) spoke of can happen behind the scenes and beneath the surface of any of the places where we interact. A specific form of a Dialogue-Spirituality might be open conversations among the members of whatever institution about the things that impel them, the values they hold, the hopes they cherish. It was often these very things that brought them to their work/profession in the first place but are now never mentioned. Creative conversations like these can re-inspire an organization simply by allowing the latent energy, long-suppressed, to come through and find new form. Similar conversations might take place across professions and sectors of society since the challenges that we face are generally not resolvable by any one perspective alone.

Yankelovich (1999) advocates for such Dialogues as a way of also developing new forms of governance. He speaks of the 'magic of Dialogue' that can advance our civility and our civilization. Perhaps, it might be suggested that this aspect of a Dialogue-Spirituality is the foundation for the true renewal of our institutions since true renewal requires changing the underpinning relationships. When this happens, we participate in the renewing power of life which is continuously making new relationships and creating new collaborations; constantly breaking down old forms that have become inadequate and replacing them with new ones that enable richer outcomes. D. H. Lawrence's poem captures the spirit of institutional redesign:

> ..we shall stamp our feet with new power
> and old things will fall down,
> we shall laugh, and institutions will curl up like
> burnt paper....

A Dialogue-Spirituality begins its redesign process with the players in the exchange. It focuses on the relationship–soul–level rather than on the material, structural forms. It is based on the realization that all life comes from one source–the Virtual–and that we can co-create by participating. This is not to devalue our contribution, but simply to put it in perspective. We are indeed co-creators of the world. All things exist in their own way. In our conscious, deliberate way we join with the energy of life through our relationships. Thomas Berry (1999), reflecting on the implications of the New Story, says that the universe is not a collection of objects but a 'communion of subjects.' There are, in fact, no objects 'out there'; rather there are the manifestations of relationships. We do not see the world as it is. We see it as we are. And our seeing calls it into being. What we see is what we get, in a sense. When we change the world changes. We control nothing in the sense that we are not the source of anything. But we do control in the sense that we have the power to bring our attention to bear in a way that calls things into existence. The real for us is truly where we bring our attention. The poem hints at this paradox and the only attitude that can make sense of it: letting go, entrusting, holding things lightly (playfully). Laughter. How many of our well-intentioned efforts founder on the hard rocks of seriousness:

> Nearby is the country they call life.
> You will recognize it by its seriousness.
> – Rilke

A Dialogue-Spirituality enables us to participate in the renewal of our institutions by getting out of our own way.

8.3   A Purpose

In a world that is increasingly materialistic, something is needed to restore balance, we say. What we mean, I believe, is that we realize that we are only partly living when we give our attention to just one level of reality. We know, both through the wisdom of our various traditions and our own experience, however rare, that there are indeed other levels of reality. And we know intuitively that we ignore these levels at our peril. No life is complete without meaning and a sense of purpose. What purpose might a Dialogue-Spirituality offer us?

In Buddhist terms, the suffering of life is caused by ignorance of reality - how things are. This ignorance is created by the ego which is imprisoned in its illusions of 'apartness', and that pushes out "..beyond what we each belong to for some empty freedom". It is the ego, thus imprisoned and thereby fearful, that creates the suffering that suppresses the unfolding of life and oppresses anything that threatens its prison. Out of fear, we attempt to preserve our world (of illusions) through defensiveness and aggression which shapes both our personal and public relationships and the structures that manifest these relationships. Perhaps a Dialogue-Spirituality might echo the purpose suggested by the Buddhist tradition: to end the cause of suffering in the world. While it seems rather grandiose to think such terms, we might keep in mind that we do indeed create our own world from the illusions of our prison of perception. To end suffering would be to transform the underpinning assumptions–the illusions–that create the relationships that constitute this world. And that clearly is the work of a Dialogue-Spirituality.

When ignorance about how life happens is lessened, and when life is experienced also at its more basic levels–the Quantum and the Virtual–suffering is decreased by this awareness. When this awareness is brought to other encounters, the work of removing suffering can continue at its most fundamental level.

To remove suffering is to free the world to participate creatively in the unfolding of the universe. To free ourselves from the symptoms of suffering that drag us into meaninglessness, is to rediscover how we belong to life and participate in its process:

> Consider that, all hatred driven hence,
> The soul discovers radical innocence
> And learns at last that it is self-delighting,
> Self-appeasing, self-affrighting,
> And that its own sweet will is Heaven's will.
> – W.B. Yeats

To live out of that place is to work creatively on behalf of the unfolding universe. In concrete terms it is to bring right relations to the world. Right relations are the foundation of true justice and wisdom. A Dialogue-Spirituality is participation in the work of life. It begins with liberation from the prison of a distorted and thereby distorting ego and ends with the liberation of the world from the creations of this distortion. Dialogue-Spirituality offers a rich program for the individual journey and a blueprint for the continuing renewal of human society.

9.   COMMENTS AND CONCLUSIONS

The hunger for spirituality experienced in a world that would seem to have everything suggests that something fundamental is missing in modern society. This has been described variously a loss of meaning and purpose in individual lives, a sense of fragmentation in our society, and an absence of justice in our world. We don't feel at home in this world. This is not meant in the sense that we would like to leave it for another heavenly home but more accurately in the sense that we don't feel as if we belong where we are, here on earth. To belong in the world is perhaps the most essential condition for a contented life. We interface with the world–we belong–through the institutions of society which are simply extensions of ourselves. However, something fundamental has shifted in our times that has rendered these extensions lifeless and ineffective so that they no longer connect us to the essential processes that underpin our lives. The emergence of a New Story of life is challenging us to redefine our very identity–who we are in this world– and to redesign our institutions–how we live in this world.

If we are to respond to this challenge–if we are in fact to survive the inexorable processes of change–we will need a new understanding of how things are and where we fit in the process. We will also need tools for reshaping our lives in response to this understanding. These reflections have suggested that a Dialogue-Spirituality can assist us in this critical task. This is because a Dialogue-Spirituality not only reflects the perspective of the New Story by defining itself in terms of the all embracing context of cosmogenesis but also offers practices and disciplines that both sharpen the tools of older spiritualities and build on the growing wisdom of modern theories of human behavior and interaction. In this way Dialogue-Spirituality is perhaps more accurately a 'trans-spirituality' in the sense that it transcends the limitations of any and all traditions as it enables and directs us (and life through us) to continue our mysterious journey of becoming.

A Dialogue-Spirituality can help free us from the illusions that bind us to old dysfunctional habits and the structures they create. A Dialogue-Spirituality can enable us to become a more creative society like a flock of birds in flight that is able to think and move together, and like a good jazz band in full swing, that is able to allow new music to flow through its interactions.

In more concrete terms, a Dialogue-Spirituality can help us address the increasingly complex problems we face in the only way that will work: a collaborative way. In this process each individual is also enriched.

Dialogue-Spirituality is ultimately the mystery of life's process. It was present before we came on the scene and will continue its journey long after we have gone. In the meantime....

REFERENCES

Aquinas T., 1946. *Summa Theologica.* Trans. English Dominicans. Benziger Brothers, New York.

Barrows, A., and Macy, J., (trans.), 1996. *Rilke's Book of Hours.* Riverhead Books, New York.

Berry T., 1999. *The Great Work.* Bell Tower, New York.

Bohm D., 1995. *Wholeness and the Implicate Order.* Routledge, London.

Chopra D., 2000. *How to Know God.* Harmony Books, New York.

Franck, F., (ed.), 1998. *What Does it Mean to be Human?* Circumstantial Productions Publishing, New York.

Isaacs, W., 1999. *Dialogue.* Doubleday, New York.

Mitchell, S., (ed. and tran.), 1982. *The Selected Poetry of Rainer Maria Rilke,* Random House, New York.

Stafford W., 1993. "A ritual to teach to each other." from *The Darkness Around Us is Deep.* Harper Perennial, New York.

Swimme B., and Berry, T., 1991. *The Universe Story.* HarperSanFrancisco, San Francisco.

Teilhard de Chardin, P., 1959. *Method in Theology* Harper and Row, London.

Wheatley M.J., and Kellner-Rogers M., 1996. *A Simpler Way.* Berrett-Koehler, San Francisco.

Yankelovich D., 1999. *The Magic of Dialogue.* Simon and Schuster, New York.

Zeldin T., 2000. *Conversation.* Hidden Spring, New Jersey.

Chapter 6

TRANSFORMING COMMUNITIES
Person-centered Encounters and the Creation of Integral Conscious Groups

MAUREEN O'HARA* AND JOHN K. WOOD**
Saybrook Graduate School and Research Center*, San Francisc,and Estância Jatobá**, Jaquariúna, Brazil

1.   PROLOGUE-THE PROBLEMATIQUE

We are living in times of unprecedented change, affecting profoundly and permanently the way we live, the environment we live in, who we are and above all, how we must relate to each other. Changes that used to occur over several generations now occur within decades. People everywhere are called upon to manage the intended and unintended consequences of not just one revolution, but hundreds occurring at the same time.

Globalization and the explosive rise of information technology means that, like it or not, we must all now deal with unrelenting information overload, trying to force coherence and meaning from the dizzying complexity and diversity. In our local neighborhoods, in the oceans and forests, and from satellite views from space, we can see around us the signs of environmental degradation, climate change and massive species loss. Biotechnology and nano-technology are changing what it will mean to say one is a "person" or that one has an "identity." The consensual status of traditional authority structures (religion, tribal and political leaders, science, parents etc) are breaking down; there is massive relocation of migrants, refugees and workers; and there is experienced in almost every community, a pervasive breakdown in established communal values destabilizing many of the psychological givens of life. In the last decade we have witnessed the triumph of American-style capitalism and consumerism over Marxism, bringing its neo-liberal democratic rationalism along with it, more often than not challenging local spiritual meaning systems with a new global myth-the "wisdom of the marketplace." Most recently we have seen the emergence of no holds barred terrorism by small groups as an overt policy of international power relations against the superpowers.

Dialogue as a Means of Collective Communication, Edited by Banathy and Jenlink
Kluwer Academic/Plenum Publishers, New York 2005

Whatever will be the long-range effects of such profound and pervasive change, the immediate effects have been radically destabilizing. We must now all deal with rising levels of uncertainty and ambiguity generated when the old rules fail to serve but before new rules have been established. There is a pervasive sense that things are coming apart. In Yeats' words, "the centre does not hold," and there is a generalized uneasiness about it. We are bombarded by more information than we can possibly use–most of which is bewildering and even terrifying–and all of it is undermining familiar certainties. The old institutions, social compacts and community structures that have historically organized civilized life no longer serve the modern context and many are unravelling altogether. In the United States, the sense of instability intensified in the wake of a 2000 presidential election in which the loser was appointed by the Supreme Court. In September 2001, four hi-jacked aircraft and several packets of anthrax spores exploded the American sense of safety and invulnerability forever.

There is also great promise in such turbulent times (Rosenau 1990). On the upside, as our new technologies change every aspect of our lives, exciting new possibilities are emerging that promise to provide humanity with benefits that surpass our grandparents' wildest dreams.

Despite the current pall that hangs over us in the wake of the terrorist attacks on the American homeland, there are also indications (admittedly less robust) that the turmoil itself may provide humanity with opportunities for evolutionary progress that are also unparalleled in human history (Tarnas 1991; Schwartz, Levden et al. 1999; Laszlo 2001)

In the historical past, whenever the life-world of a culture or group has unravelled to any great degree, if they have survived the ensuing turmoil–and often they do not–people and cultures may emerge transformed–with more complex skills and greater capacity with which to adapt and thrive in the new times. It is as if by being thrown into situations in which old habits, certainties, social conventions, mental maps and behavioral routines are obsolete and no longer serve, consciousness is able to respond by learning new ways of being that result in the ability to experience self and the world with greater depth of understanding, mastery and wonder. When a society changes so profoundly that its entire cosmology, political alignments, epistemology, socializing institutions, sense of self, relationship to others and sense of ultimate meaning, all change then we may justifiably refer to such a transition as *epochal change.*

From many quarters come signs that people alive today whether in the caves of Afghanistan or the wired skyscrapers of the developed world, are participants in such an epochal change. If that is true, then how humanity learns to face the immense challenges of our times may determine the future of humankind.

2. TRANSFORMATIVE DIALOGUE IN PERSOI CENTERED LARGE GROUPS

For close to three decades, the authors have been explorir
relationship between individual consciousness and group consciousness ɪɪɪ
large group gatherings. Along with a global network of colleagues, we have
been particularly interested in understanding the conditions that facilitate
within a group of relative strangers, not previously bound together by
cohesive forces such as family, tribe, or neighborhood community, the
emergence of a synergistic process such that the collective efforts of the
group as a whole exceed that which might be predicted by looking at the
capacities of the individuals within it. We have been trying to understand
how the values of a society that prizes the right of individuals to realize
themselves as unique and free subjects can be reconciled with the urgent
need for people to work together for the common good.

Our study focused on a series of temporary learning communities of
between 60 and 1800 people that we have personally convened or in which
we have participated. These events have been held in the United States,
Russia, Poland, Lithuania, Austria, Netherlands, Spain, Switzerland,
Germany, Hungary, Uruguay, Czechoslovakia, Brazil, Mexico, South
Africa, United Kingdom, Ireland, France, and Japan. Greece the
Philippines, and Italy. Although widely different in size of group, duration,
formats, locations, populations, facilitation styles, and languages spoken, a
common element in all the events was the work of American psychologist
Carl R. Rogers. All the organizers–or convenors as they were called–(but
not necessarily all the participants) shared a mental model of interpersonal
relationships and personal change based in Rogers' client-centered therapy
(later termed the "person-centered approach").

3. PERSON-CENTERED APPROACHES

The person-centered approach is at its core a sophisticated form of deep
multiple-view point dialogue. Through his and his colleagues' research from
the 1940s to the 1980s, in counseling, psychotherapy and later in
education and group encounters, Rogers discovered that when people are
met by another in a relationship that is characterized by what he termed
the "necessary and sufficient conditions for effective change" people will
naturally move towards psychological wholeness, growth and self-
actualization. At first called "non-directive" approaches, and mainly
applied in the arenas of psychotherapy, counseling and teaching, the key
relational conditions were identified as interpersonal warmth, genuineness,
acceptance, empathy and positive regard or respect (Rogers 1946, 1947,
1951, 1957, 1969,1979,1980; Rogers and Sanford 1989). Over the
subsequent decades Rogers' core conditions of person-centered interactions
have been shown to be the essential ingredients of all relationships in

which individual growth and consciousness development occurs (Bohart and Tallman 1999).

Rogers describes person-centered encounters as "I-Thou" dialogues (in the Buberian sense) and he believed that it was possible for I-Thou dialogue to occur in all kinds of relationships. In a conversation between them in 1957, Buber challenged Rogers' assertion that it was possible to establish a mutual I-Thou dialogue where a power or status differential exists such as that which exists between a counseling client and therapist (Kirschenbaum and Henderson 1989). We should bear in mind that Buber's view of psychiatry and psychotherapy was limited to the authoritarian Freudian model (which assumed a paternalistic, and markedly "top down" power relationship) that dominated European psychiatry at the time. Had Buber understood how radically client-empowering Rogers' view of counseling really was he might well have come to a different conclusion. For Rogers the person-centered meeting was a person-to-person, soul-to-soul encounter. As Rogers describes, "At these moments it seems that my inner spirit has reached out and touched the inner spirit of the other. Our relationship transcends itself and has become something larger" (Rogers 1986).

When our work on large group processes began, we already had extensive experience of the small group encounter process described by Rogers' in *Carl Rogers on Encounter Groups* (Rogers 1970), but we had little experience with person-centered processes in larger groups. So in 1974, Rogers, his daughter Natalie Rogers, and John K. Wood initiated an action research project to find out if the consciousness expansion that occurred in one-on-one psychotherapy or groups of ten to twelve people, might occur in groups as large as 200 or more.

Over a 16-year period our observations lead us to the conclusion that the large group process was potentially even more powerful in providing paths to growth and consciousness development than either the small group or individual therapy. In gatherings as large as 1800 people, as brief as one day in duration, participants reported, (with self-reports confirmed by family members and colleagues) significant learning and personal transformation. They found themselves reaching and maintaining higher levels of mental capacity and becoming more capable of wise and mature action and decision making. These findings were reported in earlier works (Bowen, O'Hara et al. 1979; O'Hara and Wood 1983; Rogers 1977; Rogers 1977, 1980; Rogers and Rosenberg, 1977; Wood 1984, 1988, 1994, 1996, 1999). The experiences provided new evidence of the generalizability of Rogers' "core conditions" for transformative dialogue beyond the therapeutic situation into a far wider range of potential use. We were excited by the potential of these large group events and we proposed that large person-centered groups might provide educational laboratories in which large numbers of individuals could develop the higher order capacities that are becoming increasingly necessary (Bowen, O'Hara et al. 1979).

What surprised us, however, was the observation (made often though not always) that there are moments in a group's life when a state is reached that goes beyond individual psychology. In these extraordinary states, individual participants can be deeply attuned to themselves as individual centers of consciousness, also interpersonally attuned to each other in an "I-Thou" relationship, *and* at the same time, everyone be attuned to the group as a whole entity. In such situations, the group as *another higher order entity* increases its capacity for self-organizing and becomes capable of exquisitely wise collective action that goes well beyond than any of the individual participants within the group. Even more exciting to us was the observation that in such conscious groups, individuals seem to be pulled beyond their own personal best–as if by participating in such collectivities, they are helped to enter a state of "flow" as individuals (Csikszentmihalyi 1990).

We observed people, including ourselves as convenors, gain access to deeper levels of empathy and intuition, extraordinary perception–even psychic and paranormal states of consciousness–that went beyond ordinary Western ways of knowing. People dreamed the same dreams, had premonitions of future events, read each others' minds, achieved startling levels of empathy and alignment, found innovative solutions to problems that appeared unsolvable, were able to play off each other with awesome improvisation and synergy and frequently attained spiritual trance states usually achieved only after decades of meditative practice. They also gained an extraordinary capacity to sense the community's movement and direction.

We came to refer to groups in which individual consciousness becomes expanded beyond individual ego-boundaries and voluntarily aligned with an expanded collective consciousness as *conscious communities* or *integral* groups.

After observing conscious communities develop in widely different settings and under a range of conditions, we began to suspect that if we could understand the dynamical interplay between individual and collective consciousness and learn how to create the conditions under which integral groups were likely to emerge, we might gain access to new human capacities with which to address the pressing systemic problems. We wondered if such capacities might represent a further stage in the evolution of collective consciousness.

4. MULTIPLE FRAMES

In order to discuss the results of our learning from large group events, a word needs to be said about the frames we have chosen to use. The Western psychological worldview, including its language, imagery, and epistemology, when compared to other cultures, is atomistic or "ego-centric"(Shweder and Bourne 1982). This is to say, attention ordinarily privileges either the actions of individual autonomous agents or the dynamics of clearly delineated social systems. Furthermore, in most Western discussions of about psychological processes, a simple linear causal relationship is generally assumed to exist between the actions of agents and their effects. This *modernist* frame of reference takes for granted a rational universe, and our sense of how things happen is instrumentalist. Such a frame, in our experience, is generally inadequate to describe some of the relational phenomena we have experienced in groups.

We have searched for different ways of framing our understanding and for language more adequate for encompassing the actual lived experience of participants. We are not unaware of how limited we both are, having been raised as modernists. But we hope that our repeated and sustained experience of being stretched by non-western contexts has provided us with at least a glimmer of hope that it might be possible to acquire new ways of knowing even while still inhabiting the old. Although limited by the constraints of English as a linear language, we will attempt to hold both the individual and collective levels in view at the same time and to avoid suggesting a simplistic causal relationship between particular actions and ultimate occurrences. To express this more effectively (we hope) we will be forced to shift across multiple frames of reference and language and to draw heavily on story, metaphor and analogy.

5.   CONSCIOUSNESS DEVELOPMENT IN PERSON-CENTERED LEARNING COMMUNITIES

5.1   From the Possible to the Actual

Although each group is unique, after observing many diverse gatherings, it is possible to sketch a familiar pattern to the life cycle of a person-centered group.

There is a time before the community has any being–conscious or non-conscious. There is only random, incoherent individual consciousness, in no way aligned. This is the time before anyone has even entertained any serious intention of holding a workshop and before any decision has been made by anyone. The "spirit" of the group is first evoked or called into being, and the spark of its ultimate consciousness kindled at the instant the idea of holding such an event occurs to any one individual. In its first existence, then, the community exists as a mental representation.

For a group to begin well, and for the chances of achieving higher states of consciousness to be enhanced, careful attention to initial conditions are essential. The "birth parents" of the eventual community are the convening team as it begins to imagine the upcoming gathering and the "gestation" process is their collective imagining and planning. As they design the event, as a mental phenomenon, the group already has real existence–if only in loose, inchoate form. As the weeks of planning proceed and the site is chosen, brochures produced and distributed, registrations received and all the myriad details that go into execution of a learning community are executed, the group begins to emerge and take shape at least as a meme. Convenors, potential attendees and even the staff of the facilities at which the event is to be held, begin to create mental constructs of the coming group. In a myriad conscious and unconscious ways these representations gradually establish the framing givens that the group will confront throughout its life.

The evolving group meme begins to affect its members from the outset. For example, members of the group-to-be begin to make contact with the convenors that might in turn have emotional responses to the contact. A celebrity has signed on, an entire family is coming together, there are many attendees from other countries, there are more vegetarians than usual, there are many attendees from other countries, several disabled people needing accommodation, there is a person coming who was a problem last year and so on. Each piece of mail that arrives engenders its own responses and expectations For the present geographically separated from other potential participants and still embedded in their other lives, attendees nevertheless begin to spend time imagining themselves at the workshop. They may be apprehensive about sharing a room with a room mate; they may be happy to be getting away; they may be calling other potential attendees looking to share transportation; they may dream about the group and so on. Family members sometimes report that as their loved ones anticipate the event they seem distant and withdrawn. The site staff begins to order meals, plan room arrangements and hold in their minds the logistical demands of this particular soon-to-be-real community. At one site, for instance, each year the kitchen staff received special instructions and the dining room staff made special arrangements for the PCA groups because their dietary needs were so different from their usual guests.

In the weeks and days leading up to each of these events the emerging group makes increasing demands on the mental life of everyone involved. The imagined group that until now was only the "possible group" gradually takes form and becomes the actual community, with concrete and knowable existence. Several hundred widely separated individuals are going about their lives carrying mental images of this actual group and although still existing for them only as a mental reality, in countless ways the group's imaginal "presence" is already influencing their lives.

5.2 Self-organization–From Imaginal to Concrete Being

As people arrive at the site the group's embodied presence consolidates. In the flesh interaction among members occurs and rapidly intensifies. No longer restricted by distance, people make contact with each other through the full array of senses. As embodied existence makes itself felt by the others through the multiple ways we have of affecting each other's being–scent, touch, sight, kinesthetic awareness–inevitably people begin to attune to each other. The consciousness or state of mind of everyone becomes somewhat altered. People are more aroused than usual, more aware of their environment, more sensitive to disturbance, more extreme in their responses. An ordinarily minor disappointment such as not having the first choice of main dish at dinner may become a major existential crisis; a friendly casual interaction with someone may become a defining moment. Everything seems larger and more vivid than usual.

By the time the first on-site meeting occurs, the group is already beginning to act as a self-organizing collective organism–with its own norms, language, rituals, expectations, opinion leaders, desires and agendas, and relational dynamics. Active facilitation by the convening group is minimal. In most groups it is limited to bidding the assembly welcome, providing information about the facilities, making the basic assumptions of the person-centered approach explicit. Typically the convenors express their faith in the capacity of groups to self-organize and create an agenda that will meet more of their individual and collective needs than any pre-arranged agenda the convenors could have devised in advance. The first group task is simply to begin.

Although free to begin in any way–to not meet, to meet in small groups, to appoint a committee, have someone take charge–even with no direction from a facilitator, the first meeting is usually a long meeting of the whole group. A group will usually address the most urgent issue it faces. Starting out, the most urgent issue is "who's here?" It is as if the most pressing concern is for the group to see itself fully incarnated. In a room large enough to hold everyone, people choose their own positions–usually something close to a single circle. In a recent workshop in Glasgow the shape of the room made a single circle impossible. The group spent its first three hours together wrestling with the shape of the room. They discussed at great length, how to arrange the chairs, whether to move the meeting, how decisions such as these should be made and by whom, and how to decide who would decide. In that first, seemingly chaotic, session the group confronted many of the perennial problems of community life–adequate communication, norms of behavior, power, decision making processes, the shared values that would guide the community's life, and the equitable distribution of resources–in this case space and air-time. By the time the session concluded people were emotionally and intellectually charged, and fully engaged with the existential drama of collective life.

Usually, the opening has a ritual quality, in which people share something about who they are, why they came and what they expect. Even in such simple opening sessions people nevertheless become very moved, aroused and alert, as patterns of thoughts and feelings are jostled in the diversity and newness. They become awakened and often somewhat off-balance as gradually familiar expectations and boundaries are challenged. As the process moves forward, people engage a variety of never-before-encountered experiences. There is a continuously varied assault on emotions, familiar concepts, interpretative frames of references, and patterns of behavior.

Without any techniques, group exercises, simulations or other structured interventions, self-expression and disclosure nevertheless become deepened. Without prompting people speak more intimately about core issues confronting them at home and here and now in the community. A state not unlike that which occurs in psychotherapy may occur with people speaking about deep inner symbolic and psycho-dramatic worlds–all, we emphasize, without direct intervention beyond the simple Rogerian dialogical basics. What takes many by surprise is the ease with which ordinarily matter-of-fact people with no real experience of symbolic communication, psychotherapy or even of art, understand and draw insight from symbolic content introduced by group members with more facility with imagery, symbolism and poetry. In one group, for instance, Charlie an engineer, who had initially described himself as "nuts and bolts kind o' guy," and "not into all this touchy-feely stuff," was drawn unselfconsciously into a dramatic re-enactment of a dream by a young literature student. He was willing to collaborate in Sarah's intrapsychic journey not because he was directed to by a facilitator, but simply because she asked him to and he liked her. To his surprise, while entering the flow of Sarah's dream he came up with an idea to solve a problem he was having back home with a co-worker. Although an utterly foreign experience to him prior to his participation in the group, playing a role in someone's psychodrama seemed natural while part of the group.

5.3   Tapping the Tacit Treasure House

As the group deepens and more profound experiences are shared, the hearts and minds of every member gradually become provoked by everyone else. In a process of mutual resonance, speakers tell their stories and express their truth and listeners open themselves and are moved. When Emily tearfully describes her dilemma about caring for her disabled infant and not neglecting her other children, for instance, she evokes the mental routines, emotional responses, memories, associations, cognitive schemas and images pertaining to infants, disability, mothering in everyone listening. As she speaks and connects with her listeners, the previously tacit collective wisdom becomes available to the rest of the group on conscious and unconscious levels. In any large group there will be an almost infinite storehouse of potentially relevant wisdom actually present in the room. The deeper the dialogue goes and the more associations this generates, the full synergistic potential of this vast human resource becomes available to those present.

As the hours or days together unfold this mutual awakening process is repeated many times, resonance among members deepening as it does so. Some encounters are tender, others hostile and angry, others hilarious, others tragic or hopeless, as the rich range of private human experience is brought into the public light of day. As individuals speak those listening are moved and respond, previously rigidified boundaries, frozen mental maps drawn prior to the workshop, gradually loosen and yield. New configurations of information and knowledge become possible and significant consciousness expansion occurs.

We repeatedly observed individuals who in a very short time, underwent degrees of transformation in the level of their mental maturity that are usually achieved only after extended psychotherapy, or consciousness practice. As one participant describes her experience, "When each of you spoke up I felt I reclaimed a forgotten piece of myself. I identified, I empathized and I changed because of it. I could feel the warm blood flowing back into my own life." Another person commented, "Now I can see myself as part of the big picture. I got new ideas, I could see how things all fit together, and made new connections with what I already knew and I had more to offer you in return." This is learning at its deepest and most transformative levels. It represents a gain in the capacity for systemic awareness that involves a change in epistemology–changing not only what is known, but the ways in which that knowledge can be processed and lived (Ivey 1985).

Watching this kind of experience repeatedly, we began to have faith that despite the apparently robustness or even rigidity of a person's identity and world view, transformational change in adults was possible. People have remarkable capacity to grow and to change. It is possible in these kinds of settings–though admittedly difficult and often frightening–for adults well along in years to undergo a level of psychological reorganization as to qualify as a worldview transformation.

5.4   Community Consciousness Takes Form

In the process of individual mental development it is through expanded awareness and elaboration of increasingly structured and integral cognitions, symbol and language, that higher levels of consciousness develops (Ivey 1985). So it is with collectives. As the free-flowing process in the person-centered group continues, each statement provokes another statement, a feeling or an image, gradually the group's awareness expands. As the proceedings unfold, member after member recaptures the immediacy and vibrancy of his or her unique voice and perspective and by sharing it, makes it public. The parts of the whole communicate to the others through the physicality and the utterances of its members. Through these acts of individual participation the latent potential of the ensemble–as a collectivity–becomes realized. A symphony comes into being through the combined vibrations of the instruments employed in its rendering and an individual mind becomes realized through the participation of the myriad connections among neurons. Likewise, the "group mind" begins to know itself through the interplay of the individual voices of its members.

Under the right conditions, sometimes after only hours among what were recently strangers, a new and knowable collective entity becomes manifest. Participants begin to sense the presence of this larger conscious entity and recognize that they are being influenced by it. Until this point in the process "the community" had existed only as a tacit, inchoate ground of action, but now out of the dialogical encounter itself a community emerges and becomes real to its members. The community to which people feel that they "belong" comes into focus as a conscious being with its own direction, and potential for learning, growth and transcendence.

Usually, the presence of an emergent and coherent group consciousness first becomes visible to group members when some individual member draws attention to it. This may happen by someone describing a sense of "community" or "universality" in what is occurring. For people with a religious frame of reference the presence of God or the existence of spiritual realities beyond the individual realm may be invoked. Language shifts subtly, with emphasis moving from "I" to "we," with many now referring to "our community." Scientists in the group might speak of "systems" and artists use collectivity metaphors and images such as "collage" or "quilt", psychologists frequently invoke the metaphor of the "group mind," as people try to put into their own familiar words a growing sense of some ineffable consciousness that seems to exist *beyond* any one of them as an individual yet that emerges from among them, nevertheless. It seems awkward at first for people in North American and European groups to acknowledge these trans-individual realities and they do so only timidly. In international groups, the emergence of a clear and knowable collective "we consciousness" is often first noted by non-Europeans. In our experience within groups of Euro-Americans it is religious people, artists and women who appear to have more ease expressing such collective awareness.[1]

Once acknowledged, even if only by a minority of its members at first, the group's concrete being and its effects as a collective entity upon the individuals within it, become increasingly discernible to its members. Boundaries between the group and the world sharpen. As if still too fragile to survive assaults upon its being, at this point groups can become suddenly quite xenophobic and exclusive. As a clear sense of "we" emerges, sharp and sometimes hostile distinctions are often made between "us" and "them." Not uncommonly, people from the outside world–even visiting family members or invited guests and other groups sharing the site–are somehow alien. A high degree of sensitivity to themes of harmony and disharmony among members and with the surroundings all point to the process in which consciousness of individual members is attuning to a larger collective reality. People report acting in ways that are unfamiliar even to themselves. Their sense of empathy deepens to a startling degree. They have similar dreams and "read each others' minds." They find themselves having visions, premonitions, déjà vu experiences, anticipating what will happen at subsequent meetings, and other non-rational experiences.

At an international gathering in Brazil, for instance, an emphatically rational biologist reported hearing the weeping sounds of suffering "presences" while housed in the former slave quarters of an old coffee plantation-turned-conference-center and asked to move to another room. In a workshop in Italy a delicate-looking ballerina found herself behaving with uncharacteristic fury to protect an older woman accused by a young feminist of "wasting her life cooking for her husband and raising children." People often report sensing that, oracle-like, their words seem to belong more to the group than to themselves. In some cases people report feeling taken over or "possessed" by the group process.

At this stage, there is more interest in ritual, symbol and other non-rational forms knowing and being, as people become more open to non-verbal communication, dance, music and play. Spontaneously, routines change. People might suddenly rearrange furniture or change meeting rooms. Sessions may begin with someone reading a poem, sharing a dream, an artwork, piece of music or image, as everyone becomes attuned to this new entity–the community. Consensus decisions are sought.   There is strong pressure for the entire group to meet as a whole group sometimes well into the night. There is great emphasis on what people share in common and at the same time as statements that appear to draw boundaries between "them" and "us" within the group are resisted.

Although sometimes complaining that "all we do is sit and talk and talk," groups will nevertheless resist any suggestions for activities that involve differentiation into sub-groups. Sometimes a community may discuss such a suggestion for hours and even days before a consensus is finally reached about whether the group will stay together or divide. Premature decisions imposed by fiat can be catastrophically disruptive. In one group, where a sub-group managed to precipitate a division before consensus had been achieved, the separation resulted in a violent outburst from which the disoriented community never completely recovered (O'Hara and Wood 1984; O'Hara 1997).

5.5   From "I-Thou" to "We-I-Thou"

As the sense of community deepens and members begin to pay more attention to the collective dynamics, a noticeable change occurs in the interests of the group as a whole. The deep personal sharing by individuals that is the routine early on is no longer the main focus–it may even provoke impatience and anger. Some group members will begin to question the amount of energy and time spent on individual issues, and urge the group to explore its reality as a collective.

In a recent European community a young woman had first delighted the group with her funny stories, deep personal sharing and single-minded dedication to authentic self-expression. In the opening stages she was a hero of sorts–a role model of self-expression authenticity and autonomy. After the group consciousness began to emerge, however, the same behaviors that had been approved of while the group was still in a stage of individual expression, now began to draw criticism as "individualistic" and "disruptive of group cohesiveness." As she held on doggedly to her individual style, the young woman became increasingly isolated and eventually rejected. She felt hurt, betrayed and was bewildered the group's reactions.

This sea-change in ones own or a group's preoccupations takes many by surprise. To find oneself inexplicably annoyed by stories that in other circumstances would move one deeply can be disorienting. In a group in Portugal, Sinead a rape counselor from Ireland, expressed one such moment to a fellow group member as follows:

> Nelson, until today I have been with you and very involved with your struggle, but–and I can't believe I am saying this–somehow I can't stand to listen anymore. There are so many other people I want to hear from and other deeper ways of being together I hoped we can get into, that I am pulling away from you. I am irritated by you and I feel badly about it, but I would feel worse if I sat here and did not tell you.

Earlier in the process such non-accepting, confrontational words most likely would have raised protests among the Rogerians, for whom unconditional acceptance and empathy are among the highest values. But once a palpable group consciousness has asserted itself, such an intervention might be experienced with relief–even, we might add–by Nelson, who in this event was himself growing anxious about his self-absorbed routine and was needing some help in breaking out of his isolation.

There is real vulnerability in such moments. Sinead was deeply embarrassed by her apparent lapse in empathy–a personal quality she much prized. Gradually, however, she came to realize that her considerable empathic abilities had not deserted her but had switched their focus. In place of empathic attunement to Nelson as an individual, she was attuning to the emergent consciousness of the group. Nelson's behavior, so self-assertive and unconcerned for collective needs had a relational dimension, and was potentially hurtful to those like Sinead who had made the shift to embrace the group as a whole system. By drawing attention to the threat posed to Nelson and to the group by his separateness, Sinead had acted to make the group safer for everyone. Paradoxically, breaking the empathic connection with Nelson as an individual in favor of her attunement to the whole group of which he was a member, was in actuality more in line with Nelson's deeper needs within the group. Often, an individual expresses empathy for a group through daring to be congruent and honest. After Sinead had spoken up, other members who had been unable to speak up until then, found a safe space created by Sinead's words.

The group consciousness, having become aware of itself through the sensitivity of an individual member, now becomes eager, it seems, to learn more about itself and to discover more of its potential. In order to do so it must give up its exclusive focus on individuals. Those members like Sinead, with what in some cultures would be regarded as shamanistic or mediumistic skills, who empathize easily with individuals and are especially open to attuning to the consciousness of the whole, frequently become the human means by which awareness of the group as a conscious entity occurs within a community.

6.   THE PARADOX OF RESISTANCE

Some people–notably highly educated Europeans and North Americans–re uncomfortable with this stage of the group process and may be actively resist it. There are good reasons to be cautious. Most are all familiar with science-fiction images of robotic "Borg-like" collectives made through assimilating the consciousness of autonomous and free individuals, and we have seen news reports of doomsday cults following leader into mass psychosis or suicide. More mundanely, "group think" is a well-known black to creative action in work teams and other groups.

Group consciousness can be primitive and can even sweep individuals away into mob behaviors. An inheritance from our mammalian ancestry, humans have built-in capacities for group life and it seems likely that group consciousness is older than individual consciousness on the evolutionary time scale. The limbic brain system makes all mammals acutely aware of others and we easily attune to the rhythms and moods of others–seeking one another in deeply resonant limbic partnerships that over our evolutionary history have been essential for our survival. The ability to exquisitely sense the presence, mood, desires, emotions of another, enables us to know instantly, without any need for cognitive processing, who is family or friend and who stranger or foe. The limbic system provides mammals, including humans, with the basic group-coordinating routines that in the face of either threats or opportunities enable concerted and cohesive group actions to occur automatically–and mindlessly. Throughout most of human evolution group consciousness has been a higher priority than individual autonomy.

Over the past hundred thousand years human cognition and culture have gradually emerged to buffer the effects of the automatic biological routines and to provide complex webs of tacit agreements among individuals to augment the emotional substrate. The last four hundred or so years of the history of human consciousness can be read as a journey of liberation from conformity to the demands and rewards of the tribe, family, or other collective, towards differentiation, individual freedom and individuation. Modern people are rightly ambivalent about surrendering their hard won individual identity and consciousness to the group. Drawn to the experience of unity or "oneness" because it is comforting, exhilarating and potentially ecstatic, we nevertheless fear such surrender. Most of us are well aware that if not accompanied by individual freedom and heightened awareness, such states can be fanatical, regressive, intoxicating, and when manipulated by unscrupulous or autocratic leaders, they are also enslaving.

7.   CONSCIOUS STATES

Untangling the relationship between individual consciousness and group consciousness and to draw important, and frequently neglected distinctions between different states of group consciousness, needs new language. We have found the language of holism helpful. Arthur Koestler differentiates between those behaviors of entities (which he calls holons) that are expressive of their particularity, integrity and uniqueness–in other words of their existence as separate and whole entities–and those associated with "partness" or participation and integration into some yet larger entity (Koestler 1987). Behaviors that express wholeness are termed *self-assertive*, and those that express relationality and part-ness, *integrative* or *self-transcendent*. In human systems, including systems of consciousness, self-assertive behaviors are those which highlight individuality and uniqueness and emphasize "I" as distinct from either "Thou" or "It." In self-assertive consciousness, attention is focused on clear self-expression, well-delineated boundaries, sharp distinctions and it emphasizes separation, integrity and diversity. Self-transcendent behaviors are those, which emphasize "I" only as a participant of "I-Thou", in an entity referred to as "We." Self-transcendent consciousness emphasizes pattern, connection, relationship, and belonging. For example, a person is stating an individual opinion or taking a position would be considered to be in a self-assertive mode. When listening empathetically to another and being changed by what is heard a person is probably in a self-transcendent mode.

Consciousness has both self-assertive and self-transcendent modes always co-existing in figure-ground relationships to each other. Whenever people are fully aware of themselves as unique voices and experience the ways in which they are separate and unique, they are in a self-assertive state. When they focus beyond themselves to the realities in which they are participating–such as singing in a choir or working in a team–they are in self-transcendent consciousness. When self is foreground, our relationships with others and with the universe are usually background. When our awareness is extended out beyond our own skin and embraces the wider reality of which we are part, then awareness of our individual identity usually fades into the background. In the self-assertive mode, consciousness is sharp, bounded, detailed and exclusive; transcendent consciousness at the other end of the spectrum, is fluid, impressionistic, boundary-less and inclusive.

8.   THE RELATIONSHIP BETWEEN INDIVIDUAL AND GROUP CONSCIOUSNESS

Over the course of a group's life the individual members will naturally move in and out of different consciousness states and so will the group. The stages of a group's life are well known, and need not be repeated here. Our focus has been on the way consciousness states of individuals interact and co-construct the consciousness of community.

In a young group, self-assertive consciousness is most salient. The focus is on individual initiative, autonomy, and the individual stories of participants. People go to great lengths to be seen as individuals, to clearly articulate their opinions and unique perspectives on every issue and to ensure that they are accurately heard by others. Collaboration, if it occurs at all is formal and transactional–give and take, tit-for-tat, debate, reciprocal negotiation, clear expectations and articulated contracts, majority rule and so on. When the group consciousness emerges, it may also be self-assertive. This can show up as intense discussions about group norms, concerns about membership, the unique identity of "our group", voting, leadership elections, and efforts to craft codes of conduct, manifestos, mission statements, and unifying values.

Groups in self-assertive mode may be highly cohesive but be xenophobic, unable to deal with newcomers, and may be aggressive towards others, especially outsiders. Dissenting initiatives by members are often rebuffed at least until the group as a whole is sure the initiative presents no threat to the group's power to control its members. In a Brazilian group, for example, a renowned filmmaker requested the group's permission to film the process. It was at a time when Brazil was emerging from two decades of repressive dictatorship and feelings ran high about such issues as privacy, surveillance and openness. The group could not come to an agreement about the filmmaker's request. Some people wanted the group filmed, others threatened to leave if it was, and the split threatened the group's existence as an entity. To protect itself, the group at first refused the request and embarked on a process of intense consideration of the question. The dialogue lasted several days of heated meetings. In order not to lose precious time while the group was discussing the issue, the filmmaker asked if he could audiotape. Despite the fact that the same objections and concerns about confidentiality and manipulation existed, the group nevertheless permitted the audiotaping. In their view, by delaying his film-making and accepting the will of the group, the film-maker, as an individual, had made a concession to the whole, and in doing so had demonstrated that he too was part of and loyal to the group. The group reciprocated by allowing him his self-assertiveness in the execution of his individual project.

The first awareness that group consciousness is something beyond the sum of the individual consciousness is usually accompanied by a corresponding shift towards self-transcendence in the consciousness of the individual group members. People speak far less of "I" and more of "we."

They spend more time listening, deeply empathizing, opening themselves up to be touched, moved and provoked by others. They are also more willing to accept the suggestions of others and to surrender to the group's rhythms and flow. Gradually this process seems to open people up to more self-transcendent states of consciousness.

Group consciousness also can exist in a self-transcendent state. If it does, vigilant attention to boundaries loosens and xenophobia disappears. Compromises come more easily and what might be taken as dissent in a self-assertive group is welcomed as creative input by the self-transcendent group. Whereas in self-assertive mode a group is likely to resist or reject change that comes in the form of a newcomer or an innovation, in self-transcendent mode novelty and "otherness" is likely be embraced as an opportunity for growth and renewal. The shift from self-assertive to self-transcendent can be gradual–occurring person by person–and it can be rapid–occurring almost instantaneously in response to a particular event. Phase-shifts are readily noticeable and have a "melting" feel.[2] Hardened positions soften, peoples' body postures relax, voice tones change, there are more comfortable spaces between statements, more physical expressions, more laughter, more tears, less anger, less competition and more collaboration, more dialogue, more metaphor, more graceful flow among people and topic, more nuance and ambiguity but less anxiety about it. Although less familiar in everyday life, participants often experience this state as feeling "at home."

9. STATES OF CONSCIOUSNESS IN GROUPS

From our observations of such groups, there appear to be four more or less distinct relationships between group consciousness and the consciousness of its individual members. These are self-assertive individuals participating in an integrative group; self-assertive individuals participating in a self-assertive group; self-transcendent individuals participating in a self-assertive group and self-transcendent individuals participating in a self-transcendent group.

Two of these are isomorphic–i.e. both individuals and the collective are in the same consciousness state, and two are heteromorphic where group and individuals are in different states.[3] Each configuration has its own characteristic behaviors with distinct consequences for individual and group behavior. Each state might be appropriate in some situations but not others.

9.1 Self-assertive Individuals and Integrative Group

A common individual-group relationship within groups in the United States is the "libertarian" position, where individuals are self-assertive and the group is integrative. In this configuration there may be outstanding individual achievements, a strong sense of freedom of choice, a high degree of self-awareness, autonomy and personal power, yet the group is only loosely defined and is easily entered. Individual freedom is a higher value than group loyalty and there is little common ground. In this state, the group is easily penetrated and disrupted, internal rivalry saps vitality and the group may eventually dissolve.

9.2   Self assertive Individual in a Self Assertive Group

In times of group crisis or celebration groups may be isomorphic for self-assertion. Emphasis is on individual freedom and creativity, individual and group identity and sovereignty. This is the "Superbowl" phenomenon, where individuals are highly individualistic in their expression of support for their team and the sum of these individual expressions adds up to the "team spirit". In this state even the most individualistic artistic expression refers to the identity of the group. This is the predominant situation early on in the process of American person-centered groups. It is also, not surprisingly the commonest state for the American culture in general, particularly in these days of when sub-groups such as ethnic, sexual or cultural minorities are eager to define, assert and protect their specialized identities. Americans are a self-assertive society made up of self-assertive individuals. In the aftermath of the terrorist attack on New York City and Washington D.C., we saw a myriad unique and individual expressions of grief outrage, all consolidated into a clear, unified American expression of solidarity against the "other."

As savvy political strategists and advertisers know, appeals to Americans to act collectively are most successful when made in the name of self-interest.

9.3   Self-transcendent Individuals in Self-assertive Collectives

The collectivist and militarist positions are represented by self-assertive collectives of self-transcendent individuals. Such groups have commonly provided the contexts in which individuals have achieved extraordinary performances–both constructive and destructive. These are the groups in which individuals willingly or through coercion, align their own individual consciousness to the group's purposes. Such groups produce disciplined armies, political movements, revolutions, fanatics and martyrs. There is great solidarity within and exclusivity with outsiders. In our groups, visiting family members often remark about the apparent contradiction of a community in which members speak freely to each other about "unconditional acceptance" and "openness" within the group, yet seem closed to them and fearful of strangers.

The best sports and work teams aim for this state, and their participants commonly report being aided by such groups to reach performance levels beyond their own previous best. Religious groups encourage this state as a path to their own particular version of spiritual fulfillment.

At their democratic best, such groups encourage their individual members to voluntarily offer their best efforts to the group. In exchange, the synergistic possibilities inherent in collaboration can lift individuals to new heights. Individuals seem to be able to access the permutations and possibilities of the capacities contained within their group and can be lifted to greater heights of personal development and creativity.

Such groups can be immensely powerful, as political and military leaders know, achieving feats well beyond what might be expected from a simple head count. At their worst, these groups can be extremely aggressive and violent, taking the form of warrior cultures, fanatical religious groups, cults, gangs, and sectarian or political terrorist movements. They can be self-destructive and violent as was seen in the terrorist suicide attacks on the World Trade Centers and the Jonestown mass suicide and murder.

9.4   Integrative Individuals in Integrative Collectives

The most constructive and in our experience the least frequently attained state is where the individuals are experiencing integrative, inclusive consciousness and so is the group. We refer to this state as the conscious community or integral group.

In our study, it is this state that has intrigued us the most because we believe that if we could harness its power, it provides the greatest potential as a context for higher order learning, developing collaborative wisdom and for addressing the complex challenges ahead within a global, pluralistic society.

In the integral group, individual members are in a state of integration as Subjects, i.e. they fully awake as unique centers of consciousness and are capable of processing experience at the higher levels of mental complexity and integration (Ivey 1985; Kegan 1994). In Eastern consciousness systems such as Zen or Yoga, this state might be referred to as an awakened or post-ego state. Individual awareness no longer stops at the skin, but extends beyond to embrace relationships and the broader social and environmental contexts of existence. Others entities–human beings, animals, elements of the natural world–are seen and experienced not as objects but as unique Subjects in their own right who in direct and indirect ways are co-creators of the relational dance of being. At the same time, members of integral groups are attuned to the whole larger collective–the community–which in turn exists as a conscious entity with its own Subjectivity and own participation in yet larger wholes.

In such integral groups there is a powerful sense of oneness and of enlightened collaboration that occurs voluntarily as a spontaneous self-organizing process. Furthermore, and we believe most significantly for consciousness evolution, *this occurs without the loss of individual Subjectivity or self*. On the contrary, participants usually describe feeling more empowered and cherished as unique choice-making and meaning-making individuals. In contrast to a self-assertive group of integrative individuals, here the collective is also in an integrative state; open to its constitutive parts–the individual members–accepting them, embracing each person's point of view and finding a place for everyone, and open to the wider world to which the group belongs.

We have only observed this special state at times when the group collectively aligns itself with some activity, context or cause, which requires it to act as a part of some larger whole. The community achieves self-transcendence through opening itself to its constituent parts and simultaneously surrendering its own self-assertive identity to the larger contexts in which it participates. Examples of this state include those occasions when a spiritual community dedicated to individual transcendence becomes active in an ecumenical cause, or when a non-profit organization forms a consortium with other groups and at least temporarily gives up its sovereignty to serve a greater whole. In our studies it seems that when groups composed of open and self-transcending individuals voluntarily and authentically align themselves as communities to larger systems, that the potential creativity, wisdom or higher states of consciousness accessible surpasses that achievable in all other states.

10.   CULTIVATING GROUP LEARNING AND TRANSFORMATION

10.1   Facilitating Consciousness Shifts

Sometimes events occur in integral groups that have an extraordinary or paranormal feel. Despite this, we are not ascribing any supernatural capacity to these states. We are describing what we believe are latent capacities that exist widely among all human communities, but that in modern egocentric societies like North America, frequently go untapped in everyday circumstances. As William James observed, altered states are available to us at an instant's notice. "Our normal waking consciousness ... is but one special type of consciousness, whilst all about it, parted from it by the filmiest screens, there lie potential forms of consciousness entirely different...apply the requisite stimulus, and at a touch they are all there in all their completeness" (James, 1902, p. 388).

Through our work, we have been able to identify some of the "requisite stimuli" or conditions that make it more likely that groups can access these levels of consciousness. We do not propose the following as a "manual" for creating integral groups, but rather as some "best practices" for those who wish to experiment with nurturing integral group consciousness.

Much of this we have described earlier and our observations parallel those of many other writers about the facilitation of group process. (Bohm and Edwards 1991; Gibbs 1991; Isaacs 1999; Rogers 1970; Senge 1990; Yalom 1975).

10.2   Set and Setting

Contemplatives throughout history have known that set and physical setting are vitally important in the growth of consciousness in individuals and communities. They place their monasteries in special places, bring together groups of people willing to be aligned, and cultivate symbols, rituals, music, images that provide the containers for consciousness to develop. One does not have to be a Christian to be expanded by a Gothic cathedral and one does not have to be Buddhist to be healed by the chanting of Tibetan monks. Person-centered groups housed in bucolic retreat centers respond more quickly than those crammed into urban spaces with their many distractions and less comfort. Sunshine, healthy food, the excitement of beginnings, challenge, novelty, even hardship and anxiety, and many other non-specific factors may play a role. Whatever the choice, however, it seems important that the place gives the participants a sense of location and containment. Settings shared with other groups, where it is difficult to provide safety and seclusion make it more difficult. Also, when comfortable space is not available to meet as a whole community, in small self-selected groups, and in solitude, it becomes much more difficult for an effective rhythm to be established between the development of individual and group levels of awareness.

10.3   Convening, Planning and Facilitation

Despite a large literature on facilitator training, we came to the conclusion that the important variable in the success of a convening team was not their theoretical knowledge, techniques or interventions, but who they are as persons. We mean this at the deepest level. Key dimensions of the capacity to be facilitative include the convenor's overall level of psychological maturity (consciousness) and how they are seen and experienced by other group members. Their cultural background, values, aesthetics, experience, level of anxiety or ease, imagination, physical capacities, intellectual knowledge, unconscious processes, unresolved psychological conflicts or potential and so on, all contribute to establishing the initial conditions around which all else forms. These multiple aspects of the convenors' being play out and become expressed in unpredictable but relevant ways when selecting the site, choosing participants, setting expectations and providing the initial language, frames and starting assumptions.

Every decision, phrase in a brochure, administrative choice, and the overall sense of vision and mission, is worked over endlessly and mindfully by the convening group. No detail is too small to be considered and reconsidered. Words are particularly powerful in shaping expectations and it is not unusual for a statement in a brochure to become a touchstone for discussions once the group gathers. The over-riding value in this process is the creation of conditions in which every single person present may have maximum freedom and support to be exactly what and who they are, and to be able to extend to others the same space and freedom.

The convenors are most important before the event during the planning phase of the group's life. At the start of the project, the staff of a workshop met regularly for almost a year, coming together onsite for an entire week prior to the event in order to further align and attune to each other and to become personally ready for the gathering. To become, in fact, an integral group itself. During the pre-workshop week, we meditated together, shared personal lives at deep levels, expressed feelings, hopes and dreams–even romantic attractions and spiritual and psychic experiences. Most importantly, we cleared up interpersonal misunderstandings, and hurt feelings and we finished the operational work of preparing the site. Through the course of this preparation process, the goal is to become as aligned as possible.

Such painstaking preparation is rarely an option in these hurried times, but we believe that there is a direct correlation between the amount of working together to creating an integral group of convenors and the likelihood that integral consciousness will be achieved by the entire community, once assembled.

Once the gathering starts, the convenor role shifts, becoming less concrete and symbolic. As time passes, it becomes clear to participants that despite their expectations, convenors are not functioning as directors, managers, therapists or teachers, but as empathic resonators tuned to the deeper flows of the group dynamics and as "keepers of the process." They have the effect of a tuning fork or "strange attractor," evoking empathic resonance or reverberation among those group members who may share their consciousness state. Convenors who are outspoken and confrontational are more likely to evoke similar behavior in others in the group. If they use metaphors from art, dance, science or psychology in their own communications these modes are likely to become significant to the group, if they are analytical they will evoke intellectual discussion, if they are erotically alive, eroticism will surface, an highly emotional leaders tune into emotionalism.

The empathic resonance can be extraordinarily perspicacious at times, and can have startling affects on a group. In one program, while sitting in a community group, a convenor visualized a powerful image of a child being beaten by a parent. When she described the image to the whole group, two members shared the fact that in a small breakout group earlier that morning, the self-appointed leader had bullied a member into participating in risky group project. In being so directive and leader-centered she violated basic person-centered principles. The subsequent discussion in the large group about the relationship between individual sovereignty and group participation was a turning point in the community process. After that the creative and conscious use of spontaneous imagery became a new capacity available to the group as a whole.

Another facilitative role played by the convenors is caring for the vulnerable outlyers, ensuring that space for each person to be heard is kept open.

Convenors also tune into the seen and unseen ebb and flow in group attention, focus and energy. They make sure that as the process unfolds, the Rogerian assumptions about empathy, listening, authenticity, respect, and faith in the self-organizing potential of individuals and collectives, are brought forward to be either affirmed or questioned. The convenors are not alone in this role, however. Almost from the outset participants assume their own authority and the leadership function becomes quickly distributed among those present. A successful group has not one set of leaders but is made up entirely of leaders. Even those who choose to remain silent, lead by demonstrating the importance of following.

10.4   Facilitative Attitudes

As the research on effective counseling and psychotherapy with individuals has repeatedly shown, there are certain attitudes, ways of being, and ways of being with others that seem to reliably result in personal growth, and occasionally in remarkable transformational breakthroughs (Bohart and Tallman 1999). There is, in our experience, no one overriding facilitative attitude that seems to be crucial in nurturing the emergence of consciousness in a group, but rather there are several key attitudes all interacting at the same time. It is not necessary that everyone arrive at the event with these attitudes already developed, but it does seem important that at some times during their time together they become manifest by a significant number of the group members.

In Rogers' original work a key component of the core facilitative conditions for individual growth is empathy. Empathy has since been shown to be the gold standard for effective facilitation in any growth-focused relationship (Bohart and Tallman 1999). Empathy is commonly regarded as an individual-to-individual phenomenon in which one person senses the unspoken or inchoate thoughts or feelings of another. Our observations show that group or relational empathy may be even more important that individual empathy in the formation of conscious communities. (O'Hara 1997)

O'Hara describes relational empathy as that process wherein one attunes to the whole entity–the group. Relational empathy makes it possible to sense the interpersonal dynamics, knowledge, unconscious processes, dreams, images, narratives, concerns, feelings, sensitivities, priorities, fears–in other words the tacit and explicit consciousness–of collectives.

In one Brazilian group, for instance, an impasse developed over a decision facing the community. The impasse was finally overcome through the performance of a "psychic readings" by one or two of the "sensitives" in the group. Less exotically, but just as significant, in North American or European groups the same function is often filled by artists or participants with organization or systems intervention capacities. The presence of individuals with well-developed capacities for relational forms of empathy, as we stated earlier, greatly improves the chances that a group will experience the more extraordinary levels of consciousness.

Another key attitude in facilitators is humility. It is also one that presents a significant challenge to self-assertive professionals, most of whom value their competence and technical knowledge. By humility we refer to the willingness to suspend assumptions, to open oneself up to see things afresh, to be touched by others, and learn from them, to acknowledge crystallized routines and patterns, to embrace errors and blind-spots, be open to feedback from individuals and the group as a whole, and to be willing to risk learning in public. It is also important to be open to the possibility that one can be moved by forces beyond one's ken–whether framed as a spiritual reality or scientific.

Also essential is a willingness to surrender and let go of ones certainties. We have witnessed time and time again, that at moments of anger between group members, or hostile polarization between groups for instance, that when one side is willing to yield, to accept that they may be mistaken, to apologize or accept a suggestion of another–in other words when they are willing to openly surrender a previous certainty–that a shift in consciousness occurs and the whole group moves forward.[4] It is particularly powerful when a convenor or some other kind of leader undergoes such visible shift and is seen by others in the group to be willing to learn in public.

Although we describe this as a process of surrender it is important to note that is not surrender to another individual. Among people who cherish their autonomy this might be experienced as defeat. Neither does it represent a giving up of self, or abdication of individual sovereignty. If it did, other members of the group who share the position being challenged would most certainly resist it. Instead, we are describing surrender to the larger system or community to which they all belong.

An existential, here and now focus seems to be highly facilitative. By following the moment by moment experiential references in the context of life in a particular community members seem more able to let go of previous mental maps By abandoning the world of abstraction and engaging directly with the concrete existential predicament of the group in the company of diverse others, the customary abstractions that frame expectations can be softened, if not entirely left behind.. In experiencing the present, with relatively few pre-conceptions, people are forced to learn in new and unexpected ways. When boundaries are softened in this way, new configurations of conscious become available to the individuals and to the group.

A certain amount of respectful impertinence, or iconoclasm seems necessary if the group is to tap the more creative aspects of its potential.. Unless there are group members who are willing to challenge the obvious, little of novelty or creativity is likely. In the most successful group there is continuous challenge to the obvious. The constant deconstruction and reframing, usually from several ideologies and epistemologies simultaneously, gradually undermines all past certainties and brings everyone into the experienced present. This process may have a decidedly playful quality where every fixed meaning can be put into play with hilarious or moving consequences. At other times, the battle over meaning can be conducted with the deadly earnestness of a political re-education camp. In either case, fixed understandings are overthrown and space is opened for creativity and novel solutions. Humor and irreverence are also very effective.

Everything we have been describing here represents some dimension of what we mean by deep dialogue–the mutual and reciprocal engagement of people in an open-ended encounter with Being. In the ways a dance is irreducible to the separate steps and a poem cannot be found in the sequence of words, dialogue resides in all of what we have discussed, and is more than any of it. Isaacs distinguishes between dialogue, discussion, and debate, and like Bohm makes the case that dialogue builds meaning while the others proceed by cutting meaning away(Isaacs 1999). For Isaacs, dialogue is a way of thinking together that can bring the tacit knowledge explicit, or as Bohm would say, explicate as yet implicate order (Bohm and Edwards 1991).

Person-centered dialogue is much more than merely thinking together. *It is a way of feeling, living, experiencing and being together in ways that provide a context for consciousness advancement.* The fully embodied, person-centered encounter creates the space for creative meaning making, and also provides access to seen and unseen collective knowledge or wisdom already present within the group. Some of this knowledge is in the form of thinking, but much of it is social, kinesthetic, holistic, and imaginal. It is through this open-hearted and authentic process of surrender to others that people gain access not only to the lived world of another, but they also gain access to the complex interpenetrated whole that is the emergent creation they make together. In our experience, being truly open to dialogical encounter is to participate in the mystery that rises up before us when thinking ends. Such transformative dialogue risks psychological death. To surrender ones certainties to a group of people we barely know and allow ones being to be altered in the meeting, is in a psychological sense to die and be reborn transformed in the meeting. This is an immense challenge.

Usually, risks to ones identity and psychological coherence are taken only when there is no alternative and when there is faith that something better exists at the other side. Faith comes in many forms. Whether it resides in God, Nature, "selfish genes", evolution, immutable laws of physical or biological reality, self-organizing systems, human creativity, implicate order, or all of them combined, it is faith that enables human beings to let go, move beyond themselves and risk being transformed. It is through faith rather than thought or logic that people come to believe that individuals, groups, and communities have intrinsic tendencies to self-organize and to move from disorder towards ever more complex ordered wholes (O'Hara and Wood 1984). On the individual level this faith may manifest as a confidence that people or Nature can be trusted or that shared commitments are worthwhile. On a group or organizational level it may appear as a dogged refusal of a small group to give up on a shared task, despite overwhelming odds, or perhaps a willingness to make great sacrifices in the present for the promise of a better future. Faith, like hope, is the conviction that the future is radically open and that despite turbulence and suffering in the present there are real possibilities for betterment latent in the struggle.

Faith is a powerful orienting force in a person-centered community, alerting people to the presence, perhaps as yet hidden, of an evolutionary directionality to existence that may be trusted. It is faith in the possibility of transformation that keeps eyes and hearts open even in the face of adversity. For Rogers, the object of his faith was the "actualizing tendency" which he believed was part of the intrinsic vector in all living organisms and in the universe. For others it might be faith the "God does not play dice with the Universe," as Einstein believed, and for some faith in the democratic process.

Rogers was known for his frequent assertion that he trusted the "wisdom of the group." For him this was not mystical trust, but based on personal and scientific experience, rational trust, when confronted with challenge, groups usually find their way out. Despite this trust, however, when the going got tough, Rogers himself could become as anxious as the next person about the outcome. There are times during workshops or community processes that are very difficult and painful and faith falters. Tempers flare, impasses occur, certainties dissolve, chaos reigns, anxiety spirals out of control, nothing interesting happens for hours or days, vitality ebbs and people get bored, hurt or upset. In times like these, the whole may be a good deal less than the sum of its parts. The temptation is high for individuals to withdraw from the group efforts and look out for themselves. It is the presence of people–particularly convenors–who have confidence in the group's capacity to transcend its difficulties, who have faith in human beings and in the "Rogerian story" who can convince individuals not to depart or withdraw into self-assertive individualism. They can provide the necessary encouragement to "keep the faith," stay involved and to press on.

11. THE DIALOGICAL CHALLENGE

It seems clear to us that the threats and opportunities facing humanity (and that our presence poses for our biosphere co-habitants) at this point in evolutionary history are so vast, complex and interpenetrated that it is simply beyond the capacity of individuals working alone to make much difference to collective outcomes. Although, individual creativity will always play an important role, and innovators, artists and scientists will continue to bring important breakthroughs that are the products of their individual minds, for any new ideas, new social programs, ways of organizing civic life, or adoption of new technologies on a scale broad enough to make a difference, social, political and economic systems must also be involved. Traditional patterns of life, routine behaviors, basic psychology and values of whole communities will have to change. Furthermore if resistance and backlash is to be avoided in democratic open societies, the coordination of group behavior must be achieved through voluntary agreements and mutual consent.

We have few models for generative dialogue among empowered people with diverse interests. As recently as the early twentieth century, most people lived in relatively homogeneous societies in which individual voices were largely subordinated to group survival. The person as Subject–a center of individual consciousness, agentic author and interpreter of his or her life–was unimportant. People lived out their entire lives constrained by definitions of them given by their community and bound by the multiple obligations of community life. Utterly dependent upon the community for survival, independent action was not an option. The feudal, caste-based societies of our ancestors, some tribal societies that persist today, and the totalitarian systems of the twentieth century, were built upon the backs of powerless, faceless (and expendable) masses whose individual Subjectivity and collective efforts were subordinated to the ends of leaders and elites. In such social systems, collective efforts are not coordinated by voluntary collaboration based in equality, shared values and mutual interest, but through compliance to authority and social conventions enforced by means of social coercion, violence and fear. Although still a common social form in much of the developing world, such an oppressive option is not viable in today's open and diverse societies.,

Democracy also emerged in relatively homogeneous societies. The liberal democracies of the nineteenth century, in which emancipation and individual rights provided the architecture of social progress, were highly coherent and homogeneous, with deeply embedded shared world-views and very little diversity. In 19th century Britain, for instance, John Stuart Mill could take for granted a shared cultural vision among his audience. He could not have even imagined, that by the late twentieth century, the guarantees of individual liberty he so vigorously promoted would be the basis of protection of the rights of immigrant communities from cultures that are worlds and centuries apart from industrial Britain, to establish schools, the curriculum of which sometimes challenge the very emancipatory values that made their existence possible.

In these days of high social mobility, mass migrations and expanded claims for individual and ethnic sovereignty, collaboration must occur among people who differ enormously and profoundly, and may have otherwise competing interests. The challenge for today's diverse democratic societies is to learn how to pool the efforts of their diverse citizenry and achieve voluntary collaboration on common goals while at the same time, safeguarding individual sovereignty, creativity and rights to self-determination. On a planetary scale the same challenge of human diversity faces the whole human species. Such a task requires new social learning that goes beyond any society's existing socialization processes. Because such a challenge has never been faced on such a scale before, it requires us to invent new institutions and contexts in which this social learning can occur. As evidenced by recent events, the need for contexts for dialogue and learning through dialogue is reaching crisis proportions.

12.   FINAL NOTES

We have come to see person-centered communities as pedagogy for transformational learning. These events appear to provide opportunities for people to develop the expanded capacities for individual and collective consciousness that will be crucial for human survival through the turbulent times ahead. When convened in situations where conflict exists, such as in South Africa between blacks and white, in Israel between Arabs and Jews or in Northern Ireland between Catholics and Protestants, these gatherings provide a means where people can work through their previously fixed positions and mutual estrangement, to touch their shared humanity.

In the 1960s and 1970s in the United States and beyond, large numbers of people participated in human potential group encounters with the express intentions of developing themselves as individuals and learning how to communicate better. They were eager to experience themselves and their relationships more authentically, and to develop greater levels of empathy and relational competence. For a decade or more, in church groups, classrooms, yoga centers, workplaces, growth centers, self-help groups and support groups, a whole society was engaged in a broad cultural experiment in psychologically sophisticated transformational learning.

In our view, the experiment was a great but partial success–it changed the culture but left off too soon. People certainly became more psychologically minded, more self-sufficient, learned how to be better parents, managers, and friends, and they came to enjoy deeper and more satisfying relationships with themselves and each other. People developed to greater levels of psychological capacity and reached higher levels of consciousness. But the full potential of the conscious group as greenhouses for learning in which new and more advanced relational consciousness could by cultivated, was never fully recognized by their practitioners and to this day remains largely unrealized.

In the future, as the global turbulence intensifies and staying afloat in white water becomes business as usual, there is bound to be dire need for leaders and citizens who can cope with the never-before-experienced challenges and opportunities of the sort outlined in our introduction. As we write, New Yorkers and Americans in general are attempting to process the catastrophic assault on the American psyche inflicted by terrorists on September 11, 2001. They are turning to whatever institutions exist to process their pain. Principally residents of the United States are turning to counseling, psychotherapy, spiritual traditions, talk radio, the internet chat rooms and, of course, to intimates. We are convinced that the strong emphasis on self-assertive consciousness that such services ordinarily favor, though necessary for comfort in the short term, will not be sufficient in the long run.

The level of consciousness demanded in this moment of our evolutionary history goes beyond that which we have inherited. In our view, new institutional forms for accelerated social learning are needed that can simultaneously increase group and societal consciousness at the same time as it cultivates expanded individual consciousness. We have seen such social learning and consciousness transformation occur in person-centered groups.

We end with a statement by our friend, colleague and pioneering fellow-traveler in the mysterious waters of consciousness, American psychologist Carl R. Rogers, whose revolutionary work has been translated into 20 languages and has found ready readers for over 60 years. He reflects:

> If the time comes when our culture tires of endless homicidal feuds, despairs of the use of force and war as a means of bringing peace, becomes discontent with the half lives that its members are living–only then will our culture seriously look for alternatives....When that time comes they will not find a void. They will discover that there are ways of facilitating the resolution of feuds. They will find there are ways of building communities without sacrificing the potential creativity of the person. They will realize that there are ways, already tried out on a small scale, of enhancing learning, of moving towards new values, of raising consciousness to new levels.. They will find that there are ways of being that do not involve power over persons and groups. They will discover that harmonious community can be built on the basis of mutual respect and enhanced personal growth....As humanistic psychologists with a person-centered philosophy–we have created working models on a small scale which our culture can use when it is ready. (Rogers, 1980, p. 205)

This was written two decades ago. The recent intensification in the level of ethnic warfare shows that the need for such thinking and praxis is urgent. Perhaps the recent renewed interest in-group dialogue suggests that the culture is now ready. We hope that our contribution to this volume can suggest some simple ways to facilitate the creation of powerful contexts for rapid group learning in which the skills required to mobilize the collective wisdom of diverse groups can be cultivated and nurtured. Finally we hope that we have helped remind those interested in group learning of the pioneering work of Rogers and his colleagues and help put it to the service of a culture once again in the throes of reinventing itself.

NOTES

[1] We acknowledge that in this post-modern world, it would be quite possible, and plausible to frame this process in social-constructivist terms and to understand the emerging sense of collective consciousness as the result of a gradual internalization and reification of the meme for "community" or "group consciousness." Our reluctance to do so comes from our attempt to be faithful to the language of our group co-participants, for whom this emergent reality seems more mysterious, luminous and even sacred.

[2] Conversely, a shift to a more self-assertive configuration feels like a chilly tightening or hardening.

[3] We do not mean to imply that all the individuals in a group will be in the same state of consciousness at any one time. Nor is it the case that once arrived at, a state is necessarily stable and durable. No-one ever becomes so self-transcendent, for instance, that a growling stomach will not demand someone's attention, and only serious psychopathology would prevent someone in the most self-assertive states impervious to the grief of another. What we mean is that at any one time the modal state of consciousness of individuals and collectives can often be identified as either self-assertive or self-transcendent.

[4] For a detailed description of such a shift see O'Hara 1983.

REFERENCES

Bohart, A., and Tallman, K., 1999. *How Clients Make Therapy Work*. American Psychological Association, Washington DC.

Bohm, D., and Edwards, M., 1991. *Changing consciousness*. San Francisco, Harper Books.

Bowen, M., and O'Hara, M.M.., et al., 1979. Learning in large groups: Implications for the future. *Education* 100: 108-117.

Csikszentmihalyi, M., 1990. *Flow: The Psychology of Optimal Experience*. Harper & Row, New York.

Gibbs, J., 1991. *Trust: The New Vision of Human Relationships for Business, Education, Family, and Personal Living*. Newcastle, North Hollywood, CA.

Isaacs, W., 1999. *Dialogue: The Art of Thinking Together*. Doubleday/Currency, New York.

Ivey, A., 1985. *Developmental Therapy*.

James, W., 1902. *Varieties of religious experience*. Longmans, New York.

Kegan, R., 1994. *In Over Our Heads: The Mental Demands of Modern Life*. Harvard University Press, Cambridge.

Kirschenbaum, H., and Henderson, V. L. (eds.), 1989. *Carl Rogers: Dialogueues.* Houghton Mifflin, Boston, MA.

Koestler, A., 1987. *Janus: A summing up.* Random House, New York.

Laszlo, E., 2001. *Macroshift: Navigating the transformation to a sustainable world.* Berrett-Koehler, San Francisco.

O'Hara, M., 1997. Emancipatory therapeutic practice in a turbulent transmodern era: A work of retrieval. *Journal of Humanistic Psychology,* 37(3): 7-33.

O'Hara, M., 1997. Relational empathy: From egocentric modernism to socio-centric postmodernism. In A.C. Bohart and Greenberg,. L. S., *Empathy reconsidered: New directions in psychotherapy.* American Psychological Association, Washington D.C., pp. 295-320.

O'Hara, M., and Wood, J.K., 1984. Patterns of awareness: Consciousness and the group mind. *The Gestalt Journal,* 6(2): 103-116.

Rogers, C.R., 1957. The necessary and sufficient conditions for therapeutic personality change. *Journal of Consulting Psychology,* 21: 95-103, New York.

Rogers, C.R., 1946. Significant aspects of client-centered therapy. *The American Psychologist,* 1(10) 415-422

Rogers, C.R., 1947. Some observations on the organization of personality. *The American Psychologist,* 2(9) 358-368.

Rogers, C.R., 1951. *Client-centered Therapy.* Boston: Houghton Mifflin Company.

Rogers, C. R., 1957. The necessary and sufficient conditions of therapeutic personality change. *Journal of Counseling Psychology,* 2(2): 95-103

Rogers, C.R., 1969. *Freedom to Learn.* Columbus, Ohio: Charles E. Merrill Publishing.

Rogers, C. R., 1970. *Carl Rogers on Encounter Groups.* New York, Harper & Row.

Rogers, C. R., 1977. *Carl Rogers on Personal Power.* New York, Delacorte.

Rogers, C. R., 1980. *A way of Being.* Boston, Houghton Mifflin.

Rogers, C. R., 1986. Rogers, Kohut, and Erickson: A personal perspective on some similarities and differences. *Person-centered Review,* 1(2): 125-140.

Rogers, C. R., and Sanford, R.C., 1989. Client-centered psychotherapy. In H. I. Kaplan and B. J. Sadock (eds.), *Comprehensive Textbook of Psychiatry.* Williams & Wilkins, Baltimore, pp. 1482-1501.

Rosenau, J. N., 1990. *Turbulence in World Politics: A Theory of Change and Continuity.* Princeton University Press, Princeton, NJ.

Schwartz, P., Levden, P., et al., 1999. *The Long Boom.* Perseus Books, New York.

Senge, P.M., 1990. *The Fifth Discipline: The Art and Practice of the Learning Organization.* Doubleday, New York.

Shweder, R. A., and Bourne, E., 1982. Does the concept of the person vary cross-culturally? In A. J. Marsela and G. White (eds.), *Cultural concepts of mental health and therapy.* Reidel, Boston, MA, pp. 97-137.

Tarnas, R., 1991. *The Passion of the Western Mind.* Harmony Books, New York.

Wood, J. K., 1984. Communities for learning: A person-centered approach. In J. M. Shlien and R. F. Levant (eds.), *Client-centered therapy and the person-centered approach: New directions in theory and practice.* Praeger, New York, pp. 297-316.

Wood, J. K., 1988. *Menschliches Dasein als Miteinandersein: Gruppenarbeit Nach Personenzentrierten Ansatzen.* Edition Humanistichen Psychologie, Koln, Germany.

Wood, J. K., 1994. A rehearsal for understanding the phenomenon of group. *The Person-Centered Journal,* 1 (3): 18-32.

Wood, J. K., 1996. The Person-centered approach. In R. Hutterer, G. Pawlowsky, P. Schmid & R. Stipsits (eds.), *Client-Centered and Experiential Psychotherapy.* Peter Lang, Vienna.

Wood, J.K., 1997. Notes on studying large group workshops. *The Person-Centered Journal,* 4 (Fall): 65-77.

Yalom, I.D., 1975. *The theory and practice of group psychotherapy.* Basic Books.Press, Ithaca, NY.

Chapter 7

MY DIALOGUE WITH DIALOGUE

MAURICE FRIEDMAN
Professor Emeritus, San Diego State University

1.   INTRODUCTION

The works of Martin Buber, on dialogue, have an important part of my studies on dialogue, in particular in examining the ontology of the "between" or relationship that Buber articulated in his writings on I-Thou and I-It. Concepts such as confirmation, individuation, image, wholeness, free person, otherness, imagining the self, monologue versus dialogue, "sphere of between," unification, and genuine dialogue, to name those more important in my study, are addressed in this chapter as I examine my own "dialogue with dialogue."

2.   MY MEETING WITH MARTIN BUBER

My dialogue with dialogue probably began in 1944 or 1945 when I returned to Martin Buber's *I and Thou* and read it not for its resemblance to non-dualistic Hinduism but for what it said in itself: "All real living is meeting." My 600 page doctoral dissertation on the whole of Buber's thought that I had access to was certainly another step along the way, and equally important was my dialogue with Buber himself–first by letter and later in person. Even before he had read my dissertation Buber wrote me saying he would like to help me and asked me to write him about myself without holding back but "please, no analyses." He liked my way of recounting myself but complained that I communicated how I felt about others but did not enable him to see the persons themselves. "I was not trying to write a novel," I somewhat petulantly replied.

When I first met him in person in September 1951, Buber told me that he was not mainly interested in me because I was writing a book on him but as a person. "My books are snake skins that I throw off," he said. "They are not what is important to me." He told me he had met T.S. Eliot five days before in London, that he was a shy person but one who was really frank. When I asked him if he did not find important differences between Eliot's thought and his own, Buber replied, "When I meet a person, I am not interested in his opinions but in the person."

2.1   The Ontology of the Between

The fundamental fact of human existence, according to Martin Buber's philosophical anthropology is person with person. But the sphere in which person meets person has been ignored because it possesses no smooth continuity. Its experience has been annexed to the soul and to the world so that what happens to an individual can be distributed between outer and inner impressions. But when two persons "happen" to each other, then there is an essential remainder which is common to them, but which reaches out beyond the special sphere of each. That remainder is the basic reality, the "sphere of the between." The participation of both partners is in principle indispensable to this sphere. The unfolding of this sphere Buber calls "the dialogical." The psychological, what happens within the souls of each, is only the secret accompaniment to the dialogue. The meaning of this dialogue is found in neither one nor the other of the partners, nor in both taken together, but in their interchange.

2.2   As I Say Thou I Become I

In the dialogical view we become persons in what Buber calls the "I-Thou" relationship–the direct, reciprocal, present relation between the person and what comes to meet him or her as opposed to the indirect, nonmutual relation of "I-It." I-Thou is a dialogue in which the other is accepted in his or her unique otherness and not reduced to a content of my experience. I-It is a monologue, the subject-object relation of knowing and using that does not allow the other to exist as a whole and unique persons but abstracts, reduces, and categorizes. In I-It, only a part of one's being–rational, emotional, intuitive, and sensory–enters into the relation; in I-Thou, the whole being enters in.

2.3   The Free Person versus the Unfree Individual

In contrast to the free person stands the individual who is characterized by arbitrary self-will, or willfulness, who continually intervenes in order to use the outside world for his or her purposes. This does not mean that the free person acts only from within him or herself. On the contrary, it is only he or she who sees what is new and unique in each situation, whereas the unfree person sees only its resemblance to other things. But what comes to the free person from without is only the precondition for his or her action; it does not determine its nature. The unfree person makes will to power a value in itself divorced from the will to enter into dialogue, with the inevitable result that he or she tends to use others as means to his or her ends.

Arbitrariness is a form of decisionlessness, of failure to make a decision with one's whole person. Decisionlessness makes a person divided and unfree, conditioned and acted upon. It is failure to direct one's inner power. Decision, in contrast, means transforming one's passion so that it enters with its whole power into the single deed. It is not a psychological event that takes place within the person but the turning of the whole being through which one enters once again into dialogue. Such decision means the transformation of the urges, of the "alien thoughts," of fantasy. We must not reject the abundance of this fantasy but transform it in our imaginative faculty and turn it into actuality. "We must convert the element that seeks to take possession of us into the substance of real life." The contradictions that distress us exist only that we may discover their intrinsic significance. There can be no wholeness "where down-trodden appetites lurk in the corners" or where the soul's highest forces watch the action, "pressed back and powerless, but shining in the protest of the spirit.

2.4   Wholeness, Decision, and Dialogue

True decision can be made only with the whole being, and it is decision in turn that brings the person to wholeness. Yet this wholeness is never a goal in itself but only the indispensable base for going out to meet the Thou. Decision is made *with* the whole being, but it takes place *in* dialogue. The person who decides continually leaves the world of It for the world of dialogue in which I and Thou freely confront each other in mutual effect, unconnected with causality. It is in dialogue, therefore, that true decision takes place. Decision within dialogue is a corollary of personal unification; for it means giving direction to one's passion.

In their dialogue with others and in their life with the community it is possible for persons to divert fear, anger, love, and sexual desire from the casual to the essential by responding to what comes to meet them, to what they become aware of as addressing them and demanding from them an answer.

2.5   Being and Seeming

The essential problematic of the sphere of the between, writes Buber, is the duality of being and seeming. The being person looks at the other as one to whom one gives oneself. Her glance is spontaneous and unaffected. She is not uninfluenced by the desire to make herself understood, but she has no thought for the conception of herself that she might awaken in the beholder. The seeming person, in contrast, is primarily concerned with what the other thinks of her. With the help of the human ability to allow a certain element of one's being to appear in one's glance one produces a look that is meant to affect the other as a spontaneous expression reflecting a personal being.

Whatever the word "truth" may mean in other spheres, in the realm between person and person it means that one imparts oneself to the other as what one is. This is not a question of saying to the other everything that occurs to one, but of allowing the person with whom one communicates to partake of one's being. It is a question of the authenticity of what is between persons, without which there can be no authentic human existence. The origin of the tendency toward seeming is found in the human need for confirmation. It is no easy thing to be confirmed by the other in one's being; therefore, one looks to appearance for aid. To give in to this tendency is our real cowardice, to withstand it is our real courage. One must pay dearly at times for essential life, but never too dearly. "I have never met any young person who seemed to me hopelessly bad," writes Buber. It is only the successive layers of deception that give the illusion of individuals who are "seeming" persons by their very nature. The human being is as human being redeemable.

2.6 Confirmation

True confirmation means that one confirms one's partner as this existing being even while one opposes her. I legitimize her over against me as the one with whom I have to do in real dialogue, and I may then trust her also to act toward me as a partner. To confirm her in this way I need the aid of what Buber calls "imagining the real." This imagining is no intuitive perception but a bold swinging into the other which demands the most intense action of my being, even as does all genuine imagining, only here the realm of my act is not the all-possible but the particular, real person who steps up to meet me, the person whom I seek to make present as just so and not otherwise in all her wholeness, unity, and uniqueness. I can only do this as a partner, standing in a common situation with the other, and even then my address to the other may remain unanswered and the dialogue may die in seed.

2.7 Individuation

If it is the interaction between person and person which makes possible authentic human existence, it follows that the precondition of such authentic existence is that each overcomes the tendency toward appearance, that each means the other in her personal existence and makes her present as such, and that neither attempts to impose her own truth or view on the other. It would be mistaken to speak here of individuation alone. Individuation is only the indispensable personal stamp of all realization of human being. The self as such is not ultimately essential but the created meaning of human existence again and again fulfills itself as self. The help that persons give each other in becoming a self leads the life between persons to its height. The dynamic glory of human being is first bodily present in the relation between two persons each of whom in meaning the other also means the highest to which this person is called and serves the fulfillment of this created destiny without wishing to impose anything of her own realization on the other.

3. GENUINE DIALOGUE

In genuine dialogue the experiencing senses and imagining the real work together to make the other present as whole and one. For this dialogue to be real, one must not only mean the other, but also bring oneself, and that means saying at times what one really thinks about the matter in question. One must make the contribution of one's spirit without abbreviation and distortion: everything depends here upon the legitimacy of what one has to say. Not holding back is the opposite of letting oneself go, for true speech involves thought as to the way in which one brings to words what one has in mind. A further condition of genuine dialogue is the overcoming of seeming. Because genuine dialogue is an ontological sphere, which constitutes itself through the authenticity of being, every intrusion of seeming can injure it.

Genuine dialogue can be either spoken or silent. Its essence lies in the fact that "each of the participants really has in mind the other or others in their present and particular being and turns to them with the intention of establishing a living mutual relation between himself and them." The essential element of genuine dialogue, therefore, is "seeing the other" or "experiencing the other side."

3.1 The Meeting with Otherness and Imagining the Real

There is no human situation that is so rotten and God-forsaken that the meeting with otherness cannot take place within it. The ordinary person can, and at times does, break through "from the status of the dully-tempered disagreeableness, obstinacy, and contrariness" in which she lives into an effective reality. This reality is the simple *quantum satis*, or sufficient amount, of what this person in this hour of her life is able to fulfill and to receive–if she gives herself. In order to be responsible, it is essential that we make use of that imagining the real that enables us to experience the other person's side of the relationship. Only through a quite concrete imagining of what the other is thinking, feeling, and willing can I make the other present to myself in his or her wholeness, unity, and uniqueness.

This "imagining the real" is not "empathy", as it is commonly understood, for it does not mean giving up one's own standpoint in order to enter that of the other. Rather it is a living partnership in which I stand in a common situation with the other and expose myself vitally to her share in the situation as really her share. Without forfeiting anything of the felt reality of my own activity, I at the same time live through the common event from the standpoint of the other. This "inclusion" of the other takes place most deeply and fully in marriage, the "exemplary bond," which, if it is real, leads to a "vital acknowledgement of many-faced otherness–even in the contradiction and conflict with it." In all human relations, in fact, the responsible quality of one's decision will be determined by the degree to which one really experiences the side of the other and makes the other present to one.

3.2   Monologue versus Dialogue

"Love without dialogic, without real outgoing to the other, reaching to the other, and companying with the other, the lover remaining with itself–this is called Lucifer." This "love" is evil because it is monological. The monological individual is not aware of the "otherness" of the other, but instead tries to incorporate the other into oneself. The basic movement of the life of monologue is not turning away from the other but ""reflexion" (*Rueckbiegung)*, bending back on oneself. "Reflexion" is not egotism but the withdrawal from accepting the other person in his or her particularity in favor of letting the other exist only as one's own experience, only as a part of oneself. Through this withdrawal, as Buber says, "the essence of all reality begins to disintegrate."

The soul does not have its object in itself, nor is its knowing, purifying, and perfecting itself for its own sake "but for the sake of the work which it is destined to perform upon the world." One must distinguish here between that awareness which turns one in oneself and that which enables one to turn to the other. The latter is not only essential to the life of dialogue, but is dialogical in its very nature: it is the awareness of "the signs" that continually address us in everything that happens. These signs are simply what happens when we enter into relation with occurrences as really having meaning for us. "Each of us is encased in an armour whose task is to ward off signs," for we are afraid that to open ourselves to them means annihilation. We perfect this defense apparatus from generation to generation until we can assure ourselves that the world is there to be experienced and used as we like but that nothing is directed at us, nothing required of us.

3.3   The Signs of Address

In shutting off our awareness of "the signs" we are shutting off our awareness of the address of God, for the One who speaks in these signs is the "Lord of the Voice," the eternal Thou. Every person hides, like Adam, to avoid rendering accounts. "To escape responsibility for his life, he turns existence into a system of hideouts" and "enmeshes himself more and more deeply in perversity." The lie displaces "the undivided seriousness of the human with himself and all his manifestations" and destroys the good will and reliability on which our life in common rests. The external conflict between person and person has its roots in the inner contradiction between thought, speech, and action. One's failure to say what one means and do what one says "confuses and poisons, again and again and in increasing measure," the situation between oneself and the other person. Unaware that the roots of the conflict are in our inner contradiction, we resist beginning with ourselves and demand that the other change at the same time. But just this perspective in which one sees oneself only as an individual contrasted with other individuals, and not as a genuine person whose transformation helps toward the transformation of the world, contains the fundamental error.

3.4   The Unification of the Soul

The individual with the divided, complicated, contradictory soul is not helpless: the core of one's soul, the divine force in its depths, is capable of binding the conflicting forces together, amalgamating the diverging elements. The unification of the soul is never final. Again and again temptation overcomes the soul, and again and again innate grace arises from out of its depths and promises the utterly incredible: you can become whole and one." This is no easy promise, however, but one demanding a total effort of the soul for its realization:

> It is a cruelly hazardous enterprise, this becoming a whole...Everything in the nature of inclinations, of indolence, of habits, of fondness for possibilities which has been swashbuckling within us, must be overcome, and overcome, not by elimination, by suppression.... Rather must all these mobile or static forces, seized by the soul's rapture, plunge of their own accord, as it were, into the mightiness of decision and dissolve within it. (Buber, 1954, p. 127 f.)

It is no wonder, writes Buber, that these situations frequently terminate in a persistent state of indecision. Yet even if the effort of unification is not entirely successful, it may still lay the groundwork for future success. The unification must be accomplished *before* a person undertakes some unusual work, but any ordinary work that a person does with a united soul acts in the direction of new and greater unification and leads her, even if by many detours, to a steadier unity than she had before. Thus one ultimately reaches a point where one cal rely upon one's soul because its unity is now so great that it overcomes contradiction with effortless ease.

In place of one's former great efforts all that is now necessary is a relaxed vigilance.

3.5   Spirit as the Response to the Thou

In Hasidism the holiest teaching is rejected if it is found in someone only as a content of that person's thinking. This must not be understood as a contrast between feeling and thought. It is not the dominance of any one faculty but the unity of all faculties within the personality that constitutes the wholeness of the person, and it is this that Buber calls "spirit." "Spirit is...the totality which comprises and integrates all man's capacities, powers, qualities, and urges."

But human wholeness does not exist apart from real relationship to other beings. In *I and Thou* Buber defines spirit in its human manifestation as "a response of man to his *Thou.*" These two elements are invariably linked together in the life of dialogue. Trust is a contact of the entire beings with the one in whom one trusts. True freedom comes only from personal wholeness, but it is only of value as a springboard for responsibility and communion. The true person is again and again required to detach and shut herself off from others, but this attitude is alien to her innermost being: one wants openness to and the company of others. Through relation the whole person shares in an absolute meaning which one cannot know in one's life by oneself.

> Human life touches on absoluteness in virtue of its dialogical character, for in spite of his uniqueness man can never find, when he plunges to the depth of his life, a being that is whole in itself and as such touches on the absolute....This other self may be just as limited and conditioned as he is; in being together the unlimited is experienced. (Buber, 1985, p. 176)

3.6   The "Single One" and the Thou

The child knows the Thou before it knows the separated I. But on the height of personal existence one must truly be able to say I in order to know the mystery of the Thou in its whole truth. Thus partial dialogue precedes inner wholeness but full dialogue follows it. Only one who has become a real person is able to have a complete life relation to the other that is above not beneath the problematic of interhuman relations and withstands and overcomes it. "A *great* relation exists only between real persons. It can be strong as death, because it is stronger than solitude, because it...throws a bridge from self-being to self-being across the abyss of dread of the universe" (Buber, 1985, p. 116).

This also applies to the person's relation to God. We cannot say Thou to God before we are able to say I in the fullness of our being, and this saying of Thou must include our Thou to our fellow human beings. "The real God lets no shorter line reach him than each man's longest, which is the line embracing the world that is accessible to this man." One takes up into one's life the otherness, which enshrouds one, but one takes it up only in the form of *the* other, the other who meets one, the companion. The Single One passes life in the body politic as "the reservoir of otherness"–"the basic structure of otherness, in many ways uncanny but never quite unholy or incapable of being hallowed, in which I and the others who meet me in my life are inwoven" (Buber, 1985, p. 65).

3.7   Personal Direction

It is thus that one finds one's personal direction, one's direction to God. To the extent that the soul achieves unification, it becomes aware of "direction" and of itself as sent in quest of it. This awareness of direction is ultimately identical with the awareness of one's created uniqueness, the special way to God that is realized in one's relation with the world and one's fellows. The humanly right is ever the service of the single person who realizes the right uniqueness purposed for her in her creation. "Decision" is here both the current decision about the immediate situation which confronts one and through this the decision with the whole being for God. Direction is apprehended through one's inner awareness of what one is meant to be, for it is this that enables one to make a genuine decision. This is a reciprocal process, however, for in transforming and directing one's undirected energies, one comes to recognize ever more clearly what one is meant to be.

One experiences one's uniqueness as a designed or preformed one, entrusted to one for execution, yet everything that affects one participates in this execution. The person who knows direction responds with the whole of one's being to each new situation with no other preparation than one's presence and one's readiness to respond. Direction is not meeting but going out to meet. It is not identical with dialogue, but it is, along with personal wholeness, a prerequisite of any genuine dialogue. It is also a product of dialogue in the sense that the awareness of direction comes into being only in the dialogue itself. One discovers the mystery waiting for one not in oneself but in the encounter with what one meets. Although "the one direction of the hour towards God...changes time and again by concretion," each moment's new direction is *the* direction if reality is met in lived concreteness.

3.8   *Emunah* or Trust

Closely related to Buber's concept of direction is the biblical concept of *emunah* or trust. *Emunah* is perseverance "in a hidden but self-revealing guidance." This guidance does not relieve us of taking and directing our own steps, for it is nothing other than God's making known that He is present. *Emunah* is the realization of one's faith in the actual totality of one's relationships to God, to one's appointed sphere in the world, and to oneself. "By its very nature trust is substantiation of trust in the fullness of life in spite of the course of the world which is experienced."

> He who lives the life of dialogue knows a lived unity: the unity of *life*, as that which once truly won is no more torn by any changes, not ripped asunder into the everyday creaturely life and the "deified" exalted hours; the unity of unbroken, raptureless perseverance in concreteness, in which the word is heard and a stammering answer dared. (Buber, 1985, p. 85)

The lived unity of the life of dialogue, born out of response to the essential mystery of the world, makes this response ever more possible.

4.   The Life of Dialogue

The "sphere of the between," mutual confirmation, making the other present, overcoming seeming, genuine dialogue, inclusion, or imagining the real, a personal wholeness, a responsibility, decision, direction, trust–these are all aspects of the life of dialogue. This life is a part of our birthright as human beings, for only through it can we attain authentic human existence. But this birthright cannot be simply inherited, it must be earned. We must follow Buber in not underestimating the obstacles to the life of dialogue, but we must also follow him in refusing to magnify them into an inexorable fate.

The tendency toward seeming which mars the life of dialogue has its origin not only in the interdependence and need for confirmation that Buber has indicated, but also in the specific social structures that have arisen on this anthropological base: in the ordinary amenities of civilized life which make us habitually pretend toward others what we do not feel; in the institutionalization of social life which makes us tend to relate to others on the basis of our relative positions in these institutions; in the emphasis on prestige and authority which grows out of our social differentiations; in our inner divisions which make us unable to relate to others honesty because we cannot relate as whole persons; in our unawareness of the extent to which our values and attitudes arise, not from a genuine relation to truth, but from the social attitudes of the groups to which we belong.

To emphasize the hold of seeming on our lives is to point out how difficult and also how important it is to become a "Single One." This is especially so if one understands by the Single One not Kierkegaard's person who finds truth by separating oneself from the crowd, but Buber's person of the narrow ridge, who lives with others yet never gives up one's personal responsibility nor allows one's commitment to the group to stand in the way of one's direct relationship to the Thou. Another product of the narrow ridge, one equally essential to the life of dialogue, is the realistic trust which recognizes the strength of the tendency toward seeming yet stands ready to deal with the other as a partner and to confirm her in becoming her real self. This open-eyed trust is at base a trust in existence itself despite the difficulties we encounter in making our human share of it authentic. It is the trust, in Buber's words, that the human being as human being is redeemable.

4.1   Touchstones of Reality

Two essentially dialogical approaches to human existence and meaning that I have developed on my own apart from Buber and the life of dialogue are "touchstones of reality" and the "image of the human." "Touchstones of reality," as I use that phrase in my book of that title, is not a definition: it is a metaphor. I use this metaphor in conscious contrast to all those ways of thinking that try to deal with reality in objective terms: metaphysics, philosophy of religion, theology. But I also use it in contrast to the subjective approaches that explain "reality" away, whether in terms of Freudian psychology, or Sartrian existentialism of choice–the invention of values–or the linguistic analyst who says this is what you prefer or postulate and the rest is just an unwarranted inference from your emotions, the deconstructionist or constructivist reduction of everything to social context, or any of the other cultural relativizing or subjectivizing approaches.

In contrast to both the objective and the subjective, I claim that in our lives we do have certain events that become for us touchstones of reality. We bring them with us into other life events so that they affect the way we enter these life events, and they are themselves modified in the process. While I cannot define what reality is apart from our touching, in touching we do come in contact with something really "other" than ourselves, with some otherness that has its unique impact upon us. I do not mean by touchstones of reality merely subjective experience, therefore, but what transcends our subjective experience even though we are fully part of it.

4.2   The Image of the Human

To use one obvious connecting point between my two metaphors, if religion derives from and rests upon our touchstones of reality, it also embodies and expresses our image of the human, our image not only of what human life is but also of what it can and ought to be. The image of the human means a meaningful personal and social direction that gives us some guidance in choosing between our potentialities and finding a way forward in the present that leads organically into the future.

The image of the human and personal wholeness are mutually entailed if we understand the image of the human aright–not as some universal model or ideal that we all can or ought to adopt but as a highly personal unique life-stance that every one of us chooses again and again as our personal way of being human. It is the expression of what we are in our uniqueness and in our humanity. The universality that is talked of here is one that exists only in and through the concrete, the particular, the unique.

I cannot reproduce here all the nuances of the image of the human that I depict in the first chapter of my book *To Deny Our Nothingness*, but I can give some hint of why the image of the human means both the universally human and the unique at once:

> The pole of the unique and the pole of the human stand in fruitful tension with each other: in each situation I must be concerned with what is authentic human existence and what is authentic existence for me in particular. These two can never be divided from each other, nor can they be identified. What we mean by..."human" is at once something we take for granted and something we do not know and must constantly discover and rediscover.   That we are all "human" is the commonest presupposition of social intercourse. What the human is, can be, and ought to become is continually changing, however, not only with each new culture and period of history, but also with each new individual. It is precisely in one's uniqueness, and not in what one has in common with others, that each person realizes what the human can become in one.... The image of the human is an embodiment of an attitude and a response. Whether it is an image shared by only one person or by a society as a whole, the individual stands in a unique personal relation to it. One's image of the human is not some objective, universal Saint Francis, but the Saint Francis who emerges from one's own meeting with this historical and legendary figure.[1]

Our image of the human and our personal wholeness go together not only because each person's image of the human is unique but also because our wholeness as persons is inseparable from the unique direction that we take, the attitude and life-stance that we bring to our response to the demand placed on us by the persons and world with which we stand in dialogue. Thus our individuation and our integration cannot be an end in itself, divorced from the unique direction that our image of the human and our touchstones of reality embody. These images and touchstones are our way of going out to meet what comes to meet us. We cannot use everything else merely as a means to the end of our personal integration, as sometimes seems to be the goal of Jungian therapy, or "follow our bliss" without concern for the partnership of existence.

5.   A Dialogical Theory of Knowledge

Underlying both touchstones of reality and the image of the human, as I use these terms, is a dialogical approach to knowledge that holds that it is in the immediacy of contact that we know and that our objective knowledge is derived from this I-Thou knowing. This means that in our approach to the human sciences as a whole we must be concerned with the dialectical alternation between I-Thou knowing and I-It knowledge or, to put it another way, between dialogue and dialectic.

5.1   Dialogue and Dialectic in the Human Sciences

For some time I have had the notion of writing a book on dialogue and dialectic in the human sciences in which I would like to show this dialectical alternation in such fields as psychology and psychotherapy, sociology and anthropology, literature and religion. Human existence necessarily and properly alternates between the immediate and the mediate, the direct and the indirect. As the prefix 'dia' suggests, both dialogue and dialect imply the alternation between two different points of view. In the case of dialogue, this also means real meeting with the unique otherness of an other, whereas in the case of dialectic the alternation may take place within the head of a single thinker, and the points of view may remain disembodied and hypothetical.

The tendency of by far the largest and most dominant methodology in most human sciences today is to begin with dialectic and to examine dialogue as a part of that dialectic. Putting this in Buber's terminology, it means that the mutual knowing of the I-Thou relationship is subsumed under the subject-object knowledge of the I-It relation. A radical reversal of this perspective would not mean any rejection of dialectic, which remains essential to the whole human enterprise of connected thought from one generation to another. What it does mean is a shift in emphasis toward understanding dialogue as the source of knowing and dialectic as an elaboration of that source. "The corrective office of reason is incontestable," wrote Martin Buber. It can be summoned at any moment to adjust the incongruity between my sense perception and what is common to my neighbors. In the I-It relation what is received in the I-Thou is elaborated and broken up. Here errors are possible which can be corrected through directly establishing and comparing what is past and passive in the minds of others. But reason, with its gigantic structure of general concepts, cannot replace the smallest perception of something particular and unique, cannot by means of it take part in the grasping of what here and now confronts me.

Maurice Friedman

Dialogue and Dialectic in Philosophy

___ ng with the philosophy of dialogue, we can say that the I-Thou relationship is a direct knowing which gives one neither knowledge about the Thou over against the I nor about oneself as an objective entity apart from that relationship. It is, in Buber's words, "the genuine reciprocal meeting in the fullness of life between one active existence and another." Although this dialogical knowing is direct, it is not entirely unmediated. The directness of the relationship is established not only through the mediation of the senses in the concrete meeting of real living persons, but also through mediation of the world. That means the mediation of those fields of symbolic communication, such as language, music, art, and ritual, which enable human beings ever again to enter into relation with what comes to meet them. The word may be identified with subject-object or I-It knowledge while it remains indirect and symbolic. However, it is itself the channel of expression of I-Thou knowing when it is taken up into real dialogue.

Subject-object or I-It knowledge is ultimately nothing other than the socially objectified and elaborated product of the meeting that takes place between the person and her Thou in the realms of nature, social relations, and art. As such, it provides those ordered categories of thought, which are, together with dialogue, primal necessities of human existence. But as such, also, it may be, like the indirect and objective word, the symbol of true dialogue. It is only when the full meaning of the symbolic character of subject-object knowledge is forgotten, or remains undiscovered, as is often the case, that this knowledge ceases to point back toward the reality of direct dialogical knowing and becomes instead an obstruction to it.

In his classic work *I and Thou* Martin Buber used Socrates as an illustration of the I that is made real by virtue of sharing in the dialogue between person and person. Yet Socrates is not, for all that, an adequate image of the life of dialogue. Socrates went forth to people, trusted them, met them, never suspended dialogue with them. Yet his emphasis upon dialectic thought often put him in the position of the essentially monological thinker whose dialectic, even when it brings in other people, is little more than a moving forward through the opposition and interaction of different points of view, rather than an interaction between really other persons.

Martin Buber's friend, the Jewish existentialist philosopher Franz Rosenzweig, said that the reason why most philosophical dialogues, including those of Plato, are so tedious is that there is no real other speaker. In a real dialogue the other person has not only ears but also a mouth and can say something that will surprise you. That is why real dialogue takes place in time. You cannot know the answer in advance the way Socrates teases the geometrical proposition out of the slave boy in the *Meno*.

In his reply to Robert Maynard Hutchins in the Buber section of *Philosophical Interrogations*, Martin Buber wrote:

I know of very few men in history to whom I stand in such a relation of both trust and veneration as Socrates. But when it is a matter of using "Socratic questions" as an educational method, I am against it.... Socrates overvalued the significance of abstract general concepts in comparison with concrete individual experiences. General concepts are the most important stays and supports, but Socrates treated them as if they were more important than bones–that they are not....

Socrates conducts his dialogue by posing questions and proving the answers that he received untenable; these are not real questions; they are moves in a sublime dialectical game that has a goal, the goal of revealing a not-knowing. But when the teacher whom I mean...enters into a dialogue with his pupil and in this connection directs a question to him, he asks, as the simple man who is not inclined to dialectic asks, because he wants to know something: that, namely, which this young person before him, and precisely he, knows to report on the subject under discussion–a small individual experience, a nuance of experience that is perhaps barely conceptually comprehensible, nothing further, and that is enough. The teacher will awaken in the pupil the need to communicate of himself and the capacity thereto and in this way bring him to greater clarity of existence. But he also learns, himself, through teaching thus; he learns, ever anew, to know concretely the becoming of the human creature that takes place in experiences; he learns what no one ever learns completely, the particular, the individual, the unique. (Rome & Rome, 1964, p. 67)

5.3   The Spokenness of Speech

This contrast between dialogue and dialectic has much to do with the importance of the spokenness of speech in which the between becomes real in the relationship of two persons or more. When the word really becomes speech, when it is really spoken, it is spoken in the context of relationship, of the meeting with what is other than us, of mutuality. It takes its very meaning from the fact that it is said by one person and heard by another. The hearer adds a different dimension and relationship to the word that is spoken, even as he or she stands on a different ground from the speaker. One must keep in mind, therefore, the genuinely two-sided and dialogical character of the word as the embodiment of the between when it is spoken.

The mystery of word and answer that moves *between* human beings is not one of union, harmony, or even complementarity, but of tension, for two persons never mean the same thing by the words that they use, and no answer is ever fully satisfactory. The result is that at each point of the dialogue understanding and misunderstanding are interwoven. From this tension of understanding and misunderstanding comes the interplay of openness and closedness and expression and reserve that mark every genuine dialogue between person and person. Thus the mere fact of the difference between persons already implies a basic dramatic situation as an inherent component of human existence as such which drama only reproduces in clearer and heightened form.

It is this recognition of *difference* that explains the polarity, the vis-a-vis *and* the tragic conflict that may arise because "each is as he is."

But this is also at the heart of the distinction between dialogue and dialectic, even Socratic dialectic. *Dialogue* recognizes differences and never seeks for simple agreement or unanimity. *Dialectic,* in contrast, begins with the categories of "the same" and "the other," but excludes the reality of "the between" and with it the recognition of real otherness as that which can be affirmed even in opposing it. Thus both the original assumption and the goal of dialectic is a unified point of view. The dialectician's faith in logic as the arbitrator and common denominator not only of his inner reflections but also of the dialogue between person and person is essentially single-voiced, monological, and pseudo-universal.

I like to think (and I admit that this is sheer speculation, since aside from Plato's *Dialogues* we have only Aristophanes' *Clouds* and Xenophon's mention of Socrates to go on) that Socrates himself was a very dialogical person but that Plato, who bewailed in his epistles that he had to write down Socrates' dialogues, was already moving over to dialectic. Aristotle took over from Plato the categories of same and other on which he built his logic and on which most of the logic that has followed in the Western world was built. Plato cherished the form of dialogue enough to reproduce it in literary form, albeit replete with characters who seemed to be there mostly to say, "Yes, Socrates," and "No, Socrates." But for Aristotle even the form of dialogue was no longer important!

5.4   Dialogue and Dialectic in Social Psychology and Sociology

The alternation between dialectic also applies to social psychology and sociology, as I shall illustrate with some thoughts from my book *The Confirmation of Otherness: In Family, Community, and Society* (Friedman, 1983).

We need to be confirmed by others. They make us present, and this, as Martin Buber points out, induces our inmost self-becoming. One of he paradoxes of confirmation that I elaborate is that we are all too often confirmed with strings attached. Another is that we do and must live in a world in which we have both personal uniqueness and social role.

Everyone has to play a social role as a basic prerequisite not only to economic livelihood, but also to relations to other people and families in society. Yet we cannot resolve this tension between personal uniqueness and social role by sacrificing personal confirmation; for that results in an anxiety that can only become greater and greater. To stand in this tension is to insist that one's confirmation in society also be in some significant sense a confirmation of oneself as a unique person who does not fit into a social category.

To be confirmed in personal uniqueness is to be confirmed directly. That is dialogue. To be confirmed only as a certain social role is to be confirmed indirectly. That is dialectic. Both are necessary. We cannot altogether dispense with the idea of social role, though we can guard ourselves against taking it as a reality in itself. We must see it, instead, within the interaction between more or less static conceptions of roles and the actual dynamic of our relationship to them. We cannot deny the specialization of labor. Neither can we deny the continual rationalization of that specialization in terms of job descriptions and problems of decision-making and authority. This includes the obvious need to call for people not as the unique persons that they are but as abstractions, such as professor, secretary, machinist, crane operator, doctor, or bank clerk.

What we need not accept is that the convenient label and the social role exhaust the reality of the person for the hours during which she works. On the contrary, her own unique relationship to her work is of crucial importance not only for the success or the meaning of the work but for the human reality that here becomes manifest as event. What is more, we can recognize the necessity for a continual critique of abstractions, to make them more and more flexible and more and more in line with the actual situation at any one time.

In terms of this critique, it is a part of the task of man and woman alike to reject the unfair burden of always responding to a situation in a catalogued way. This means rejecting the life in which the human has been all but smothered under the weight of technical, social, and bureaucratic abstractions.

5.5   Dialogue and Dialectic in Psychology and Psychotherapy

Dialogue and dialectic are also central to psychology and psychotherapy. Even the patients' sicknesses are part of their uniqueness, for even their sicknesses tell us of the unique life directions to which they are called. If, instead, therapists make patients into objects to themselves, the therapists will have robbed the patients of part of their human potentiality and growth.

This is not a question of choice between scientific generalization and the concrete individual, but of which direction is the primary one. Is the individual regarded as a collection of symptoms to be registered in the categories of a particular school, or are the theories of the school regarded as primarily a means of returning again and again to the understanding of the unique person and his or her relationship with his or her therapist?

An increasingly important trend in psychotherapy suggests that the basic direction of movement should be toward the concrete person and her uniqueness, and not toward subsuming the patients' symptoms under theoretical categories or adjusting them to some socially derived view of the ideal. This trend emphasizes the *image* of he human as opposed to the *construct* of the human. The image of the human retains the understanding of human beings in their concrete uniqueness: it retains the wholeness of the person. Only a psychotherapy that begins with the concrete existence of persons in their wholeness and uniqueness and with the healing that takes place in the meeting between therapist and client will point us toward the image of the human. In the last analysis, the issue that faces all the schools of psychotherapy is whether the starting point of therapy is to be found in the analytical category or the unique person, in the construct or the image of the human.

The former Jungian therapist Hans Trueb contrasts the dialectical psychological approach with a dialogical anthropological one. He does not ask us to choose between them, but he wants to enclose he dialectical within the dialogical. The dialectical approach of the psychologist entails a methodological and systematic focus on the contradictory multiplicity of the psyche. This approach has to be coordinated with and subordinated to the dialogical attitude of the partner in relationship that rejects both method and system in favor of the person-to-person meeting, each and every time unique, each and every time demanding a decision.

No matter how significant and reliable the self-illuminating insights achieved by the analyst through depth psychology may be in any given case, they demonstrate their curative force decisively only when the patient abandons the stand he took during the analysis and throws himself as himself into the world of real objects and real meetings. The uncovering of these inner psychic defense mechanisms by means of depth psychology can succeed only if it recognizes that they are based in the self's personally executed flight from meeting. The reconstruction of the capacity for dialogue must go hand in hand, writes Trueb, with the methodical attempt to loosen and dismantle the complex defense mechanisms in the psychic realm of expression as fast as the recuperating self permits. When the psychological cooperation and dialectical interaction of patient and therapist is conducted dialogically with mutual personal trust between therapist and patient, then there gradually awakens and grows in the patient a new confidence in himself and in the other.

There are two kinds of therapists, Martin Buber asserted at the seminars he gave in 1957 for the Washington (D.C.) School of Psychiatry. One knows more or less consciously the kind of interpretation of dreams she will give to the patient. The other is the psychologist who does not know, who does not want something precise, who is ready to receive what she will receive. She cannot know what method she will use beforehand; for she is, so to speak, in the hands of the patient. "The real master responds to uniqueness," says Buber.

Such a master uses that type of intuition which Buber calls imagining the real, or "inclusion." Inclusion, as we have seen, does not mean empathy but experiencing the other side of the relationship–concretely imagining what the other is thinking, feeling, and willing, while at the same time remaining on your own side of the relationship. Imagining the real is the very stuff of betweenness because it is, in the first instance, the stuff of immediacy that only later becomes something that one reflects upon and thinks about. It is dialogue that only later becomes dialectic.

The therapist with years of experience and the knowledge of the many case histories that are recorded in the literature will naturally think of resemblances when a client tells her something. But if she is a good therapist, she must discover the right movement back and forth between her patient as the unique person he is and the categories and cases that come to her mind. She cannot know through scientific method when a particular example from case histories, her earlier clients, or even her own experience applies. This is where true intuition, where imagining the real, or "inclusion," comes in.

5.6   Dialogue and Dialectic in Anthropology

Let us look at one brief example of dialogue and dialectic from anthropology. Kurt Wolff, a distinguished American sociologist and anthropologist, lived among the Loma Indians for three years after which he wrote an essay and later a book entitled *Surrender and Catch*. Instead of coming with his questions and categories already formed, he lived with the Loma Indians long enough to understand from *their* side what was unique to them. The "surrender" was the surrender to their uniqueness. The "catch" was his response.

The contrasting and much more usual approach of imposing one's categories on what one is studying is illustrated in extreme form by a distinguished psychoanalyst and direct disciple of Freud. In the late 1950s this man gave a talk about a society where children were raised differently from those of any other society, pointing out all the nefarious effects of such child rearing. Since he was unmistakably talking about the kibbutzim in Israel, I asked him after the lecture about his stay in Israel. "I've never been to Israel," he replied. "I am a Park Avenue anthropologist. I send my students to Israel, and they bring back to me the results of the T.A.T. [Thematic Apperception Tests] that they administer."

5.7   Dialogue and Dialectic in Phenomenology

The concern for both the typical and the unique in phenomenology may serve as our final example of the necessary interaction of dialogue and dialectic. In true phenomenological research there must be a constant movement between dialogue and dialectic so that the ideal types that evolve can continually be corrected by the particulars and so that there is room for the unique. In contrast to the scientist who is only interested in particulars insofar as they yield generalizations, we can derive valid insights from the unique situations in which we find ourselves without having to claim that they apply to all situations. We take these insights with us into other situations and test the limits of their validity. Sometimes we find that these insights do hold for a particular situation and sometimes that they do not or that they have to be modified. Yet that does not mean that they cannot be valid insights for other situations.

I chaired for five years a phenomenological dissertation in psychology studying Jews who had gone to Oriental religions. Midway through the process the acting dean of the college insisted that the student deal with thirty cases on the ground that this would help her in her future career. The result was that she could not do an in-depth study but had to limit herself to two out of the ten categories that she had developed in the course of her work. At her doctoral oral I pointed out the loss and with it the fallacy in the notion that thirty would give her more valid "evidence" than six would. Precisely because in good phenomenological research the researcher is a part of the knowing involved, real evidence is not a matter of a statistical population and of generalization but of valid insight based upon an in-depth dialogue with each subject and the interplay between ideal types that develop and the uniqueness and particularity of each case

A number of years ago I taught a contract course on Philosophy and Psychology in a professional school of psychology where I had once been on the core faculty and where I had introduced and directed a non-statistical dissertation track, including theory, case history, and phenomenology. This track was continued by a former student of mine for a few years until it was abolished on the grounds that that might make it easier to get postdoctoral fellowships from the American Psychological Association. At the first session of the course I asked the question, "What is the philosophical assumption underlying the notion that the only proper way to train clinical psychologists is through a statistical dissertation. The answer, of course, was the assumption that the so-called "scientific method" of generalizing from data (induction) and then applying that generalization to individual cases (deduction) best enables the psychologist to work with his patients. This is far from what Amedeo Giorgi has called "psychology as a human science," and it is equally far from the recognition that the most important source of knowledge for the therapist is the dialogue with the unique patient and only after that the dialectic of diagnoses and cases.

NOTES

[1] Maurice Friedman, *To Deny Our Nothingness: Contemporary Images of Man*, 3rd rev. ed with a new Preface and Appendix (Chicago: The University of Chicago Press, Phoenix Books, 1978), p. 18. I have amended the text slightly to remove what today would be considered sexist language.

REFERENCES

Buber, M., 1958. *I and Thou*, (trans. by R. G. Smith). Chas. Scribner's, New York.

Buber, M., 1985. *Between Man and Man*, (trans. by R. G. Smith). Macmillan, 1985, New York.

Buber, Martin. *The Knowledge of Man: A Philosophy of the Interhuman*, ed. with an Introductory Essay (Chap. 1) by Maurice Friedman, trans. by Maurice Friedman and R. G. Smith. Atlantic Highlands, NY: Humanities Press International, 1988 (now distributed by Prometheus Books, Amherst, NY.

Friedman, M., 1983. *The Confirmation of Otherness: In Family, Community, and Society.* Pilgrim Press, New York.

Rome, S., and Rome, B., (eds.), 1964. *Philosophical Interrogations.* "Martin Buber" section conducted, ed. & Buber's responses, (trans. by Maurice Friedman). Holt, Rinehart & Winston, New York, pp. 13-117.

Wolff, Kurt H., 1976. *Surrender and Catch. Experience in Inquiry Today.* D. Reidel, Boston.

SECTION II

PERSPECTIVES ON
DIALOGUE CONVERSATION

Chapter 8

THE FIVE DIMENSIONS OF BOHM'S DIALOGUE

MARIO CAYER
Laval University

1. INTRODUCTION

In the past few years, we have witnessed an interest for dialogue in many disciplines such as education, psychology, women's studies, sociology, management, etc. The popularity of dialogue, in the form proposed by physicist David Bohm, has spread in many of these disciplines. However, this enhanced popularity also gave rise to a greater confusion surrounding the practice of dialogue.

The first part of this chapter will describe the two strategies usually adopted to deal with the confusion surrounding the practice of Bohm's dialogue. The first strategy consists in presenting and practicing dialogue in a way that makes it simpler by focusing on only one or two of its dimensions. This strategy is called narrowing dialogue. A counterpart to this tendency is the attachment to a model. The persons adopting this strategy consider as complete the description of dialogue given in Bohm's texts and therefore the practice of dialogue must conform to the description without regard to the environment. The forces underlying these strategies will be explored as well as the consequences on the development and spreading of dialogue.

In an attempt to clarify the practice and to find a common ground amongst the practitioners of Bohm's dialogue, the second part of this chapter proposes a descriptive model of dialogue which brings to the fore its five most important dimensions. These dimensions, which came out of empirical data and of Bohm's writings, include dialogue as conversation, as inquiry, as creation of a shared meaning, as a participatory process and as a collective meditation. Each of these dimensions is explained and tensions and paradoxes amongst the dimensions are brought to light.

Dialogue as a Means of Collective Communication, Edited by Banathy and Jenlink
Kluwer Academic/Plenum Publishers, New York 2005

2.   THE FIVE DIMENSIONS OF BOHM'S DIALOGUE

As part of a research study I conducted on Bohm's dialogue, I had the opportunity to meet many people who had practiced this form of dialogue for many years. Most of them showed great interest to better their comprehension and practice of dialogue and, in many cases, to spread it around. I noticed that some participants, as it is unfortunately often the case, had grown attached and had identified themselves to their vision of dialogue; this attachment and identification made dialogue very hard between them! Many of the comments in this chapter were written in the hope to provide a common ground that would facilitate dialogue in that very situation.

I would like to emphasize that this text should not be viewed as the conclusion of a long reflection but rather as a long reflection in process. I invite the readers to view my comments, despite the affirmative form, as an on-going questioning.

3.   PART I: THE OBSERVATIONS

In this first part, I will talk about two observations, which ensue directly from my participation in many dialogue groups and from my formal and informal conversations with the participants in my research as well as with other actors involved in the practice and spreading of dialogue. The first observation brings to light the state of confusion and ambiguity surrounding dialogue. I will talk about how this confusion manifests itself and I will suggest some hypotheses on its origins. The second observation, which could be a corollary of the first one, reveals a certain polarization in the way dialogue is presented and practiced. I will talk briefly about these two tendencies and about the possible consequences they may have on the evolution and spreading of dialogue.

3.1   First Observation: The Confusion Surrounding Dialogue

In his article, Schein (1993) states" Some proponents [of dialogue] have made it sound like a most esoteric experience" (p. 43). Some of the findings in the research I conducted can shed light on the source of such a perception. They reveal that some participants have experienced transpersonal states of consciousness. When translated into words, these experiences can seem esoteric for those who are not familiar with such experiences or did not study them. The study also shows that some participants want to preserve Bohm's vision of dialogue and are reluctant to introduce into the practice of dialogue techniques and methodologies that could be contradictory to Bohm's vision. Moreover, some participants hesitate to promote dialogue as the new miracle-technique that can solve all our problems or to make consumers' good out of it. I think that we have here some of the factors that can explain why certain persons have the impression that some participants have made dialogue sound like an esoteric experience.

My first observation agrees with Schein's comment on one point: for many people, dialogue is hard to understand,[1] hard to grasp. For many, the practice of dialogue is confusing and vague. However, I do not think that we can attribute this solely to some proponents; it is also a consequence of how dialogue was developed and presented by Bohm. Maybe we should look at how the difficulty to grasp dialogue manifests itself before dwelling on the causes.

When I was conducting my research, I frequently heard comments such as: "Everything is allowed in dialogue." "Dialogue must be open to everybody and to everything." And, moreover: "Everybody is welcome to a dialogue group whatever their intentions may be." I think that such comments reflect the difficulty people have in defining the practice of dialogue and acknowledging its boundaries and limitations. Not being able to acknowledge the limitations of an approach does not demonstrate, in my view, its omnipotence but is rather revealing of the confusion it generates.

Another clue about the difficulty people have in grasping dialogue, was revealed during my participation in certain dialogue groups. There were occasions where participants requested permission to play musical instruments, dance, sing together, etc. (In fact, among the persons interviewed, some mentioned having witnessed the same type of request in other groups.) The effect on a group of this type of request and the ensuing discussions demonstrate each time the confusion and vagueness surrounding the concept and practice of dialogue.

Finally, everyone who is involved in a dialogue group knows how difficult it is to gather enough people and sustain the group over time. Obviously, all kinds of reasons can be stated to justify the fact that very few persons sustain the practice. Among these, Peat (1992) mentions that, in his last years, Bohm was disappointed that so few people had the necessary courage to sustain the practice of dialogue. I do believe that a lack of courage is one of the reasons for abandoning the practice. But I venture the hypothesis that one of the reasons for abandoning the practice of dialogue is the fact that many persons never really understand, grasp or make sense of dialogue. I think this is the most serious manifestation of the difficulty to understand dialogue.

I cannot see any advantage in having dialogue misunderstood, in not defining its boundaries and in spending a lot of time in a group discussing why we should or should not sing and dance together. Mostly, I cannot see any advantage in having many people abandon the practice because they do not grasp what it is all about or because they are bored with dialogue becoming itself the topic of dialogues. I am not saying this because I think dialogue should be practiced by each and everyone: individuals, organizations, etc. This would be going from esotericism to salvation. People must know about dialogue and understand it in order for them to make a sound decision on the value and pertinence of such a practice for them and for society.

Let us now come back to what constitutes, in my view, two important causes (but certainly not the only ones) of the difficulty in grasping dialogue and understanding the meaning of its practice. I already mentioned above that one of the causes would be the way Bohm developed and presented dialogue. Another reason would be, on one hand Bohm's capacity to access Learning Level III and, on the other hand, the fact that he refrained from suggesting concrete means for helping participants access this third level of learning. Let us consider each of these causes. Obviously Bohm had brilliant insights into the functioning of thought and its role in the crises our society is facing; he had also insights into the importance of practicing dialogue to help grasp the perverted effects of the functioning of thought. It seems that Bohm wanted to experience with dialogue and develop his vision of dialogue in a dialogical, experiential way, namely during his introductory seminars on dialogue. In my view, Bohm's insight into dialogue was developing, getting richer and more complex as he advanced and initiated dialogues with participants in his seminars and people close to him. In other words, Bohm took the idea of dialogue seriously and embodied it well. For him the practice of dialogue was something that was alive and grew with time and through contact with the people who engaged in the experience with him.

Bohm's most important works addressing dialogue and its foundations come from transcripts from his seminars or conversations.[2] But, as mentioned above, these seminars allowed Bohm to engage in dialogue with the participants on the topic of the functioning of thought and on dialogue itself. Therefore, these texts present a concept in progress which partly "unfolded" from the interests of the persons participating in these seminars and from their questions. A disadvantage to this was that, over time, many dimensions, many aspects of dialogue were addressed, many links were made with other approaches (for example, with de Maré socio-therapy, with meditation, with anthropology through the references made to the hunter-gatherer bands, etc.). I think Bohm did not have time before he died to present a complete image of dialogue, a synthesis–in other words, to organize the different aspects of dialogue and present them in a coherent whole (maybe he did not think it was pertinent to do so). The consequence of this is that the texts addressing dialogue present it as something complex, progressive and alive but, nonetheless, hard to grasp.

The comments in the previous paragraphs are directly linked to what I identified as the second cause of the difficulty in understanding dialogue, that is, on one hand Bohm's capacity to access Learning Level III,[3] and on the other hand his refraining from proposing concrete means to help participants access this third level of learning. Bohm's capacity to access Learning Level III is shown by the fact that he was not only able to challenge his own beliefs, assumptions within a dialogue but also challenge, "suspend" his assumptions towards dialogue itself. He was not afraid to change his mind, to let his thoughts evolve, to be influenced by the content of the dialogues and by the very process of dialogue. He took this non-attachment to his positions seriously, "...that no fixed position is so important that it is worth holding at the expense of destroying the dialogue itself"[4] (Bohm & Peat, 1987, p. 242). He was ready to modify his own point of view towards dialogue if he had good reasons to do so. In other words, Bohm was able to challenge his assumptions and beliefs towards his proposed approach in order to challenge the individual and collective assumptions. It seems clear that this capacity falls within the province of Learning Level III. Hawkins (1991) describes very well what is Learning Level III:

> What seems to me crucial in understanding this distinction between Learning II and Learning III is that the latter occurs when the person cannot only replace one underlying framework by which he lives with another–e.g., deciding to quit being a Christian and to become a Buddhist; or to quit being an alcoholic and become an ex-alcoholic–but must also be aware that both these paradigms or world views are systems, frameworks, or spectacles through which we view the world. It is when we are able truly to let them go that we enter the domain of Learning III. (p. 177)

There is no doubt Bohm had this capacity to work at the level of Learning III. But how is this statement pertinent to our topic? What I want to bring to the fore is that Bohm was not only able to access Learning Level III but that he also proposed an approach which was at the level of Learning III, that is, an approach that redefines itself at the moment it is happening. Therefore, we find ourselves with an approach developed in a Learning III mode and developed mostly to function in a Learning III mode. In my view, to be able to work with such an approach, one must be able to access Learning Level III. However, Bateson (1972) emphasizes that very few people have reached that level.[5] In the practice of dialogue, people are not only invited to challenge their assumptions and beliefs but also experience the practice of dialogue itself being challenged; the result of this, particularly for people who are at the level of Learning I and Learning II, is that they have no longer any reference point, nothing is stable anymore, everything is changing. I think the experience of absolute relativism must be much alike this experience of losing every frame of reference. Expressions such as "Everything is allowed in dialogue," "Dialogue must be open to everybody and to everything," or "Everybody is welcome to participate in a dialogue whatever their intentions may be," are, in my view, manifestations of this relativism.

I am not saying that only Bohm could work with dialogue. I think that only the persons able to access Learning Level III can work with dialogue the same way Bohm did. In this respect, it would have been very useful if Bohm had proposed some kind of "bridge" to help Learning I and Learning II people (the vast majority) understand and make sense of the experience of dialogue. Bohm refrained from proposing means, methodologies to help build this bridge.[6] Taking into account the previously mentioned difficulty to gather enough people and to sustain a dialogue group over time, I wonder whether or not building this bridge is necessary in order for dialogue to survive, at least in the form proposed by Bohm. In dialogue's present state, I think the criticism directed towards Krishnamurti's teachings could apply to dialogue. In reference to an analysis by Marco Vassi in his book *Lying Down*, Berman (1990) writes:

> In denouncing all methods and worldviews, Krishnamurti failed to come up with any positive alternative. Year after year, says Vassi, Krishnamurti would chide his aging fans for having made no breakthrough in terms of their attachments, but he categorically refused to discuss how such a breakthrough might be made. (p. 313)

In the case of dialogue, people simply abandon the practice. They do so, in my view, not because dialogue lacks values and pertinence but rather because people have a hard time making sense of it. I think the challenge is to make the practice of dialogue more accessible without losing its essence. This leads to my second observation.

3.2   Second Observation: Polarization in the Ways of Presenting and Practicing Dialogue

Observing different groups led to identifying two tendencies in the way dialogue is presented and practiced (there are more than two tendencies but I will focus on these two because they seem archetypal). I called them A) narrowing dialogue and B) attachment to a model of dialogue. In the following pages I will describe each of them in detail and insist on the consequences they have on the spreading of dialogue.

3.2.1   A) Narrowing Dialogue

I previously mentioned that Bohm had insisted during his seminars on the diverse dimensions or aspects of dialogue (the second part of this chapter addresses the more important dimensions of dialogue). One way of presenting and practicing dialogue is to focus on one or two dimensions and leave out the others. For example, some persons present dialogue as a "good and profound conversation". Their presentation of dialogue consists only in asking the participants to remember a profound and significant conversation they had and to act in the same spirit and the same way in the dialogue. For these people, dialogue is a good and profound conversation. I am not saying that I disagree with that. *Dialogue is indeed a profound conversation, but it goes beyond that, it is not limited to that.* Another example comes from the persons who see dialogue as a technique to help them discover their mental models and those of other people and as a technique to create a shared meaning or a strong culture. Again, *dialogue can help mental models surface and create a shared meaning, but it is more than that.* What I am trying to say is that one way of presenting and practicing dialogue consists in making it simpler by focusing on only one or two of its dimensions. I would like to explore the forces underlying this tendency to narrow dialogue.

The first force that drives people to simplify is precisely our reflex to simplify any situation when it gets too complex and we cannot make sense of it. Unable to deal with great complexity in dialogue, people extract what suits them or what they understand and, in the process, they sometimes leave essential dimensions of dialogue behind. The fact, that dialogue is not well defined and that its boundaries are not clear contributes to its simplification yet to its distortion.

If from the great complexity of dialogue ensues an almost natural reaction of simplification; sometimes this drive towards simplification has a cultural nature. In fact, one characteristic of our culture, particularly North American, is to look for weekend enlightenment, easy solutions, quick fixes, and how-tos. When dialogue gets too demanding and challenging, one must transform it into something easier and more accessible. How can one sell a complex product that may lead to confusion, pain and questioning? This is a very difficult task. Therefore, people must make it marketable by bringing to the fore its attractive qualities and insisting on its usefulness. Cultural pressure is another driving force explaining the narrowing of dialogue.

A third force is related to the system protection mechanism (meaning institutions, our way of living, predominant values, etc.) now in place. This mechanism has an astonishing co-optation capacity for any approach that can potentially challenge the values and assumptions on which the system is based. Dialogue has a subversive potential. Therefore, a very powerful force is at work to control it and render it compatible with the dominant system. (The same mechanism that is at work at the social level is also at work at an individual level.)

It is very ironic to observe that dialogue was proposed namely to explore these forces, face them and free ourselves from the grip they have on us. In this respect, it seems that dialogue does not carry out its role since these forces control, at least partly, the way many people practice dialogue. There are two common reactions to this observation; the first one consists in stating that this is precisely an illustration of dialogue not fulfilling its role and consequently justifies adapting it. Those who adopt this position usually have not experienced dialogue in the form proposed by Bohm or have experienced it over a very short period of time. The other reaction is to blame people for their lack of courage, their lack of perseverance, their inability to understand the essence of dialogue.

This first way of presenting dialogue obviously has consequences on the development and spreading of dialogue. A summary of the consequences includes:

- Makes dialogue more accessible;
- Spreads the practice of dialogue;
- "Plants seeds" and, as a result, people can go deeper into their practice;
- Applies dialogue to concrete situations; consequently there may be short-term results;
- Underuses the potential of dialogue;
- Subjects dialogue to the cultural and utilitarist imperatives and therefore, takes away its potential for challenging these aspects of the culture;
- Spreads a vision of dialogue that is reductionist;
- Nurtures the confusion surrounding the concept of dialogue (because everyone has his or her own model of dialogue);
- Carries the risk of transforming dialogue into another transient fad.

I observed a counterpart to this tendency to narrow and simplify dialogue. I called it the attachment to a model of dialogue.

3.2.2   B) Attachment To A Model Of Dialogue

It would probably be more appropriate to talk about an attachment to the writings on dialogue because, generally, the persons adopting this tendency consider as complete the description of dialogue given in Bohm's texts and therefore the practice of dialogue must conform to the description without regard to the environment. These persons forget that Bohm presented dialogue as a proposition that could evolve if need be. Far from following Bohm's example and consider "...that no fixed position is so important that it is worth holding at the expense of destroying the dialogue itself" (Bohm & Peat, 1987, p. 242), it seems that sometimes precedence is given to the writings on dialogue rather than to maintaining dialogue itself.

People who show this tendency seem to lose their critical mind and do not want to challenge their way of presenting and practicing dialogue despite the following facts: 1) very few groups succeed in recruiting the number of participants proposed by Bohm (for example, when I participated in different on-going groups, none had more than 20 people, the majority having from 12 to 15 people) and 2) very few groups succeed in sustaining the group over a long period of time. The usual scenario of long-lasting groups consists in a core of persons who persevere and a high turnover of participants making up the rest of the group.

Obviously, this attitude is different from the one, nonetheless legitimate and courageous, that consists in wanting to persist in the practice of dialogue in order to learn to resist to the quick-fix reflex or to face the anxiety arising from the complexity and the unknown. But this attitude of wanting to confine oneself to Bohm's works on dialogue must not prevent someone from asking questions about the actual state of the practice of dialogue: is it possible to form groups of 20 to 40 people that will sustain the practice of dialogue over a significant period of time? In its form proposed by Bohm, is dialogue only possible for those who personally knew David Bohm or for admirers of his works and those of Krishnamurti? If so, it makes the practice of dialogue rather limited. If it is not possible to form groups of 20 to 40 persons and sustain practice, we must then have the courage to face this reality and ask why it is not possible. Is it because dialogue is too counter-cultural or too demanding? Is it because the theory on dialogue is too hard to communicate and to grasp? Is it because there is in the very way we see dialogue something that makes its practice only accessible to a few initiates and thereby makes dialogue a contradiction in terms since it is suppose to encourage diversity?

Among the people who have the tendency to attach themselves to the writings on dialogue, this type of questioning is rather rare. I would like to explore the underlying forces to this attachment to the literature on dialogue.

A first force underlying this attachment comes from the difficulty in dealing with uncertainty, which drives people to hang on to something stable and certain. People find comfort in the certainty and stability provided by the literature on dialogue especially when confronted with the uncertainty and the anxiety coming from constantly calling everything into question, which is the essence of dialogue.

Another force comes from the difficulty of developing the practice of dialogue. It is not that obvious to suggest avenues of development for dialogue, avenues that would respect the essence of dialogue as well as take into account the environment in which dialogue is practiced. Facing this enormous challenge, many choose to stick with the literature on dialogue (while those who adopt the first tendency choose to adapt to the environment sometimes at the expense of the essence of dialogue).

This second way of presenting and practicing dialogue also has consequences on its development and spreading. A summary of these consequences includes:

- Allows participants to have the same reference;
- Prevents the practice of dialogue from being subjected to cultural and utilitarist imperatives;
- Does not encourage the development of the practice of dialogue;
- Does not take into account the environment (the environment must adapt to dialogue);
- Makes the practice of dialogue look like something not easily accessible.

Before ending the first part of this chapter, I would like to add one last comment. It is my assumption that one person cannot control the development and evolution of the practice of dialogue, in the form suggested by Bohm. The practice of dialogue does not happen in a closed vase: it is subjected to all sorts of influences coming from inside as well as outside. People interested in dialogue, those who practice it and those who practice approaches that are similar, all have an influence on the development of dialogue. The use and co-optation of the practice of dialogue by businesses as well as the institutionalization of dialogue by prestigious universities all see to it that it is not possible to "preserve" dialogue, to keep it from outside influences and stop its evolution. This is all the more true since dialogue is very open to outside influences.

For those who believe that the practice of dialogue in the form proposed by Bohm can help deal with the many difficulties human beings and modern societies are facing, the challenge is not becoming attached to a static vision of dialogue but rather to: 1) clarify Bohm's ideas about dialogue in order to make it more understandable, clearer, more defined; 2) open oneself to outside influences, and 3) trust and have the courage to follow Bohm's steps and be ready to explore and challenge the very practice of dialogue if there are good reasons to do so (and, in my view, one of these reasons would be the fact that it is not possible to attract enough people to sustain dialogue).

I think the first stage is to provide a clearer image of the diverse dimensions of dialogue. The second part of the chapter addresses this task.

4. PART II: DIALOGUE AND ITS DIMENSIONS

Even though one of the objectives of this section is to make the practice of dialogue more precise, one must recognize from the start that it would be utopic to try to completely define such a practice. Bohm himself, paraphrasing Korzybski, emphasized that:

> whatever we say a thing is, it isn't. First of all, whatever we say is words, and what we want to talk about is generally not words. Second, whatever we *mean* by what we say is not what the thing actually is, though it may be similar. For the thing is always *more* than what we mean and is never exhausted by our concepts. And the thing is also *different* from what we mean, if only because no thought can be absolutely correct when it is extended indefinitely. (Bohm & Peat, 1987, p. 8)

Therefore, one must avoid giving too much detail or over-analyzing a concept because the risk here is, at best, coming back to the initial complexity or, at worse, losing oneself in the confusion of interpretations. I would add to this that one of the aspects of dialogue is precisely developing our capacity to deal with ambiguity and paradox. Zohar and Marshall (1993) eloquently talk about the role of ambiguity in communication:

> our many ambiguous feelings are like a background pool of potential relationships that can in time be made more precise according to circumstances...Ambiguous or double meanings in words and sentences allow shared meanings to form. Such ambiguity and duality is basic to letting creative social relations emerge. (p. 99)

Seeking the right balance must guide our effort to clarify the practice of dialogue. This is the first objective and the first challenge of this section. The second challenge is that this effort for clarification should also extend to the issue of polarization in the way dialogue is presented and practiced. In other words, is it possible to present a proposition that will enlighten those who practice a simplified version of dialogue as well as those who strictly conform to Bohm's works on dialogue?

It is from such a perspective that I propose a descriptive model of dialogue which 1) brings to the fore what I consider as its five most important dimensions and 2) links each dimension to authors, approaches which explored, in depth, a specific dimension of the model. In this model, I insist on the similarities between dialogue and each of its dimensions and I do not mention the differences. For example, regarding the fifth dimension entitled "dialogue as collective meditation," I focus on the similarities between dialogue and meditation but I do not mention how dialogue is different from meditation. It is the same for each dimension.

This model was developed from the data gathered in my research without, however, neglecting the influence of Bohm's writings. In my view, this model should meet, at least partly, the need for clarification. As for the topic of polarization, it will be addressed the following way: by presenting the diverse dimensions of dialogue, I hope to inform those who focus on one or two dimensions that there are other dimensions to dialogue. The idea here is not to imply that practicing a simplified version of dialogue is without value. My point is that choosing to focus on a subset of the dimensions of dialogue should be a deliberate and well-advised choice and not the result of ignorance. This would greatly help clear up the confusion surrounding the practice of dialogue. But it must be understood that I am not saying that everyone practicing an approach that resembles dialogue should know about dialogue. What I am saying is that everyone who claims to be practising dialogue in the form proposed by Bohm (and this includes consultants who change the name of their type of intervention and call it "dialogue" in order to take advantage of the popularity attached to the term) or in a form derived from Bohm's dialogue should be aware of the many dimensions of dialogue and should know how their practice is different from Bohm's.

Regarding those who strictly conform to Bohm's works on dialogue, I hope that presenting other thinkers or other approaches focusing on similar dimensions than that of dialogue, will encourage them to consult these resources and be open to what they have to offer. Maybe, with the help of these resources, they will find a way to keep dialogue alive which is something, in my view, that requires that one respects and adapts to the environment while preserving the essence of dialogue.

Obviously, dividing dialogue into its main components can give the impression of fragmenting it or changing its nature. However, the greater clarity that will result from this way of presenting dialogue is worth the risk. One must not consider each dimension of dialogue as independent from the others because many overlap. Moreover, the specificity of Bohm's dialogue resides precisely in the fact that dialogue encompasses each of these dimensions and that each one is necessary to its integrity. (Although it is not necessary that they all be there at the same time, at every moment.) Figure 1 provides an overview of the five dimensions of Bohm's dialogue.

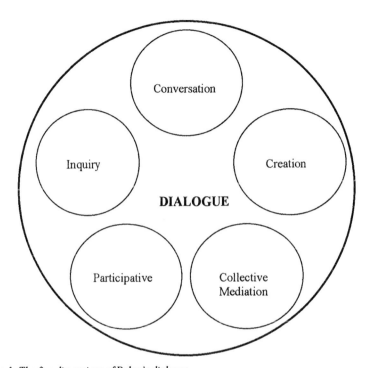

Figure 1: The five dimensions of Bohm's dialogue

In the following sections, each dimension is briefly described, in relation to Bohm's dialogue.

4.1   First Dimension: Dialogue As A Conversation

Bohm insisted in presenting dialogue as the simple fact of people sitting together for the purpose of talking, listening, and sharing together. For him, this very simple activity, yet so rare in our society, is at the roots of dialogue. Bohm was referring to this particular dimension when he talked about the hunter-gatherer tribes who got together to talk, without apparent agenda or predetermined purpose. Some participants in this research also mentioned this dimension of dialogue. The following quotation constitutes a typical example:

I've become more interested in people just being able to sit down together in one room and being able to hear each other out about the things that they feel are important in their lives. And being able to listen very attentively without making a lot of judgment and without interrupting a lot.

As shown in this quotation, this dimension of dialogue refers to listening, to a non-judgmental way of listening. This dimension also calls for empathy, respect and receptivity towards the other. The meaning of this activity resides in the conversation, in the relationship with the other. There is something disinterested in the simple act of sitting and talking with other human beings. If the participant does not expect anything else from this activity, he or she must, nonetheless, intentionally participate. For me, intentionality is an essential element in the practice of dialogue.[7] The participant gets involved in this dimension of dialogue not for the purpose of getting more content but rather to understand the experience of the other.

4.1.1   Resources

This dimension of dialogue is related to Buber's I-Thou relationship and Carl Rogers' insistence on listening. Readers who are interested may consult their books, which are, respectively, *I and Thou* and *Client-Centered Therapy*. An article from Cissna and Anderson (1994), *The 1957 Martin Buber-Carl Rogers Dialogue, as Dialogue*, is also most interesting owing to the fact that it not only provides a kind of compared analysis of the thinking of these two proponents of dialogue, but also shows how their conversation was a dialogue.

During the past few years, feminist scholars brought to the fore feminist principles and values that embodied this dimension of dialogue and in a way much more topical than that of the hunter-gatherer bands. For example, Carol Gilligan's (1982) book *In a Different Voice: Psychological Theory and Women's Development* proposes an ethic of care focusing on relation and attention. Women's ways of knowing have been explored by Belenky et al. (1986) in their book *Women's Ways of Knowing: The Development of Self, Voice, and Mind*. These authors emphasize the importance of dialogue, reciprocity, and cooperation as an alternative way of knowing.

Nel Noddings, professor of Education at Stanford University where she teaches courses in Ethics and Feminist Studies, has developed, in the past few years, what she calls *interpersonal reasoning* characterized by an attitude of solicitude, a special form of attention, flexibility in both ends and means, continual effort at cultivating the relation and the search for the appropriate answer to a situation rather than for "the" good answer (Noddings, 1994). She thinks we must take on the challenge of developing "the capacity of moral agent to talk appreciatively with each other regardless of fundamental differences...". She stresses the importance of dialogue which she defines as "... that exchange of words, feelings, and solicitude that reaches outward to care for others and inward to build a stronger and more reflective self" (1994, p. 5). Her articles *Stories in Dialogue: Caring and Interpersonal Reasoning* and *Learning to Engage in Moral Dialogue* should be read by those interested by the spreading and development of dialogue.

Finally, it is important to underline that this dimension of dialogue seems to answer an emerging need in our society. The March/April 1991 edition of the *Utne Reader* magazine addressed the issue of increase in number of groups and approaches advocating the *art of conversation*. Among the approaches presented we could find *salons, councils* and *Bohm's dialogue*. Figure 2 a summary of the key points related to dialogue as conversation.

Dialogue as Conversation

To talk together without agenda;
To listen to the other;
Respect, empathy, care,
receptivity and solicitude
To understand the experience of
the other
Intentionality
Interpersonal reasoning
Reciprocity

Figure 2. Dialogue as Conversation Dimension

4.2 Second Dimension: Dialogue As Inquiry

This is certainly the most well known dimension since it is used to describe dialogue in Bohm, Factor and Garrett's proposal (1991):

We are proposing a kind of collective inquiry not only into the content of what each of us says, thinks and feels but also into the underlying motivations, assumptions and beliefs that lead us to do so.

In this dimension, focus in on the exploration of individual and collective assumptions, beliefs, ideas and feelings that control the participants' behaviors and interactions. It is important to emphasize that the purpose of this inquiry is not the search for truth or the right answer, but rather the surfacing of our individual and collective assumptions and becoming aware of the conditioning they impose on us. But, if each participant believes he or she has the "correct" version of reality (or worse, believes that it is not a version of reality but reality itself), this exploration is not possible. Each participant must show openness to alter their view of reality, they must not hold on too tight to their points of view, their beliefs, etc. This kind of openness requires a great deal of courage.

There is a learning aspect to this dimension of dialogue. But it is not learning in the sense of accumulation of knowledge but in the sense of renewal of knowledge. In this respect, it would be necessary to accept to unlearn before learning.

One must emphasize that this inquiry is not directed solely towards intellectual knowledge but also towards feelings and emotions, which are linked to our knowledge and to our interactions with other people. If there is a certain tradition of challenging our knowledge, we are rather "illiterate" in regard to acknowledging and challenging our feelings and those of others.

Many participants mentioned this dimension of exploration and for some it constitutes the main reason for their involvement in dialogue. For others, this spirit of inquiry must imbue the content and process of dialogue since they describe dialogue as "an inquiry into what is".

4.2.1   Resources

By its focus on questioning and its refusal of previous learning, this dimension of dialogue brings us closer to its Greek roots and to Socrates' dialogues (however, it differs from it since the purpose is not to lead the participants towards a predetermined truth). Socrates was interested in education and philosophy. These two basic subjects went deeper into the art of asking questions, the mastery of which is essential in order to surface individual and collective assumptions and beliefs. Thus, it would be very enriching to consult the literature addressing these two basic subjects in order to learn more about this dimension of dialogue. An excellent place to start is Burbules' (1993) work *Dialogue in Teaching*. Accessible and very well documented, this book places dialogue at the interface between philosophy and education. Burbules' book does not talk about dialogue in the form proposed by Bohm but addresses many issues at the very heart of Bohm's dialogue, such as: rules in the dialogue, moves in the dialogue, dialogue and authority, etc.

I believe our ability to inquire would be better if we could develop our capacity "to reflect-in-action" (which is a form of inquiry). The work of Donald A. Schön deserves our attention, namely his books *The Reflexive Practitioner* and *Educating the Reflexive Practitioner*. In the same line of thought, one must not forget Argyris works which explore the defense mechanisms preventing learning and propose a theory of reasoning and action to overcome these mechanisms both at the individual and organizational levels. His books *Reasoning, Learning, and Action, Action Science* (with Putnam and Smith) and *Knowledge for Action* present his work.

An inquiry into our individual and collective assumptions is something that is close to Freire's raising of social consciousness. For him, social consciousness must be raised through dialogue, which becomes a method to increase awareness and pedagogy of individual and social liberation. I think Freire's (1970) book *Pedagogy of the Oppressed* is a must for those interested in spreading and developing Bohm's dialogue. Figure 3 provides a summary of the points related to dialogue as inquiry.

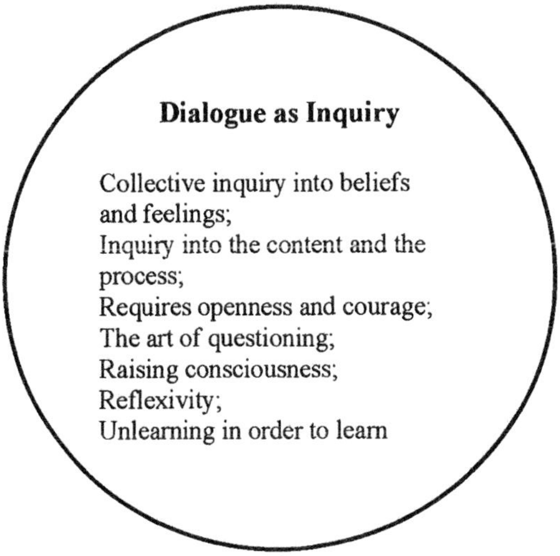

Dialogue as Inquiry

Collective inquiry into beliefs and feelings;
Inquiry into the content and the process;
Requires openness and courage;
The art of questioning;
Raising consciousness;
Reflexivity;
Unlearning in order to learn

Figure 3. Dialogue as inquiry

4.3   Third Dimension: Dialogue as Creating Shared Meaning

Bohm often brought the role of dialogue in creating shared meaning to the fore. From the flow of meaning circulating through the participants should emerge a shared content of consciousness, a shared meaning created by the participants. They should then be conscious of the fact that this meaning has been created by them and must be continually recreated. Bohm also mentions that this shared meaning acts as a cement that must hold the diverse parts of society together. That is the role of culture. Bohm also referred to this dimension of dialogue when he talked about the hunter-gatherer tribes.

For sharing to take place there must be more than one point of view. And, for Bohm, there must be a great diversity in points of view since dialogue must be a microcosm of society. Moreover, to construct shared meaning, participants must let the words of the other penetrate deep inside them. They must suspend any judgmental thoughts, points of view in order not to take away the transformational power of words. In other words, for there to be true shared meaning (rather than simply being exposed to ideas of other people), participants must accept the risk of being transformed by the experience of dialogue.

Bohm attributes a dimension to our meaning-making capacity that Weber (1990) qualifies as mystical: he proposes that through this capacity we are co-creators of the universe. The following quotation illustrates the depth of Bohm's ideas on the subject:

> [David Bohm] proposes that meaning is a form of being. In the very act of interpreting the universe, we are creating the universe. Through our meanings we change nature's being. Man's meaning-making capacity turns into nature's partner, a participant in shaping her evolution. The word does not merely reflect the world, it also creates the world. (Weber, 1990, p. 18)

What Bohm is proposing is that collectively and through dialogue we become aware of and responsible for the effects of this meaning-making capacity.

Some participants in the research also mentioned this creation of meaning as an essential aspect of dialogue. In fact, one participant even considers the role of facilitator as "the capacity to help the group understand the dynamics of the flow of meaning" and "the capacity to listen while keeping in mind that he or she must 'shepherd' the group towards certain levels of meaning".

4.3.1   Resources

Bohm's insistence on meaning resonates with the existentialist tradition. To those interested in going deeper into this tradition, I suggest looking at it through existential psychology since "professional existential philosophers surpass even psychoanalytic theoreticians in the use of turbid, convoluted language" (Yalom, 1980, p. 16). Works from May, Frankl, and Yalom can be read to learn more about this facet.

To really understand this dimension of dialogue, namely our capacity to create and recreate meaning, I think it would be helpful to get acquainted with the constructivist and post-modernist perspective. Accessible authors are Kenneth Gergen (1991), *The Saturated Self: Dilemmas of Identity in Contemporary Life* and Walter Truett Anderson (1990), *Reality Isn't What It Used To Be.* Zohar and Marshall's (1993) book *The Quantum Society* is particularly interesting since it puts emphasis on the importance of dialogue to give meaning to a more and more alienated and fragmented society.

It is not possible to talk about the cultural aspect of dialogue without referring to Patrick de Maré (de Maré et al., 1991). In his works, Bohm often gives credit to de Maré. Using a psychoanalytic approach, de Maré claims in his book *Koinonia* that the socio-cultural level plays a major role in shaping and controlling collective human experience. He argues that a large group offers a structure able to link together the inner world with the cultural context and, consequently, allows people to be aware of the cultural assumptions prevailing in society and thus modify them. As such, people engage in a form of "socio-therapy" that allows them to confront, through dialogue, the sources of mass conflict and violence and reach what was known to the Greeks as *Koinonia*, the state of impersonal fellowship. De Maré's contribution to Bohm's dialogue is important but Bohm distinguishes himself from it by the emphasis put on the fundamental role the activity of thought plays in being a source of the crises presently shaking our societies.

I would also like to mention that this search for a shared meaning through dialogue is desirable not only on a collective level but also on an individual level. Breaking from the myth of the monolithic self, many authors maintain that people are made up of many parts that they call subpersonalities (Assagioli, 1965), voices (Stone & Winkelman, 1993), or I positions (Hermans & Kempen, 1993). Generally, these authors insist on 1) acknowledging these diverse I positions, and 2) establishing a dialogue between these I positions. The reading of these works shows us the many parallels between group dialogues and dialogues with the multiple voices of the self. In this respect, Bohm often referred to the fact that a dialogue group could be imagined as a microcosm of society. In my view, it may be possible that each person in a dialogue group be imagined as a microcosm of the whole group and thus of society. The boundaries between the inner and the outer world then become less and less defined. For those interested in knowing more about this aspect of dialogue, Hermans and Kempen's book *The Dialogical Self: Meaning as Movement* is highly recommended. For those who like pop psychology, the book *Embracing Our Selves* by Stone and Winkelman can be consulted.

Finally, few things have been written on the mystical dimension of our meaning-making capacity.[8] The best place to start may be philosopher Renée Weber's (1990) book *Dialogues with Scientists and Sages* from which the last quotation was extracted. Figure 4 provides an overview the Creating Shared Meaning Dimension, noting the more important actions that individuals taking part in dialogue must consider.

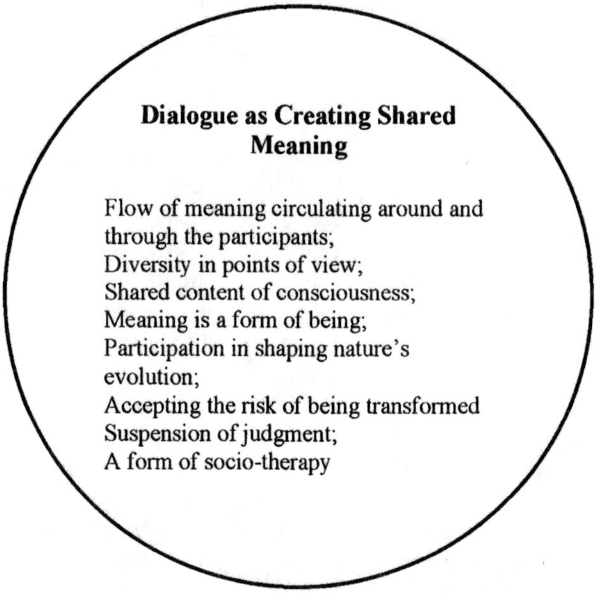

Dialogue as Creating Shared Meaning

Flow of meaning circulating around and
through the participants;
Diversity in points of view;
Shared content of consciousness;
Meaning is a form of being;
Participation in shaping nature's
evolution;
Accepting the risk of being transformed
Suspension of judgment;
A form of socio-therapy

Figure 4. Dialogue as Creating Shared Meaning Dimension

4.4   Fourth Dimension: Dialogue As Participatory Process

Bohm often refers to the participatory nature of dialogue and does so in many ways. First, dialogue welcomes each and everyone's participation in a spirit of openness and non-hierarchy: "a dialogue is something more of a common participation, in which we are not playing a game against each other but with each other" (1989, p. 1). This aspect of participation brings us back to the concept of democracy, non-hierarchy, empowerment of participants, egalitarianism. However, for Bohm, the participatory nature of dialogue goes well beyond a simple participation in a group. It lies at the heart of his vision of the universe. The following quotation is very eloquent:

> Participation is a different way of looking at the world and experiencing it. The people in the past who thought in terms of participation in some sense experienced a different world than we do. The way we experience the world depends on our general thoughts about it. If there is participation, then everything participates everything–as it partakes of everything and takes part in everything–so that the very being of each thing arises in that participation. That includes us especially. We in this room are participating, and each one of us is partaking of the whole and also contributing in some way.
>
> This is what was meant in my book about the implicate order. It's another way of looking at it—to say everything enfolds everything. (1989, p. 74)

This "way of looking at the world" is very different from the usual way we experience the world, which is characterized by separation and unconnectedness. This notion of participation is intimately linked to the notions of interconnectedness, embeddedness in the wholeness, transcendence of the observer/observed dualism, etc. This "way of looking at the world" is a new form of consciousness described by many authors. In order to grasp the different aspects of this form of consciousness, I quote Reason (1994a) who gives a good description of the qualities of this participatory form of consciousness (which he calls *future participation*):

> First of all, future participation will be self-aware and self-reflective. Neither submerged in unaware union with the other nor seduced by the brilliant promise of a completely autonomous rational consciousness, the mind in future participation will learn to attend to its own processes...[9]

A second quality of future participation is that the mind will move beyond the world in which all is immersed in a seamless web, and beyond the world of separate objects, into a world of pattern and form, of relationships within an interdependent whole...

A third quality of future participation is the active conscious use of imagination....The world defined by conceptual language, categorizing, pruning and pinning down, reduces this vast range of imaginative possibility to a world of fixed things...future participation...is less attached to conceptual language and to paradigmatic knowing... (pp. 33-35)

The practice of dialogue would represent a way of developing this new form of consciousness. In their comments, many participants referred to this dimension of dialogue. Some talked about dialogue as a cosmic process. Others stressed the empowerment and democratic aspects of dialogue. Others described their own experience of expansion, of their sense of self, and their feeling of communion. All these comments show how dialogue is a participative process.

4.4.1   Resources

This dimension of dialogue is extremely subtle and complex and has not been very much explored yet, at least by mainstream disciplines. However, I would like to suggest a few clues. Psychology is starting to cast doubt over the modern Western view of "self-contained individualism" and proposes "a decentralized, nonequilibrium conception of personhood that allows our multiplicity and interconnectedness" (Sampson, 1985, p. 1210). Two excellent papers introduce the readers to these new tendencies in mainstream psychology: one is by Sampson (1985,) *The Decentralization of Identity: Toward a Revised Concept of Personal and Social Order*, and the other is by Guisinger and Blatt (1994), *Individuality and Relatedness: Evolution of a Fundamental Dialectic*. These articles also include many references that can be helpful to those wanting to know more about this aspect.

In the last few years, transpersonal psychology has been developing particularly outside academic settings. The purpose of this new discipline is namely the development of participative consciousness and many approaches are suggested to access our interconnectedness. The following works can be consulted and are of interest: Stanislav Grof's *Beyond the Brain: Birth, Death and Transcendence in Psychotherapy*, Ken Wilber's *No Boundary: Eastern and Western Approaches to Personal Growth* and *The Atman Project: A*

Transpersonal View of Human Development, and Walsh and Vaughan's *Beyond Ego.*

Philosopher Henrik Skolimowski also wrote very eloquently about the participatory nature of the mind. Among other things, he proposes a methodology of participation to make the transition from objective consciousness to *compassionate consciousness.* His book *The Participatory Mind: A New Theory of Knowledge and of The Universe* can shed light on the participation aspect of dialogue.

I would like to bring your attention to Mindell's process psychology which, in my view, is very close to the participative dimension of dialogue. The basis for Mindell's approach are the works from Jung, Taoism (which put emphasis on the flow), and quantum physics. His way of working with groups, although much more interventionist than dialogue, resorts to awareness, empathy, capacity to deal with tension, conflict, etc. For those who want to know how to be more interventionist in their way of facilitating a dialogue group, Mindell's books can be of valuable help, namely the following: *The Leader as Martial Artist: An Introduction to Deep Democracy, Techniques and Strategies for Resolving Conflict and Creating Community* and *Sitting in the Fire: Large Group Transformation Using Conflict and Diversity.*

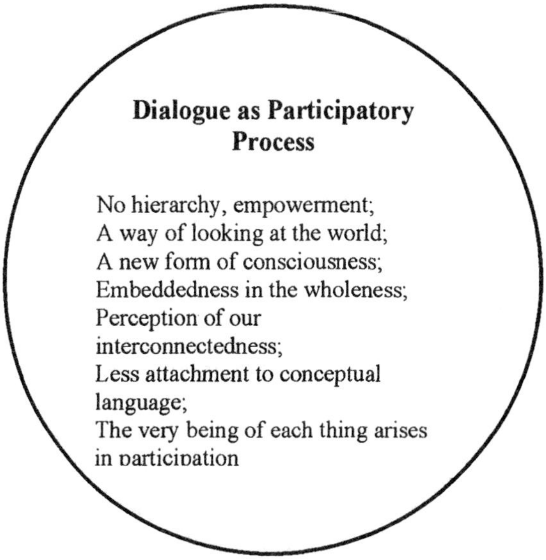

Dialogue as Participatory Process

No hierarchy, empowerment;
A way of looking at the world;
A new form of consciousness;
Embeddedness in the wholeness;
Perception of our interconnectedness;
Less attachment to conceptual language;
The very being of each thing arises in participation

Figure 5. Dialogue as Participatory Process Dimension

Finally, we must mention the authors who addressed the evolution of human consciousness toward a form of participative consciousness. Figure 5 provides an overview of this dimension.

Among those we find Berman and his two volumes: *The Reenchantment of the World* and *Coming to our Senses* (the latter is particularly important for those who have a tendency to practice dialogue in a very cerebral and intellectual way).   Again, I must mention Wilber and his volumes: *The Spectrum of Consciousness* and *The Atman Project: A Transpersonal View of Human Development.* One must not forget Georges Feuerstein's *Structures of Consciousness* and Owen Barfield's *Saving the Appearances.* These authors do not address dialogue but I mention them to those interested by dialogue in order for them to see where dialogue stands in a much larger context and to better judge whether or not dialogue can contribute to the evolution of consciousness.

4.5   Fifth Dimension: Dialogue As Collective Meditation

A few times, Bohm specifically referred to dialogue as a collective meditation.[10] There are many forms of meditation. I believe the type of meditation that comes the closest to what Bohm had in mind when he talked about dialogue as a meditation, is mindfulness meditation. This type of meditation is presented the following way by Kabat-Zinn (1994): "[Mindfulness] has to do with examining who we are, with questioning our view of the world and our place in it, and with cultivating some appreciation for the fullness of each moment we are alive. Most of all, it has to do with being in touch" (p. 3). He adds: "Mindfulness means paying attention in a particular way: on purpose, in the present moment, and nonjudgementally. This kind of attention nurtures greater awareness, clarity, and acceptance of present-moment reality" (p. 4). There are many aspects of dialogue which are similar to meditation. Dialogue does not attempt to change people, behaviors, or situations, but brings people to simply be aware and be attentive to what is without judging. Bohm describes the function of dialogue as one "to free the mind from being attached to definite goals, aims, and purposes, with their rigid assumptions, so that it can explore new meanings freely" (Bohm & Kelly, 1990. p. 463). And he states: "This kind of dialogue, where people are not trying to do anything in particular, is a collective meditation" (p. 463).

Dialogue insists on the development of attention. As mentioned in Chapter 3, this attention is a form of subtle intelligence that allows one to go beyond the duality content/process or, even more, beyond the duality observer/observed which is the basis of the fragmentary functioning of the mind. Dialogue provides a space within which participants can individually and collectively cultivate this form of attention. This attention is directed toward the process of thought (which, as we recall, is not limited to the cognitive aspect but also includes the emotions, the body and, moreover, has a collective dimension).

The practice of dialogue makes space for creativity, insight and a form of enlightenment, which are all aspects related to the practice of meditation. Bohm recognizes this potential when he talks about dialogue in the following way:

> We need a kind of social enlightenment to help that [experiencing our wholeness together] take place. In the past, people have developed ways to foster individual enlightenment, a higher intelligence for the individual through meditation or mystical insight or what-have-you. But we haven't worked on ways to develop a higher social intelligence. (Briggs, 1989, p. 111)

This dimension of dialogue is, in my view, what distinguishes it the most from the other models of dialogue such as those of Freire or Buber. It is also the dimension, which is the closest to the essence of dialogue. On the other hand, it is also the most counter cultural aspect in the sense that it does not have any utilitarian function and is not aimed at doing but at being and, like meditation, it requires intentionality and perseverance.

Many participants mentioned the parallels between dialogue and the practice of meditation, while I felt some resistance from others (a resistance Bohm did not have) to link dialogue to meditation.

4.5.1   Resources

It is not possible to talk about meditation, attention, awareness, mindfulness without referring to Buddhism which has explored systematically the human's inner world for more than two thousand years and has developed techniques to train the mind. For a few years now, many Western scientists have become interested in meditation[11] and it is possible to get a grounding in the practice of meditation without having to adopt any kind of religion or philosophy.

The work of Dr. Kabat-Zinn at the University of Massachusetts is relevant. He proposes cultivating a more mindful life through the practice of meditation to transform society (1995). His book (1994), *Wherever You Go There You Are: Mindfulness Meditation in Everyday Life*, is highly recommended to those wanting to become initiated with this dimension of dialogue.[12] Other excellent works on the practice of meditation are also recommended: Jack Kornfield's (1993), *A Path with Heart* and Golstein, and Kornfield's (1987), *Seeking the Heart of Wisdom*. In his book *Living the*

Mindful Life, psychologist Charles Tart provides a list of readings on meditation.

It is also important to mention the work of German philosopher and psychologist Georg Kühlewind (1984, 1988). He, like Bohm, sees in our capacity to develop a form of attention subtle enough to grasp the functioning of thought when it operates, a stage in the evolution of human consciousness. In his volumes *From Normal to Healthy* and *Stages of Consciousness*, he proposes many exercises to develop concentration, attention and attention to the process of thought; moreover, he provides an in-depth discussion on the functioning of thought.

Not to talk about the work of Krishnamurti would be unfair to those wanting to go deeper into this dimension of dialogue. In fact, as mentioned in Chapter 3, those who are familiar with the work of philosopher Krishnamurti will find many parallels between Bohm's thinking and Krishnamurti's. That should not come as a surprise since these two great thinkers were close friends and this friendship lasted until Krishnamurti's death in 1986. Among the many books written by him, I would recommend: *The Flame of Attention, The Network of Thought, Freedom from the Known* and *The Only Revolution*.

Finally, one aspect of this dimension of dialogue refers to the importance of being in the here and now, of being in contact with one's body, emotions and thoughts.

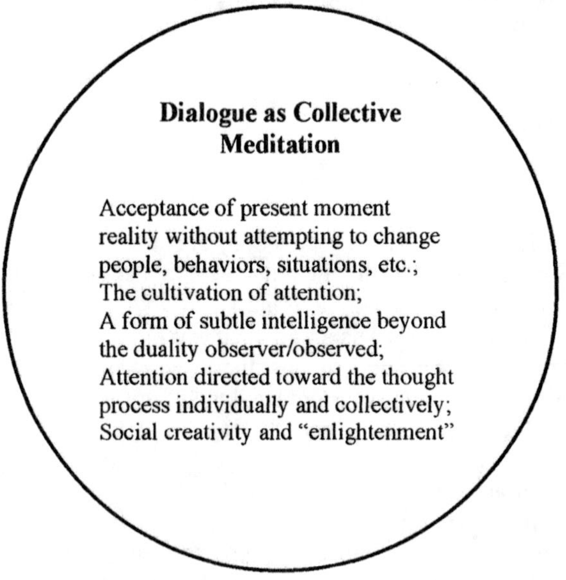

Dialogue as Collective Meditation

Acceptance of present moment
reality without attempting to change
people, behaviors, situations, etc.;
The cultivation of attention;
A form of subtle intelligence beyond
the duality observer/observed;
Attention directed toward the thought
process individually and collectively;
Social creativity and "enlightenment"

Figure 6. Dialogue as Collective Meditation Dimension

Figure 6 provides an overview of this dimension, noting the attributes of dialogue as collective meditation. Being in the here and now is at the heart of Gestalt therapy. Taking into account the comments from some participants in regard to the difficulties in dialogues to express one's emotions and deal with the emotions, which are expressed, it would be helpful to consult a volume from Perls, Hefferline, and Goodman *Gestalt Therapy* and get acquainted with this form of therapy. Regarding emotions, Goleman's (1995) *Emotional Intelligence* is a must for those interested by self-awareness, empathy and the relationships between emotions and thoughts.

5.   FINAL THOUGHTS

Here I will mention one last thing about this model: It is not free from tensions and paradoxes. For example, how can one reconcile conversation, which puts emphasis on empathy, listening and receptivity with inquiry that explores and questions? This tension can be illustrated by one example. In one of the dialogue groups I visited during my research, one woman only wanted to talk, share with others; she did not want to focus on the individual and collective assumptions and wanted even less to reflect on the process. Her attachment to conversation and the attachment of other participants to inquiry degenerated into a violent argument and resulted in the woman leaving and never coming back.

How can one reconcile the no-goal characteristic of meditation with the purposes of other dimensions, for example the creation of a shared meaning, the surfacing of the collective assumptions, etc.. In other words, the different dimensions of this model can very easily be in contradiction with one another. And it is precisely in such a situation that it is imperative to initiate a dialogue.

One must not be naive and think that the presentation of this model will resolve all problems. No model can resolve problems. Models are a creation of the human mind. And when we grow attached to our models, to the creations of our minds, we then give up our capacity to create. That price is much too high. Let us hope that individually and collectively we have the courage not to become too attached to the creations of our minds and, consequently, keep our capacity to create. It is what the practice of dialogue invites us to do.

NOTES

[1] The expression "difficult to understand" is one of the three meanings attributed to the word "esoteric" by *The American Dictionary of the English Language* (Houghton Mifflin, Boston, 1981). The two other meanings are: "Intended for or understood by only a small group" and "Not publicly disclosed; confidential."

[2] I am referring to the following texts: *On Dialogue, Thought as a System*, and *Changing Consciousness*.

[3] For those who are not familiar with Bateson's work (1972) on the different levels of learning, I include a brief description of these levels of learning taken from Berman, 1984, p. 354:

> Learning I: The simple solution of a specific problem.
>
> Learning II: Progressive change in the rate of Learning I. Understanding the nature of the context in which the problems posed in Learning I exist; learning the rules of the game. Equivalent to paradigm formation.
>
> Learning III: An experience in which a person suddenly realizes the arbitrary nature of his or her own paradigm, or Learning II, and goes through a profound reorganization of personality as a result...

[4] A comment made by one of the participants illustrates this very eloquently. To the question "What are the most profound, significant experiences you've had in dialogue?" he answered the following:

> P: ...he [David Bohm] was presenting an idea that he wanted to pursue, that he believed to be true, and he could see that I couldn't go with what he was saying.
>
> R: You couldn't...
>
> P: No. And he let go of the idea. I feel that was a lot for him to do, because he was a deep thinker and a professionally qualified person and the main attraction of the whole activity. He let go of what he had prepared in favor of our friendship, because he felt that our movement together was more important than the idea. I was very moved by that."

[5] Argyris (1982) who dedicated a lot of time to help individuals and organizations shift from Learning I to Learning II, goes even further when he says that he met very few individuals and organizations practicing Learning II.

[6] I can only speculate on the reasons for his refraining to do so. The most obvious one would be that he could not find any methodology that was not contrary to the essence of dialogue.

[7] I believe it is important to show the difference between the "dialogues" of the hunter-gatherer bands and dialogues of today. For hunter-gatherers, participation in "dialogues" was something obvious; it was natural and cultural. Moreover, participation to the life of the band meant roof, food, and survival. For us, participation in a group comes from deliberate involvement, intention, and voluntary choice. Furthermore, there is an "opportunity cost" to our decision to join a dialogue group. Our cultural and social environment offers so many activities that the practice of dialogue occupies time that could be used many different ways. Consciously or not, our participation in dialogue is often compared to other activities with objectives more or less similar.

[8] Skolimowski (1994) addresses this topic. His book is presented in the next section.

[9] In my descriptive model, this first quality is part of the fifth dimension "dialogue as collective meditation".

[10] The boundaries between the dimensions of "participative process" and "collective meditation" become very vague when we look at the evolution of human consciousness. Participation, as described above by Bohm, seems to be at the heart of the next stage of the evolution of human consciousness. Many people see in meditation and in attention a privileged way to acknowledge and become aware of our interconnectedness.

[11] In this respect, it is appropriate to mention the Symposium organized by the Harvard Medical School's Department of Continuing Medical Education and held in 1991 at MIT and attended by leading authorities from the fields of medicine, psychiatry, psychology, neurobiology and education as well as by His Holiness the Dalai Lama and other Indo-Tibetan scholars. The transcript of the Symposium has been published in a volume entitled: *MindScience: An East-West Dialogue.*

[12] Some of the participants in this research showed some hesitation to practice meditation while others mentioned that the practice of dialogue spared them from practicing meditation. I strongly believe that daily practice oriented towards cultivating mindfulness and self-awareness nurtures the practice of dialogue and makes it richer.

REFERENCES

Anderson, W.T., 1990. *Reality Isn't What It Used To Be.* Harper & Row, San Francisco.

Argyris, C., 1982. *Reasoning, Learning and Action: Individual and Organizational.* Jossey-Bass, San Francisco.

Argyris, C., 1993. *Knowledge for Action.* Jossey-Bass, San Francisco.

Argyris, C., Putnam, R., and Smith, D., 1985. *Action Science.* Jossey-Bass, San Francisco.

Assagioli, R., 1965. *Psychosynthesis: A Manual of Principles and Techniques.* Hobbs, New York.

Barfield, O., 1965. *Saving the Appearances: A Study in Idolatry.* Harcourt, New York.

Bateson, G., 1972. *Steps to An Ecology of Mind.* Ballantine, New York.

Belenky, M., Clinchy, B., Goldberger, N., and Tarule, J., 1986). *Women's Ways of Knowing: The Development of Self, Voice, and Mind.* Basic Books, New York.

Berman, M., 1984. *The Reenchantment of the World.* Bantam, New York.

Berman, M., 1990. *Coming to Our Senses: Body and Spirit in the Hidden History of the West.* Bantam, New York.

Bohm, D., 1989. *Thought and 'felt'.* David Bohm Seminars, Ojai, CA.

Bohm, D., 1990. *David Bohm: On dialogue.* David Bohm Seminars, Ojai, CA.

Bohm, D., 1992. *Thought As a System.* David Bohm Seminars, Ojai, CA.

Bohm, D., and Edwards, M., 1991. *Changing Consciousness: Exploring the Hidden Source of the Social, Political and Environmental Crises Facing Our World.* HarperCollins, San Francisco.

Bohm, D., Factor, D., and Garrett, P., 1991. *Dialogue-A proposal.* (Available from Dialogue, Hawthorn Cottage, Broad Marston Lane, Mickleton, Glos. GL55 6SF England).

Bohm, D., and Kelly, S., 1990. Dialogue on science, society, and the generative order. *Zygon,* **25**:449-467.

Bohm, D., and Peat, D.F., 1987. *Science, Order, and Creativity.* New Bantam, New York.

Briggs, J. (1989, Sept./Oct.). Quantum leap: A New Age Journal interview with David Bohm. *New Age Journal, 44-49,* 110-114.

Buber, M., 1958) *I and Thou.* Scribner, New York.

Burbules, N.C., 1993. *Dialogue in Teaching: Theory and Practice.* Teachers College Press, New York.

Cissna, K. N., and Anderson, R., 1994. The 1957 Martin Buber-Carl Rogers dialogue, as a dialogue. *Journal of Humanistic Psychology,* **34**: *11-45.*

de Maré, P., Piper, R., and Thompson, S., 1991. *Koinonia: From Hate, Through Dialogue, to Culture in the Large Group.* Karnac, London.

Feuerstein, G, 1987. *Structures of Consciousness: The Genius of Jean Gebser–An Introduction and Critique.* Integral Publishing, Lower Lake, CA.

Freire, P., 1970. *Pedagogy of the Oppressed.* Herder and Herder, New York.

Gergen, K.J., 1991. *The Saturated Self: Dilemmas of Identity in Contemporary Life*. Basic Books, New York.

Gilligan, C., 1982. *In a Different Voice: Psychological Theory and Women's Development*. Harvard University Press, Cambridge, MA.

Goldstein, J., and Kornfield, J., 1987. *Seeking the Heart of Wisdom: The Path of Insight Meditation*. Shambhala, Boston, MA.

Goleman, D., 1995. *Emotional Intelligence*. Bantam, New York.

Goleman, D., and Thurman, R.A. (eds.), 1991. *Mindscience: An East-West Dialogue His Holiness the Dalai Lama et al.* Wisdom Publication, Boston.

Grof, S., 1985. *Beyond the Brain: Birth, Death and Transcendence in Psychotherapy*. SUNY, Albany, NY.

Guisinger, S., and Blatt, S. J., 1994. Individuality and relatedness: Evolution of a fundamental dialectic. *American Psychologist*, 49: 104-111.

Hawkins, P., 1991. The spiritual dimension of the learning organization. *Management Education and Development*, 22: 172-187.

Hermans, H.J., and Kempen, H.J., 1993. *The Dialogical Self: Meaning as Movement*. Academic Press, San Diego.

Kabat-Zinn, J., 1994. *Wherever You Go There You Are: Mindfulness Meditation in everyday Life*. Hyperion, New York.

Kabat-Zinn, J., 1995. The contemplative mind in society. *Noetic Sciences Review*, 35: 14-21.

Kornfield, J., 1993. *A Path With Heart: A Guide Through the Perils and Promises of Spiritual Life*. Bantam, New York.

Krishnamurti, J., 1982. *The Network of Thought*. Harper & Row, New York.

Krishnamurti, J., 1984. *The Flame of Attention*. HarperCollins, New York.

Krishnamurti, J., 1969). *Freedom From the Known*. Gollancz, London.

Krishnamurti, J., 1970). *The only revolution*. London: Gollancz.

Kühlewind, G. (1984. *Stages of Consciousness: Meditations on the Boundaries of the Soul*. Lindisfarne Press, Great Barrington, MA.

Kühlewind, G., 1988. *From Normal to Healthy: Paths to the Liberation of Consciousness*. Lindisfarne Press, Hudson, NY.

Mindell, A., 1992. *The Leader As Martial Artist: An Introduction to Deep democracy*. HarperCollins, New York.

Mindell, A., 1995. *Sitting in the Fire: Large Group Transformation Using Conflict and Diversity*. Lao Tse Press, Portland, OR.

Noddings, N., 1991. Stories in dialogue: Caring and interpersonal reasoning. In C. Witherell, and N. Noddings (eds.), *Stories Lives Tell: Narrative and Dialogue in Education*, Teachers College Press, New York, pp. 157-170.

Noddings, N., 1994. Learning to engage in moral dialogue. *Holistic Education Review*, 7: 5-12.

Peat, D., 1992. Un pionnier du troisième millénaire: Hommage à David Bohm. *3e millénaire*, 26 : 72-75.

Perls, F.S., Hefferline, R.F., and Goodman, P., 1965. *Gestalt Therapy: Excitement and Growth in the Human Personality*. Dell, New York.

Reason, P., (ed.), 1994. *Participation in Human Inquiry*. Sage, London.

Rogers, C.R., 1965. *Client-centered Therapy: Its current Practice, Implications, and Theory*. Houghton Mifflin, Boston, MA.

Sampson, E.E., 1985. The decentralization of identity: Toward a revised concept of personal and social order. *American Psychologist*, 40: 1203-1211.

Schein, E.H., 1993. On dialogue, culture, and organizational learning. *Organizational Dynamics*, 22: 40-51.

Schön, D.A., 1983. *The Reflective Practitioner: How Professionals Think in Action*. Basic Books, New York.

Schön, D.A., 1987. *Educating the Reflexive Practitioner: Toward a New Design for Teaching and Learning in the Professions.* Jossey-Bass, San Francisco.

Skolimowski, H., 1994. *The Participatory Mind: A New Theory of Knowledge and of the Universe.* Penguin, London.

Stone, H., and Winkelman, S., 1993. *Embracing Ourselves: The Voice Dialogue Manual.* Nataraj, San Rafael, CA.

Tart, C.T., 1994. *Living the Mindful Life.* Shambhala, Boston.

Utne Reader (March/April 1991). Salons: *The art of conversation.* **44**: 66-88.

Walsh, R. N., and Vaughan, F., (eds.), 1980. *Beyond Ego: Transpersonal Dimensions in Psychology.* J.P. Tarcher, Los Angeles.

Weber, R., 1990. *Dialogue With Scientists and Sages: The Search for Unity.* Penguin, London.

Wilber, K., 1977. *The Spectrum of Consciousness.* Quest, Wheaton, IL.

Wilber, K., 1979. *No boundary: Eastern and Western Approaches to Personal Growth.* Shambhala, Boston, MA.

Wilber, K., 1980. *The Atman project: A transpersonal view of human development.* Quest, Wheaton, IL.

Yalom, I.D., 1980. *Existential Psychotherapy.* Basic Books, New York.

Zohar, D., amd Marshall, I., 1993. *The Quantum Society: Mind, Physics and a New Social Vision.* Bloomsbury, London.

Chapter 9

FACILITATING A GLOBAL CONVERSATION THROUGH THE UNIVERSAL DEMOSOPHIA FACILITY

MATTHEW A. SHAPIRO
Research Associate, CWA Ltd. and President, Mary Parker Follett Foundation

1. INTRODUCTION AND RATIONALE

Demosophia is a word derived from Greek roots to mean "wisdom of the people," (Christakis, 1993). It is not something that is already extant, lying there ready to be used, nor is it something that can be tapped through opinion polls and voting. It is something that must be produced continually and which can only be manifested through human interaction of a progressive nature. For its full expression, demosophia requires two other conditions, whose names are also derived from the Greek: democracy and sizitisis. Democracy is literally "power of the people," and sizitisis means "searching together through conversation." These three–demosophia, democracy, and sizitisis–form a great triad of authentic power, the absence of any one of them significantly diminishing the quality of the whole.

If we conclude that democratic process, policy-making and power should be grown from the innermost units of family, neighborhood, village, or clan outwards, and that this is based on the ability of people to engage in dialogue and co-creation, and that in a complex world various issues require various degrees of scope of deliberation, then we see a need for a means of facilitating such deliberation in a way which maximizes the involvement of the innermost unit and minimizes the need for representatives as proxies.

If we further conclude that conversation at the community level is the best method for making decisions affecting the common interest, then we must seek ways in which such conversation can be facilitated for efficiency and to better allow the creativity and demosophia of the communities to emerge. There is in particular a need for means to effectively grapple with

Dialogue as a Means of Collective Communication, Edited by Banathy and Jenlink
Kluwer Academic/Plenum Publishers, New York 2005

complexity, for so many of the issues that we face today involve more than just a few elements and relationships. This condition calls for some discipline and structure to our collective thought-process.

We now have three working premises: (1) Open yet structured conversation at the community level is the decision-making mode of choice. (2) Various issues require various degrees of scope of deliberation in a complex world. (3) We need a means of facilitating such deliberation in a way that maximizes the involvement of the innermost unit and minimizes the use of intermediaries. Given these premises, we need a method that can facilitate inter-group and trans-group deliberation on a very large scale. Given that a large-scale deliberation among groups could include thousands or even millions of conversations, it is not feasible for our facilitation process to be based mainly upon direct communication between or across groups, for the latter could only be done meaningfully between a few groups at a time.

If, however, the distributed communities were to agree to common triggering questions, a common format, and the use of a global communication system, there may be a way to meet both needs. A system can be created that will portray the essential products of all policy conversations and to allow each community to observe their own, any other, any combination of others, and a total picture simultaneously, thereby portraying a trans-group conversation which can then be supplemented or complemented by inter-group conversation.

The following are the features that we would seek in a "demosophia facility" that expresses this vision:

- Unlimited participation
- Collaborative decision-making
- Preservation of the uniqueness of issues and solutions
- Elimination of redundancy in issue-presentation and ideas
- Communication of relative quantities and dominance of views and ideas
- Conservation of variety, saliency, and parsimony, and other factors required for the effective, participatory management of complex situations.

These, then, become the specifications behind the development of the Universal Demosophia Facility.

2.   THE UNIVERSAL DEMOSOPHIA FACILITY

The Universal Demosophia Facility (UDF) is a proposed system for the enabling of inter-communal and trans-communal communication that minimizes the need for intervening vertical structures and maximizes the emergence of demosophia through participatory modes of decision-making, with unlimited potential for numerical and ethno-linguistic inclusiveness. By "facility" is meant a mind-set and a skill-set as well as the technology and physical space designed to support the surfacing and application of demosophia locally and globally.

In order to fulfill the specifications given above, a combination of powerful technologies is required. UDF represents integration of four such technologies. The first of these is called Interactive Management, which will be represented here by its leading example, CogniScope^{TM}. The second is the United Nation's Universal Networking Language. The third we will call the Semantic Aggregator. The fourth is the Internet. There is a fifth and non-technological aspect to the UDF: access. This includes issues of technology transfer, financing, and cross-cultural adaptation. Access will be addressed later when we consider issues of implementation. At present, we will go through each of the four technological aspects and the significance of each.

2.1 Interactive Management: Collaborative Decision-Making and Complexity Management

Interactive Management (IM) is a decision-making methodology that is designed for the complexity of real-world issues and is based upon dialogue among stakeholders in an issue or set of issues. IM employs computer support models that help participants overcome cognitive limitations related to complexity. CogniScope is the trademarked name of the best-proven implementation of IM. CogniScope integrates open and focused dialogue with consensus methods, skilled facilitation, and computer-aided Interpretive Structural Modeling (ISM) to make sense out of complex issues. The process engages the creativity and diversity of the participants and it helps them to build consensus and converge on "collaborative action plans" that have a high degree of coherence and likelihood of success when implemented. This extraordinarily successful methodology is based upon the work of organizational consultant Alexander Christakis and IM pioneer John Warfield, and it has been widely applied through the services of consulting firm CWA, Ltd. It was through Christakis and the pioneers of Interactive Management that the Greek word *demosophia* entered the lexicon of progressive community-builders (Christakis, 1993).

2.2   The Universal Networking Language: The Language of the Inter-Facility

The Universal Networking Language (UNL) is a computer-based language that has been designed by an agency of the United Nations to enable people to communicate in their mother language with peoples of different languages. The system consists of a network and a conversation system between UNL and native languages utilizing "enconverters" and "deconverters" designed by native speakers. Its purpose is to provide a linguistic bridge for harmonious information exchange, ultimately in the cause of reconciliation and peace among nations. One of the key features distinguishing UNL from machine translation systems is that a passage of text or speech need only be translated *once* for it to be accessible to speakers of any language who have the deconverter at their disposal. Another key feature is that the system minimizes the imposition of meaning through the de-centralization of enconverters and deconverters and through its capacity to accept new concepts into the set of "universal words."

UNL has been under development since 1996 by the Institute for Advanced Studies at the United Nations University, based in Tokyo, Japan. The development work has shifted to the UNDL Foundation, based in Geneva, Switzerland. The UNL itself has been completed and partners in various nations have been developing the enconverters and deconverters for their respective languages. The first stage of the UNL project is to create conversion modules for 16 languages. Those include the six official U.N. languages–Arabic, Chinese, English, French, Russian and Spanish–as well as German, Hindi, Indonesian, Italian, Japanese, Latvian, Mongolian, Portuguese, Swahili and Thai. Conversion software for each language is being developed in partnership with governments, research institutes, universities and participating companies. The aim is for the languages used by all U.N. members–now 185 countries–to be supported by UNL by the year 2005. UNL will be available globally through software plug-ins designed for the medium of the Internet.

2.3   Semantic Aggregator: Global Participation and Conversational Integration

The Semantic Aggregator is the name given to a means of taking a theoretically unlimited number of discrete ideas that have been generated in response to a common triggering question, assessing their closeness in meaning, sorting them into the categories of "identical, "similar," and "unique," and displaying a "map" of these ideas in a useful way. The purpose of this system will be to provide participants with an accurate picture of their collective thought-in-progress by reducing redundancy, preserving uniqueness, and conveying the relative quantities of contributions. This is a key to lateral or horizontal collaboration among a large number of groups who are pursuing a common inquiry while seeking to avoid "groupthink" and the watering down of input.

The Semantic Aggregator would incorporate an automatic text analysis engine that draws from (a) a pre-determined set of "affinity ratings" within groups of concepts from the UNL's universal pool, (b) a weighting system, and (c) an automatic pair-wise comparison process for the generation of clusters of uniques, similars, and identicals on a continuous basis.

2.4   The Internet: The Medium

The Internet is a network of electronic networks through which information is transmitted among millions of computers, from PC's in the home to mainframe systems. The hallmark of the Internet is a relative lack of regulation and centralized control. In its current form the Internet can deliver data, text, and audio at high speed. Video transmission remains slow, but is improving. Faster and higher-capacity Internet facilities are under development. The Internet is the medium of choice for the UNL system and will most likely also be the medium of transmission for the UDF.

2.5   The Integrated System

When we bring together the local demosophia facility represented by the use of IM/CogniScope, the cross-lingual bridge of Universal Networking Language, and the mass-leveling Semantic Aggregator across the global electronic network of the Internet, we may come close to achieving our goal of a Universal Demosophia Facility: a union of distributed demosophia facilities. Its use would facilitate a disciplined and creative conversation among people across nations and across the globe, with each group speaking as an individual. Within each community of participants, however, it is essential that dialogue and co-creation be the chief mode of decision-making; this is the humanistic, non-technological foundation of the system.

3.   COGNISCOPE: A CLOSER LOOK

The CogniScope system is a specialized process aimed at collaborative teamwork by a community of stakeholders, leading to the definition of a complex situation and the design of an action plan for the resolution of that situation. The process enables stakeholders to merge language, cognition, and action. Through open and focused dialogue the community generates and clarifies a large number of elementary ideas (sometimes over 300) and design interactively an "action plan" which is co-owned by the stakeholders because it has been co-created. This is achieved with great efficiency through the combination of effective facilitation, computer support, appropriate consensus tools, and participants' commitment to an intensive effort. To date, CogniScope has seen hundreds of applications in a wide range of contexts and cultures in the public and private sectors.

After developing a knowledge base about the issue they are grappling with, the stakeholders employ the CogniScope system to perform three principal activities (Christakis, 1996):

- Generation and clarification of the meanings of ideas contributed by the stakeholders in response to properly framed *triggering questions* that are specific variations on "What should we do?" and "How can we do what we should do?"
- Production of "idea patterns" which result from exploring relationships among ideas in the context of carefully-framed *generic questions*.
- Evaluation of idea patterns and action packages in response to agreed-upon *criteria*.

These activities are embedded in four distinct but interrelated stages in the application of the CogniScope system.

- Defining the problem or design situation by making statements in a round-robin fashion in response to the initial open-ended triggering question, clarifying these statements, clustering these by affinity in order to reveal the dimensionality of the problem or challenge, and exploring the influence and enhancement relationships to produce a visual pattern;
- Designing alternatives by generating solution ideas, clustering them, exploring their likely enhancement relationships and how they would address the issues identified in the Definition stage (again generating a visual pattern of influence), and then choosing from among key options within clusters of affinity;
- Choosing a preferred alternative according to agreed-upon criteria, usually employing trade-off evaluation; and

- <u>Planning</u> for action, which includes considering the most effective sequence for implementation of the preferred solution alternative.

To assist users in grappling with complexity, CogniScope employs a computer-assisted methodology known as Interpretive Structural Modeling, which allows the exploration of relationships among a great number of elements without overwhelming the short-term memory capacities of the participants. ISM helps reveal influence relationships among elements, which in turn helps participants focus their priorities as well as learn about their own assumptions and decision preferences.

Christakis and Bausch (2002) describe this integration of dialogue and technology as "technologue," and describe what its users are able to achieve:

> In contrast to many group encounters where an initial euphoria is drained away in linguistic Babel, the technologue advances further dialogue that clarifies, surfaces values, and generates enhancement patterns. The results of this process are emancipation of the stakeholders, individual and collective learning, integration of diverse viewpoints, discernment of salient priorities for design, and the emergence of a situation-specific consensual linguistic domain that enables understanding and meaningful action.

Through the use of this "technologue," the group is not only able to generate highly effective action plans while constructing shared meaning, but they are able to do it far more efficiently. The software program embedded in the system is said to increase the speed of group work by up to 20 times and to deepen analyses as much as five times for large-scale applications involving 150 observations and twenty participants. It would not be possible to construct the observed patterns of influence and interaction of issues and ideas in a reasonable amount of time without the use of this software.

The CogniScope process, and the science that it represents, is founded upon six laws that have been observed at work in situations wherein stakeholders are identifying issues and solutions – what Christakis and Bausch (2002) call the "construction of observations". These six laws have been distilled from the work and the field experience of key cognitive researchers, semanticists, and facilitators throughout the 20th century. They are discussed extensively in the literature, but the following provides an overview (Christakis and Bausch, 2002):

- The Law of Requisite Variety (Ashby's Law) says that a design must possess an amount of variety that is at least equal to the variety of the problem situation. This means that the group dealing with a complex situation must surface the full dimensionality of an issue. This may be achieved, at least in part, by ensuring that there is adequate representation of observers.

- The Law of Requisite Parsimony (Miller's Law) says that human beings can only deal simultaneously with between five and nine observations at one time. This is based on knowledge about limitations in human short-term memory.
- The Law of Requisite Saliency (Boulding's Law) addresses the importance of an observation, such as a problem or a solution, relative to other observations in a set. Ignoring relative saliency typically results in low productivity and in the under-conceptualization of the issue that the participants are dealing with.
- The Law of Requisite Meaning (Peirce's Law) says that it is essential that the observations and meanings of the stakeholders be surfaced through inquiry into the relational structure amongst observations. In the context of an Interactive Management deliberation, these relationships include those of affinity, difference, influence, and temporality (time sequence).
- The Law of Requisite Autonomy of Distinction-Making (Tsivacou's Law) says as the group seeks the best path of exploration through an issue and develops through their observations a "consensual linguistic domain," no participant must be allowed to monopolize the power of distinction-making, and the autonomy of individual distinction-making must be ensured. This is achieved, for example, by allowing each participant to retain authorship of his or her contributions and by providing every participant with an equal chance to speak and to persuade.
- The Law of Requisite Evolution of Observations (Dye's Law), the most recently discovered, states that

> Whenever observations made by stakeholders in the context of a complex design situation are interdependent, assigning priorities for action on the basis of aggregating individual observer's "importance voting" leads to erroneous priorities and ineffective actions. The effective priorities for action emerge after an evolutionary search of interdependencies among the observations through a dialogue focusing on 'influence voting.'

It is important to again emphasize the necessity for skilled facilitation in ensuring that these laws are taken into account to guide the participants toward the most powerful, implementable, consensus-based resolution to their collective inquiry.

As of today, CogniScope has been employed almost exclusively in a synchronous mode and within single groups. The key challenge when taking it to a multi-group and asynchronous mode will be to maintain the integrity of the process, i.e., that it remains a place for open and focused dialogue among stakeholders with equal voice in the group and allows them to find consensus through converging on a set of priorities and actions.

4.   UNIVERSAL NETWORKING LANGUAGE: A CLOSER LOOK

The Universal Networking Language (UNL) is an artificial language in the form of a semantic network for computers that enables people to communicate in their mother tongue with people of different mother tongues. The UNL has been in development since 1996 by the United Nations University's Institute for Advanced Studies.

The UNL has three key components: the *editor*, which allows users to write into UNL without any knowledge of the UNL structure; the *enconverter*, which converts a natural language into UNL; and the *deconverter*, which converts the UNL into a natural language. Once a text has been converted into UNL, it can be accessed directly into any language connected to the UNL system. Enconverters and deconverters are now in service for a limited number of languages. There are plans to make the UNL available to all of the languages spoken by the UN's 185 member nations by the year 2005.

4.1 How the UNL Expresses Information

The UNL expresses information and meaning sentence by sentence, utilizing a set of *Universal Words* ("UWs") and a variety of relations between those words. The Universal Words, for which there is a very large database, are taken from English to represent discrete concepts. They are supplemented by words from other languages in cases where it is not possible to capture their meaning effectively using English words or phrases.

There are three different kinds of Universal Words: Basic, Restricted, and Extra. The first type of UW represents a general concept. Restricted UWs are used to further restrict the range of meaning of Basic UWs. Extra UWs are introduced as extra categories in the UNL statement when there is no satisfying match for a Basic UW.

The UNL represents relations among these UWs with a set of binary relations. There are 41 different types of relations used. Examples include "agt" or Agent (a thing which initiates an action), gol (Goal/Final State, the final state associated with the object of an event), and Rsn (Reason, a reason that an event or a state happens).

While the Universal Words and the Relations serve to describe the "objective" aspect of statements, the subjectivity of statements is conveyed through *attributes*. Attributes show the speaker's point of view, including such things as speech acts, propositional attitudes, truth values, etc. There are four major types of Attributes, which address a range of factors such as time perspective, the focus of the speaker, the degree of generality or specificity, where the speaker places an emphasis, and the speaker's attitudes toward what is being said or who it is being said to.

Finally, the UNL features a Knowledge Base that defines possible binary relations among Universal Words.

4.2   How the UNL Functions

When someone uses the UNL, they enter a statement using the Editor. The Enconverter recognizes the "meaning" of the statement and matches words from the natural language (for example, Urdu) with Universal Words. The statement is now held in the UNL as a set of UWs oriented to each other by Relations, with Attributes attached to the UWs for subjective meaning. The user may then deconvert their statement back into their native language to check for accuracy and make changes if necessary. Upon final approval, the statement is now ready for direct deconversion into any language used in the UNL system.

A Deconverter (e.g., a French language deconverter) matches the UWs with concepts in French words and reads the relations and attributes so as to be able to reconstruct the entire statement in French, anywhere in the world, through the Internet.

Information expressed in UNL must ultimately be handled by any network system in the world. In order to achieve this aim, UNL is being designed for technical interface as an extension of HTML convention. Conforming to the HTML convention, the description of the UNL will be all made in plain text, and the format will be open to the public.

4.3   Capacity for Continuous Improvement

The UNL system retains a capacity to "learn" because the pool of Universal Words and the "word dictionaries" that are used to match natural language words with UNL concepts can be expanded and revised to improve the capability for users to express meaning. This process is being automated to the extent possible. Users are allowed to register as many Universal Words as they need. In doing so, they need to define not only a UW label, but also the correspondence with a word in their own language, together with a classification in the conceptual hierarchy. Provided this information, the UNL system will automatically manage UWs and provide deconversion capability. Universal Words with no access by users will be removed from the register.

5.   THE SEMANTIC AGGREGATOR

The Semantic Aggregator will be critical for integrating large numbers of issue and idea statements received in response to common triggering questions. It will compare and cluster statements according to their similarity of meaning *in the context of all other statements received*. In other words, this clustering must go on continuously until every response has been integrated. The result would be a display–in every participating Local Demosophia Facility–of every *unique* statement, a representative statement from a set of *similars*, and a representative statement from a set of *identicals*. Each local group will have the capability to look at all of the statements in a set of similars, and will also have the capability to determine the source of every statement displayed in the system.

To achieve this end, the Semantic Aggregator will likely consist of the integration of three elements:

- the **UNL enconversion process**, by which statements are parsed within the Universal Networking Language as an arrangement of Universal Words, relationships, and attributes;
- a set of **concept domains** in which every pair of different concept-terms (drawn from the universal pool of UNL) have been give *affinity ratings* in the context of all the other concept-terms in their domain;
- an **automatic text analysis engine** which (a) compares different elements of statements according to the similarity ratings within their respective concept domains, (b) weights them appropriately, and (c) conducts a pair-wise comparison of statements received in response to a common triggering question in order to classify them as uniques, similars, or identicals.

The parsing process is already an integral part of UNL. The proposed concept domains and affinity ratings between Universal Words will have to be generated in advance, and updated periodically, by a multi-cultural team of persons. This team should probably consist of both linguists and lay-speakers. To provide an example of their task, let's take "Conversation" as a concept domain. Such a domain might include the terms conversation, talk, intercourse, dialogue, discourse, discussion, deliberation, debate, gossip and chat, along with non-English words whose meaning cannot be effectively captured using any of those English words. Affinity ratings would be created prior to the implementation of the UDF, and updated on a continuous basis. Affinity might be assessed by "spatially" laying out and clustering the terms, the relative distance between each of them becoming the rating for that pair.

5.1   One Method of Semantic Aggregation

Determining the best approach to semantic aggregation will require a thorough survey of the state of the art in qualitative analysis. We will, however, explore one possible method here. As a statement enters the UDF from a Local Demosophia Facility, in response to a common triggering question for an issue of common concern, it is in the enconverted form of UNL. While in that condition, the statement can be assigned a *semantic code* based on two factors. The first factor would be the location of Universal Words in the statement within the pre-determined concept domains. For example, the term "nuclear waste" would be distinguished as being part of the concept domain "pollution" or "energy," and given a specific difference or affinity rating in relation to other Universal Words in that domain.

The second factor would be a weight assigned to the various relationships and attributes within the UNL statement. For example, the central dynamic and the object upon which that dynamic is acting would be weighted most heavily. The following is one possible hierarchy of weighting in a statement:

The **Dynamic**: The verb, the central action theme.
The **Object**: That upon which the dynamic is acting.
The **Actor**: That which is carrying out the dynamic.
The **Manner**: How the dynamic is being carried out.
The **Type**: The type of dynamic or object or actor; a modifier.
The **Reason**: The rationale or justification for the dynamic.
The **Negator**: The indicator of opposition or reduction of any element.

Not all statements will have all of these elements in them. All statements, however, will probably have a dynamic+object kernel. Many will have an actor and/or a manner. Some will have a type and/or a reason and/or a negator. It will require a careful analysis of the UNL relationships and attributes to determine how they might be best adapted to this weighting system.

The ideal next step would be to conduct a pair-wise comparison between the new statement and every other statement received, comparing the semantic codes with pre-determined affinity thresholds to determine the clusters of Uniques, Similars, and Identicals on a continuous and ultimately relative basis. However, this degree of comparison would be extremely demanding technically (involving up to *trillions* of automated comparisons in a full-scale, global CogniScope session with tens of thousands of participating communities). Furthermore, it may not be necessary for effective clustering.

What I would propose instead is each new statement be compared for affinity in a pair-wise fashion with each of the Uniques but only the *representative* Similars and Identicals currently in the system. This would dramatically reduce the processing power and time required to perform the semantic aggregation. The new statement would be matched with those of the greatest affinity.

If this affinity is within the first designated threshold, it will be aggregated into that cluster as an Identical (although it will remain accessible, with the click of a mouse, to anyone who wishes to see it). If the affinity is not within the first designated threshold but within the second, the statement will be aggregated with the representative Similar that it is closest in meaning to. (Again, even though it is not visible on the surface, any UDF user can examine it if desired). If it is simpler than this representative Similar, then it may even takes its place as the representative Similar for that cluster. If the closest statement happens to be an Identical, then that statement and the new one will form a new Similar. In other words, statements may be pulled out of the Identical clusters and into Similar clusters.

Finally, if the affinity between the new statement and the closest one is not within the second threshold, it will not be aggregated with any other statements; it will be displayed as a Unique. The same method would be used to display all of the products of the "Local Demosophia Facility" (LDF) sessions that are jointed in the UDF session, including clusters of issues, the enhancement patterns that show the influence and enhancement relationships, options fields (in which different solutions are displayed according to cluster and chosen from to form alternative action scenarios), criteria for choosing among options, and action sequences.

5.2   Adapting the UNL to the UDF

Developing the Semantic Aggregator for the UDF will require some additions to the existing UNL system. First, the development of an enconverter and deconverter for the English language may be required. English is the language used in the core of the Universal Networking Language. The Universal Words, although they might be configured to express virtually any word in any other language, are English words. It is not surprising that the developers of the UNL did not see a need for the creation of an English enconverter and deconverter, because people speaking to each other in English would have no need for language translation. However, when there are many English-speaking communities participating in the UDF, the comparison and sorting functions of the Semantic Aggregator must come into play.

Second, an interface will have to be developed between the UNL and the UDF. As indicated above, with the enconversion of statements into the UNL form, half of the work of the Semantic Aggregator is done. Upon the parsing of statement components according to their role and relationship and the conversion of key words into Universal Words, the Semantic Aggregator is ready to carry out its comparison and sorting functions. However, the UNL will need to be modified to interface with the Semantic Aggregator in order to enable the integration of distributed CogniScope applications.

5.3   The Visual Display of Uniques, Similars, and Identicals

The visual display of Uniques, Similars, and Identicals should convey a clear distinction between the three different types of clusters.

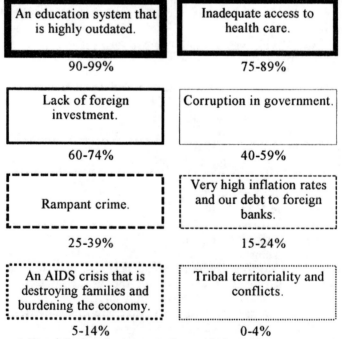

Figure 1. Visual display of uniques, similars, and identicals

This might be achieved through the use of different colors for the Uniques (Red), Similars (Blue), and Identicals (Green). The visual display should also convey the frequency of statements as a percentage of all communities participating in the UDF session, so that the viewer can quickly ascertain the relative predominance of a given issue or idea. This may be achieved through the use of different thickness of text boxes (see figure 1).

A very general triggering question in this example might be "What are the greatest obstacles to our development as a community?" The same general display strategies would be used for products of all of the phases of the UDF session.

6.   ASSESSING THE SPHERE OF INTERDEPENDENCE AND ESTABLISHING THE SCOPE OF DELIBERATION

The Universal Demosophia Facility concept is based upon the idea that decision-making should maximize the involvement of the most intimate community units and minimize the need for representatives. As the range of systemic impact and influence of given issues increases–due, for example, to cultural, economic, or environmental relationships–the scope of deliberation must therefore expand.

In preparing for a UDF conversation, it will be necessary for participating communities to establish an idea of the Sphere of Interdependence for their particular issue. The Sphere of Interdependence is the geographic, social, and political scale of the issue that creates stakeholders with a common interest in that issue. For example, educational policies might be more locally made: it's not easy to cross borders to "get" them, and their impacts will probably be more directly local. However, if it's easy to cross between communities in order to do something, such as buying and selling certain products, then deliberation should be larger in scope. Things that no one has exclusive access to at a given scale would need to be dealt with on a larger scale. Examples are oceans, the air, rivers, major forests and wildlands.

We might also look at a set of generic criteria such as the following:

(a) Can something be done without the help of others?
(b) Can something be done *well* without the help of others?
(c) Will an action taken here affect people in other places?
(d) Will an action taken in other places affect people here?
(e) Will an issue cross community boundaries?
(f) *Should* an issue cross community boundaries?
(g) Will an issue or issues *related* to this issue cross community boundaries?

The scope of deliberation might be defined using units such as the following, from innermost to outermost:

1. Neighborhood / Village / Town / Clan
2. City / County
3. Bio-Region
4. State / Province
5. Macro Bio-Region
6. National Region
7. Nation
8. World Region
9. World

7.   PLANNING AND COORDINATING A UDF CONVERSATION

Once the scope of deliberation has been established for a particular issue, communities within that particular sphere of interdependence would be invited to plan and to engage in the conversation on that issue. The UDF would need "channels" dedicated to various conversations in various spheres of interdependence.

CogniScope typically involves four major phases: Definition, Designing Alternatives, Choice, and Action Plan. Within each phase there are activities that can be described as either synchronous (activities requiring working together at the same time) or asynchronous (activities that can be performed alone). A single CogniScope application can be completed within two to three days. Sometimes it is broken up into two sessions of two days each. With a global UDF conversation, however, we need to allow for some differences in timing.

A typical CogniScope application is synchronous, meaning that the participants are on the same schedule. The aggregate schedule is roughly predictable based on how fast the individuals are able to work and how fast the interaction between them is. The overall effect is a normal range of four hours for the generation and clarification of observations, four hours for clustering and pair-wise relation activities, etc. In a UDF application involving hundreds, thousands, or even tens of thousands of communities, small differences in time requirements for the various CogniScope phases will become magnified to the point where at least some, if not all, of the phases will have to become asynchronous. This is true even without taking into account the time-zone issue when UDF sessions span broad areas of the globe.

The challenge then becomes, how do we preserve the interactivity between the Local Demosophia Facilities when they are working independently in time? Can the UDF be completely asynchronous, or does the integrity of the process of mutual learning and decision-making require at least some synchronous activity? We can best consider these questions by going through the principal activities of a typical CogniScope session.

In the Identification and Design phases, let's say that each Local Demosophia Facility conducts its generation of issues and solutions in response to the common triggering questions. In an asynchronous mode, the LDFs would not have the benefit of seeing what other communities' were generating in response to the triggering question until after all have completed this phase. This is probably acceptable because each LDF could use the lag time to review and utilize the Uniques, Similars, and Identicals from across the region or the globe. These would, include the Clarifications that accompany issues or ideas of particular interest. The individuals within those LDFs to decide whether they would like to expand or revise their own set thanks to the triggering of new ideas, determination of better phrasing, etc. The lag time could even be used for direct communication between LDFs for further clarification, using the UNL for language conversion.

A second principal activity in the UDF session will be the clustering of issues so that the dimensionality of the problem can be observed. If this were conducted independently by each LDF, without immediate reference to the dimensionality emerging in the other LDFs or on a global scale, mutual inspiration and learning could also be afforded during the lag time between the next phase. For example, an LDF in Cairo, Egypt could consider the classifications of problems generated by an LDF in Qatar, an LDF in Jerusalem, and an LDF in Paris. It might see how a different community located the same issue in a different cluster, or combined it with issues in a more effective way. A community would have a chance to revise its own characterization of dimensions during this time, which in turn would alter the global picture of dimensions. So this activity may be suited to asynchronous work as well.

A third principal activity in the UDF/CogniScope session will be the exploration of influence and enhancement relationships among issues and solution ideas. This is essential to revealing the relative leverage of problems and potential solutions. This leverage often remains hidden, or even worse, mistaken because it is typically assessed using flawed processes that do not take into account cognitive limitations. In a typical CogniScope session, participants might explore relationships among 20 different problems (or, in the design phase, solutions), going in both directions (e.g., "Does the persistence of issue x significantly aggravate the existence of issue y?" and vice-versa). The answers to these types of questions are determined by near-consensus among the local group, with the facilitator helping the group explore areas of disagreement.

This is one activity in which asynchronous work will not readily convey reflection and learning across the boundaries of LDFs. The LDFs can look at the resultant enhancement patterns generated by other groups, and some insight and thought can be triggered through this comparison, but an LDF will not be able to reproduce the thought that went into the individual pair-wise comparisons of another LDF which ultimately drove the creation of their enhancement pattern. This could represent a major potential breakdown of the system because just as a non-participant cannot look at an enhancement pattern (also known as a "problematique") and immediately grasp the logic of *why* Issue *x* was determined to be a deeper driver than Issue *y*, another group will not be able to do this, either. They might even disagree based on casual opinion.

On the other hand, there may not be significant differences between the way one group would have discerned leverage relationships and the way that another group would. Or it may depend upon the issue, on cultural factors, etc. It will require empirical evidence to properly assess whether or not this would create a significant gap in the progression toward highly effective and consensus-based action plans that is intended to be afforded by the UDF. In any event, the UDF will have the capability to display the differences and similarities between enhancement patterns. This alone, together with time for reflection of the nature of those differences and similarities, may afford us the cross-group stimulation and learning that we seek.

If there is a synchronous alternative, it would involve scheduling windows of time when all LDFs can participate in pair-wise relationship activity together, both among individuals within groups and then across groups where there is disagreement. Facilitation would be provided by a "facilitator-general" whose only window to the participating LDFs is the universal display of UDF work products. If thousands of LDFs are involved, however, such an activity would be rendered too unwieldy to be efficient.

Other activities involve the generation of options fields for the creation of alternative scenarios, the creation of criteria and weighting for trade-off evaluation and selection of solutions, and the sequencing of steps in the collaborative action plan. I believe that all of these can be conducted in an asynchronous mode without compromising the effectiveness of the methodology, provided that there is enough time between steps for reflection, inquiry, and revision.

In sum, it is likely that a UDF application or conversation can be conducted in a purely asynchronous mode. What takes a local CogniScope group (or LDF) three days to accomplish would need to be expanded to six or seven days, but the time expansion would be well worth the result gained. There are two more major intervening factors, however, that may expand this time-frame. The first is that if participation in the LDF is truly participatory and community-based, then it will require a method for mass citizen participation that is atypical of CogniScope experiences to date. This is addressed below. The second factor is that if there is disagreement at major decision points that can make or break the creation of a national law or the negotiation of an international treaty, such as the weighing of evaluation criteria during the Choice phase, it might be wisest to pause for an extended time period to allow for deeper exploration of the particular issue at hand.

Participating LDF communities could always teleconference with other communities during the pause periods if the other community or communities are agreeable to it. This would allow further opportunity for inquiry and interaction. Individual LDFs could even watch and listen to the dialogue in another LDF, and individuals could ask questions or even offer suggestions. The Universal Networking Language would be well-suited to enabling language conversion to take place during these direct community-to-community interactions.

7.1 Providing for Generative Dialogue

It is essential that diverse people who are working together develop an appreciation for the humanity and good will of those that they are working with. It is also essential that they develop some sense of shared meaning and understanding prior to, and while engaging in, a decision-oriented inquiry. To facilitate this development, we need to encourage a form of conversation called *generative dialogue*. This is distinguished from the decision-oriented form of inquiry, which can be called *strategic dialogue*.

It is important that we interweave the generative and strategic forms of dialogue in UDF conversations. To this end, a UDF conversation should begin with one to two weeks of local dialogue and inter-LDF teleconferencing that is not oriented toward agenda-setting, negotiation or decision-making, but simply toward the exploration of backgrounds, culture, and assumptions. These dialogues should probably involve clusters of only two or three LDFs that are diverse geographically, culturally, socially, and politically.

7.2 Adapting CogniScope for Mass Participation

If the Universal Demosophia Facility is to facilitate authentic community and provide an empowering experience for the general public, rather than only a select few who can sit at the table in an LDF facility, then the CogniScope component must be opened up for broad participation. How might this be done without compromising the direct, interpersonal encounter that allows a consensual linguistic domain and community to emerge? By sharing the work associated with a UDF conversation in a given community.

Specifically, there are stages of the CogniScope methodology that can be carried out by a large number of distributed groups, each with perhaps 10 to 20 participants, the integration of the product of these groups carried out by an integrating body that utilizes the computer technology essential to ISM and to the UDF. The key is to balance the work activity with the critical learning experiences so that all parties are full participants. Trust is also a major factor here, as the integrating body must effectively capture and conserve the diversity of what they have received and carry out their integrative tasks with the benefit of their whole community in mind.

In the proposed approach, an unlimited number of small discussion groups comprising the body of the community would do the bulk of the deliberative work, including the generation of issues, the generation of options, the creation of alternative models, and the development and weighting of evaluation criteria. The integrating body–which ideally is representative of all of the stakeholder groups in that community for the particular issue(s) under consideration–would help to organize the information generated in the aforementioned tasks by drawing relationships between issues and options, constructing the enhancement patterns, creating options fields, assigning scores to various options, and scoring alternative models. They might also be responsible for developing action sequences and designing implementation processes. This integrating body would be the body using the UDF to actualize a second-order integration with all of the other participating communities.

We have already seen how using the UDF in asynchronous mode among LDFs will expand the time frame for creating an action plan from two or three days to six or seven days. Adapting the process for mass participation at the local level expands this significantly further, as we must now take into account the scheduling of small groups of individual citizens – those stakeholders who are ultimately affected by the UDF conversation, thus being those with a right to participate in that conversation.

8.   THE LOCAL UDF FACILITY

Here we will address the physical setting for local UDF sessions. First, these facilities must meet all of the requirements for general CogniScope and small-to mid-size group deliberative activities. These requirements include a comfortable work space capable of accommodating up to 20 people sitting close enough to hear one another and facing each other in a non-hierarchical orientation. There must be a table for the facilitation team to work from, and a surface on which to project computer displays.

For the UDF application, additional requirements include the capacity to view three displays simultaneously: a display of the local group's work, a display of the cumulative global conversation, and a display of the work of any other participating LDF that is of interest. This calls for either three separate data projectors and a large projection surface, or the use of a split-screen display projected onto a large area. The LDF will also require a Internet connection, the specifications of which are not yet known.

If UDF conversations are to be public and involve extended communities, then there may be a large number of people who wish to observe the sessions. This would require a large-capacity viewers gallery or other seating facility, from which the observers could see the three UDF displays. In other words, a Local Demosophia Facility might need to be an auditorium type of setting with very large projection areas.

9. THE GLOBAL NETWORK: TECHNICAL CONSIDERATIONS

Let's use 100,000 as the absolute potential for number of participating Local Demosophia Facilities. This is equivalent to one LDF for every 70,000 people on the planet. This is the size of a small city, a cluster of neighborhoods in a large city, or a cluster of small towns. Precisely how the LDFs are distributed depends on spheres of interdependence, communities of place, and population distribution.

If during a Semantic Aggregation cycle the UDF had to analyze 100 statements from every one of the 100,000 LDF communities sent in response to a triggering question, then the system would–if every statement was determined to be a "Unique"–have to perform nearly 5 trillion comparisons over the course of a few hours. This might be feasible given adequate computing power. However, it is highly unlikely that every statement would be determined to be "Unique". Furthermore, we have already explored the reason why a comparison between every statement or item in a given phase is not likely to be necessary to accurately discern Uniques, Similars, and Identicals.

In order to spread the burden of computing power and to increase the integrity and security of the system, it might be preferable to link up the LDFs to regional node-servers operating in parallel. Each node-server would have to accommodate custom requests for information, such as the integrated maps of any two or more specified communities, or the specific items behind a cluster of "Similars." This would include requests from inside its own region for information from outside, as well as requests from outside for information within. In cases where a node-server fails, other node-servers would be able to assume their load.

Finally, it has been assumed that the Internet would be the means of linking LDFs to their various computer servers, both for the purposes of Semantic Aggregation, transmission of UDF data, and for the Universal

Networking Language function. However, many areas of the globe still do not have a sufficient telecommunication infrastructure to support this function. In order to make the UDF a reality before such infrastructure is in place, it may be necessary to consider Internet connection via satellite.

10.   SCOPE OF WORK

The development of the UDF would involve contributions from the fields of linguistics, computer programming and artificial intelligence, communications, multimedia, interactive management, anthropology, community development, and international relations.

10.1   Key Activities

Some of the key activities necessary for the development of the UDF are outlined below.

Assessment of Organizational and Social Requirements. This involves the question of "who" would develop and coordinate the UDF. Closely related is the assessment of social and cultural factors necessary to bring the spirit of the UDF to life, i.e., capacity for democratic interaction among citizens at the most local levels.

Assessment of Technical Requirements. This involves a complete assessment of the computer, working facility, audio-visual, and telecommunications equipment necessary to conduct UDF applications.

Assessment of Financial Requirements. This will involve assessing the cost of creating the software necessary for the UDF. It will also involve modeling the cost of implementation based on the cost of establishing and maintaining local facilities in nations and regions of different economic and technological readiness. This includes the cost of training and certification, licensing fees where applicable, requirements for regional node-servers, technical requirements applicable to all participating facilities, and personnel factors.

Procurement of Financial and Technical Resources. This involves identifying who would pay for the development of the UDF and how the costs of implementation would be covered, particularly in nations where resources are scarce. It also involves identifying the most suitable vendors and service providers for development and implementation.

Development of Concept Domains and Affinity Ratings. This will require a diverse group of persons working the UNL's Universal Words pool to create domains (if necessary) and pre-assign affinity ratings to concepts within domains, setting the stage for the Semantic Aggregator.

Development of the Semantic Aggregators. This will involve studying the UNL's relationships and Attributes, developing a weighting system, setting affinity thresholds, and developing the algorithm for aggregating statements and other factors that are generated through the UDF conversation. It will have to incorporate the technical requirement for aggregating items at a high rate and volume.

Development of the Visual Interface for the UDF. This involves designing the manner in which Uniques, Similars, and Identicals are displayed, as well as the display of individual statements and items, enhancement patterns, menus, help files, interactive maps, etc.

Creation of an English Enconverter and Deconverter for UNL. As described earlier, this is necessary so that the Semantic Aggregator can serve English-speaking communities. This may have already been accomplished by the UNL staff. If not, it will have to be commissioned.

Development of Additional Technical Dimensions. These dimensions include a Geographic Information System that can be integrated into the UDF, the specification and configuration of the UDF servers, and the various files that will need to be written to support the system, such as Installation and Help files.

Advancing the CogniScope Methodology. This needs to take place on two tracks. The first track is to create an interface between the CogniScope software, the UNL software, and the UDF software, once the latter is developed. The second track is simply extending the "technologue" to the community level and across the globe. The availability of the UDF technology does not substitute for the development of Interactive Management capacity. The application of a UDF will depend on the widespread extension of the mind-set and skill-set associated with the use of CogniScope to resolve system dilemmas in a democratic manner. This involves training and certification in the CogniScope methodology in order to preserve its integrity and effectiveness. This will, in turn, depend upon the continuous fostering of a democratic consciousness across the globe, which is of course a complex and long-term endeavor that is beyond the scope of this chapter.

Development and Testing of a Prototype. Once all of the components have been developed and integrated, a UDF prototype can be tested on any scale, from two groups who speak the same language to a large number of groups speaking different languages.

Full-scale Implementation. Once the prototype has proven successful, the UDF can move to full-scale pilot conversations conducted in a distributed mode across the world.

Continuous Expansion of the UDF. Expanding the UDF to be within reach of every community on the planet is the natural long-range goal. This would require substantial investment on the part of governments and/or private industry and could not be considered separately from general economic and educational development, particularly in regions challenged in this regard.

11. CONCLUSION

We need a democratic process that is capable of releasing the creativity of people and communities, of growing power from human interaction, and for dealing with the change and complexity of today's world. A new democratic consciousness will have at its root the development of the capacity for dialogue and co-creation at local levels. Should this capability become widespread, a means for extending the conversation will be necessary because of the complex and inter-dependent nature of public issues. We will obtain the greatest creativity and commitment from stakeholders if we can maximize the involvement of the smallest, innermost units of community and minimize the need for layers of representation. Should this groundwork of democratic consciousness be lain, the Universal Demosophia Facility concept may help to support its manifestation on a global level.

REFERENCES

Christakis, A.N., 1973. A new policy science paradigm, *Futures*, 5(6): 543-558.

Christakis, A.N., 1987. High technology participative design: The space-based laser. In John A. Dillon Jr. (ed.), *General Systems*, International Society for the Systems Sciences, Vol. XXX, New York, pp. 69-75.

Christakis, A.N., 1988. The club of Rome revisited. In W.J. Reckmeyer (ed.), *General Systems*, International Society for the Systems Sciences, Vol. XXXI. New York, pp. 35-38

Christakis, A.N., 1993. The inevitability of demosophia. In Ioanna Tsivacou (ed.), *A Challenge for Systems Thinking: The Aegean Seminar*, University of the Aegean Press, Athens, Greece, pp. 187-197.

Christakis, A.N., 1996. A people science: The cogniScope system approach, *Systems: Journal of Transdisciplinary Systems Sciences*, 1(1).

Christakis, Alexander N. and Kenneth C. Bausch. (2002). Technologue: Technology-Supported Disciplined Dialogue, in: *Transformative Power of Dialogue*, Nancy Roberts, (ed.), Elsevier, New York.

Uchida, Hiroshi, Meiying Zhu and Tarcisio Della Senta (1999). *The Universal Networking Language: A Gift for a Millennium*. Tokyo: The United Nations University / Institute of Advanced Studies.

Uchida, Hiroshi (2001). The Universal Networking Language: Beyond Machine Translation. Submitted to the International Symposium on Language in Cyberspace, 26-27 September 2001, Seoul, Korea.

Chapter 10

BECOMING AWARE
A Dialogical Approach To Consciousness

MAURICE FRIEDMAN
Professor Emeritus, San Diego State University

1. INTRODUCTION

> The limits of the possibility of dialogue are the limits of awareness.
> – Martin Buber, *Between Man and Man*

> A world of consciousness mutually illuminating one another.
> – Mikhail Bakhtin, *Dostoyevsky's Poetics*

> Consciousness is not the sum total of reality, Jung to the contrary; nor is Freud's goal of making the unconscious conscious an adequate aim for either therapy or personal or social fulfillment. The world in which we live is more than consciousness, and our existence itself is more than consciousness. An alteration of consciousness, even in the form of an intercourse between the archetypal depths and the personal unconscious and conscious, can never be the sum and substance of concrete existence.
> – Maurice Friedman, *Touchstones of Reality*

So far as I know, no one, including Martin Buber and Mikhail Bakhtin has ever attempted to write an essay on consciousness from a dialogical point of view. I do not feel myself equipped to do the fresh anthropological investigation that the subject calls for. What I shall try to do here instead is, first, to set down some reflections on our ordinary approach to consciousness, including even that heightened awareness that people think of as mystical consciousness. Second, I shall examine several aspects of Martin Buber's philosophy of dialogue and philosophical anthropology to

Dialogue as a Means of Collective Communication, Edited by Banathy and Jenlink
Kluwer Academic/Plenum Publishers, New York 2005
217

see if it is possible to distill from them implications for consciousness that he himself did not make fully explicit. Third, I shall conclude with some phenomenological reflections of my own. This too, to the best of my knowledge, no one has attempted.

2.   INDIVIDUAL MYSTICAL CONSCIOUSNESS

Even in our approach to higher consciousness, we all tend to remain prisoners of Descartes' *cogito ergo sum.* We assume that our individual consciousness is our "touchstone of reality," to use my own phrase, and we proceed from there to discovered what we can about altered states and higher levels of consciousness that we see as accessible to the Eastern mystic and to the New-Age Westerner. Although we imagine we are becoming one with the All, we do not, in fact, go beyond the borders of our individual consciousness, deepened and reinforced perhaps by our ideas of Jungian archetypes or transpersonal realms. We accept unquestioningly, as I did once, Gerald Heard's dictum that consciousness is *sui generis,* and we absolutize it.

Strangely enough, this tends to remain true for those who turn from Western psychology to Eastern mysticism. We assume that we have gotten beyond our petty egos to the realization that Brahman is Atman–*tat twam asi* when, in fact, we are still ensconced in our own consciousness or, still worse, our own world-view.

An excellent example of this approach to consciousness is a summary of the third stage set forth at an Australian conference by Kenneth Wilber and both summarized and quoted in a journal appropriately named *Consciousness*:

> Continuing practice still further, the spiritual master reaches the Non-dual stage where objects and images of the world reappear once more. But now, the instant they become aware of something arising they also spontaneously become aware that it is merely the play of consciousness.   All that arises in awareness is recognized as the projection and expression of consciousness itself–thoughts, the world, other beings–all is simply consciousness manifesting itself as the Universe. This is Zen's One Mind, Aurobindo's Supermind, Brahman for the Hindus, or Atman and Sat Chit Ananda, or the TAO (manifest and unmanifest for Taoists). "Consciousness has now awoken to itself and sees itself in all things, unbound by space and time because it creates space and time: both utterly transcendent to the world and immanent in and as the world. This is said to be the profound realization, enlightenment, salvation, moksha, the goal of goals, the end of all seeking and the highest good and goal of human existence. (Barton, 1994, p. 10)

I wonder if Ken Wilber is aware that his perennial philosophy is actually philosophical idealism in new guise!

The next stage, to be sure, is to "become aware of the world's pain and suffering" which calls deeply to the spiritual contemplative who is now a sage and goes back into the world to attempt to heal and teach. This too is an old tradition, but what is taught is still a perfecting of individual consciousness into what is assumed to be universal or absolute consciousness.

Many years ago when I was immersed in the *advaitin* Vedanta–the non-dualistic Hindu teaching of Sankaracharya and Sri Ramakrishna–I was struck by the saying that as our dreams are to waking consciousness so is our waking consciousness to *samadhi*–the superconsciousness attained by the enlightened. Only years later, after I had made my own Martin Buber's philosophy of dialogue, did I reflect that all three terms in this equation are individual consciousness, that nowhere is there that coming to the border of one's own consciousness and meeting with others that is the touchstone of reality for the dialogical. To say with Buber that "all real living is meeting" does not mean that everything else is unreal, only that here we touch on what Paul Tillich calls the "really real," or what I call the "touchstone of reality." Human life touches on absoluteness in virtue of its dialogical character, for in spite of his uniqueness man can never find, when he plunges to the depth of his life, a being that is whole in itself and as such touches on the absolute.... This other self may be just as limited and conditioned as he is; in being together the unlimited and the unconditioned is experienced (Buber, 1985, p. 158).

This recognition meant for Buber an ascetic renunciation of his natural tendency toward mystic ecstasy in favor of the task of hallowing the everyday. The event that precipitated this renunciation: After a morning of religious ecstasy Buber was visited by a young man with a "question of life and death"–someone for whom he failed to be present because of his mystic ecstasy.

This ecstasy was so important in Buber's life that five years before then he had published *Ecstatic Confessions*–one of the earliest anthologies of mystics from all over the world. Buber's description of this ecstasy is worth restating here because it throws light on his later understanding of dialogical consciousness:

In my earlier years the "religious" was for me the exception. There were hours that were taken out of the course of things. From somewhere or other the firm crust of everyday was pierced. Then the reliable permanence of appearances broke down..."Religious experience" was the experience of an otherness which did not fit into the context of life. It could begin with something customary, with consideration of some familiar object, but which then became unexpectedly mysterious and uncanny, finally lighting a way into the lightning-pierced darkness of the mystery itself. But also, without any intermediate stage, time could be torn apart–first the firm world's structure then the still firmer self-assurance flew apart and you are delivered to fullness.... Over there now lay the accustomed existence with its affairs, but here illumination and ecstasy and rapture held, without time or sequence. Thus your own being encompassed a life here and a life beyond, and there was no bond but the actual moment of the transition. (Buber, 1985, p. 13)

It was June of 1914, two months before the onset of the first "World War." The young man who visited Buber did not later commit suicide, as many have supposed, but, as Buber both wrote and told me, was killed at the front "out of a despair which did not oppose his own death." Buber's meeting with the young man was friendly, but he was not present in spirit. Buber had not offered him "a presence by means of which we are told that nevertheless there is meaning."

Buber experienced this event as a judgment, not just on his meeting with the young man but of his whole way of life with its division into the exalted hours and the everyday hours.

Since then I have given up the "religious" which is nothing but the exception, extraction, exaltation, ecstasy; or it has given me up.... I know no fullness but each mortal hour's fullness of claim and responsibility. (Buber, 1985, p. 14)

In this same essay, "Dialogue," Buber speaks of "The Wordless Depths," acknowledging from his own unforgettable experience the state in which the bonds of the personal seem to have fallen away and we experience an undivided unity. But now he rejects what he once willingly assumed, namely, the assumption that in this mystic state he had attained to a union with the primal being or godhead. Rather he sees this "undifferentiable unity without form or content" as a pre-biographical one—one that "is hidden unchanged beneath all biographical change, all development and complication of the soul." But the person in such a moment is not above but beneath the creaturely situation and the life of dialogue. "He is not nearer the God who is hidden above *I and Thou*, and he is farther from the God who is turned to men and who gives himself as the *I* to a *Thou* and the *Thou* to an *I*."

In its place Buber offers the lived unity of the life of dialogue: "the unity of *life*, as that which once truly won is no more torn by any changes, not ripped asunder into the everyday creaturely life and the 'deified' exalted hours; the unity of unbroken, raptureless perseverance in concreteness, in which the word is heard and a stammering answer dared." (Buber, 1985, p. 24 f.)

Almost forty years ago it fell to my lot to translate, among a dozen other of his works, Buber's collection of essays *Pointing the Way*. Although he had written in his *Vorwort* to the German original *Hinweise* that he had selected only those essays that he could stand by in the present, I pointed out to him that he could not really stand by his mystical essay on "The Teaching of the Tao," which introduced his 1909 translation of selected *Talks and Parables of Chuang-tzu*. Buber responded that I was right but that

he had to include it because it belonged to a stage that he had to pass through
before he could enter into an independent relationship with being.

> One may call it the 'mystical' phase if one understands as mystic the
> belief in a unification of the self with the all-self, attainable by man in
> levels or intervals of his earthly life. Underlying this belief, when it
> appears in its true form, is usually a genuine 'ecstatic' experience. But
> it is the experience of an exclusive and all-absorbing unity of his own
> self [understood]…as the experience of *the unity*.
> When this man returns into life in the world and with the world,
> he is naturally inclined from then on to regard everyday life as an
> obscuring of the true life. Instead of bringing into unity his whole
> existence as he lives it day by day, from the hours of blissful
> exaltation unto those of hardship and of sickness, instead of living
> this existence as unity, he constantly flees from it into the experience
> of unity, into the detached feeling of unity of being, elevated above
> life. But he thereby turns away from his existence as a man…. In the
> 'lower' periods he regards everything as preparation for the 'higher.'
> But in these 'higher hours' he no longer knows anything over against
> him: the great dialogue between I and Thou is silent; nothing else
> exists than his self, which he experiences as *the* self. That is certainly
> an exalted form of being untrue, but it is still being untrue. (Buber,
> 1974, p. ix f.)

3.   THE CONSCIOUSNESS OF DIALOGUE

Buber's classic presentation of his philosophy of dialogue is his poetic book *I
and Thou* (Buber, 1958). Here he distinguishes between the "I-Thou"
relationship that is direct, mutual, present, and open, and the "I-It," or
subject-object relation, in which one relates to the other only indirectly and
nonmutually, knowing and using the other. What is decisive is the
relationship itself–whether it is sharing or possessing, imposing on the other
or helping her to unfold, valuing the relationship in itself or valuing it only
as a means to an end.
    Buber's I-Thou philosophy is concerned with the difference between
mere existence and authentic existence, between being human at all and
being more fully human, between remaining fragmented and bringing the
conflicting parts of oneself into an active unity, between partial and fuller
relationships with others. No one ever becomes a "whole person." But one
may move in the direction of greater wholeness through greater awareness
and fuller response in each new situation.
    The I of the I-It relation is a partial one, the I of the I-Thou
relationship a whole one. As the I of I-It is different from the I of I-Thou,
so the consciousness of the two relations differ. The consciousness of I-
Thou is not only a fuller consciousness than that of I-It; it is a qualitatively
different one. Only in I-Thou is the unique known of and for itself; only in

I-Thou is there real presence and presentness. Only in I-Thou is the ineffable "suchness" of the particular met and recognized in itself.[1]

4.   THE INTERHUMAN

The sphere in which person meets person has been ignored because it possesses no smooth continuity. Its experience has been annexed to the soul and to the world, so that what happens to an individual can be distributed between outer and inner impressions. But when two individuals "happen" to each other, there is an essential remainder which is common to them but which reaches out beyond the special sphere of each. That remainder is the basic reality, the "sphere of the between." In an essential relation the barriers of individual being are breached and "the other becomes present not merely in the imagination or feeling but in the depths of one's substance, so that one experiences the mystery of the other being in the mystery of one's own." This is the heart of true friendship and of genuine love. The two persons participate in one another's lives not merely psychologically, as images or feelings in one another's psyches, but ontologically as a manifest, even if not continuous reality of the between.

In us something takes place that takes place nowhere else in nature. One person turns to another as this particular being in order to communicate with the other in that sphere of the between that reaches out beyond the special sphere of each. In that sphere what happens cannot be exactly distributed between an "outer" event and an "inner" impression. This realm of the between exists on the far side of the subjective and on this side of the objective "on the narrow ridge where *I* and *Thou* meet." This sphere of the interhuman is where the human comes into being, and it is our contact with the really real.

The unfolding of the sphere of the between Buber calls the "dialogical." Since "the between" is not a fixed object but a reality that comes and goes, it cannot be objectified. "What unfolds in the between during the dialogical process," says Royal Alsup, "is the invisible made visible on the interhuman plane." The psychological, what happens within the soul of each, is only the secret accompaniment to the dialogue. The meaning of this dialogue is found in neither one nor the other of the partners, nor in both added together but in their interchange. What is essential is not what goes on within the minds of the partners in a relationship but what happens *between* them. For this reason, Buber is unalterably opposed to that "psychologism" which wishes to remove the reality of relationship into the separate psyches of the participants. This distinction between the "dialogical" and the "psychological" constitutes a radical attack on the psychologism of our age.

"Individuation is only the indispensable personal stamp of all realization of human existence." writes Buber in *The Knowledge of Man*. "The self as such is not ultimately the essential, but the meaning of human existence given in creation again and again fulfills itself as self" (Buber, 1988, p. 75).

The meeting between persons is hardly a mere going outward; for in its depth such meeting includes our penetrating to the very heart of the other by what Buber calls "imagining the real"–a bold swinging to the life of the other so that to some extent one concretely imagines what the other is thinking, feeling, and willing. Only from such a meeting, in fact, can we know that there is not just one inner–myself, and one outer–others. Only if we can get beyond this deep-seated prejudice of inner and outer can we understand the sense in which our existential meetings–whether with persons, animals, plants, or rocks–are, in their betweenness, meeting with the reality that can be known only in the between. As every electron has a finite center and an infinite circumference, so we each have our own ground yet meet each other from that ground. Our existences interpenetrate. Inner versus outer is thus not only a distortion of the primordial human wholeness of the person, but also a distortion of the reality of our existence as person *with* person.

Every genuine dialogue is unique.[2] An ever-renewed presentness and presence can be fully concrete and meaningful only insofar as it is unique, whether it be a beloved person or a ghost cypress at Point Lobos. There is, at the same time, a decisive difference between the revelation in dialogue of the uniqueness of a human and a non-human existing being. The latter, whether it be a tree or a flower, will not hide from us by any conscious act of will. Man, in contrast, cannot and will not allow another to "see into his soul" if he senses that that other comes merely as objective observer, scientifically curious analyst, or prying manipulator. That is why a friend can know one better than the psychologist with his TAT tests even though the psychologist may know more about one "objectively."

5.   BECOMING AWARE

It might appear from the epigraph that I have placed at the head of this essay that if the limits of dialogue are the limits of awareness, all we need to attain dialogical consciousness is that very enhancement of awareness that so many have striven for from the sixties until now.

If we look at this sentence in context, it appears otherwise. *Becoming aware* is only one of three modes of perceiving a person that Buber puts forth in "Dialogue." The other two are the *observer*, who knows the other as the subject knows the object–as a collection of traits–and the *onlooker*, who has no goal or intention but allows the object to present itself to him without traits or special characteristics, which is the perception common to all great artists.

In contrast to both of the above is that knowing or consciousness in which I allow the person before me to say something *to me*, to claim my attention and demand my response, not by anything the other intends but by the other's very being. To understand what Buber means by this one must understand his phrase "signs of address," for it of these that one must become aware.

By "signs of address" Buber does not mean fixed signs that have one universal meaning for all time. This is what characterizes all knowing by rule from the crudest superstition to the highest reaches of gnosis. Rather the true signs of address are unique. They stand in the stream of "happening but once." "Lived life is tested and fulfilled in the stream alone." The signs of address speak to me in my life, but not in such a way that they can be interpreted or translated, explained or displayed. They offer no information or appeasement. They are inseparable, incomparable, irreducible—what Buber in an earlier essay called the "bestowing side of things" which blazes up to meet us if we bend over it with our fervor.

> It is not a *what* at all, it is said into my very life; it is no experience that can be remembered independently of the situation, it remains the address of that moment and cannot be isolated, it remains the question of a questioner and will have its answer. (Buber, 1985, p. 12)

It is from this awareness of the signs of address that Buber distills his concept of responsibility. Buber was one of the earliest to point out that the root of responsibility is response. "Genuine responsibility exists only where there is real responding." "Responding to what?" Buber asks and answers, "the events of everyday life." We can still avoid responding by wrapping silence around us or stepping aside into the accustomed way. Yet if we venture a stammering answer, we enter into the situation that has at this moment stepped up to us, a situation "whose appearance we did not and could not know, for its like has not yet been."

What Buber then says is a marvelous indication of just how seriously he means becoming aware of and responding to the address of everyday life.

> A situation of which we have become aware is never finished with, but we subdue it into the substance of lived life. Only then, true to the moment, do we experience a life that is something other than a sum of moments. We respond to the moment, but at the same time we respond on its behalf, we answer for it. A newly- created concrete reality has been laid in our arms; we answer for it. A dog has looked at you, you answer for its glance, a child has clutched your hand, you answer for its touch, a host of men moves about you, you answer for their need. (Buber, 1985, p. 17)

6.   INCLUSION OR IMAGINING THE REAL

It is clear then that meeting, dialogue, the "between" are Buber's touchstones of reality. But is there really such a thing as dialogical consciousness apart from or in addition to that individual consciousness with which we are all so familiar that we take it for granted?

To answer this question we must look at three central concepts in Buber's philosophy of dialogue and his philosophical anthropology. The first of these is inclusion, or "imagining the real." Buber's earliest use of inclusion was in his discussion of the actor and the theater in his 1913 book *Daniel: Dialogues of Realization*. In his 1925 essay "Education" Buber extended the notion of inclusion to the human in general.

By inclusion Buber means not what is narrowly called "empathy" but a remarkable swinging over to the side of the other with the most intense activity of the being so that one to some extent experiences concretely what the other person is thinking, feeling, and willing. Buber also calls this experience "imagining the real," for in contrast to the free play of the imagination this fantasy is directed to the concrete other to whom one says Thou. This other can be perceived in her wholeness, unity, and uniqueness only as a partner and not at all as an object.

Inclusion, as a result, must be distinguished from every type of intuition which sees through a person and finds out what makes them "tick." Inclusion means a reversal of the single instinct. It is a bipolar reality. Unlike both identification and, in the narrow sense of the term, empathy, inclusion means remaining on one's own side at the same time that one goes over to the side of the other.

Buber gives two examples of inclusion in "Education":

A man belabors another, who remains quite still. Then let us assume that the striker suddenly receives in his soul the blow which he strikes: the same blow; that he receives it as the other who remains still. For the space of a moment he experiences the situation from the other side. Reality imposes itself on him. What will he do? Either he will overwhelm the voice of the soul, or his impulse will be reversed.

A man caresses a woman, who lets herself be caressed. Then let us assume that he feels the contact from two sides—with the palm of his hand still, also with the woman's skin. The twofold nature of the gesture, as one that takes place between two persons, thrills through the depth of enjoyment in his heart and stirs it. If he does not deafen his heart he will have—not to renounce the enjoyment but—to love. (Buber, 1985, p. 96)

In the "Eros" section of "Dialogue" Buber gives us another illustration that he does not identify as "inclusion" but which is unmistakably that:

Those who are loyal to the strong-winged Eros of dialogue know the beloved being. They experience his particular life in simple presence—not as a thing seen and touched, but from the innervations to his movements, from the "inner" to his "outer". But by this I mean nothing but the bipolar experience, and—more than a swinging over and away in the instant—a contemporaneity at rest. That inclination of the head over there—you feel how the soul enjoins it on the neck, you feel it not on your neck but on that one over there, on the beloved, and yet you yourself are not as it were snatched away, you are here, in the feeling self-being, and you receive the inclination of the head, its injunction, as the answer to the word of your own silence. In contemporaneity at rest you make and you experience dialogue. The two who are loyal to the Eros of dialogue, who love one another, receive the common event from the other's side as well, that is, they receive it from the two sides, and thus for the first time understand in a bodily way what an event is. (Buber, 1985, p. 29)

To these three examples we can add something of Buber's own adumbrations. In "Education" he asserts that, in contrast to empathy, inclusion "is the extension of one's own concreteness, the fulfillment of the actual situation of life, the complete presence of the reality in which one participates." Inclusion is the heart of genuine conversation–its shared silence, the continual potential presence of the one to the other even when they are separated in space, the "acknowledgement" of the actual being of the partner in conversation (Buber, 1985, p. 97). All this in preparation for a deeper understanding of education that, because it is one of pure dialogue, is also one of inclusion.

A quarter of a century later Buber places inclusion and "imagining the real" at the center of his mature philosophical anthropology. In "Distance and Relation" he defines imagining the real as "the capacity to hold before one's soul a reality arising at this moment but not able to be directly experienced." This capacity is essential to making the other present, which is essential, in turn, to confirmation–a principal factor in the life between persons:

"Imagining" the real means that I imagine to myself what another is at this very moment wishing, feeling, perceiving, thinking, and not as a detached content but in his very reality, that is, as a living process in this man.... I experience...the specific pain of another in such a way that I feel...this particular pain as the pain of the other. This making present increases until...the pain which I inflict upon him surges up in myself, revealing the abyss of the contradictoriness of life between man and man. (Buber, 1988, p. 60)

In "Elements of the Interhuman" Buber focuses again upon inclusion and imagining the real in the section entitled "Personal Making Present." In this section Buber asserts that to be aware of a person means to perceive her wholeness as a person determined by the spirit–the dynamic center which stamps her every utterance, action, and attitude with the recognizable sign of uniqueness. Such an awareness is impossible so long as the other is a separated object of contemplation or observation, and it is particularly hindered by the analytical, reductive, and deriving look that prevails today and that threatens radically to destroy the mystery between person and person.

This implies, of course, that a person's wholeness and uniqueness can only be perceived in dialogue, in which, in contrast to monologue, one allows the other to exist in her otherness and not just as a content of one's experience. But this dialogical perception demands that Cinderella gift, one day to become a princess, which Buber calls "imagining the real." Buber describes imagining the real here as "a bold swinging–demanding the most intensive stirring of one's being–into the life of the other." It is not, again, the all-possible which is imagined, but just the particular real person who confronts me and whom I can make present only in this way.

Inclusion is not a possession of a spiritual elite. On the contrary, it is a gift that every human being has, even though it mostly sits by the ashes of the fireplace and seldom goes out to the ball where there is intercourse between human beings. It is evident from what we have said above that it is just such an extension of consciousness beyond the individual as we hypothesized might be the case with dialogical consciousness. Most people imagine that we are imprisoned within our individual experience and find it hard to believe that Buber's imagining the real can actually enable us to make our own what the other experiences. The Gestalt therapist's "empty chair" technique is a vivid proof to the contrary, for it is based on the fact that we can always imagine quite concretely our mother's or father's or lover's or friend's part of any conversation or dialogue. A graduate student tells me that now that her mother has died a great burden has lifted off her. She is sad, of course, about the death of her mother. But during her mother's long illness from cancer she not only felt her own approaching loss but also directly experienced the pain of her mother–a true case of imagining the real.

Almost forty years ago I moderated the now famous "dialogue" between Martin Buber and the great American psychologist Carl R. Rogers. The plan of the dialogue was that Rogers should ask questions to which Buber would respond. The first question that Rogers asked, was "What were the channels of knowing that enabled you to learn so deeply of people and relationships?" The second part of Buber's long response concerned an inclination to meet others, "to change something in the *other*, but also to let *me* be changed by *him*." At the end of this section Buber spoke of what was must have been the single most important instance of inclusion in his own life. Although he does not speak of him by name, he unmistakably alludes to the murder of his close friend Gustav Landauer by German soldiers who kicked him to death in a courtyard under the direct orders of their Junker lieutenant. Along with his "conversion" and the First World War itself, this was one of the turning points in Buber's life.

I could not resist what was going on, and I was compelled to, may I say, to live it. Things that went on just at this moment. You may call this *imagining the real*. Imagining what was going on. This imagining, for four years, influenced me terribly. Just when it was finished, it finished by a certain episode in May 1919 when a friend of mine, a great friend, a great man, was killed by antirevolutionary soldiers in a very barbaric way, and now again once more...I was compelled to imagine just this killing, but not in an optical way alone, but may I say so, just with my *body*. And this was the decisive moment, after which, after some days and nights in this state, I felt, "Oh, something has been done to me. (Buber, 1988, p. 158)

For many days and nights Buber lay on his bed, feeling in his own body every blow that the soldiers had inflicted on his murdered friend.

7.   THE ESSENTIAL WE

Once Buber proposed to write a book entitled *The Place of Faith.* In connection with this project he wrote to the great psychiatrist Ludwig Binswanger asking him to tell him all he could about schizophrenia. Later all mention of the book disappeared from Buber's correspondence, and the book itself never saw the light of day. Yet I am convinced that this book found its inheritor in Buber's seminal essay "What Is Common to All?" and that his interest in schizophrenia gives us an essential clue to both the concern and the significance of this essay.

Although Buber is most famous for the "I-Thou" relationship, the heart of "What Is Common to All" is what he calls "the essential We." He does not deny the validity of ordinary individual consciousness in this essay, but he extends the human beyond that to what the pre-Socratic philosopher Heraclitus spoke of as "the common" which one should follow.

If by "the common" Buber meant only some moral obligation to serve the community or society, it would no more modify the individual character of our consciousness than Jeremy Bentham's assumption that making laws according to the utilitarian calculus of maximizing pleasure and minimizing pain would result in a harmonious society. But to Buber, as to Heraclitus before him, it means far more than that.

We learn at the outset that the heart of the essay's concern is maintaining unmixed the oppositeness of two states of human consciousness–that of waking and that of sleeping. This in itself demonstrates the essay's significance for our investigation of the consciousness of dialogue. "The waking have a single cosmos in common," says Heraclitus in one of his aphorisms, providing a clue to what I found missing in the Hindu contrast between waking and dreaming and between superconsciousness and waking. They were regarded as three states of individual consciousness, I pointed out above. But in waking consciousness we have the possibility of becoming a co-worker in building the common cosmos as we do not in dreaming or in superconsciousness.

Particularly important here is the fact that Buber speaks of the full mutuality of human being together as "a spiritual reality." This spiritual reality only comes into existence, writes Buber, if human beings "do not sleep while waking and spin dreamlike illusions which they call their own insight." The pure duty and responsibility of waking togetherness which

Heraclitus places upon us means the rejection of "that dreamlike refusal of the We through whose illusion the common day is broken asunder."

This task of establishing in common a common reality clearly implies that there is a consciousness of the We, the common, that is more than the sum of individual consciousness. That this is so Buber makes clear by contrasting Heraclitus' teaching with Chuang-tzu's idealist version of Taoism and with the ancient Hindu teaching of identity–*tat twam asi*. In the latter discussion he makes fully explicit how "the ancient Hindu 'That art thou' becomes the postulate of an annihilation of the human person." The identification of the other with oneself has as its corollary the devaluing and destruction of the uniqueness of the person–"the affirmation of the primally deep otherness of the other."

It is not surprising that Buber carries his critique over to Aldous Huxley's advocacy of the use of mescaline to take "chemical holidays" that give us a glimpse of what the artist and mystic experience.

> Man may master as he will his situation, to which his surroundings also belong; he may withstand it, he may alter it, he may, when it is necessary, exchange it for another; but the fugitive flight out of the claim of the situation into situationlessness is no legitimate affair of man. And the true name of all the paradises which man creates for himself by chemical or other means is situationlessness. They are situationless like the dream state and like schizophrenia because they are in their essence uncommunal, while every situation, even the situation of those who enter into solitude, is enclosed in the community of logos and cosmos. (Buber, 1988, p. 90)

Once during the seminars on the unconscious and dreams that Buber gave for the Washington School of Psychiatry in 1957 he remarked that the reason the so-called "normal" person prefers the real world to the world of the schizophrenic is not because it is a better world but only because it is a real world!

Had Buber written this essay during the sixties instead of the fifties, he would undoubtedly have made the same stricture against Huxley's and Timothy Leary's celebration of the use of LSD. Aldous Huxley, who in his last novel *Island* showed some awareness of the flight from the common accompanying acid trips, deliberately "went out" on LSD at the time of his death. It was during the sixties, I believe, that Timothy Leary remarked that he had taken LSD so often that ordinary life now seemed to him play–a denial of the task of building together the common cosmos if ever there was one! What Buber says of the common logos adds to our understanding of the common consciousness that is attained through the We. The logos does not attain to its fullness in us but rather between us. It is the eternal chance for speech to become true between human beings and in this sense it is common to them. Persons who genuinely think with one another because they genuinely talk to one another existentially effect the communal guarding of meaning. Thus logos is not law or word to Buber nor even simply meaning.

It is the interhuman event of speech-with-meaning, the sensuous meaningful human word in which human talk becomes true.

Through our common logos the cosmos becomes the shaped world of human beings–a total order formed and revealed. "Only through our service to the logos does the world become 'the same cosmos for all.'" This working together, however is not that of a team hitched to the great wagon. It is, rather, a tug of war in which each from the ground of his or her uniqueness contributes to building the common order. "This cosmos from which we come and which comes from us is, understood in its depth, infinitely greater than the sum of all special spheres of dreams and intoxication into which man flees before the demand of the We" (Buber, 1988, p. 95).

In the last section of "What Is Common to All" Buber explicitly recognizes that the human being has always had both his thoughts and his experiences with others and with himself as I. It is as I, moreover, that the human being transplants his ideas into the firmament of the spirit. But it is as We that the human being has constructed and developed a world out of his experiences, and it is as We that the human being has ever again raised them into being itself which, in distinction from both the psychic and physical realms Buber identifies with "the between"–"the mode of existence between persons communicating with one another."

> It is to this that the seventh Platonic epistle points when it hints at the existence of a teaching which attains to effective reality not otherwise than in manifold togetherness and living with one another, as a light is kindled from leaping fire. Leaping fire is indeed the right image for the dynamic between persons in We. (Buber, 1988, p. 97)

This We begins, to be sure, with the meeting of I and Thou: "He who existentially knows no Thou will never succeed in knowing a Thou." But it does not remain on the one to one of I and Thou. "In our age, in which the true meaning of every word is encompassed by delusion and falsehood, and the original intention of the human glance is stifled by tenacious mistrust, it is of decisive importance to find again the genuineness of speech and existence as We" (Buber, 1988, p. 98).

8.   THE UNCONSCIOUS

Buber's uncompleted but nonetheless pregnant speculations concerning the unconscious add one more necessarily element to our understanding of the consciousness of dialogue. In contrast to Freud and Jung, who held that the unconscious must be psychic since they would not recognize it as physiological, Buber has suggested that the unconscious may really be the ground of personal wholeness before its elaboration into the physical and the psychic.

Buber bursts the bounds of psychologism by recognizing that the division of inner and outer that applies to the psyche and the physical need not apply to the unconscious. Here, in contrast, there might be direct meeting and direct communication between one unconscious and another. Obviously this paves the way for inclusion and imagining the real. Of course, each of the contents of the unconscious can in any moment enter into the dimension of the introspective and thereby be explained and dealt with as belonging to the psychic province.

The physical and the psychical represent two radically different modes of knowing: that of the senses and that of the "inner sense." Pure psychic process is not to be found in the physical. Our memory retains the process, to be sure, but by a new process in time. Physiology deals with things that are to be found, psychology with things that are not to be found. The psychic is pure process in time. In order to grasp the physical as a whole, we need the category of space as well as time. But for the psychic we need time alone.

The unconscious is a state out of which these two phenomena have not yet evolved and in which the two cannot be distinguished from one another. The unconscious is our being itself in its wholeness. Out of it the physical and the psychical evolve again and again and at every moment. The unconscious is not a phenomenon. It is what modern psychology holds it to be–a dynamic fact that makes itself felt by its effects, effects the psychologist can explore.

This exploration, as it takes place in psychiatry, is not of the unconscious itself, but rather of the phenomena that have been dissociated from it. Modern psychology's claim that there are unconscious things that influence our life and manifest themselves in certain conscious states is one that Buber, in contrast to the phenomenologists, does not contest.

But we cannot, Buber reminds us, say anything about the unconscious in itself. It is never given to us. The radical mistake that Freud made was to think that he could posit a region of the mind as unconscious and at the same time deal with it as if its "contents" were simply repressed conscious material which could be brought back, without any essential change, into the conscious.

Dissociation is the process in which the unconscious "lump" manifests itself in inner and outer perceptions. This dissociation, in fact, may be the origin of our whole sense of inner and outer. The conscious life of the person is a dualistic life. One can have, to some extent, the consciousness of the coming together of one's forces, one's acting unity, but one cannot perceive one's unity as an object.

If the unconscious is not of the nature of the psychic, then it follows that the basic distinction between the physical and the psychic as "outer" and "inner" does not apply to the unconscious. Yet Freud, holding that the unconscious must be simply psychical, places the unconscious *within* the person, and so do all the schools that have come after Freud. As a result, *the basis of human reality itself comes to be seen as psychical rather than interhuman, and the relations between person and person are psychologized.*

If the unconscious is not something psychic that can be preserved in the underground but just a piece of human body and soul existence, it cannot at all again be raised as it was. We do not have a deep freeze which keeps fragments, but this unconscious has its own existence. It can again be dissociated into physical and psychic phenomena, but this means a radical change of the substance. (Buber, 1990, p. 166)

Not only philosophical psychologists such as Jung but mystical philosophers such as Bergson and the mystics themselves may have made a corollary mistake when they assume that it is only in our inwardness that we find our touchstones of reality while the outer, and particularly the social, is relegated to an inferior status. To take only three illustrations out of what could be thousands, two mystically inclined friends of mine have founded a "Center for Inner Work," the title of a Friends journal is *Inward Light*, and the title of a new mystical journal (to which I myself contributed an article on the essence of Hasidism) is *Inner Directions*.

If the unconscious *is* that part of the existence of a person in which the realms of body and soul are not dissociated, then *the relationship between two persons would mean the relationship between two nondivided existences.* Thus the highest moment of relation would be what we call unconscious. More precisely, the unconscious and the conscious are integrated in the spontaneity of personal meeting. The unconscious should have, may have, and indeed will have more influence in the interhuman than the conscious, Buber insists. Through it there is a direct contact between persons in their wholeness, of which the unconscious is the guardian. This is so because the whole person is not pictured here as divided into a conscious part with which she identifies and a hidden unconscious part which operates as her "shadow" or "not me," to use Harry Stack Sullivan's term. It is what undergirds and guarantees our wholeness as persons, hence what enters into any act that we perform as whole persons.

It should be evident that Buber's philosophy of the unconscious suggests an essential foundation for the consciousness of dialogue that we have discussed in connection with imagining the real and the essential We.

9.   THE PARTNERSHIP OF EXISTENCE

I shall close this essay with some of my own reflections on the phenomenology of dialogical consciousness in lived life.[3]

What we have said about becoming a self with others does not imply that we do not exist as a self when we are not with some other person, any more than that in being with another we are automatically in mutual relationship. There is a distinction between our awareness of our self as some sort of continuity and our becoming ourselves in the meeting with others.

The simplest fact of our existence together is that we are neither self-sufficient entities nor are we able to come together in such a way as to overcome our separateness and our uniqueness. Deeply satisfying as the ecstasy of oneness is in romantic love or mystic meditation, we cannot remain in it.

10.   MEETING OTHERS AND HOLDING ONE'S GROUND

To me the two central statements of Buber's *I and Thou* are "All real living is meeting" and, speaking of the I-Thou relationship, "By the graciousness of its comings and the solemn sadness of its goings, it teaches us to meet others and hold our ground when we meet them."

We must distinguish between holding our ground and rigidity, even as we must distinguish between going out to meet the other and dissolving all boundaries between person and person in a symbiotic clinging. To live means to venture, but it does not mean giving up one's own ground in doing so. There is a difference between openness and self-denial, between risk and suicide. Seventy-five years before Jesus the Jewish sage Hillel wrote: "If I am not for myself, who will be for me? If I am for myself alone, what am I? And if not now, when?" If I not for myself, who will be for me, indeed? But what am I if I am *only* for myself?

How does one know when to emphasize going out and when to emphasize holding one's ground? There is no easy formula. It takes a lifetime to learn the wisdom of responsiveness, the right alternation for this person in this situation between centering oneself and moving out of oneself. What the America poet, Theodore Roethke, calls "the long journey out of the self" is not achieved by losing touch with oneself any more than it is achieved by aiming at oneself.

If we ask the question, "Does the partnership of existence give us 'security' and protect us from tragedy, contradiction, and absurdity?" our answer must be, "No." There is a basic insecurity in our existence itself that arises from the fact that we cannot live without others and yet often cannot live with them. That is why the psychologist, George R. Bach, speaks of the necessity of infighting with one's partner in marriage, one's "intimate enemy." Because this insecurity is the human condition, there is an existential anxiety that no amount of psychoanalysis can remove. Again and again, as long as we live, our existence will be endangered by the openness of leaving our ground and the closedness of not leaving it! So far from the partnership of existence excluding tragedy and the absurd, it provides the very ground for them—when meeting becomes mismeeting, when our being face-to-face, or opposite, each other, crystallizes into a fixed and polarized opposition, when the mingling of understanding and misunderstanding that we call communication freezes into the terrifying solitude of the absurd.

These are not inevitable expressions of the human condition. They are real events that happen again and again but do not happen necessarily. We are not fundamentally alone. If we were we would not feel lonely. But we again and again find ourselves alone and isolated, "lonely and afraid/in a world I never made" (A. E. Housman).

The loneliness of mismeeting is a real happening, an existential event that may protract into permanence, as happens in some relationships, but *may* also be overcome in deeper meeting. This latter *may* pertains to those situations and relationships in which the partnership of existence proves to have stronger resources than the contradictions and absurdities that pull us apart.

11.   DIALOGUE AND AWARENESS

Our resources in each situation are limited, of course, but we do not know what that factual limitation will be before and apart from the situation. Our freedom is a "finite freedom," as Paul Tillich says, and that finite freedom varies from moment to moment. Insofar as we have freedom within the situation, we have the possibility of responding more wholly. But to respond more wholly we must be more fully aware. Full awareness here is the awareness of dialogue itself, the awareness of what addresses you.

In talking with another person, for example, you may pick up only the intellectual level of what she says while, consciously or not, she is addressing you on many levels at the same time. To recognize and respond to that address may make you anxious. Therefore, you block off your awareness of it. Later on, though, the anxiety will probably come into the circle of your awareness–through dreams, fantasies, memories, twinges of pain or embarrassment. When that happens, it might become possible in a new situation to enter into relationship with a greater awareness and a more whole response than before.

A patient of mine came to me with the problem that he had met a woman for the first time with whom he had no intention of getting romantically involved but wanted to know because she was interesting and might possibly become a friend. He had resolved not to be as outgoing as he often was. But at the end of their meeting he was surprised by the mutual openness between them and felt that he had, in fact, made a new friend. Yet he also carried away with him a troubling sense that he had met her without fully holding his own ground and this made him anxious. Since in the past precisely such situations led him into embarrassing involvements that he could not handle, I might have suggested to him that his anxiety was a warning to drop the relationship altogether. If I had done that, he might have reacted against my advice and preferred to ignore his anxiety rather than not continue the relationship. What I did suggest to him instead was that he go back into the relationship with equal openness yet with greater awareness and not treat responsiveness and awareness as an either/or. Only thus could he do justice to the partnership of existence.

Much of our guilt is not deliberate commission or omission but simply that fuzzy awareness: "If only I'd really known!" We are responsible even for our lack of awareness, for that failure to hear which eventually turns into an inability to hear.

What is true of our awareness is also true of our response. We can be guilty even when we do and say all the right things if we do not respond with our whole being. One of the most terrible responsibilities in the world is that of really being present, of being a *presence* for the other. We cannot achieve dialogue by an act of will, for dialogue is a genuinely two-sided affair. We cannot know in advance that there can *not* be dialogue in a particular situation, but neither can we know that there *will* be dialogue. We cannot will that the other respond, nor can we even will our own presence and presentness. We are, nonetheless, responsible for what we are, for our presentness or lack of it.

To know that it is you that the other is demanding and nothing that you can hand out, whether it be prescriptions or wise sayings, to know that what is really demanded is that you be present for and to him is terrifying. The demand is total and uncompromising, and we are often not able to be fully present even when we really want to. Our lack of awareness is the limitation of the *given* situation. But in the long run our degree of awareness is not necessity but possibility, something for which we can be responsible.

When I become aware and do respond, I respond not to the way you are regarding and treating me but to that in you that calls out to me even when you do not speak to me. Even though you are not conscious of my answering your call, in some way you will feel my response. You may be asking me for help without knowing that you are doing so. If I refer your existence only back to myself and how you regard me, I shall fail to hear the question that you put, fail to answer the real need that you have. Because we repress our awareness of our own negative characteristics, we dislike those people in whom they are manifest. Yet even then, it is possible to ask ourselves whether, over and above what upsets us in them and what we find so threatening, there is something they are trying to tell us, something to which we are called to respond. This applies even to those who are unjust to us. If someone upbraids and accuses us falsely and with great passion, that very excess and unfairness suggests that there is some hurt in this person that is expressing itself in this distorted way. In the depths she may be asking for understanding and reassurance from us.

Listening and responding at a greater depth is the direction away from a specious individualism to the reality of the partnership of existence.

12.   AWARENESS AND PERSONAL WHOLENESS

Those people who relate to the world only as a function of their own becoming will not change no matter how concerned they are about changing. But those people whose trust is grounded in the partnership of existence are changed every time they go out to meet another. They become anew and are reborn in each new situation. We can help allow this, and in this sense we can will it. But there is another will that easily falls into despair because it sees everything as depending on it alone. If we change, it is because someone or something comes to meet us as we go to meet it–not because we decide to change. Our will may be necessary to break the inertia, to overcome the obstacles, but then we have to allow ourselves to be taken up into the flowing interaction.

We are all persons to a certain extent by courtesy of one another. We call each other back into being persons when sleepiness, sickness, or malaise has divested us of our personhood. What makes us persons is the stamp of uniqueness, of personal wholeness, and this is not anything that can ever be looked at or grasped as an object or known directly in ourselves. We know it of each other as we enter into relationship, but we know it of ourselves only in that dim awareness that has to do with becoming more and more uniquely ourselves in responding to what is not ourselves. Rabbi Pinhas of Koretz stressed that there is no person who is not incessantly being taught by the soul. "If this is so," asked one of his disciples, "why don't people obey their souls?" "The soul teaches incessantly," Rabbi Pinhas explained, "but it never repeats." The reason why the soul never repeats is that it does not teach in generalities but always only the message and demand of the unique situation in which the person finds herself.

Knowledge has to do with the general. Truth has to do with the unique. The unique does not mean he different, but the particular, that which is related to for itself and as of value in itself. The Baal Shem Tov, the founder of Hasidism, once spoke to a group of people, and afterwards each person asserted that he had spoken to him alone, until all fell silent. The Baal Shem did not seek the least common denominator or generalities that might easily be taken in by the crowd, as does the politician. Rather, he spoke with such directness and concreteness that what he said addressed *each* of his hearers as the unique person he was. (See Friedman, 1988, Chap. 3)

There is no end of what we might say about genuine personal awareness. We are surprised at our own resources or we discover deep convictions that we did not know we had. Or we may become aware that what we are doing is not what we are called to do, like the man who told me that after years of training he had become a practicing dentist and after still more years a practicing architect. Yet as soon as he was financially able to do so, he walked away from both professions, convinced that what he had planned for and become was at variance with the deeper call to his being of which he had become aware.

The whole self is not what I am aware of when I am simply self-conscious. For then I am turning myself into an object and lose my intuitive grasp of the person that I am. That intuitive awareness that comes in responding is not incompatible with objectivity, analysis, or psychoanalysis. But it *is* incompatible with making these latter the final court of appeal as to what is real.

It is ultimately an interhuman awareness that is in question here. Our awareness has to guard itself against becoming completely reflective self-consciousness or completely objective analysis. Our intuitive awareness of ourselves grows in listening and responding if we use ourselves as a radar screen: hearing not just how the other responds but also how we ourselves respond to him or her. We can do this without turning our self into an object.

Our wholeness is most there when we have forgotten ourselves in responding fully to what is not ourselves. It is not just *ekstasis,* mystic ecstasy, that occasionally lifts us out of the burden of self-consciousness; any genuine wholehearted response–"When the music is heard so deeply that you are the music while the music lasts" (T. S. Eliot)–can bring us to this immediacy. Our self-consciousness returns when we go back, as we must, from immediacy to mediacy. Yet even it need not get in the way as much as we usually suppose. I had a donnee at Sarah Lawrence College who was a gifted pianist. I faithfully attended her concerts, but somewhere in the middle of each one she would forget what she was playing and stop dead. This was the point where the consciousness of Schubert or whomever she was playing would be lost to her because of her consciousness that *she* was playing the piano. The Hasidic Maggid of Mezritch said to his disciples that they must say Torah in such a way that the Universe of the Word speaks through them. "As soon as you hear yourself speaking, you must stop."

The fact that we are reflective can be handled lightly instead of heavily, as every gifted performer knows. The followers of one Hasidic *rebbe* could not understand what riveted his gaze to the foolish spectacle of a rope dancer. "This man is risking his life, and I don't know why," he replied when questioned. "But I am sure he is not thinking of the hundred gulden he will get at the end of the performance, for if he did he would fall."

To learn how to handle our self-consciousness lightly, we must in particular avoid the mistake of identifying our "I" with that reflective consciousness and regarding the rest as just the objects that the "I" looks at. The more we do that, the more we become Dostoyevsky's "Underground Man," "twiddling our thumbs" and totally unable to act. One of the forms of lack of personal wholeness, correspondingly, is that endless self-preoccupation which splits us into two parts, one of which is the observer and the other the actor who is being observed. This bifurcation of consciousness prevents us from having any sort of spontaneous response, from ever really going outside of ourselves.

The person finds his full reality in the present, and personality exists in an actualized form only in the present. When we speak, as we must, of the personality extending over time, it is the alternation between actual and potential personality that we really mean. The existence of the person in time is not a smooth process but an alternation between moments of real presentness and other moments–of sleep, of semiconsciousness, of distraction, inner division, illness–when a person falls from actualized presentness into mere subsistence, or potentiality.

13.   ADDRESS AND RESPONSE AS MORE THAN
CONSCIOUS AWARENESS

We address others not by conscious mind or will but by what we are. We address them with more than we know, and they respond–if they really respond–with more than they know. That is because our gestures, stance, and tone of voice, of which we are often unaware, are as important in our communication as the words we consciously utter. Address and response can never be identified merely with conscious intent or even with "intentionality." Our resources have to do with what calls us and with the way in which we bring or do not bring ourselves into wholeness in response to this call. The courage to address and respond sees life as a giving and a receiving, but it does not mean a "trust that" life will always be a flowing.

NOTES

[1] In his essay on "The Unconscious Functions of the I-It and I-Thou Realms" William G. Heard offers a useful summary of this qualitative difference between the consciousness of the I-It and that of the I-Thou realms:

I-It: "The ongoing unconscious structuring of our psyche limits the extent of our awareness. We are conscious only of certain emotional characteristics of the world that are determined and shaped by the structure of our psyche. We may be conscious of the world in ways that we find useful, amusing, interesting, or necessary to us in the moment, but always after they have been shaped by our psyche.

"Our conscious experiences are always reflective in nature, that is, they are made possible by our apperceptive ability. We are conscious because there is a part of ourself that observes what has transpired. Our observations are always of something that has already occurred, be it only an instant before, that has been shaped by our psyche. What we are conscious of is a representation of our direct experience, a representation that is not presented in an isomorphic fashion. The representation is shaped and elaborated by our current disposition in conjunction with the structuring activities of our psyche. As such we are not presented our unmediated, direct experience but a representation that has been altered and shaped by our psychic structure to produce consistency and coherence in our experiences.

"In the I-It realm of our existence we do not have conscious contact with our unmediated and immediate experience of the world or of others. We are conscious of a reality that is mediated and abstract in nature that allows us to know the other in a rational sense, to know that part of the other that is predictable and most often certain in our encounters with him–but this is only to know him as an object."

I-Thou: "We are never conscious of our personal wholeness. Our ontology is such that it always eludes us. When we exercise our conscious function there is a part of ourself–our perceptual ability–that provides the content of our consciousness. There is yet another part of ourself–our apperceptive ability–that is conscious of this content. It is this latter part that must remain outside our perceptions to be conscious of them. As we can see, our conscious function requires us to separate a part of ourself from the rest in order to be aware, thus, fragmenting the unity of our wholeness. Because of this, our consciousness cannot encompass our personal wholeness, for it too is a part of our wholeness and cannot encompass itself.

"In dialogue we are able to relate to the personal wholeness of the other in a reality that appears by grace between us. The between is not a conscious phenomenon but an ontological occurrence–ontological in the sense that our relating takes place not within us but between us."

William G. Heard, "The Unconscious Functions of the I-It and I-Thou Realms," *The Humanistic Psychologist*, Vol. XXIII, No. 2, Summer 1995, pp. 239-258.

[2] A tribal member, the liberation psychologist Royal Alsup points out from his twenty years of work counseling and championing Native Americans, takes the risk of singing his or her new dance song in a ceremony. The confirmation by other tribal members telling him or her that was a great jump dance (a world renewal ceremony) or brush dance song (a healing ceremony for children) enables the individual tribal members to feel their own uniqueness: they feel that they are called to be a singer in the ceremonies.

[3] These phenomenological reflections draw from Friedman, 1972, and Friedman, 2001.

REFERENCES

Barton, P., 1994. July Meeting Review: 'ITA Conference Report, *Consciousness*, **Spring**: 6-11.

Buber, M., 1958. *I and Thou*, 2nd ed. (with postscript by author added, trans. by R. G. Smith). Chas. Scribner's, New York.

Buber, M., 1985. *Between Man and Man*. (Introduction by Maurice Friedman, trans. by R.G. Smith with new "Afterword," trans.   by Maurice Friedman). Macmillan, New York.

Buber, M., 1988. *The Knowledge of Man: A Philosophy of the Interhuman*. (Ed. with an Introductory Essay (Chap. 1) by Maurice Friedman, trans. by Maurice Friedman and R.G. Smith).   Appendix: "Dialogue between Martin Buber and Carl R. Rogers." Humanities Press International, Atlantic Highlands, NJ. (now distributed by Prometheus Books, Amherst, NY).

Buber, M., 1990. *A Believing Humanism: My Testament*. (Trans. with introduction and explanatory comments by Maurice Friedman). Humanities Press International, Atlantic Highlands, NJ. (now distributed by Prometheus Books, Amherst, NY).

Friedman, M. S., 1972. *Touchstones of Reality: Existential Trust and the Community of Peace*. E. P. Dutton, New York.

Friedman, M. S., 1988. *A Dialogue with Hasidic Tales: Hallowing the Everyday*. Human Sciences Press, Insight Books, New York.

Friedman, M. S., 2001. *The Partnership of Existence: Our Road to True Community*

Chapter 11

DOING AND TALKING
Schools, Complexity, and Conversation

ALEXANDER M. SIDORKIN
Bowling Green State University

1. INTRODUCTION

This chapter is an attempt to use the category of conversation for analysis of schools as complex social systems.

2. SCHOOLS AS SYSTEMS

The Russian version of Educational Systems Theory began in the mid-80-s by a group of Moscow scholars lead by Dr. Liudmila Novikova. This was an extension of a long-standing theoretical tradition known as the educational collective theory. The notion of the collective has acquired somewhat derogatory meaning in the West, mainly because its association with totalitarian Communism of the Soviet Union. The Cold war sealed the negative connotation of the word, and Star Trek the movie with its semi-robotic faceless members of the Collective finished the job. However, the Russian theory and practice of the collective draws its roots clearly from American and European Progressivism and social psychology of the early 20-s century. This is not a good place to tell the full story of the educational collective. I only would like to point out that its basic theoretical premise made a lot of sense.

The fundamental fact of schooling is that one adult teaches and supervises many students. The early school was nothing but a form of division of labor: while most of adults worked, some were charged with minding the children and teaching them some skills. This essential configuration changed very little throughout human history. Teaching still involves facing of a multitude of children. Early Soviet practitioners of collective education correctly reasoned that meaningful teaching requires personal relationships, but it is difficult for one teacher to influence many

Dialogue as a Means of Collective Communication, Edited by Banathy and Jenlink
Kluwer Academic/Plenum Publishers, New York 2005

children at once. It is difficult not only because of the difference in numbers, but also because children and especially adolescents tend to resist adult influences. However, children and adolescents are very likely to be influenced by peers. Therefore, educators must try to create a modified peer group called the collective. This peer group will generally support the educational influences, and limit negative behaviors. In other words, the collective education is simply use of peer group relations for educational purposes. This line of reasoning is not entirely unknown in the West. Some recent examples could include various peer mediation efforts, the Just Communities experiments by L. Kohlberg and his associates(Power, Higgins, Kohlberg, 1989), and the experiences of many volunteer youth organizations (see, for instance, McLaughlin et.al, 1994). However, Western equivalents of collective education have never entered the mainstream educational practices. Consequently, Western, especially English-speaking educational theory never tried to understand how peer groups can be modified for educational purposes.

The Russian collective education from the very beginning had two schools of thought, one authoritarian and one democratic. Anton Makarenko, the founder of the collective theory and practice, believed that the collective development goes through two stages. During the first stage, the collective is the goal of teacher's efforts. The second stage turns the collective into a tool for educational purposes oriented toward an individual student. The authoritarian school of thought emphasized the first stage and viewed the collective as an excellent instrument of behavioral control. The democratic school was looking for the forms of communal life that would enrich individual development. Sometimes no more than difference in emphasis, sometimes a bitter political issue, this basic division survived to this day in Russia.

Liudmila Novikova, who in the 70-s has become an unofficial dean of the democratic wing of the collective theory, by the mid-80-s realized that the language of the traditional educational theory is no longer adequate to describe the new realities of Russian education. I do not think she ever stated explicitly her reasoning, but here is my interpretation based on many conversations with her. Novikova always made it a point to keep very close ties with several excellent schools throughout Russia, both to conduct research, and to try out her ideas in schools. At some point she and people around her realized that good schools have become too different from one another. As educational experiments diversified, it became more and more difficult to say that certain things work in all schools. The traditional language of the collective education was very sophisticated and highly nuanced to analyze peer relations and student-teacher relational dynamics (Novikova, 1978). However, it was structured so that a theorist could recommend specific strategies for teachers (which is how American educational theory is unfortunately structured, too). As the real-life educational collectives were becoming more and more diverse, the theory of the collective ran into some problems. Frustrated by the lack of observable commonalities among the best schools, Novikova started to use the systems approach in an attempt to understand deeper structures of schools as social organisms. For that purpose she created a special laboratory of the educational systems in the mid-80-s within the Russian Educational Academy.

The Novikova group took schools as holistic social systems, where all components are interrelated and equally important for education – formal curriculum and informal peer interaction, school walls and inside jokes, assemblies and rumors, little habits and serious traditions. They saw the school as something like a living organism, with its own culture and ecology, its own cycles of activity. Education was thought to be a function of the entire system, not only of conscious and organized efforts of teachers and administration. They realized that a school is not fully controllable, at least not with the means of direct management. The good schools did not become such strictly by design; there was always an element of unexpected. The mechanisms of self-control and self-regulation were found to be much more effective that administrative control.

Novikova's group quickly realized that emphasis on complexity (non-determinism) of school systems and interdependency of all its components presents a specific theoretical problem. Any sort of description implies separation of important from unimportant, of figure from the background, of key features from secondary features. Yet the assumption of the system theory was the interdependency of all components. But how does one describe such a system, let alone give recommendations on how to create or improve one? It is one thing to give examples of seemingly unimportant details of school life that turn out to be educationally significant; it is very different to give a more or less comprehensive description of a school. With so many elements to consider, school systems could become indescribable, and therefore untheorizable.

One could use the methods of qualitative research, and Novikova encouraged her doctoral students to use those extensively. Yet even an ethnographic study would have to come up with some theoretical framework that could explain the system as a whole. And this is something very difficult to do, because the holistic assumptions also imply some sort of ineffability. The system approach forbids reducing the whole system to the sum of its components. However, no description is possible without breaking down the whole into some sort of components. Novikova's group set out to search for new units of analysis and for methodology that would avoid traditional analytical breakdown of the whole into parts. The search is still going on with various degrees of success (see, for instance, Karakovsky, Novikova, and Selivanova, 1996).

3.   THE CORE ACTIVITY

What follows is not so much a rendition of Novikova's group findings as examining some possible implications of the group's research.

One fundamental implication of Novikova's work was finding that good schools have to maintain a certain level of complexity. The good schools cannot be monolithic and homogeneous. Rather, they are conglomerates of heterogeneous groups, including peer groups, teacher associations, clubs, sport teams, etc. Significantly, all these groups have overlapping memberships and means of communication with each other. Karakovsky, Novikova and Selivanova describe this as a "web of memberships and relations enveloping a student"(1996). The multiplicity of school activities seems to ensure that no rigid hierarchies of successful versus unsuccessful groups will emerge. In Russia, it was always assumed that schools cannot and should not limit themselves to strictly academic learning. Novikova's associates found empirical evidence suggesting that outside of the selective elitist schools, only schools with a sufficient variety of activities can be successful both socially and academically.

Another implication is that school as a system cannot be meaningfully presented in one coherent description; instead, it should be presented as at least two different and complementary descriptions (school as an organization and school as a community). This distinction is similar to the German notions of Gezelleschaft and Gemeinshaft (Sidorkin, 1990). The important point here is epistemological–a system as a whole cannot be adequately described only once. 3-D computer imaging could serve as an imperfect analogy. In order to get a 3-D image, one needs to take numerous 2-D pictures of an object. One very good image, even an X-ray does not create the sense of reality of the three-dimensional object. With complex social systems, the same principle applies. One description of the system, no matter how detailed or how sophisticated, does not do justice to the complexity. Two or more different descriptions, however, can do just that.

Extending Novikova's distinction between the school as a community and the school as an organization, I suggest another pair of categories that can both describe a school as a whole, but still can be thought of as components of the system. To address the difficulty of describing a complex system that I mentioned above, one needs units of analysis that would not reduce the system to the sum of its components. The problem could be solved should one use *processes* rather than things of objects, or concepts as such units. One can describe a complex social system such as school as a number of key processes without diminishing the system's complexity. In other words, it seems almost impossible to describe a good school; however, it is quite possible to describe what is going on in a good school.

Any school can be described as having "core activity" and "core conversation." The notion of core activity (*Vedushchaia, kliuchevaia* or *sistemoobrazuiushchaia deiatelnost'*) has a long history in the Russian theory of educational collective. The core activity makes creation of the school community possible, because it in some way requires collaboration, differentiation of roles, and motivation. Here is how Alexander Pashkov explains the role of core activity in an education: "Cultivating humanity in various kinds of activity helps the transition from objective, super-personal knowledge to subjective, personalized, phenomenological knowledge of experience. This involves understanding activity as a special mechanism that transforms outside influences into internal developmental changes" (Karakovsky, Novikova, Selivanova, 1996, 115). One can clearly see the connection to Vygotsky-Leontiev tradition of Russian psychological theory of activity. Learning is understood as a function of social activity, and not as just any kind of cognition. Simplifying to the extreme, this is the position "knowing is doing."

Novikova's group took the activity theory beyond the problematic of learning into the theory of educational systems, which could be viewed as applying Vygotsky's idea of Zone of proximal development to large social systems. They consider the dominant activity the main system-forming factor (Vygotsky, 1996, p. 25). This means, simply, that a school must be held together by some sort of shared activity. A good school, in their view, has both a variety of activities, and one common core activity.

The notion of core activity is similar to John Dewey's (1916) concept of experience. Dewey discovered a general principle of social organization: for any given group, the type of predominant shared activity directly affects the type of social relation within the group. His views here are similar to one of the main Marxist heuristics about the relation between the mode of production and the social relations in society. He analyzed the activity/relation link for a traditional school as a particular case of that principle. Dewey's conclusion was that the regular object-lesson learning as an activity provides a very poor foundation for a "social spirit" or a "social glue" which could hold a school together as a group. Dewey's interpretive tool is very valuable indeed in explaining the many ills of contemporary education. It shows that revising policies, introducing better teaching methods, or investing more resources into schooling cannot significantly affect the fundamental well being of schools. Following Dewey's idea, schools are organizations that are very hard to manage, which becomes more and more apparent with the passage of time and with the disappearance of some form of extrinsic social control (such as the threat of corporal punishment or expulsion). One needs to insert a different foundation (different activity) under the whole school in order to affect its predominant social relationships.

What, according to Dewey was so wrong with the activity of learning that it could not provide the "social spirit" or "the cement of social organization?" His critique of the traditional learning, and especially his apology of active "occupations" primarily focus on the fact that traditional learning is not like real life; it is not aimed at achieving some real results, and therefore is not engaging for students. From Dewey's point of view, the active "occupations" are better because they provide a "genuine motive."

The main problem with "occupations" is connected to the very essence of learning. If learning, in whatever active form, becomes too close to the real "adult" occupation, it simply ceases to be learning. Let us take, for instance, Dewey's favorite example, "a busy kitchen, in which a group of children is actively engaged in the preparation of food." For such an activity to provide a real motive it should be as "real" as possible; that is as close to real cooking as possible. However, if children are there mainly to cook food, their activity ceases to be learning, and is no different from routine adult cooking. By moving closer the active occupation, learning looses its meaning as learning. Cooking, as any other learning activity, must remain somewhat unreal, non-utilitarian to preserve its essence.

Dewey understood these boundaries of learning; he made sure to specify that in active learning, "The aim is not the economic value of the products, but the development of social power and insight" (Dewey, 1900 18). But this is exactly what will always keep learning separated from the world of real professional occupations. The problem of learning motivation lies not with the form of learning–traditional object-lesson or progressive active occupations. This problem will be intrinsic to *any* learning, as long as it stays within its boundaries. Dewey confused the excitement of novelty, which can really motivate children to learn for some time, with long-term motivation. Deweyan "active occupations" invariably face the same issues of motivation as soon as they become a normal, routine part of school life. The only true, long-term, reliable motivation known to humankind is the paycheck; it will never be applicable to schools.

Dewey's second, more general solution seems to be far more careful and broad. "Learning? Certainly, but living primarily" (Dewey, 1900 36). Centering educational enterprise around the "life of the child" from my point of view, means that schools really must cease to be educational institutions. Learning, no matter how broadly understood, no matter passive or active, cannot provide the "social spirit" for the schools. Following Dewey, and despite Dewey, learning cannot be placed at the center of a good school. What we want from schools from the point of view of social relations cannot be achieved with learning as its foundational activity.

Some evidence supports this theoretical conclusion by Novikova's group. Among the large number of best schools they studied, only very few had learning at the center of their communal life. (See, for example,

Baliasnaya, 1995). Now, all the schools had excellent academic achievement levels, sometimes despite socio-economic odds. However, the overwhelming majority of good schools did not place academic learning into the center of their lives. This can be explain by the specifics of academic learning as an activity that does not invite much cooperation, especially on the scale of the whole school. In addition, learning does not provide good basis for a large conversation.

4.   THE CORE CONVERSATION

Curiously, Novikova's group considered in detail the core activity – the process that describes the organizational aspect of school, – but has never considered an analogous process that would describe the school as a community. Instead, the group only examined the static elements of the communal aspect (goals, shared visions, communal self-portraits, etc.) Similarly, Sara Lightfoot who studied different American high schools, come to the following conclusion: "Yet despite the extreme material contrasts, there are ways in which each institution searches for control and coherence. Gaining control seems to be linked to the development of visible and explicit ideology"(1983, 320). I am not questioning Novikova's or Lightfoot's conclusions. Indeed, every good school seem to have a set of shared beliefs of goals (ideology). However, what I found is that in reality, these ideologies do not explain the schools very well. In fact, they are often a collection of myths and commonplace proclamations. Moreover, some of very mediocre schools sometimes have very elaborated and clever ideologies (Sidorkin, 1990 and 1990a). One cannot determine the character of a system from analysis of stable components of its ideology. However, one can learn about the system by learning about its core conversation–a dialogical process by which the school community attempts to interpret itself.

The core conversation is like a plot of a novel–it usually includes a number of issues that are discussed by a school community via a number of channels, some formal and some informal. The core conversation is a way for a school community to make sense of itself. The core conversation is an on-going dialogue of multiple players, which does not require a consensus or even shared values or beliefs. The conversation itself is a connecting factor, and paradoxically, it requires certain amount of disagreement. Therefore the system constantly produces dissent to preserve its coherence.

The moral vision or an ideology in school matters only when there is an opportunity for all to talk about it. The public conversation creates disruptions in the settled framework of a school's ideology, its habits and organizational ways. It is a type of situation where students and teachers actively engage in conversation about the fundamentals of school ideology. It is a public talk about the most important community issues.

The forms of the public conversation may be different. A school may employ a straightforward form of democratic government. A.S. Neil, who had the luxury of a very small school, could afford to run general meetings that held the supreme power of decision making, and where teachers and students had equal vote. Only some essential provisions for safety were beyond the general meeting's power (Neil, 1961, 45-55). Another famous example of full-blown democracy in an educational setting would be L. Kohlberg's "just communities" (Higgins, 1991). Neil saw the democratic form as "practical civics," that is an exercise in democratic discussion, as well as the fulfillment of children's right to govern themselves. Kohlberg argued that just community meetings might serve as vehicles of moral education. Very similar ideas of democratic schools were tried, if only inconsistently, in Russian education of the 20's, and then resurfaced in the 60's. I certainly endorse these experiments of democratic government in schools, with two reservations.

My first reservation is about the purposes of self-government. Neither "learning democracy," nor implementing more effective management should become the priorities of self-government. The main purpose of democratic institutions in schools is a symbolic one, and I do not use the word "symbolic" lightly. A democratic assembly is important because it evokes images of democracy, which is a particular normative vision of good life. Now, this image is very much consistent with the mainstream liberal ideology of the larger society, which makes it more plausible to defend. Yet I would state that the purpose of self-government in schools is mainly a symbolic one. This means that other forms of public conversation should supplement self-government.

I have witnessed numerous attempts to introduce democratic forms of student government in Russian schools during the early years of perestroika. Most of these attempts ended in a spectacular failure precisely because there was nothing underneath the new democratic forms (Sidorkin, 1990a). Even Deborah Meier, who considers developing democratic communities to be a purpose of schooling, notes: "Representative bodies are surely a legitimate form of democracy, just not very effective for the kind of school culture we are trying to create"(Meier, 1995, p. 24). A good school does not evolve from the elections. I do not think this thesis requires extensive argumentation for support. Everyone has come across examples of democratic conversation without much coherence. The reversed case, of good school without democracy, is worth illustrating, though.

Sara Lightfoot describes Bill Oates, rector of St. Paul school, who wields great power. There is nothing like a formal democracy in St. Paul. For example, even decisions made by the admissions committee are subject to final approval by the rector, "but he is wise enough to recognize when an overturned decision would greatly violate a difficult and consuming selection process or offend an important constituency" (Lightfoot, 1983, p. 238).

> Faculty rarely disagree with the rector, or even dare to disagree strongly. No one risks being late to meetings with him. People who normally seem strong and sturdy in their roles appear strangely submissive and accommodating in his presence...

> Even though his dominance is without question, his style is not dominating. Rather he appears supremely civilized and benign in manner. He takes on the demeanor of the rectors who were his predecessors....As a matter of fact, many students describe him as friendly and approachable....Every Saturday night, he and his wife host an open house with punch and their famous chocolate chip cookies. (Lightfoot, 1983, pp. 237-238)

This description of "enlightened authoritarianism" strikes me as very familiar. It is exactly the style of leadership exercised by Boris Polianskii, a principal of a school that is as different from the privileged world of St. Paul as it is possible to imagine. Polianskii rules in the small rural school of Zorino village, Kursk region in Southern Russia. This is a school that combines a family-like atmosphere with very high learning achievements. This is how Alexander Pashkov, who closely studied this school for a number of years, describes the role of its principal:

> He is not only a generator of ideas, and organizer of these ideas' fulfillment; he is also a mediator, a tuner of relations in the collective, and a communications expert. Most of his time (according to our timing, up to 80%) is spent on support, adjustment, and correction of relations among teachers, counselors, and coaches from sports department, leaders of clubs, students and support staff. This allows him to know everything that happens in the school, to keep his finger on the school's pulse, to regulate quickly all the components of organization. (Selivanova, 1989, p. 51)

Both Polianskii and Oates are leaders of schools where public conversation does not entail formal democracy. Yet I would insist both schools fall under my definition of a good school. First, they do satisfy students, teachers, and parents, which seems to me to be a true and effective criterion of a good school. And second, these schools create dialogical situations, if in different forms than more conventionally democratic schools. In both schools there exists some space and occasion for public conversation, even though this conversation may be mediated by one person, or occur mainly through informal channels.

In some schools, like in that of Karakovskii in Moscow, there exists a peculiar mixture of democratic and non-democratic forms of public conversation. The school has a so-called Big Council, which includes faculty, administration, and student representatives, with the last group making a clear majority. This body assembles two or three times a year, making some important decisions. But the regular life of the school is run through channels very similar to those Oates and Polianskii use. Yet I found that everybody in the school knows what everybody else's position is on any given issue. It always escaped me how such information gets exchanged. Autocracy does not necessarily mean that certain voices are not heard. Informal consultations may very well play the role of a public conversation. I think, the notion of a public conversation means that information about different opinions is freely distributed, not censored, and is available on demand. It also means that anybody is able to make his or her opinion known to all at any time. There is not an absolute need for the physical presence of the conversant at the same time in the same place.

The difference between a good school and a bad one is the existence of a public conversation. There should be channels for every voice to be heard, and for every ear to listen. In non-civic schools such channels are absent or not functional. There is no assurance that what you think can be known to everyone, especially those individuals in authority. In such schools, authorities are not interested, nor have they established any effective ways to find out, who thinks what and why. This defines the absence of public conversation.

The model of "enlightened authoritarianism" does not seem to be functional at the level of large societies. The procedural aspect of democracy has proven to be a necessary (although not sufficient) condition for a large-scale democracy. It is not so in smaller social entities like schools. Formal democratic procedures of decision making are neither necessary nor sufficient conditions for initiating what I call the public conversation.

The type of core conversation directly depends on the type of the core activity. In other words, a volunteer fire department and a criminal gang will produce two different types of conversations not only because they are populated by different people, but because the nature of common activity implies different core conversation. Schools differ not because they implement dissimilar policies, or have dissimilar social make-up; they differ because they have dissimilar core activities *and/or* dissimilar core conversations. Schools are self-regulating systems; the type of core conversation will generally follow the type core activity. This does not mean, though that there is an automatic link between the two. The main point of this chapter is to show that the core conversation is just as important factor of school system as the core activity. A school succeeds as a community if it has an important common project (the core activity), but also if it is able to realize an adequate form of core conversation. Any misbalance between the two will create tension and conflict.

The internal driving force of the school histories is the tension between the core activity and the core conversation. The core conversation tends to mutate much more rapidly than the core activity, and school's communal mentality outgrows the activity-based foundation of the community.

5. IMPLICATIONS FOR SCHOOL REFORMING

There are two main concepts of school reforming: policy-driven and movement driven. The former implies that certain policies will produce certain effects. If a policy had a certain effect in one instance, it will produce similar effect in all other instances. Reforms fail either because of the faulty policy or faulty implementation; the individual differences among schools are "noise." The movement-driven concept of reforming has similar assumptions: schools are simple, deterministic, and homogenous systems. One school's success could be translated into few key components, which than could be transplanted into another school. The only difference between the two concept is that the movement-driven one believes that individual schools select for themselves which model to assume, and whose success to follow.

I would argue that it does not matter whether schools are given exact directive from above, or their teacher truly believe they can emulate someone else's success. For most reformers, most of the deep structure of a school remains invisible. For example, schools can be on different periods of their development, and have different core activities/core conversations in them. To understand a school, one needs to attend to its core conversation, and those are by definitions very unique for each school.

The matter is complicated by the fact that many successful educators often do not realize the reason for their own success. Some of the great school principals who were able to create wonderful vibrant school communities, sometimes have very silly ideas about why they were able to succeed. As successful principals, they enjoy tremendous respect and acquire followers. Unfortunately, great principals are not necessarily great theoreticians. In fact, it is very difficult to be enmeshed into complexities of everyday reality of school life and be able to produce meaningful generalizations.

Educational reforming should be based on assumptions of the systems approach: every school is a complex non-deterministic system, the key components of which are the core activity and core conversation. To change a school means to change its core activity and core conversation. One cannot arbitrarily change the core conversation without changing the core activity. However, introduction of a new activity does not necessarily bring about a change in core conversation. One cannot count on changing the conversation (and therefore the culture) of a school, if the foundation of an activity is missing, or does not fit. At the same time, just changing the core activity is not sufficient; the new and adequate core conversation is also needed.

Traditional academic learning is a very poor activity to build a system on, because it does not require true cooperation. Therefore, school reformers must attempt to find some forms of youth activity that would cause educationally beneficial forms of conversation to appear.

School reforming should be informed by analysis of an individual school's core activity and the core conversation. It is a one-at-a time, individualized process. An outside expert can bring certain analytic tools, but cannot offer a model for a change.

REFERENCES

Baliasnaya, L.K., (ed.), 1995. Vospitatel'nye sistemy sovremennoy shkoly: opyt, poiski, perspektivy [Educational systems in contemporary schooling: experiences, explorations, perspectives]. Moscow: Russian Educational Academy, Institute for Educational Theory and Pedagogy.

Dewey, J., 1900. *The School and Society.* The University of Chicago Press, Chicago.

Dewey, J., 1916. *Democracy and Education: An Introduction to the Philosophy of Education.* The Free Press, New York.

Karakovsky, V.A, Novvikova L.I., and Selivanova N.L., 1996. Vospitanie? Vospitanie... Vospitanie! Teoriia i praktika vospitatel'nykh sistem. [Character Education? Character Education... Character Education! Theory and Practice of Educational Systems]. Novaia Shkola, Moscow.

Lightfoot, Sara L., 1983. The Good High School: Portraits of Character and Culture. Basic Books, New York.

McLaughlin, M.W., Irby, M.A., and Langman, J., 1994. *Urban Sanctuaries: Neighborhood Organizations in the Lives and Futures of Inner-city Youth.* Jossey-Bass Publishers, San Francisco.

Novikova, L.I., 1978. *Pedagogika Detskogo Kollektiva. Voprosy Teorii.* [The Pedagogy of the Children's Collective: Theoretical Issues] Znanie, Moscow.

Power, F.C., Higgins, A., and Kohlberg, L., 1989. *Lawrence Kohlberg's Approach to Moral Education.* Columbia University Press, New York.

Sidorkin, A.M., 1990. Razvitie vospitatel'noi sistemy shkoly kak zakonomernyi protses. [Development of school system: driving forces and contradictions] Kand. diss., Research Institute for Theory and History of Education, Moscow.

Sidorkin, A.M., 1990a. Posobie dlia nachinaiushchikh robespierov [Beginner revolutionary guide]. Znanie, Moscow.

Neil, A.S., 1961. *Summerhill: A Radical Approach to Child Rearing.* Hart Publishing, New York.

Higgins, A., 1991. The just community approach to moral education: Evolution of the idea and recent findings. In W.M.Kurtines and J.L. Gewit (eds.), Applications, vol. 3 of *Handbook of Moral Behavior and Development,* Erlbaum, Hillside, NJ, pp. 111-139.

Meier, D., 1995. The power of their ideas: Lessons for America from a small school in Harlem. Beacon Press, Boston.

Selivanova N., (ed.), 1989. Vospitatel'naia sistema shkoly: problemy i poiski, Znanie, Moscow.

Chapter 12

BOHM'S JOURNEY TO DIALOGUE
A Look at Its Roots

LINDA ELLINOR
The Dialogue Group

1.   INTRODUCTION

> Bohm's world was holistic, as holistic as the unanalyzable
> interconnections of the quantum or his unified vision of matter and
> mind. Holism extended, he believed, into human psychology and
> society itself. He dreamed of developing a group mind and spent his
> last years organizing dialogue circles in its pursuit. (David Peat,
> 1997, p. 4)

Many groups today are exploring dialogue through the inspiration of the
work of the late David Bohm, a quantum physicist and philosopher. This
paper examines David Bohm's worldview out of which his vision of
dialogue unfolded in the mid-1980s. Dialogue represents an important
culminating aspect of Bohm's lifework: a far-reaching inquiry into the
nature of reality and the ramifications it suggests for human society.
Because few thinkers in our day have grappled so thoroughly with making
connections between the physical sciences and the problems facing our
world today, it seems apropos to examine the journey Bohm took on his
way to developing his proposal of dialogue.
    My interest in Dialogue began in 1991after first reading Peter Senge's
Fifth Discipline and attending one of David Bohm's seminars on Dialogue
in Ojai. The draw for me was intuitive. It seemed that Dialogue might be
one remedy for some of the self-defeating ways of interacting that are
unconsciously fostered in our society. In the West, we learn from an early
age in school and in our families how to defend our position on things. We
learn that being right is more important than listening to others. When
we grow up, we take these ways of defending our need to be right into our
most intimate relationships with others and then wonder why things do
not go the way we like. We rarely examine the ways in which we
communicate. We rarely consider that the interpersonal problems we
encounter may lie with the *process* rather than with the *content*. One of

the important values of Bohm's proposal of dialogue is that it brings into conscious relief the process by which we share meaning with others. And this rests on the values, skills, and worldview that underpin it. What are these assumptions about the nature of reality that Bohm came to from his work in quantum physics that led him to dialogue? Do they make sense in our world today? Should we take his proposal of dialogue seriously?

After first learning about dialogue, I started practicing it in a community group I started in Temecula, California. Later, with my business partner, Glenna Gerard, I began to train others in how to use dialogue in organizational contexts. After a decade of exploring dialogue and co-authoring a book with Glenna, entitled *Dialogue: Rediscover the Transforming Power of Conversation*, I began to wonder more deeply about the roots of Bohm's proposal of dialogue. How did a quantum physicist come to the conclusion that something like dialogue was imperative in our world today? Why was I, a practicing organizational consultant, coming to the same conclusion as a physicist?

The interconnectedness of life, holism, and the constant flowing nature of reality were fundamental for Bohm. In the context of these beliefs, Dialogue is a conscious act of man, representing the élan vital, the force, and the spirit that holds the entire universe together.

I will attempt to trace the development of Bohm's thinking from his vision of quantum reality to dialogue.[1] I will do so mainly by drawing upon his biography by David Peat, *Infinite Potential: The Life and Times of David Bohm*. Other sources that have been important to me in my personal work with dialogue have been Bohm's own writings: *Wholeness and the Implicate Order*, *Science, Order, and Creativity* (co-written by Bohm and Peat), *On Dialogue*, and *Changing Consciousness* (a dialogue by Bohm and Mark Edwards). Also helpful have been interviews with Bohm by Renee Weber in *Dialogues with Scientists and Sages*, as well as a collection of writings in *Quantum Implications: Essays in Honour of David Bohm*, edited by B.J. Hiley and F. David Peat.

2.   THE JOURNEY TO DIALOGUE BEGINS

> That ability to touch preverbal processes at the muscular, sensory level remained with (Bohm) all his life. It was not so much that Bohm visualized a physical system as that he was able to sense its dynamics within his body: 'I had the feeling that internally I could participate in some movement that was the analogy of the thing you are talking about.' (Peat 1997, p. 68)

Bohm seems to have come into the world with a natural inclination for seeing the big picture and being in touch with how his own intuitions of wholeness and constant flux are at the essence of reality. His way of operating from a very early age was to sense how something felt true within himself and then to extrapolate these truths broadly into his work as a quantum physicist and later as a philosopher. He seemed to live by the hermetic dictum of "as above, so below", a medieval idea that holds each individual is the microcosm of the macrocosm. Bohm felt that "by giving attention to his own feelings and sensations, he should be able to arrive at a deeper understanding of the nature of the universe" (Peat 1997, p. 36). Later, when he became interested in dialogue, he would talk about how a dialogue group could serve as a microcosm for the whole society of which it was but a part. In other words, what one group might experience in a dialogue about the changing nature of thought might be projected into society at large. (For those interested in pursuing this assumption of Bohm's further, this idea of "as above, so below, and "the microcosm of the macrocosm" can be traced to Hermes Trismegistus, an ancient Egyptian god. Hermetism was a religious amalgam of Greek philosophy with Egyptian and other Near Eastern elements that arose between 100AD and 300AD. Hermetism was reintroduced into Western Europe during the Renaissance and inspired philosophers, scientists and magicians of the fifteenth and sixteenth centuries. (*Concise Routledge Encyclopedia of Philosophy*, 1999, p. 349)

Peat tells the story of Bohm as a small boy being somewhat uncoordinated, having to plan his physical movements in sports step by step. When, once, he had to cross a river, stepping from stone to stone he had a sudden flash that the only way to make it across was to do it as one continuous movement. He knew at that moment that he couldn't stop to think about how to cross the river, and "suddenly realized that security does not require control and stillness but can come in a freely flowing movement...(from this moment on) David began to see the world in terms of flows and transformations, processes and movements" (Peat, 1997, pp. 14-15).

As a youth he became fascinated with science fiction with led him to the idea of a fourth dimension. This idea later appeared in his work as a quantum physicist in terms of his Hidden Variables Theory of Quantum Phenomenon. Could it be, he hypothesized as a boy that a fourth dimension might exist that operates on our three dimensionality in ways that are hidden? As he mastered Euclidian geometry in high school, he began to explore his idea of the fourth dimension more formally. "Now he was in a position to show that what appear to be separate objects in our world could be, in four dimensions, aspects of a single whole. His ambition was, as he wrote in his notebook, to show how 'all the apparent laws of the universe' have the same source...'This correlation has long been sought, and if it is true, I believe it will aid the future progress of science greatly.' In effect, he sought a cosmology, a scientific account of the interconnection of all things" (Peat, 1997, p. 25). Later, in his proposal of dialogue, Bohm makes this same assumption of interconnection and includes the nature of mind. Mind and matter, it will be seen for Bohm are inseparable. If we study one, we study, by definition, the other.

Other subjects of fascination for Bohm included light, energy, power and transcendence. "Throughout his life Bohm yearned for contact with the transcendent and for moments of "breaking through" (Peat, 1997, p. 21). Although, from a psychological point of view, his thirst for power and transcendence might have stemmed from difficulties he experienced within his early family environment (an emotionally unstable mother and a father focused on the practical matters of a furniture business which had little interest for Bohm), these subjects came to dominate in his quest for knowledge as an adult.

He also had an early interest in politics, which carried through to his adult years to his development of dialogue. He was always interested in ways of ordering society that would alleviate the problems he saw around him from his youth in the depression era. For instance, the miners from his hometown in Wilkes-Barre, PA suffered economically during this time when the New York market for coal dried up. "Later in life David took the world's troubles, (like these), onto his shoulders and dreamed of a life that could be ordered, harmonious, and free..." (Peat, 1997, p. 21)

During his college years and a few years there after he flirted with communism. Unfortunately, while he found fleeting moments of community within the communist party, his involvement led to his need to leave the country. He was a victim of McCarthyism and lost his professorship at Princeton.

One of his main driving forces in becoming a theoretical physicist was what could be learned from natural science that could help the world at large. He had the belief in the importance of science for everyday life and how to make his scientific ideas, no matter how abstract, accessible to ordinary people. He also believed that science could transform society (Peat, 1997, p. 19). Communism for him held out a promise of radical societal transformation. While he later changed his mind regarding communism after learning of the atrocities under Stalin, he never let go of the idea of a transformation of society. Dialogue later became for him the transforming vehicle. Interestingly, Hegel, who inspired Marx and Engel also inspired Bohm's thinking about quantum phenomena and led him into seeing how his findings could also impact society.

His belief was that there were universal laws at work in nature that were harmonious. "If only human beings could realize that the entire universe was rational, he thought, they would begin to apply reason and seek harmony in their own lives" (Peat, 1997, p. 24). Bohm's quest for rationality and harmony eventually led him to his conception of the implicate order which allows for an infinite number of levels of order. What appears irrational at one level of perception makes perfect sense at a deeper level of perception. This is why in dialogue we seek deeper and deeper levels of understanding as well as the broadest number of perspectives. In this way, we try to see a larger whole from the collection of individual perspectives. What one person sees is but a small part of what might actually be happening. Together, collective meaning creates a fuller tapestry.

Moving into his college work and beyond there were three main thrusts that led him to his focus on dialogue: his work as a quantum scientist, his study of Hegel, dialogues with J. Krishnamurti, an eastern mystic, and his exposure to the work of Patrick de Mare, a Freudian psychologist who began doing a form of social psychotherapy in his work with groups.

3. INSIGHTS FROM QUANTUM PHYSICS

There can be few physicists who have delved as deeply into the philosophical implications of their subject as has David Bohm. (Roger Penrose, *Quantum Physics and Conscious Thought*, cited in Hiley, 1987, p. 105)

Unfortunately for the broad advancement of his ideas, Bohm was considered a maverick among his physicist peers with much of his work that we might think important in the development of dialogue, not being taken seriously. But, isn't this the way for visionaries? Bohm was not interested in research just because they solved certain short-term problems. And his goal wasn't an equation for equation sake, but rather to further a deep understanding of quantum phenomenon. He says over and over again in interviews and in his writings, that the positivist, pragmatic approach that dominates main street physics loses sight of the very reason quantum physics can be important in the world today. "Bohm was really a throwback to an earlier age, in which physics involved deep and quiet contemplation of nature; when it was more concerned with discovering the underlying order of cosmos than with making predictions and solving practical problems" (Peat, 1997, p. 35).

A bit like Einstein, David thought out-of-the-box using his intuitions gained earlier about wholeness and interconnection. The research projects influencing him most directly in his development of dialogue were with plasma and his quest for an alternative explanation to quantum mechanics leading him to his hidden variables theory.

3.1 Plasma

In a plasma...there is a subtle relationship between the free individual and the collective. (Peat, 1997, p. 67)

Just as Bohm was completing his Ph.D. at Berkeley, McCarthyism was on the upswing. Because of his affiliation with the communist party, he was denied access to his own on-going research work, which would have led to his dissertation. This was because those working on the Manhattan

Project, the research project that eventually resulted in the development of the atomic bomb, saw his research as valuable to the effort. Eventually, Oppenheimer (the head of the department at the time who was also appointed to head up the Manhattan Project) intervened on Bohm's behalf so that he could be awarded his PhD in 1943. Bohm then immediately was asked to turn his attention to work with plasma, another way that supported the work of the Manhattan Project.

Plasma is a fourth state of matter that is different from a solid, liquid, or gas. Although we can only create plasma artificially in a laboratory because incredible heat is required – around 20,000 degrees Celsius, Peat points out "plasmas constitute over ninety-nine percent of the matter of the universe – most stars and interstellar gases exist in this fourth state of matter" (Peat, 1997, p. 65). What Bohm discovered was that plasma operates in two ways: collectively and individually at the same time.

> Seen from a distance, a plasma appears to be a series of collective oscillations, involving an astronomical number of particles. Examined at a high magnification, however, only the random motion of individual particles is visible. Bohm worked out a technical way to show mathematically how both collective vibrations and individual movement could be a part of a single whole: a collective motion of the whole enfolded within the random, individual movement, and vice versa. (Peat, 1997, p. 67)

At the time, Bohm had been drawn to Marxism. And, he felt his work with plasma corroborated Marxist idealism. "Marxist society was the rational ideal for humanity, (Bohm) was convinced, one in which each individual would experience perfect freedom while serving the common good." This was in contrast with how he viewed capitalism, as a collection of self-motivated individuals somehow contributing to the common good through their random actions. "Bohm realized that plasma was a perfect metaphor for (his ideal) for society. A plasma functions in a collective way, oscillating as a whole. Yet it is built out of particles, each of which moves freely with its own individual movement" (Peat, 1997, p. 67).

Later when Bohm began to develop his notion of dialogue, he drew from this metaphor in that people are relatively free but, yet, are influenced through their common perceptions, meanings, and values of society. It is culture that creates the connection between the individual and the collective. Dialogue is that which helps to surface what the connections are and it is that which can change both the individual and the collective while doing so.

Bohm's plasma research led him to his first outstanding contribution to physics. "His theoretical treatment of diffusion in a turbulent plasma has since become known as Bohm diffusion" (Peat, 1997, p. 68). Even back in the 40s, Bohm was looking for societal ramifications of his work in physics. He was trying to see how nature fundamentally lies at the crux of social systems.

The way we look at the world, he reasoned, determines how we act toward it, how we structure our society and derive the tenor of our individual lives. Equally, the society in which we live conditions our values and the way we think about and perceive the world. Science, society, and human consciousness were for Bohm, all aspects of a greater whole. (Peat, 1997, p. 68)

3.2   The Hidden Variable Theory/The Causal or Ontological Interpretation of Quantum Mechanics

The mystic sees in matter an immanent principle of unity, and this is implicitly what the scientist is also doing. (Bohm, interview with Renee Weber *in Dialogues with Sages and Scientists*, 1997, p. 144)

It was Einstein who had said, referring to the need for a radical new quantum theory, 'if anyone can do it, then it will be Bohm'. (Peat, 1997, p. 104)

That a creative mind may not necessarily be aware of what it has given birth to is as true in science as in the arts...Over the next forty years, Bohm pushed his hidden variable theory in new directions.... [He] expressed these changes in the differing names he gave the theory; hidden variable, the causal interpretation, and finally the ontological interpretation. (Peat, 1997, p. 115)

In the late 70s and early 80s, Renee Weber conducted a series of interviews with scientists such as David Bohm, Rupert Sheldrake, Ilya Prigogine, and Stephen Hawking as well as with mystics such as J. Krishnamurti, the Dalai Lama, and Father Bede Griffiths. She had a conviction that both these scientists and mystics were driving towards the same discovery of unity in universal reality. Weber states:

If I did not see a connection between science and mysticism, there would have been no need for this book. The connection I perceive is this: A parallel principle drives both science and mysticism–the assumption that unity lies at the heart of our world and that it can be discovered and experienced by man. (Weber, 1986, p. 13)

Bohm seems to have taken his own personal intuition of unity, a kind of mystical insight, from his boyhood and found it first in his research with plasma in the 40s. Later he extended it into a whole cosmology resulting in the implicate order that was first implicit in his development of an alternative interpretation of quantum mechanics, called his hidden variable theory. This was contrasted with the Copenhagen Interpretation of quantum mechanics put out by Niels Bohr which had became the accepted and standard way in which quantum phenomenon are understood and worked with within the physics community. Later Bohm renamed his theory the Causal Interpretation (Peat, 1997, p. 115), trying to differentiate it from another physicist's (de Broglie's) earlier, but similar theory that bore the same name, hidden variables. Still later, towards the end of his life, he renamed it the ontological interpretation to even further differentiate it from its former connections.

Many complex factors came together that caused his ideas, like those of one of his colleague's, de Broglie, to be largely overlooked by the mainstream of the physics community. Bohm explains this in an essay he wrote for Hiley's book published posthumously, *Quantum Implications: Essays in Honour of David Bohm* (1987), in that one of the main objections to his alternative theory was that it gave the exact same predictions for experimental results as does the accepted one. The positivist empiricist attitude that pervaded physics at the time couldn't see the relevance of what Bohm had done. Although Einstein at one point thought that Bohm was the most likely to come up with what he had struggled to do in his lifetime, a unified field theory; he was not to endorse Bohm's causal interpretation either. Einstein had a strong conviction that non-locality could not be accurate. (Non-locality comes from experiments with quantum particles where it is observed that one particle can impact another without it being close by or local. In Newtonian physics, this make no sense, but in the quantum world, it has become accepted.) And, he could not give up his need for a completely objective universe which does not necessitate the observer effecting the observed (as does Bohr's accepted quantum interpretation).

What Bohm tried to do was to resolve the different assumptions or attitudes involved in classical, Newtonian physics with those used in quantum physics. In effect, he was trying to connect Einstein's theory of relativity with quantum mechanics (Bohr's interpretation).

> I felt particularly dissatisfied with the self-contradictory attitude of accepting the independent existence of the cosmos while one was doing relativity (Einstein's strongly held conviction), and, at the same time, denying it while one was doing the quantum theory, even though both theories were regarded as fundamental. I did not see how an adequate way to deal with this could be developed on the basis of Niels Bohr's point of view. So I began to ask myself whether another approach might not be possible. (Bohm, 1987, p. 34)

Without going into the technical details, what Bohm's hidden variable theory does is to provide in scientific terms an alternative explanation and mathematical formulation to the Bohr's interpretation, and it does so by providing a logical, cosmological explanation of why Bohr's interpretation will predict accurate, statistical results. Basically, Bohm came up with a way to show how his original idea of a fourth dimension (hidden variables) to reality was not only a possibility, but offered a satisfying explanation for not only quantum phenomena, but for reality in its everyday perception (for classical phenomena). His basic postulation is that there is what he came to call the 'quantum potential' (a hidden variable) that carries information of the whole universe and is the ordering principle.

> With the quantum potential...the whole has an independent and prior significance such that, indeed, the whole may be said to organize the activities of the parts. For example, in a superconducting state it may be seen that electrons are not scattered because, through the action of the quantum potential, the whole system is undergoing a coordinated movement more like a ballet dance than like a crowd of unorganized people. Clearly, such quantum wholeness of activity is closer to the organized unity of functioning of the parts of a living being than it is to the kind of unity that is obtained by putting together the parts of a machine. (Bohm, 1987, p. 38)

So, while in classical physics we make the assumption that the parts add up to the whole, Bohm turned this around and showed how the whole affects the parts and is more primary. In dialogue, we learn to pay attention to the collective meaning that is flowing through the conversation. In so doing we are able to see how the whole effects the individuals who partake in the group and we can then see how this same effect might be extrapolated to society at large.

3.3 The Implicate Order and the Holomovement

> So the thought occurred to me: perhaps the movement of enfoldment and unfoldment is universal, while the extended and separate forms that we commonly see in experience are relatively stable and independent patterns, maintained by a constant underlying movement of enfoldment and unfoldment. This latter I called the holomovement. (Bohm, 1987, p. 41)

> ...the implicate order provided an image, a kind of metaphor, for intuitively understanding the implication of wholeness which is the most important new feature of the quantum theory. (Bohm, 1987, p. 41)

At the same time that he was devising his notions that moved his hidden variable theory to be renamed his causal interpretation, he was also playing with his earlier boyhood ideas of the constant flux of the universe. This resulted directly in his conception of the implicate order.

After finding little acceptance of his hidden variable theory, he began to direct his attention to the importance of order. He felt that this might lead to a different kind of resolution between the divergence in assumptions he saw between classical and quantum physics.

As he describes it, there were two metaphors that helped him develop his conceptions of the implicate order. One he saw on a BBC television show, a device

> in which an ink drop was spread out through a cylinder of glycerin and then brought back together again, to be reconstituted essentially as it was before. This immediately struck me as very relevant to the question of order, since when the ink drop was spread out, it still had a 'hidden' (i.e. non-manifest) order that was revealed when it was reconstituted. On the other hand, in our usual language, we would say that the ink was in a state of 'disorder' when it was diffused through glycerin. This led me to see that new notions of order must be involved here. (Bohm, 1987, p. 40)

The second metaphor that led him to postulating the implicate order was the hologram.

> I began to reflect on the hologram and to see that in it, the entire order of an object is contained in an interference pattern of light that does not appear to have such an order at all. Suddenly, the similarity of the hologram and the behavior of the ink drop struck me. I saw that what they had in common was that an order was enfolded; that is, in any small region of space there may be 'information' which is the result of enfolding an extended order and which could then be unfolded into the original order (as the points of contact made by the folds in a sheet of paper may contain the essential relationships of the total pattern displayed with the sheet is unfolded). (Bohm, 1977, p. 40)

How I conceive of the implicate order is that there are subtler and subtler levels to reality. What we see in our everyday world, Bohm likens to what he calls the explicate order. This is the order of classical, Newtonian physics. We can measure and predict this level of reality by making the assumption of the independent nature of matter and its existence. In this level of reality we do not need to worry about how the parts of a system are impacted by the whole, or how an observer might impact on what is being observed. Rather we can treat the parts as though they have independent existence apart from both the observer and other parts of reality. But, actually, what Bohm is saying in terms of his implicate order is that what we see in our every day reality, the explicate, is affected by a more subtle level of reality, that which he calls the implicate order, and below that the super-implicate order. Bohm postulates, in fact, that there may not be an end to levels of order; that there are an infinite number of levels.

The holomovement is based on his idea of flux and change being at root in nature. There is nothing but the changing nature of reality. What appears stable and solid, at closer scrutiny, at a quantum level, can be found to be nothing but waves of energy, light, and information, all interacting in ways that are informed by the whole.

This is what stands the positivist empiricist attitude on its head. Bohm states:

> Instead of supposing that extended matter (what we see in our everyday reality) and its movement are fundamental, while enfoldment and unfoldment are explained as a particular case of this, we are saying that the implicate order will have to contain within itself all possible features of the explicate order as potentialities, along with the principles determining which of these features shall become actual. The explicate order will in this way flow out of the implicate order through unfoldment, while in turn it 'flows back' through further enfoldment. The implicate order thus plays a primary role, while the explicate order is secondary, in the sense that its main qualities and properties are ultimately derived in its relationship with the implicate, of which it is a special and distinguished case. (Bohm, 1987, p. 41)

In the realm of human life, what this says to me is something akin to my understanding of the work of Carl Jung and his ideas regarding the Self and the collective unconscious. Jung felt that the human ego was but sub-part of a much larger whole that was connected by the Self to what he called the collective unconscious. The Self was that part of the psyche that has access to the collective unconscious and it is the collective unconscious that is most like Bohm's super-implicate order, or the order that provides the patterning that moves through the implicate through to the explicate order (or ego level reality).

There are other areas in which Bohm's conception of the implicate order and the holomovement play out. Renee Weber drew Bohm into a discussion about the work of Rupert Sheldrake and his theory of morphogenetic fields, for instance. Bohm was clear that Sheldrake's theory might be considered a subset of his implicate order. Bohm's work also touches on chaos theory as he likens non-linearity and seeming chaos to the need to look to deeper layers of understanding that reside within the implicate order. These deeper layers can then bring order or meaning to the chaos (Weber, 1986).

In dialogue we usually begin with something known or from within the explicate realm. In attempting to unfold a larger whole, we draw from the implicate order by uncovering underlying assumptions that might be hidden to us consciously at first.

Bohm's implicate order is an all-encompassing cosmology. If we were to consider any theory which might predict good results within a given range of phenomena, Bohm would say that in that domain it can hold, but beyond it, there are more and more subtle levels of order that need to be considered. And, that all our theories that help us explain phenomena are in some ways connected (although we may not obviously see the connections) through a deeper level of reality that may be hidden from our awareness. What is important in all of this, is Bohm's conviction that we must stay open in our quest for deeper levels of understanding. In his later development of dialogue, the implicate order underlies the assumption of no end point. Dialogue can not be dialogue if there is a need for closure or resolution to a problem. If there is then the dialogue dissolves into the need for one opinion or perspective to be right and this will curtail the free flow of meanings.

One of Bohm's most important objections to Neil Bohr's accepted quantum interpretation was that it was closed ended. In other words, once you accept the formalism of the mathematics involved in predicting quantum results (which is all based on statistical accuracy), there is n o where else you can go with it. It does not attempt to explain the results nor does it allow one to push the theory into a deeper level of understanding. It simply asks one to accept based on faith, the mathematical formulas will by themselves give you good statistical results.

Bohm felt that knowledge had infinite depths to it and that it was most important that we never lose sight of this. In fact, he felt that his implicate order was merely one potential cosmological conception and that many more would be developed as more and more understanding is unfolded in future years.

Ultimately, his ideas moved into the philosophical domain when he began to be interested in consciousness and meaning. Bohm was a master at the conceptualization of an all inclusive, cosmological understanding of the universe. This conceptualization needed to include both mind and matter. It is to this connection we turn to next which involves first his discovery of Hegel and then his relationship with J. Krishnamurti.

3.4   Hegel

It was Hegel's belief that he had discovered the true nature of thought - not in terms of particular content but its actual underlying dynamics, and not simply human thought but Thought with a capital T, the World Soul itself, which evolved through a process of dialectical creation and differentiation. (Peat, 1999, p. 156)

This claim about the deep dependence of individuals on one another (even for their very identity), even while they maintain their independence, is one of the best-known examples of Hegel's attempt at a dialectical resolution of many of the traditional oppositions and antinomies of past thought. (Audi, 1999, p. 367)

[Bohm felt that] The whole movement of consciousness must be considered, that was what he had previously left out of his calculations. (Peat, 1999, p. 180)

During the years Bohm was exiled in Brazil, a fellow physicist, Mario Schonberg, introduced him to the philosopher B.W.F. Hegel. The influence on Bohm of Hegel's thinking was to be profound. Like Bohm, Hegel was a systems thinker who attempted to integrate the philosophical currents of his day, such as rationalism and empiricism, by stating that from a larger perspective, both are valid.

Hegel often argued that what appeared to be contraries in philosophy, such as mind/body, freedom/determinism, idealism/materialism, universal/particular, the state/the individual, or even God/man, appeared such incompatible alternatives only because of the undeveloped and so incomplete perspective within which the oppositions were formulated. (Audi, 1999, pp. 367-368)

Like Bohm, Hegel also held that reality was in constant movement. "Hegelian dialectics is a ceaseless process, a movement of thought that is constantly creating and building" (Peat, 1999, p. 156). His most popular contribution to society at large was what has become known as the dialectical process wherein a thesis is countered by its opposite, or antithesis, only to be transcended by its synthesis. Now with Hegel's dialectical framework, Bohm was able to take his reformulation of quantum theory further. No longer did he need to oppose chance and causality. He now could show how at one level, what seemed like chance or chaos, could at another level of thought or consciousness, be seen as necessary or rational. "Now he realized that dialectics could take him much deeper and that his earlier essays and letters must be revised" (Peat, 1999, p. 157). It was during this time in Brazil that he completed *Causality and Chance in Modern Physics* which incorporated this new thinking based on Hegel.

From the perspective of dialogue, I have often seen the dialectic process unfolding. When considering a particular topic, for instance, two points of view will often come into conflict. If the topic holds a lot of energy for group members, it may feel at first like an unsolvable clash of opinions–a clash that might split the group apart. As judgment is suspended, and other opinions are shared and underlying assumptions explored, the group begins to build a fuller perspective. As this larger view unfolds, the two contrasting views are still there, but now they are held relative to this much larger group perspective. In this state of suspension, wherein all views may be held and heard, the contrariness of the original two perspectives diminishes in intensity. It is often in this holding of oppositions in paradox that a new and often creative breakthrough becomes possible in dialogue–thesis and antithesis transcended by synthesis.

Hegel was interested in searching for a broad philosophical approach that could take in all of human history, the arts, religion, etc. While Hegel was grounded in theology, the classics, and philosophy, as opposed to Bohm in theoretical physics, both men attempted to synthesize their worldviews across multiple disciplines. And, it is in the realm of politics, that the two thinkers, Bohm and Hegel, went down similar paths.

Hegel attempted to integrate politics with his dialectical worldview. He did not buy the Christian view of "human beings as permanently divided against themselves in terms of living an ethical or moral life" (Audi, 1999, p. 368). He didn't buy Kant's dualist idea either, that we are torn between duty and inclination or between rationality and desire. Hegel felt that:

> the dualisms of morality could be overcome in ethical life, those modern social institutions which, it was claimed, provided the content or true 'objects' of a rational will. These institutions, the family, civil society, and the state, did not require duties in potential conflict with our own substantive ends, but were rather experienced as the 'realization' of our individual free will. (Audi, 1999, p. 368)

In other words, like Bohm with his ideas on plasma showing compatibility between the movement of individual molecules and the movement of the whole, Hegel believed that the individual is not in ultimate conflict with collective institutions. If man could act from a position of 'rational self-determination' (which I interpret as being from the perspective of the whole–or what Hegel came to call 'Absolute Knowledge') (Audi, 1999, p. 367), then there would be a harmonious relationship between man and society. This integration of or connection between the individual and the collective was one of Bohm's life-long callings. Hegel's thinking on this subject certainly validated his own.

Bohm left Brazil for Israel in 1955 and shortly thereafter met Mashulan Groll, an active proponent of the kibbutz movement and an authority on Hegel's philosophy. It was through his influence that Bohm shifted away from a materialistic dialectic, which is more intrinsic to Marxist thought, and more towards a dialectic of thought (based on the "idealism of Hegel's logic"). Up until then he felt that "Nothing existed except matter, and human behavior arose out of material processes" (Peat, 1999, p. 179).[2]

Through his talks with Groll, he began to move towards a "form of idealism, giving a fundamental role in the cosmos to thought" (Peat, 1999, p. 179). He felt now that Marx and Engles had gone wrong and had distorted Hegel's basic position. He was coming to the realization that it was the "entire process by which thought operates that was of fundamental importance" (Peat, 1999, p. 180).

His fundamental error had been to assume that mind would be transformed through matter. He had focused on the surface, he now realized, on matter and its transformations. But actually matter could be viewed as a symbol or manifestation of the deeper movement, Universal Thought. (Bohm includes as thought, feelings, sensations, and the whole content and structure of consciousness.) (Peat, 1999, p. 180).

Eventually, Bohm was to come to a non-dualistic position on this, that mind and matter are aspects, or sides, of a deeper whole. If Hegel was the influence that started him towards this final insight, it was Krishnamurti's influence that was its culmination.

3.5 Krishnamurti

Krishnamurti's observations that 'the thinker is the thought' and 'the observer is the observed' struck Bohm as resembling his own...meditations on the role of the observer in quantum theory. Bohm had personally experienced the way in which the observation of a particular thought changes the movement of thought itself. His study of Hegel had led him to similar conclusions about the movement of thought. The physicist was well prepared for his engagement with Jiddu Krishnamurti. (Peat, 1999, p. 199)

Bohm compared (Krishnamurti) to Einstein in his ability to explore deeply in a spirit of impersonal friendship. (Peat, 1999, p. 200)

After moving to England in 1957, Bohm began to have the feeling that there "was more to the world than physics could explain, or rather, that there had to be something qualitatively different" (Peat, 1991, p. 193). What began as his shift away from Marxism in his quest for a transformed society, led him through Hegel to a search which took consciousness into account. He cast his net wider at this point by turning first to the work of such mystics as P.D. Ouspensky and G.I. Gurdjieff to an eventually long relationship with the eastern mystic, Krishnamurti. From Ouspensky and Gurdjieff, Bohm was struck by the notion of how people live their lives as though half asleep. Like a rider on horseback, we have forgotten that we are in charge of the horse. Rather, we allow the horse to take us where it will while we unconsciously go along. He was beginning to see that it was our unconsciousness that was getting the world into trouble.

When his wife, Saral, came upon Krishnamurti's book in a local library in 1959, *The First and Last Freedom*, and showed it to Bohm, he felt an immediate connection. "...here was a thinker who had seen deeply and authentically into the essence of the human problem. Gurdjieff had warned of the trap of unconscious conditioning; Krishnamurti was pointing to a way out. He wrote of the transformation of human consciousness through the operation of the 'intelligence,' or the 'unconditioned'"(Peat, 1999, p. 195).

Over time, Krishnamurti and Bohm began to meet regularly and even record their talks on a variety of subjects. Bohm was continually trying to clarify Krishnamurti's spiritual insights in light of his own ideas coming from his work as a physicist and philosophical interests.

Krishnamurti talked about a direct awareness of a universal ground, the same ground Bohm was trying to describe in his physics. Bohm felt that if we could act out of an awareness of this wholeness, we could bring a kind of harmony to our lives. And, it is this experience of wholeness that Bohm eventually was to promote to others through his proposal of dialogue.

Krishnamurti spoke about the "nature of thought and the transformation of consciousness. Thought, for Krishnamurti, is a constant activity of the physical brain. Again, this validated Bohm's notion of the constant flux of the universe. This activity, Krishnamurti further explained, operates in response to memory, a record of the past or a sort of internal image" (Peat, 1999, p. 223).

This idea of memory affecting the thinking process would prove to be essential in Bohm's subsequent work with dialogue. It led him to propose the metacognitive aspect of his dialogue: we attempt to identify our underlying assumptions, beliefs, and values in a conversation so that we can consider more deeply the nature of our different opinions we hold. In this way, we are able to transcend the surface nature of the opinions and our habitual ways of interacting with each other.

It is this metaphysical principle from Krishnamurti that most distinguishes Bohm's dialogue from that of other forms of group conversation, such as might be found within the Native American traditions.[3]

Another important influence of Krishnamurti on Bohm's proposal of dialogue is a quality of presence that he called 'choiceless awareness'. It is a kind of present attention that we attempt to bring to a dialogue that contains no judgment or memory. It is an awareness that is open to the moment in a way where deep listening to another becomes more possible. We attempt in this way to suspend our normal distortion in listening that come as a result of the many internal filters we develop through memory.

Bohm's relationship with Krishnamurti lasted from 1961 to 1984, when the Indian teacher for a variety of reasons began to distance himself from Bohm. This change in their relationship hit David very hard and threw him into a period of depression. "As Krishnamurti confronted Bohm in a way that others later described as 'brutal,' the physicist was thrown into despair. Unable to sleep, obsessed with thoughts, he constantly paced the room to the point where he thought of suicide" (Peat, 1999, p. 285). I mention this fact of Bohm's life because it was this depression that led him to the work of Patrick de Mare, a Freudian analyst in London who was doing a form of social therapy. It was de Mare's influence that was the final stepping-stone to Bohm's proposal of dialogue.

3.6   Patrick de Mare

> Essentially, it (the book, Koinonia,) is about an operational approach to dialogue, culture, and the human mind, through the medium of a larger group context....We have tried to link the most intimate aspect of individual beings naturally and spontaneously in the sociocultural setting of the larger group...Psychoanalysis and small groups till now have not been able to handle this aspect empirically. The larger group now shows us the other side of the coin to the inner world, namely the socio-cultural dimension in which these interpersonal relationships take place. (de Mare, 1991, p. 3)

Though Bohm was devastated by the growing distance he was experiencing with respect to Krishnamurti, his psychotherapy with de Mare gave him a new avenue for his ideas on consciousness and eventually dialogue. de Mare was worked with groups greater in size than what would normally result in family dynamics being played out, usually 15 or more.
de Mare believed, as Peat (1997) notes, that:

> in the hunter-gatherer stages of human social development, when people had lived and traveled in groups of thirty to forty, social and psychological tensions had been dealt with as they arose, through a process of dialogue. It was after the growth in size and complexity of human societies, following the transition from farming to city building and finally to industrialization, that the power of the group disappeared. But human beings are not psychologically well adapted for life in complex societies, de Mare believed, and require continuous, active social therapy. (p. 286)

Peat goes on to explain that earlier in his life, Bohm had speculated that "simply being in the presence of Krishnamurti and engaging in an active inquiry was sufficient to induce a transformation of consciousness." Bohm thought that "even if only a handful of persons could participate in this transformation...they would still be sufficient to induce a radical change in general human consciousness." Bohm believed that "such change could come about through the operation of group dialogue" (Peat, 1997, p. 288).

Bohm saw in de Mare's work something that he found missing in Krishnamurti's work, the social dimension. While Krishnamurti gave him an approach to transformation of consciousness, it did not appeal to Bohm's quest for social transformation. While working with de Mare on his own therapy, he also attended some of de Mare's groups for patients. He joined a group that was run for therapists. Out of this exposure, he came to the conclusion that something like dialogue in which the group thinking process is slowed down so that underlying assumptions can be looked into, social problems could be unfolded with cultural transformation forthcoming. How I like to look at it is that Bohm took Krishnamurti's suggestion of attending to one's thinking process and he applied it to the group or cultural level. Many people liken Bohm's dialogue to a kind of group meditation. It aims to break through blocks to both individual and cultural creativity.

Bohm seems to have been influenced also by de Mare's reference to "impersonal fellowship" which can come about between people in sustained, ongoing dialogue. de Mare talks about "Koinonia" as being first coined within Greek culture between 495 BC and the death of Aristotle in 322 BC. He felt that this period in our western history "whether considered in itself or with reference to the effect which it has produced upon the subsequent discoveries of civilized man is the most memorable in the history of the world" (de Mare, 1991, p. 1).

Koinonia refers to "the atmosphere of impersonal fellowship rather than personal friendship, of spiritual-cum-human participation in which people can speak, hear, see, and think freely, a form of togetherness and amity that brings a pooling of resources" (de Mare, 1991, p. 2). In reading Peat's biography of David Bohm and in reflections on my own time spent with him in dialogue at Ojai, I was struck how Bohm modeled this form of relationship with colleagues and others with whom he interacted. I feel that with de Mare's work, Bohm found a process that validated his inclination to and enjoyment of the open and free sharing of ideas. This stands in contrast with our culture's way of withholding open communication due to the need to protect or defend in order to hold to power or privilege.

Based on his exposure to de Mare's work, he began to look at the blocks in interpersonal communication that tend to cause what he called 'fragmentation' in society. It starts at the individual level, where non-negotiable positions are created in thought–positions that are based on strongly held beliefs about the way things are or should be–and then at the interpersonal level where conflicts form and as these non-negotiable positions meet. Bohm had long been aware of this tendency within his own professional community. He has pointed out in *On Dialogue* and elsewhere that even Einstein and Bohr were unable to continue their interactions after a certain period of time because each held non-negotiable positions about the nature of quantum reality.

Bohm felt that if opposing scientific theories could be allowed to hold together for a while and both exist in their own right, something new might come about through that tension. Rather, what happens is that one or the other is judged as being superior and the other eliminated as quickly as possible. In so doing, we often eliminate subtle distinctions too fast without considering the value that they offer in a larger synthesis.

By applying his ideas from his work with plasma, wherein he found the individual particles co-exist within a collective order, continuing through on into his work on consciousness and thought, dialogue was a natural result. It was practical in that he felt it could greatly effect how complex problems could be thought about, and it transformed those who practiced it.

Bohm would often say that a 'change of meaning is a change of being'. This is the heart of what can happen in a group practicing dialogue. For me, this is where Bohm's lifetime of exploration in both the physical sciences and human consciousness finally led him. In dialogue we learn to follow the meaning that is being shared. In so doing, we attend to the thinking, the feelings, and all the insights, etc. Something happens when we have attended long enough. A subtle shift in how people regard each other may happen. There is a sort of 'group mind' that builds through the meaning being attended to. This is the change of being or the transformation to which Bohm alludes.

FINAL THOUGHTS

So deeply have his ideas permeated the general cultures that they are becoming part of the shared way we look at the world. Their influence can be found in areas as diverse as education, psychology, art, and literary criticism, appearing even in novels. Bohm became something of a guru to those seeking renewal through education and psychotherapy or seeking to build new communities or understand the internal dynamics of society. (Peat, 1997, p. 3)

At the beginning of this chapter I asked the questions: 'What are the assumptions about the nature of reality that Bohm came to from his work in quantum physics that led him to dialogue? Do they make sense in our world today? Should we take his proposal of dialogue seriously?'

To me I would summarize his worldview in this way: for Bohm the nature of reality is an interconnected whole within which infinite levels of reality co-exist and interact with each other in an unending flow. Reality is based on this ceaseless flux, where matter and consciousness are ultimately indistinguishable, two-sides of the same coin. Reality is ordered by the very nature of its being one integrated whole. What looks like chaos or a mystery at one level of reality, is in harmony when considered from a broader or more complex level of reality. Time and space disappear at certain levels of existence, making way for mystical and other forms of conscious experience. Synchronicity, paradox, and opportunities for creative transformation become inexhaustible.

While Bohm himself did not think of his worldview as an absolute truth, it makes sense for me to live life as if it were. It is a more inclusive world view than is our existing Newtonian/Cartesian one. What we adopted as the way things are based on Newton's clockwork universe and Decarte's mind/matter dualism has contributed to many of the problems in our world today, such as rampant individualism, materialism, and the many forms of conflict based on absolute notions of right and wrong. Too much has been written about these problems for me to go into them here. Most of us are well aware of these paradigm-based issues facing us as a world community right now.

I believe that Bohm is an early new paradigm thinker whose contributions perhaps will be seen even more in the future. His proposal of dialogue makes sense to me because it is a process approach to change and transformation. It does not try to nail down a solution to world problems, but merely asks us to consider an open-ended process that we might try for this purpose.

How we are in our relationships with each largely comes from what we believe to be true about the nature of things. Most of us today are well versed in notions of how things work based on the Newtonian/Cartesian paradigm. Even if we say we have moved beyond it, our everyday ways of interacting may not suggest that we have. I believe that Bohm's proposal of dialogue presents us with ways of being in the world that supports a broader view of mankind and of physical nature. When we dialogue, we open ourselves to unlimited potential.

Paradigms change slowly. Most organizations I have experienced have not yet seemed ready for the slow pace of Bohmian dialogue. However, I am beginning to see aspects of dialogue being integrated into organizational life in small ways making a difference. As aspects of dialogue such as suspension of judgment and assumption identification become more consciously understood, they can be practiced with more discipline until they become engrained in the fabric of our social lives.

I began this chapter well over a year and one half ago. During this time, I have looked increasingly towards the field of depth psychology for inspiration in my own search for ways to promote individual and group wholeness. As I see it, Bohm's own practice of dialogue fell short only in the arena of helping participants to move into the sharing of intense emotional material. Bohm, after all, was an intellectual, which colored how he was able to model and facilitate the dialogues he led. This more intellectual or thinking style is not always helpful in bringing emotional material into the dialogue that might shed light on unconsciously held assumptions, lying hidden below the surface of what is being said.

From early childhood (Bohm) learned to escape into the world of the mind and the imagination. Yet his life was accompanied by great personal pain and periods of crippling depression. He never achieved wholeness in his own personal life, and the fruits of that life, which are still with us, were gained only at great sacrifice. (Peat, 1997, p. 4)

Though it is beyond the scope of this chapter to speculate where Bohm might have gone with his work, were he able to transcend his own personal pain, at another time, this exploration might be a fruitful one in which to engage.[4]

When complex problems are being discussed, something approaching Bohm's dialogue is essential. Whether in the political, social, educational, or interpersonal arenas, there are many opportunities for group conversation that can take advantage of Bohm's proposal of dialogue. Bohm's proposal has practical value when used in whole or in part–such as in a facilitated approach to dialogue (in Bohm's proposal the leadership or facilitation of dialogue is shared and not held by one person as the dialogue unfolds. For examples of how this might be done, see *Dialogue: The Transforming Power of Conversation*).

There is also merit to Bohm's ideas on dialogue in individual change work, as well as within a variety of group settings. I am in the midst of my own explorations of combining ways of working in groups that combine dialogic principles with the psychotherapeutic. I have been influenced lately by the work of Stanislav Grof, Arthur Janoff, and many of the post Jungians in my own continuing search for ways of working towards our inherent wholeness as individuals and groups.

I hope this chapter will be a useful to you the reader in your own journey to Bohm's dialogue and beyond.

NOTES

[1] Bohm was not particularly concerned about acknowledging the roots of his own ideas. He preferred to absorb ideas from a broad number of sources and then to make his own unique synthesis, having little patience for conventional ways of source notation (as might be found in academic research). David Peat speculates about this in his biography. He feels that Bohm may have been impacted in this by his many dialogues with J. Krishnamurti who felt it was most important that we develop our own insights rather than to rely on the insights of others. For whatever reason, Bohm does not make this journey to the roots of his ideas an easy one. For this reason, I cannot say that this paper makes any pretension to completeness; rather it is just my own personal start at understanding Bohm's path to dialogue.

[2] Though Peat does explain that "by matter Bohm meant something that went far beyond naïve materialism for, to him, matter was inexhaustible and could never be contained within fixed physical laws" (Peat, 1999, p. 179).

[3] Note: in our training (The Dialogue Group), for instance, we often show a short film on a Native American council process and then contrast it with how group decisions are often made in our culture. While the council process demonstrates many of the characteristics found within Bohm's dialogue, it lacks the metacognitive aspect.

[4] I recently took a transcribed dialogue from the internet between Bohm, E. T. Nada, and Colleen Rowe that has never been published. In it Bohm shares his understanding of the nature of the tri-partite of the brain and how its functioning might have an impact on the current state of society. It is from this work on brain structure, that some of the newer ways of working therapeutically are emerging such as are found in Janoff's work and in pre- and peri-natal therapies. These are of interest to me presently in my own work and they may have been for Bohm, as well. (www.simurgh.net/nada/planet/dbohm.htm; copyright NADA–1998.)

REFERENCES

Audi, R., (ed.), 1999. *The Cambridge Dictionary of Philosophy, Second Edition.* Cambridge University Press, Cambridge.

Biederman, D.B., 1999. *Boh-Biederman Correspondence: Creativity and Science.* Routledge, London.

Bohm, D., 1980. *Wholeness and the Implicate Order.* Routledge, London.

Bohm, D., 1987. Hidden variables and the implicate order. In B.J. Hiley and F.D. Peat, (eds.), *Quantum Implications: Essays in Honour of David Bohm.* Routledge & Kegan Paul, New York, pp. 33-45.

Bohm, D., 1992. *Thought as a System.* Routledge, London.

Bohm, D. (1996). *On Dialogue.* London: Routledge.

Bohm, J. K., 1999. *The Limits of Thought.* Routledge, London.

Edwards, M., and Bohm, D., 1991. *Changing Consciousness: Exploring the Hidden Source of the Social, Political and Environmental Crises Facing our World.* Harper Collins Publishers, New York.

Gerard, G., and Ellinor, L., 1998. *Dialogue: Rediscover the Transforming Power of Conversation.* John Wiley & sons, Inc., New York.

Griffin, D.R., 1986. *Physics and the Ultimate Significance of Time.* State University of New York Press, Albany, NY.

Grof, S., 1985. *Beyond the Brain: Birth, Death and Transcendence in Psychotherapy.* State University of New York, Albany, NY:.

Hiley, B., Peat, F.D., 1987. *Quantum Physics and Conscious Thought.* Routledge, London.

Kolb, D., 1986. *The Critique of Pure Modernity: Hegel, Heidegger, and After.* The University of Chicago Press, Chicago.

de Mare, P., Piper, R., Thompson, S., 1991. *Koinonia: From Hate, Through Dialogue, to Culture in the Large Group.* Karnac Books, London.

Peat, F. D., 1997. *Infinite Potential: The Life and Times of David Bohm.* Addison-Wesley Publishing Company, Inc., Reading, MA.

Rosen, S.M., 1994. *Science, Paradox, and the Moebius Principle.* State University of New York Press, Albany, NY.

Weber, R., 1986. *Dialogues with Scientists and Sages: The Search for Unity.* Routledge, London.

Chapter 13

CARNIVAL AND DIALOGUE
Opening New Conversations

ALEXANDER M. SIDORKIN
Educational Foundations and Inquiry, Bowling Green State University, Bowling Green, OH 43403

1. INTRODUCTION

This chapter will examine the theory of polyphony and carnival by Bakhtin in its relation to opening new conversations within such social systems as schools. Opening new conversation is a metaphor for educational change that I suggest should replace that of reforming. One can argue about the quality of American educational system in general, but I do not believe anyone would argue that the various efforts of educational reforming during past fifty years or so were successful. In fact, the record of educational reforming in most developed countries is abysmal. The only sort of educational reform that proved to be workable is when educational system is created, and the majority of students become students. After that point any sort of reform has proven to be extremely difficult.

Schools change over the years, no doubt about it. The question is whether these changes are result of organized reforming, or are they almost natural gradual changes that no one can predict and shape. Is educational change a subject of history or social science? Yet most of industrial nations engage into one or another form of educational reforming almost incessantly. Before one reform runs its course, another one is usually underway. It would be too easy to attribute the persistence of educational reforming to politicians that use education as a safe ground to demonstrate their usefulness. Of course, such an explanation is partially true, at least in the US. The politicians discovered long ago that one could not damage education too badly by experimenting with its reform. The remarkable inertia of educational institutions prevents them both from radical improving, and from radical deteriorating. However, there exist a theoretical fallacy of equating educational change with educational reform. The assumption here is two-fold: that educational system is reformable,

Dialogue as a Means of Collective Communication, Edited by Banathy and Jenlink
Kluwer Academic/Plenum Publishers, New York 2005

and that the only way to effect changes in education is reform. This assumption is not entirely unique for education, but is much more prevalent in our field as compared to other social sciences. No one, for instance, wants to come up with a new model of financial market reform every two years or so; yet there is an understanding that governments can somehow affect or regulate the financial market. The economy is generally viewed as much less reformable than education. The same could be said about the politics.

My intention is to try to develop a new metaphor for educational change. Let us assume, following John Goodlad (1994), that an individual school is an agent of change, not state officials, not school districts, and not individual teachers. For a school to change, it needs to develop new conversation, not only (and not as much) a new model or idea, or a concept. My central assumption is this: educational models do not change schools, but they may or may not serve as reasons (or excuses) for new conversations, which in turn change the reality of school life. This view would require a healthy dose of respect for complexity and the non-deterministic character of school as a culture and as an organization.

A simple argument can show that education is a process that is possible only within complex non-deterministic systems. The "product" of education is a person, an agent with his or her freely exercised will. Teaching is a purposeful and organized human activity, yet its results are unpredictable. The results are not unpredictable because we *cannot* predict, but because we *must not*. An educational process with fully predictable outcome is not so much impossible as it is immoral, because such a process will destroy the free agency of a student. In other words, whatever are the insides of the black box called "education," we know one sure thing about the box: it may not contain a simple, linear, and deterministic system. This would contradict the desirable output of the box. In much of educational theory, education is still viewed as complicated, but not complex process. In other words, even though it is difficult to explain fully, researchers nevertheless have an ideal of fully explainable and therefore fully predictable system.

Another way of avoiding complexity is often associated with use of probability. Even though, the thinking goes, it is impossible to predict behavior of each individual school, one can statistically predict behavior of an average school. Yuri Sachkov describes the role of statistics in physics, which is very similar to that in educational research:

In scientific minds, probability and chance became inseparable. Yet the fundamental nature of chance was long ignored in the theoretical constructs. Statistical theories were considered incomplete, that is temporary and logically inferior. It was assumed that we need statistical theories because, for one reason or another, we cannot get a full description of the analyzed system. One assumed also that scientific progress will obtain more and more full knowledge of such systems, and that chance will be eliminated from the theoretical constructs (Sachkov, p. 131).

Similarly, educational researchers often assume that the systems in question are in theory fully predictable, but we need to use statistical approximations for now. This is, of course, a mistake. Education can only be reasonably presented as a complex non-linear system, where unpredictability is so important, it defines the system itself.

I will not attempt even a brief literature review on complexity theories, and will only point to one bibliography source (Heylighen, 1995) and offer my rendition of selected basic facts. The complex systems theory, however notoriously unorganized and heterogeneous, has nevertheless developed certain categories to describe a non-linear system. Chaos is the central category that describes the specifics of complex system's path toward organization. Complex systems of very different nature seem to develop through either limited periods of chaos or permanent zones of chaos. Complexity as a form of organization depends on disorganization (chaos) to develop.

One faces a fundamental problem when applying the complexity theory to social systems. Social sciences have always meant to inform human practice, but any constructive human practice seems to be antithetical to the notion of chaos. Practice is a force that counteracts, and if successful, overcomes chaos. Yet chaos appears to be a constructive element of complex systems. An idea of creating chaos seems to be counterintuitive and not terribly useful. This paper is an attempt to address this contradiction. Using Bakhtin's theoretical framework, the generic systems theory notions of complexity and chaos can be understood as polyphony, and carnival, respectively.

2.   PARADOX OF SCHOOLING

I will assume a school to be a system, where education is the central organizing process. This means simply that we call certain group of people, building and other things a school when they are brought together for the purposes of educating students. Of course, they enter a number of other relationships that have nothing or little to do with education, but educational relations proper take precedence over all others. In other words, teaching and learning take privileged position in schools.

This initial assumption does seem self-evident and circularly defined. Yet the next logical step that directly follows this assumption is something I find troubling and am willing to dispute: The more organized is the school as an educational system, the more effective is education in it. Why I dispute this will become apparent later, but for now I need to state another assumption. Following the critical theorists whose argument stems from the Marxist analytical tradition, education may not be understood as limited to transmission of value-neutral knowledge and skills to students. There is no value-neutral knowledge, therefore education will inevitably involve the core of human personality–the beliefs, agency, and the ability to chose. If one was to understand education as simply training, my argument will make very little sense.

The language of efficiency, effective schools, and effective education is the foundation of many current trends in educational policy-making. As John Goodlad comments: "Much of so-called effective schools movement that grew out of some solid research on factors characteristics of good schools foundered on efforts to reduce complexity to a few simple concepts"(1994, p. 204). A school that wants to get recognition is pressured to come up with a simple explanation of its success. And yet most successful schools are very complex and not fully explicable.

The notion of school accountability, a rhetorical pet of the last presidential campaign, is based on some idea of effective schooling. To hold schools accountable, one must not only believe that schools control the outcomes of education, but also that effective schools are good for student's education. Let us imagine that schools would have been found to be a necessary, but also dangerous and unreliable technology, say, like nuclear power plants. In such a case, politicians would not be able to speak about efficiency only, but also about containing the negative aspects of the technology. Nothing like this shows up in educational politics. Schools are simply assumed to be unequivocally good, free of side effects, fully controllable and therefore the public is free to pursue the goal of effective schools without limitations. But what is an effective school? Can there be different interpretations of effectiveness? And most importantly, are there limits of school effectiveness?

If we understand schools as social systems clearly organized around their educational purposes, then their unchecked effectiveness is detrimental both to democracy and to personal development. On one hand, extraordinary successful schools will inevitably reduce pluralism by imposing a particular set of values on all students. On another hand, effective school education will limit the freedom of choice. Paradoxically, schools cannot be organized as purely educational institutions. Consistently effective education cannot be the main principle of school organization. To the contrary, schools must be systems that prevent education from being overly successful.

Paradoxically, good schools cannot be very effective. Education itself is a paradoxical process, as I have shown previously. Its purposes are contradictory. Education must normalize, make everyone somewhat the same, and provide the same knowledge and trains the same skills. The idea of public education is in many ways a reflection of this normalizing side of education. At the same time education has a differentiating side. It has to make everyone different, free, and able to make independent choice. When such a contradictory process as education is used as a corner stone for building a social system such as school, one discovers quickly that it is not easy to do. How do you "align" a system in relation to a contradictory set of goals? Most often schools simply ignore the second set of goals and pretend that education is all about normalizing. This happens, not because educators do not value individual free agency, but because they are faced with a much more immediate task of building an organization called "school." And the organization must be coordinated, run smoothly, have a clear set of priorities, be controllable, and effective.

Luckily, schools comprise of a multitude of conflicting interests of teachers, administration, different groups of students, parents, political and ideological parties, etc. Not many schools are very effective organizations yet, but such "imperfection" exists entirely by accident, and for wrong reasons. No one *consciously* tries to prevent schools from becoming effective. Moreover, I worry about a relatively recent school reforming trend that is called different names in different states, and has no clear identity beyond being clearly influences by business quality management techniques. Sometimes this trend is openly aligned with the Total Quality management movement; sometimes it is called something else like continuous improvement plans. Its essence is to let schools and school districts to develop their own ideas and procedures of self-reforming under strictly defined guidelines. This is not a classical top-down reform, but a reform developed at the local level. Here is the catch: the process of developing every school's ideas is strictly prescribed and monitored. This reforming trend should be properly analyzed in another work. I only want to suggest that it may prove to be effective, at last, and thus very dangerous. The industrialized nations grew so used to very ineffective attempts of educational reforming, they may miss a moment when one particular reform will be successful and will wipe out any complexity from schools.

The paradoxical nature of schools as educational systems can be further understood with a notion of complex non-deterministic systems. If we can learn to treat schools as such systems, perhaps we can also alter our ideas about their effectiveness and the concept of educational reform.

3.   COMPLEXITY

I have pointed out above that the notion of chaos is very difficult to apply in social sciences. Similarly, one of the main difficulties of using the concept of complexity with social systems is that complexity is an essentially a negative concept. Complexity is something we cannot predict, explain and understand. I do not know how many philosophy papers use the same rhetorical device I will call "complicating the picture." They take a particular notion or a theory, analyze and conclude that well, this seem to be a much more complex thing than originally thought.

Theorists have done this trick immeasurable number of times with democracy, liberation, dialogue, power, race, class, gender, identity, etc., etc. A fair theoretical move, it nevertheless uses the concept of complexity without much thought. The "complicating the picture" technique often assumes that one can clarify the picture by complicating it. One very clear example is the ever-complicating descriptions of gender and gender identities. From a simply binary opposition it has changed into a very complicated taxonomy, each class of which is characterized by unstable and fluid membership. Without questioning the validity of each separate paper of book that uses the "complicating the picture" technique, I would only point out that this technique takes complexity as a sum of many simplicities. The technique assumes that we can explain complexity away.

Complex systems are not necessarily to be described with complicated texts. Rather, we need to move away from the negative complexity toward the positive complexity. The negative complexity is something difficult to explain. Once explained and understood it disappears in the shadow of newly understood causality. A positive description of complexity "reserves" certain areas as not explainable with cause-and-effect relationships. It must then offer a strategy useful under conditions of unpredictability. How a theory of complex systems should be useful to a school principal? For instance, she has to understand that she cannot create certain events that would improve school, but can wait for them to happen. Or, instead of asking why some negative things keep happening in her school, she could seek to break the routine of school life hoping that the negative things will not be a part of new school organization.

After researching many successful school transformations both in Russia and the US, I am convinced that most of good schools' leaders have no idea why their schools are so good. They simply attempt an energetic shake-up of their respective schools, which result in opening up some new conversation, and the systems react with some inexplicable self-adjusting mechanisms. In other words, it is not that important what exactly the successful leaders do with their schools; it is even less important what the leaders believe they do with their schools. The quality of interaction between the system and its leader is much more important. Especially important is the leader's ability to part easily with his or her theories, to react and adapt quickly, and the courage to disturb equilibrium. Luck is critical, too.

Complexity demands respect by setting limits for how much we can hope to know about complex systems. But knowing what cannot be known is also a positive and extremely practical knowledge. Getting ourselves rid of illusions about fully controllable and explainable universe may be an important discovery. The next step is to develop a language of complexity suitable for social systems. I will use Bakhtin's concept of polyphony to do just that.

4. POLYPHONY

Bakhtin defines polyphony as both a literary artistic method, and as a principle of human relationship. He develops the concept mainly in his *Problems of Dostoevsky's Poetics* (1963) in conjunction with his concepts of dialogue and carnival. Bakhtin claims that Dostoevsky created a new form of novel that he calls the polyphonic novel. In the polyphonic novel, the author does not position himself above his heroes, but is, so to speak, alongside with them. The authorial voice is only one of many, and it does not have a privilege of knowing and understanding everything. In Dostoevsky's novels, Bakhtin claims, each of the main heroes is also a novelist with his or her comprehensive worldview. It is fairly obvious that Bakhtin's theory of the polyphonic novel is a vehicle for advancement of his philosophical views. With certain reservations, one can assume that the polyphonic novel is Bakhtin's social theory, and the description of Dostoevsky's heroes presents his theory of the self.

Polyphony is engaged co-existence of many independent but mutually addressed voices. Polyphony, according to Bakhtin, does not bring synthesis or merger of multiple voices. In this regard he sharply distinguishes himself from both German idealism and the hermeneutics. The multiplicity of voices is not an accident, not something to be overcome for the sake of human understanding of unity. Rather, this multiplicity is an essential condition of human existence. The continuation of dialogue is the end, and everything else is the means. Bakhtin develops a very interesting notion of the polyphonic epistemology. He observes a very simple fact that different people have different opinions about the same things. Idealist philosophy, against which Bakhtin is arguing, simply assumes that if two people know differently about the same thing, at least one of them must be mistaken.

For an idealist, one person can know the truth. I would only extend this argument well beyond idealism, for most of contemporary philosophers will agree with that statement. However, Bakhtin asserts that one person cannot know the truth, and that truth requires, so to speak, a multiplicity of bearers. In other words, only several people can know the truth, if their individual voices interact with each other. The truth is inaccessible to an individual.

It is both plausible and conceivable that a single truth requires a multiplicity of consciousnesses, that it is not containable within the limits of one consciousness, and that it is, essentially, so to speak, *event-specific [sobytiina]* and born where different consciousnesses touch. (Bakhtin, 1963, p. 107)

Polyphony does not only describe complexity of social systems, but also clarifies some epistemological difficulties of complex systems. One person cannot claim to understand a complex social system such as school for reasons stated earlier. In fact, no one inside or outside of a particular school can fully understand how it functions. However, all involved together may understand it as a group, although this knowledge cannot be presented by one voice or one opinion. One must learn to perceive conversation as a form of knowledge; not the result of conversation, not an outcome of conversation, and not a conclusion made at the end of conversation, but a conversation itself.

Now, a school leader or a researcher could try to understand this collective understanding, but not the system itself. One can understand a conversation about the school, but could not understand the school. This would be a violation of long-standing tradition of social science research. Social sciences always prefer the direct information to the indirect. An eyewitness account is often preferable to a hearsay account. Even when interviewing participants, social scientists tend to "triangulate" their data. Now, triangulation and similar procedures throw out data that is individual, unique to a specific person, and only selects data that are the same for many different sources. But this achieves exactly the opposite of Bakhtin's polyphony. The polyphony of school life often gets lost, and artificial monologicality is achieved. I wonder what would happen if a researcher throws out the data that is the same for different sources, and instead concentrates on differences.

Bakhtin uses dialogue and polyphony as very close, almost interchangeable notions. However, for the purposes of this chapter, I will consider polyphony to be the systemic description of dialogue; it is an ability of a social system to maintain complexity. It is important to emphasize that not any multiplicity of voices makes polyphony, but only when these multiple voices are engaged in one conversation. In many schools, the many voices do not notice each other, talk pass each other, and have no common conversation. Cacophony and polyphony both imply multiple voices, but only polyphony makes music. Polyphony exists as long as teachers, parents, and students are able to maintain dialogue, as long as they disagree, but willing to carry on the "big conversation" of the school life. As soon as general agreement or consensus is reached, polyphony is no longer possible, and the complex system collapses into an effective school.

Polyphony is especially important to emphasize in view of constant demands of theorists like William Damon (1995) for coherence and consistency of expectations towards students. He suggests that despite the obvious diversity of pluralism of opinions, the society can reach a certain consensus pertaining to moral messages intended for the youth. He sees no other way to avoid moral confusion, and ultimately, cynicism among young people. It is a very common error to believe that conflicting messages students receive from different teachers, or from parents are somehow detrimental to the students' development and moral growth. Not only psychologists of such an outstanding reputation as Damon, but also many of my undergraduate students share this common-sense belief. Yet from the point of view of developmental psychology, there is no evidence that this maybe true. Some of the great moral leaders of humanity grew up amidst much struggle and confusion. Some of the most morally corrupt societies controlled by Nazis and the Communists achieved remarkable unity of moral message for their youth. Conflict seems to be the engine of cognitive and moral development, thus the notion of cognitive conflict. From the point of view of complex systems theory, the consistency of educational messages is a sign of system's degradation and slide into entropy. What educators really need to do is to maintain and cherish a certain kind of inconsistency best described by the concept of polyphony. In other words, we should stop worrying about coming to a consensus, and concentrate on the quality of our conversations.

5. CARNIVAL

Assuming that polyphony is something important to have in schools, what is the mechanism that keeps the system from entropy? Bakhtin analyzes Dostoevsky's novels and finds that the situations of dialogue, where a person meets the other, are often triggered by scandals. Bakhtin also noted that the scandals are remarkably similar to carnival. He called both the threshold situations (Bakhtin, 1993, p. 195). These are events out of ordinary, unique events that let people come together without the limitation of conventions and prejudices. Bakhtin made direct connection between carnival and dialogue. In his view, carnival-like situations are more conducive to the genuine dialogue than the mundane every-day life.
Bakhtin examined the history of carnivals in Europe, and their influence on literature and other spheres of culture. Carnival is a temporary suspension and inversion of established social norms, a moment of chaos and creativity. Carnival and carnivalesque elements of culture constitute an important mechanism of tipping the social equilibrium. Carnival is a way of ensuring that human culture remains a non-linear, non-deterministic system. The carnival is a social equivalent of what the nonlinear system theory calls bifurcation, where something new arises from chaos.
What are some of the specific processes that make carnival a positive source of cultural change? One may theorize the carnival as a conscious mutation of existing discursive patterns, which lead to evolving new patterns of discourse. The only way of producing new cultural meanings includes producing a text of nonsense, which then becomes meaningful. Bakhtin describes the carnivalesque sense of the world as one of "merry relativity" (1963, p. 143). Carnival relies on humor to mock and subvert existing social conventions and hierarchies. It is a symbolic rebellion against the common sense and traditions, a reversal of the normal.

Carnival is "life knocked out of its *usual* rut; it is, to some degree, a life 'inside out,' 'an inversed world' ('monde à l'envers') (1963, pp. 163-164). Carnival allows living through a new mode of human relationships, familiar and free. Another important category of the carnival sense of the world is eccentricity, which, according to Bakhtin, allows for the suppressed side of human nature to be revealed and expressed in concretely sensual form (1963, p. 164).

Remarkably, Bakhtin shows that carnival is not, so to speak, absolute chaos. He traces down the specific mechanisms of the constructive side of carnival's destructiveness:

> Carnival celebrates the change itself, the process of changing itself, and not what specifically is being changed. Carnival is, so to speak, functional, not substantial. It makes nothing absolute, but proclaims everything relative... it is not a naked, absolute negation and annihilation (carnival knows neither the absolute negation, nor the absolute affirmation). (Bakhtin, 1963, p. 167)

The carnival-like events in school life are Dionysian elements of what I would call the "structured chaos." Not every situation of chaos, of breaking down the routine has the constructive potential. It is important to remember, however, that any significant change requires something like carnival. School leaders will benefit from developing an eye for the carnival-like situations of school life, and using them for renewal of the school culture. The alternative is to react to outbreaks of unstructured chaos with which the system will self-regulate itself to ensure complexity but at much higher cost.

6.   CARNIVAL AND NEW CONVERSATIONS

I have observed a highly developed carnival tradition in Moscow school #825 at the end of 1980s. It would not be useful to describe what exactly that school did, partly because of contextual gap an English-speaking reader would need to fill, partly because the behaviors associated with carnival are not that important. Briefly, once a year the school holds a retreat that can be very accurately described as carnival. The most remarkable is not the carnival itself, but the time *after* it. I observed that the entire frame of reference changes in multiple conversations throughout the school. Students and teachers are not simply talking about different things now, but school also develops new inside jokes and idiosyncratic words and expressions.

Carnival is an instrument of change. Here is how it works, in first approximation. The school uses the state of the carnival to laugh at itself. The most serious, even sacred beliefs, traditions, and roles are mocked and challenged. The school's principal Vladimir Karakovsky, who is normally treated with utmost respect and reverence, suddenly becomes an object of pranks and jokes. The serious language of school's traditions becomes an object of parodies. In other words, the carnival is a ritual self-destruction of the school culture. Yet the carnival also provides the stock of new meanings, new ideas, and new language. Some of these in time become elements of the official "serious" school culture. For example, the school developed a new decision-making body (the so-called Big Council) out of mostly non-serious experiments during one of the first carnivals.

Social systems of every level–from a family to the global system–can be said to have one or more recurring conversations. According to Bakhtin, such conversations always include a multitude of unmergeable voices, and none of the "big" cultural conversations ever gets resolved. This is the polyphony of school life that must be maintained. However, the polyphony cannot simply maintain itself. The resource of meaningful conversation within each particular culture is not inexhaustible. It may reach a point where the parties have said and argued everything they could. One can only make so much sense in any given conversation before it runs its course. What happens next is of utmost importance for educational institutions. When a conversation is exhausted, one of the voices may prevail, or a compromise reached. The group will achieve a consensus and thus lose its polyphony. In other words, such a social system will lose its complexity and shift towards being a linear, deterministic system. But this, as I have shown earlier, would be detrimental for education. Another outcome for such a system is to get through a carnival-like situation in order to replenish its conversational resource. The multitude of voices thus prevails. Carnival is a mechanism of sustaining cultural polyphony.

7. CONCLUSION: POLYPHONY, CARNIVAL AND SOCIAL CHANGE

One can give many different reasons for schools to change. Addressing social injustice, remedying brutalities of school life, or boosting students' academic achievement–all these goals certainly deserve our attention. However, we should not lose sight of a fundamental problem of school as an educational system. Like Alice in Wonderland, it has to keep running just to stay in one place. It needs to possess polyphony to provide some meaningful education. To do that, schools must go through cycles of constant change, so they can have some new conversations.

Would such a view imply that no actual progress is possible (as some Postmodernist thinkers seem to imply?). Bakhtin embraces a concept of social change that is neither ethical nor purely esthetical. For him, change should occur not because it brings progress, but because it brings new things to life. His is a Dionysian ethics of rebirth and renewal. It seems especially suitable for educational world.

REFERENCES

Bakhtin, M., 1963. *Problemy Poetiki Dostoevskogo*. Sovetskii Pisatel', Moscow.
Damon, W., 1995. *Greater Expectations: Overcoming the Culture of Indulgence in America's Homes and Schools*. Free Press, New York.
Sachkov, Yu.V., 1994. Sluchainost' formoobrazuyushchaya [Shaping Chance], Samoorganizatsiya i Nauka: Opyt filosofskogo rassmotreniya [Self-organization and science: An attempt of philosophical analysis], Russian Academy of Sciences, Philosophy Institute, Moscow.
Heylighen, F., 1995. Bibliography "The Evolution of Complexity", http://pespmc1.vub.ac.be/evocobib.html.
Goodlad, J., 1994. *Educational Renewal: Better Teachers, Better Schools*. Jossey-Bass Publishers, San Francisco.

SECTION III

MODALITIES OF CONVERSATION

Chapter 14

POST-FORMAL CONVERSATION

RAYMOND A. HORN, JR.
Penn State University at Harrisburg

1.   INTRODUCTION

As we begin the new millennium, a significant question that needs to be asked is, what kind of society do we want to become? Implied in this question is the assurance that the status quo will not be maintained and society will indeed change. In this question, the word "want" implies the possibility that we can design our future society, or at least use design techniques to affect the evolution of society. Obviously, the important question is what can we do to bring about the kind of society that we want?

> We are not at the mercy of evolutionary forces but have the potential and the opportunity to give direction to societal evolution by design, provided we create an evolutionary vision for the future and develop the will and the competence to fulfill that vision in our own lives, in our families, in the systems in which we live, in our communities and societies, and in the global system of humanity. (Banathy, 1996, p. 313)

Banathy's call for a conscious evolution addresses both of these questions. Banathy (1996) sees "a crisis of consciousness" in our current society because "we have yet to create a unity of consciousness" (pp. 315-316). Banathy maintains that "this is a crisis that we created, and we are responsible for acting upon it" (p. 316). One of the actions that can be taken is to promote the development of evolutionary learning as opposed to "maintenance learning" (Botnik & Maltiza, 1979). Maintenance learning "involves the acquisition of fixed outlooks, methods, and rules of dealing with known events and recurring situations" (Banathy, 1996, p. 318). On the other hand, "evolutionary learning empowers us to anticipate and face unexpected

Dialogue as a Means of Collective Communication, Edited by Banathy and Jenlink
Kluwer Academic/Plenum Publishers, New York 2005   291

situations. It will help us to progress from unconscious adaptation to our environment to conscious innovation, coevolution, and cocreation with the environment and the development of the ability to direct and manage change" (Banathy, 1996, p. 318).

Evolution is characterized by Banathy (1996), as a multidimensional unfolding that has to be designed and implemented in all of our human systems (p. 324). His evolutionary guidance system, which would enable this unfolding, includes dimensions containing social and economic justice; social and ecological ethics; physical, mental, emotional, and spiritual wellness; a scientific and technological dimension that serves human and social betterment; aesthetics in relation to beauty, as well as cultural and spiritual values; and a political dimension of self-determination, genuine participation in self governance, peace development, and global cooperation (Banathy, 1996, pp. 324-325).

In addition to Banathy, Barbara Marx Hubbard also espouses conscious evolution. Hubbard (1998) presents conscious evolution "as an emerging idea of the nature of reality that can guide us in the ethical and creative use of our power toward the next stage of human evolution" (p. 2). Hubbard feels that the development of a conscious evolution is imperative since "we entered a period of confusion–a loss of vision and direction" (p. 9). She reports that "during the past 30 years, our basic social and economic systems have attempted to maintain the status quo despite the many warnings that the old ways, particularly in the developed world, were no longer sustainable. In many instances our existing systems are not humane; homelessness, hunger, disease, and poverty consume the lives of hundreds of millions of people and the environment continues to degrade" (p. 11).

According to Hubbard (1998), the solution is an evolution from the human potential movement, characterized by the humanistic work of Abraham H. Maslow, Victor Frankl, Robert Assogioli, and others, to a "social potential movement that builds on the human potential movement" (p. 17). This movement "identifies peaks of social creativity and works toward social wellness the same way the human potential movement cultivates personal wellness. It seeks out social innovations and designs social systems that work toward a life—enhancing global society" (p. 17). Hubbard's vision is based on many ideals, such as syntony, which is a "spiritual resonance with the patterns of creation" (p. 71). She sees the attainment of conscious evolution through the transformation of our memes–"ideas woven into complex thought systems that organize human activities according to a specific pattern" (p. 77). Through the transformation of these memes, the social potential movement "seeks out innovations now working in health, environment, communication, education, government, economics, technology, and other fields of human endeavor while designing new social systems that lead toward a regenerative and life-enhancing global society" (pp. 97-98). In this way humanity can become cocreators, in which "the most fundamental step on the path of the cocreator is a new spirituality in which we shift our relationship with the creative process from creature to cocreator–from unconscious to conscious evolution. Through resonance with the metapattern that connects us all, we learn to take responsibility for our part in the creation of our own evolution" (p. 99).

I share Banathy and Hubbard's evolutionary visions because inherently it is about thinking and feeling differently. It is about the development of a new knowledge base that also includes old knowledge seen in a different more critical context, and it is about language and the politics of communication. New thinking, feeling, knowledge, and language translate into new attitudes and new practice.

In the context of education, as we in the United States look at a nation that most see as still being at risk, once again we must decide how we will *see* this problem. What processes will we use to understand the problem, and to evaluate the action that we will take? What sort of conversation will enable us to make sense of our efforts? The purpose of this chapter is to propose a type of conversation that can be a lens that allows us to *see* differently, and also can be a pragmatic process that can guide our critical action. Post-formal conversation will be proposed as a process that can facilitate ideas such as Banathy's, and act as an oppositional process to the entrenched dominant culture that resists the development of an evolutionary consciousness. The ensuing explanation of post-formal conversation will be in the context of Banathy and Hubbard's visions of conscious evolution and S. J. Goerner's (1999) thoughts on the emerging science and culture of integral society. These contexts will not only situate the relevance of post-formal conversation to the debates that need to be held and to the actions that need to be taken, but also will provide an opportunity to showcase the nature of post-formal conversation.

In her book, *After the Clockwork Universe*, Goerner (1999) discusses the emerging science and culture of integral society. She extensively critiques the clockwork science and culture of the modern age, and argues that a vision of a web world is taking its place. Understanding her web metaphor requires the acknowledgement that all systems are not just chaotic and complex, but also *intricate*. "Intricacy refers to the order which arises from interweaving" (Goerner, 1999, p. 135). Goerner (1999) argues that the space between the elements of a system (i. e., the space between people in a human activity system) "is actually filled with intricacy–the patterns, structure and organization produced by interdependence" (p. 136). Her position leads to the conclusion that "most traditional methods are *inappropriate* for intricacy. If you try to break intricacy down, you miss the point–its organization. If you use statistics, you glimpse order fleetingly but have no idea what caused it or how it works" (Goerner, 1999, p. 137). In addition, a central idea of her thesis is the idea that human systems are self-organizing, and in order to understand and facilitate the evolution of a system requires the ability to affect the self-organizing processes. How then do we discern the intricate patterns, structures, and organization of a human system in order to move the system along a different path?

This is a significant question for those who want to realize the greater potential of their society, local community, school, or family. More traditionally, this question can be rephrased as how do we effect and sustain change that is not only just and caring but also change that facilitates the development of a web of relationships that are characterized by an evolutionary consciousness?

In this chapter, post-formal conversation will be proposed as a philosophy toward change, as a method to discern the hidden patterns and structures of human organizations, and as an on-going assessment of the self-organizing process. First, post-formal inquiry will be situated in relation to other postpositivistic paradigms such as postmodernism, poststructuralism, and critical theory. This will be followed by an explanation of post-formal conversation that will discuss what it is, where and when its use is appropriate, and how to engage in post-formal conversation. Post-formal conversation will be posed as an intricate process that can help us understand a web world containing hidden patterns and processes that are essential to an understanding of self-organizing human systems. Post-formal conversation will be further proposed as an integral mediating process in the conscious evolution of our thinking, feeling, knowledge, and language.

2.   BEYOND MODERNISM

Whether entertaining the idea of a conscious evolution or a web world of intricate order, requires movement away from the reductionist and mechanistic understandings and methodologies of modernism toward those of the post-modern. However, replacing a reductionist view with a holistic view does not automatically guarantee the on-going identification and eradication of oppressive structures. The discernment of intricacy, implicate order (Bohm & Edwards, 1991; Bohm & Peat, 1987), and a different kind of consciousness does not, by itself, guarantee the emancipation of the marginalized and the promotion of an egalitarian and caring society.

The well-documented insidious nature of human intellectual and emotional activity raises questions about ideas such as conscious evolution and integral societies in a web world. Are these ideas merely extensions of modernistic thought and methodology, or do they represent a significant rupture with the anachronistic aspects of modernistic rationality? What are the safeguards that will protect against the development of uncritical essentializing metanarratives related to an information age, and new metanarrtives that merely replace the outdated ones that are grounded in an industrial society? At first glance in the ideas promoted by Banathy, Hubbard and Goerner, there is the inherent assumption of a natural emancipatory component; however, what are the mechanisms that will facilitate the development of this component instead of reproducing the inequity historically associated with rational systems?

As mentioned, post-formalism will be promoted as a mechanism that can address these questions. To provide a theoretical foundation for post-formal conversation, post-formality will be situated within the postmodern landscape through a review of its postpositivistic antecedents. By locating post-formality in relation to the postpositivistic paradigms of postmodernism, poststructuralism, and critical theory, the commonality and distinctiveness of post-formal thinking to these antecedenal paradigms will become clearly apparent.

2.1   Postmodernism

Postmodernism can be used in an attempt to make sense of our postmodern society. Pinar, Reynolds, Slattery, and Taubman (1995) list the ideas articulated by postmodernism: "the death of the subject, the repudiation of depth models of reality, metanarratives, and history itself, the illusion of the transparency of language, the impossibility of any final meaning, the movement of power as it represents and discourses on the objects it constructs, the failure of reason to understand the world, the de-centering of the Western logos and with it the 'first world,' the end of belief in progress, and the celebration of difference" (p. 468). The critique of modernity as articulated by Pinar, et al. is echoed by Lawrence Cahoone (1996) in that "for some, postmodernism connotes the final escape from the stultifying legacy of modern European theology, metaphysics, authoritarianism, colonialism, racism, and domination" (p. 1). Cahoone (1996) continues by noting that "at a minimum, postmodernism regards certain important principles, methods, or ideas characteristic of modern Western culture as obsolete or illegitimate. In this sense, postmodernism is the latest wave in the critique of the Enlightenment, the critique of the cultural principles characteristic of modern society that trace their legacy to the eighteenth century" (p. 2).

From a philosophical point of view, Patti Lather (1991) claims that "the essence of the postmodern argument is that the dualisms which continue to dominate Western thought are inadequate for understanding a world of multiple causes and effects interacting in complex and non-linear ways, all of which are rooted in a limitless array of historical and cultural specificities" (p. 21). Lather further proposes that the inadequacy of Western thought is a "crisis of representation," which "is an erosion of confidence in prevailing concepts of knowledge and truth. Whatever 'the real' is, it is discursive. Rather than dismissing 'the real,' postmodernism foregrounds how discourses shape our experience of 'the real' in its proposal that the way we speak and write reflects the structures of power in our society" (p. 25).

At this point in the discussion, the question needs to be raised as to what is the relevance of postmodernism to the visions of conscious evolution and a web world of intricacy? There are two aspects to the answer of this question. The first deals with the origins, methods, and desired outcomes of those who support these idealized visions. Undoubtedly, the origins of these visions are rooted in modernistic totalizing theories and expert descriptions (Lather, 1991, p. xviii). These origins need to be recognized, deconstructed, and critically interrogated on an on-going basis. The methods (old and new) used to propagate these visions need to be deconstructed in order to discern the circular, linear, and critical meanings constructed by the methods. Finally, the desired outcomes of these visions also need to be deconstructed to expose the modernistic fallacies that will denigrate any emancipatory or egalitarian intentions. The significance of the postmodern critique of these visions is that without a rigorous deconstruction they will prove to be modernistic and marginalizing; in other words, not significantly different in how they see the world and in how they affect the world.

The second aspect deals with the nihilistic tendencies of the postmodern technique of deconstruction, which appear to be at odds with the view of the idealized visions. Lather (1991) maintains that "the goal of deconstruction is neither unitary wholeness nor dialectical resolution. The goal is to keep things in process, to disrupt, to keep the system in play, to set up procedures to continuously demystify the realities we create, to fight the tendency for our categories to congeal" (p. 13). Pinar et al., (1995) find it difficult if not impossible, after encountering deconstruction, "to take for granted the unity and autonomy of the self, of systems and structures, the phenomenological claims to present a prediscursive reality, the claims of humanism, the truth of history, the traditional ways of conceiving power, the possibility of a final or true or original meaning, or finally any thought which is based on or posits universals, foundations, origins, absolutes or essences, or that does not take its own language into account" (p. 468). Another description of deconstructive postmodernism is that of a relativistic and nihilistic fog that "stems from its [postmodernism's] opposition to all forms of assessment or grounding and the latter from its rejection of ethical theories and humanistic concerns with progress" (Willower, 1998, p. 454). This fog arises because all postmodern discourses are "deconstructive in that they seek to distance us from and make us skeptical about beliefs concerning truth, knowledge, power, the self, and language that are often taken for granted within and serve as legitimation for contemporary Western culture" (Flax, 1990, p. 41).

Just as the technique of deconstruction can be utilized to discern the ambiguities and contradictions of the foundations of modernistic thought, that are to be displaced by the aforementioned idealized visions, so can this technique be used to critique those visions. The challenge lies in determining how the techniques of postmodernism be utilized without encountering the enervating fog of relativism and nihilism. What other postpositivistic methods of inquiry can help address this change?

2.2 Poststructuralism

Poststructuralism and postmodernism are often used interchangeably, and in many cases the term postmodernism has subsumed poststructuralism (Pinar et al., 1995). Initially, poststructuralism was a response to humanism and structuralism. Postmodernism initially referred to radical innovations in the arts, technology, and in science, but recently has become used to refer to an epistemic and cultural break with modernism (Pinar et. al., 1995, p. 451).

One distinction is that poststructuralists criticize the structural belief that has meaning residing in invariant structures, systems, and sets of relations that are essentially foundational (Pinar et al., 1995). Structuralism rejects a focus on the self and instead focuses "on the super-individual structures of language, ritual, and kinship which make the individual what he or she is. It is not the self that creates culture, but culture that creates the self" (Cahoone, 1996, p. 5). One poststructural problem with structuralism is that while it avoids the subjectivity inherent in the idea of a unitary self (as characterized by Marxism, existentialism, phenomenology, and psychoanalysis), it retains objective, scientific method in its analysis of reality (Cahoone, 1996). As a reaction to the oppressive nature of all modern institutions, including the representations of modern science, poststructuralists critiqued the structural positions by revealing the "hidden paradoxes and modes of social domination operating within all products of reason" (Cahoone, 1996, p. 6).

Another area of contention deals with structural analysis "which emphasizes wholeness and totality, not units and parts. The focus on wholeness comes from concentrating on systemic relationships among individual elements, not on their unique characteristics" (Cherryholmes, 1988, p. 18). "Structural analysis also deals with transformations. If a structure is determined by relationships among its units, then those relationships, if the structure is to survive, must regenerate and reproduce the structure. Furthermore, structures are self-regulating, their relationships governing which activities are and are not permitted. A structure, then, is constituted by relationships among elements that are self-regulating and generate transformations. The relationships of a structure define it; they are its reality. As a consequence, structuralism decenters the subject by emphasizing relationships and not individuals" (Cherryholmes, 1988, pp. 18-19). Cherryholmes' understanding of structuralism is relevant to the previously described visions in that within the construction of an evolutionary consciousness and an intricate web of relationships, an essential element of constructive activity will be a mechanism(s) that critiques the structural tendencies of the activity. This does not mean that the structural foundations of both visions are irrelevantly deleterious to the construction of the desired ideal outcome of the visions, it simply means that methods must be employed to discern the ambiguities, contradictions, and oppressive tendencies in the construction process.

Additionally relevant to our exploration of the use of post-formal conversation in societal and political projects, such as the promotion of conscious evolution and an understanding of an integral society, is poststructural feminism. Fraser and Nicholson (1990) describe the complementarity between the poststructural emphasis on antifoundational metaphilosophy and the social criticism of feminism. "Postmodernists offer sophisticated and persuasive criticisms of foundationalism and essentialism, but their conceptions of social criticism tend to be anemic. Feminists offer robust conceptions of social criticism, but they tend at times to lapse into foundationalism and essentialism" (Fraser & Nicholson, 1990, p. 20). They note that postmodern social criticism is limited to "smallish, localized narrative," and "with philosophy no longer able to credibly ground social criticism, criticism itself must be local, *ad hoc*, and untheoretical" (Fraser & Nicholson, 1990, pp. 24-25). Fraser and Nicholson (1990) then argue that "a phenomenon as pervasive and multifaceted as male dominance simply cannot be adequately grasped with the meager critical resources to which they would limit us. On the contrary, effective criticism of this phenomenon requires an array of different methods and genres" (p. 26).

They then venture away from postmodernism in their suggestion that these different methods require "at minimum large narratives about changes in social organization and ideology, empirical and social-theoretical analyses of macrostructures and institutions, interactionist analyses of the micropolitics of everyday life, critical-hermeneutical and institutional analyses of cultural production, historically and culturally specific sociologies of gender, and so on" (p. 26). However, they issue a caveat that these methods can be conceived and utilized "in ways that do not take us back to foundationalism" (p. 26). What Fraser and Nicholson report about feminism in relation to postmodernism is analogous to the task before those who wish to construct new visions of society.

The lack of significant social critique in postmodern and poststructural thought is bolstered by "feminism's long-standing tendencies toward self-reflexivity [that] provide some experience of both rendering problematic and provisional our most firmly held assumptions and, nevertheless, acting in the world, taking a stand" (Lather, 1991, p. 29). Lather argues that "feminism has pushed poststructuralism in directions it might otherwise not have gone in terms of political engagement" (p. 31). However, Lather recognizes that "postmodernism offers feminists ways to work within and yet challenge dominant discourses. Within postmodernist feminism, language moves from representational to constitutive; binary logic implodes, and debates about 'the real' shift from a radical constructivism to a discursively reflexive position which recognizes how our knowledge is mediated by the concepts and categories of our understanding" (1991, p. 39).

Once again this relationship between feminism and postmodernism/poststructuralism is informative for those who wish to promote idealistic visions. The key is to include or develop mediating mechanisms that allow a critical and metaphysical critique of the project without denigrating the idealized intent of the project. One mechanism that is ubiquitous in all human activity systems is conversation. The type of conversation can be the mediating mechanism. However, before post-formal conversation is proposed as a mediating conversation, one more postpositivistic paradigm needs to be discussed.

2.3   Critical Theory

"Critical theory is, above all else, a way to ask questions about power" (Hinchey, 1998, p. 17). Whether power arrangements in a society are just and caring is the central concern of critical theory. Critical theory is centered on social justice and caring. Critical theorists, like David Purpel (1989) recognize "our culture's discomfort with making moral choices" (p. 8). For example, Purpel (1989) writes about the trivializing of education in America, especially in relation to "the evasion or neglect of larger, more critical topics and the stress put on technical rather than on social, political, and moral issues" (pp. 2-3). This trivializing and avoidance of dealing with the moral context of issues inhibits the generation of an evolutionary and ecological consciousness by fostering "responses that are at best ameliorative [and] have the danger of deepening the crisis by further strengthening social and cultural policies and practices that endanger our deepest commitments" (p. 3). In his critical assessment of technicist responses, Purpel (1989) notes that "this basic difference in assumptions about the human condition represents a historic and continuous struggle between fundamentally different consciousness and orientations toward human nature and destiny" (p. 10).

The moral nature of critical theory is an integral part of post-formal conversation and must become an important lens through which idealized projects can critique their center and critique who they are marginalizing by establishing that center. David Purpel (1989) "believes that there is an urgency not only to be critical, not only to deconstruct, debunk and unmask, but also simultaneously to affirm, commit, and advocate" (p. x). Not only must visionary projects be responsive to the critique of their activity by the postpositivistic paradigms, but they also must not lose sight of the aspect of their vision that centers their activity, and the necessity to advocate for that center. As mentioned, the deconstructive nature of postmodernism does not allow for the recognition of a moral or ethical center. First, a center implies foundational support, which is not possible under postmodern and poststructural scrutiny. Second, the establishment of a center immediately marginalizes others. Therefore, a postmodern analysis of a center based on social justice and caring would claim that the center actually creates a marginalized group, and casts doubt on the definitional and ethical nature of the concepts of justice and caring.

As we have seen, poststructural feminism has addressed this issue. Other poststructuralists, like Cleo Cherryholmes (1988, 1999) have posited a critical pragmatic poststructuralism. Cherryholmes (1988) recognizes that the deconstructive poststructuralism and poststructural criticism that investigates the effects of history and power "question the liberal faith in rationality, control, and progress" (p. 14). However, "when criticism turns to action, when poststructural analysis is projected onto the world in what we say (discourse) and do (practice), critical pragmatism as a generalized approach to discourses and practices is a possible response" (Cherryholmes, 1988, p. 14). Cherryholmes describes critical pragmatism as a process that brings "a sense of crisis to considerations of standards and conventions. Critical pragmatism considers not only what we choose to say and do, along with their effects, but also what structures those choices. Critical pragmatism pursues the fundamental questions asked by poststructural analysis into the design as well as operation of our social practices and institutions. Critical pragmatism is concerned with evaluating and constructing the communities, educational and otherwise, in which we live and work" (Cherryholmes, 1988, p. 14).

Cherryholmes' critical pragmatism is reminiscent of the interplay between postmodern critique and social criticism reported by Fraser and Nicholson. Recognition of this interplay is the essential centering process. Pragmatically, human activity needs to be morally and ethically centered; however, postpositivistically, the center needs to be constantly deconstructively and critically challenged. Therefore, the center is not a fixed point with a modernistic foundation, but a moving target, a dynamic juxtaposition of socially constructed and criticized realities.

In relation to a center as a moving target, Alexander M. Sidorkin (1999) calls for a center based on civility. Sidorkin's (1999) view is that the complexity of difference in any society can have deleterious effects in the establishment of community, therefore necessitating some type of social cohesion that can lead to an "institutionalized dialogue" (p. 126). Sidorkin (1999) warns that "complexity must not become an absurd theater of broken conversations, dislocated phrases, and meaningless encounters" (p. 126). Sidorkin (1999) proposes civility " as a quality of organization that enables the organization to include the ideas of the dialogical and to limit dialogue and polyphony" (p. 127). However, can civility be defined to satisfy the postpositivistic critique?

Sidorkin (1999) proposes that "civility involves a moral self-assessment of a community with such a concept" (p. 127). Of course, the moral center of a community is an ideological construct. How can this ideological center withstand a postpositivist scrutiny? Sidorkin addresses this concern by dealing with the type of conversation in which the center is nested. "The ideology of a good school is principally negotiable and unstable. This is why it should be balanced by another element of civility, the public conversation" (Sidorkin, 1999, p. 129). Sidorkin's moral center becomes a continuously negotiated center; however, a center anchored by an ideological concern for social justice and caring. In addition, this negotiated center is mediated by the ongoing inclusion of postpositivist critique by all of the community members. In the context of a school community, Sidorkin writes that " the public conversation creates disruptions in the settled framework of a school's ideology, its habits and organizational ways. It is a situation where students and teachers actively engage in conversation, while still keeping the fundamentals of the school ideology in mind" (p. 129).

To better differentiate between the various types of postpositivistic inquiry, Lather (1991) distinguishes between the deconstructive purpose of inquiry, which is represented by poststructural and postmodern inquiry, and emancipatory inquiry, which includes critical theory and feminism. Emancipatory intent is the key ingredient in the development of a moral center. Intent, rather than foundational critical structures, drives the need to center a visionary project. Grounding one's center in a specifically defined and structured metanarrative, whether of a political or religious nature, is a cognitive illusion easily critiqued by postpositivistic inquiry, as well as by positivistic inquiry. However, using emancipatory intent as the guiding principle, in conjunction with the constant employment of the tools of postpositivist inquiry, creates a critically oriented intricacy or evolutionary consciousness.

This critically oriented intricacy is another way to characterize post-formal conversation. Through the employment of post-formal conversation, critical concerns about generalizing structures, such as race, gender, and social class, would not become universalizing narratives, but comparativist inquiry attuned to changes and contrasts (Fraser & Nicholson, (1990). Post-formal conversation replaces unitary notions of race, gender, and social class with "plural and complexly constructed conceptions of social identity, treating gender as one relevant strand among others, attending also to class, race, ethnicity, age, and sexual orientation" (Fraser & Nicholson, 1990, pp. 34-35).

A significant portion of this chapter has been devoted to a discussion of postmodernism, poststurcturalism, poststructural feminism, and critical theory. The reason is that whatever new vision is proposed, if the vision does not properly align with the modernistic thinking of the dominant culture, significant resistance will be encountered. In addition to the response of the dominant culture, the vision will be rigorously scrutinized by postpositivistic paradigms. Whether conscious evolution, an intricate web world, or a new educational reform, the proponents of the new vision need the tools that will allow an on-going critical and rigorous construction of the vision, and help the vision withstand the oppositional discourses and resistance that will be encountered. Post-formal conversation is a paradigm that will facilitate the critical and rigorous construction, and provide a means to answer the both positivist/modernist and postpositivistic critics.

3.   POST-FORMAL CONVERSATION AS METACONVERSATION

Early in the chapter Banathy, Hubbard and Goerner's visions were provided as contexts to situate the relevance of post-formal conversation and also to showcase the nature of post-formal conversation. The emancipatory potential of the idealism that is the basis of these visions was questioned by the possibility of these visions representing extensions of modernistic thought and methodology rather than representing a significant break with the anachronistic aspects of modernistic rationality.

The brief review of postpositivistic thinking had two purposes. The first was to clearly establish that what modernistic thought represents is only one singularly fallible lens in discerning reality. Prior to the postpositivistic critique of modernism, rational empiricism with all of its related metanarratives was the dominant *consciousness*. As idealists like Banathy, Hubbard and Goerner propose, there is a new consciousness or perception of reality, and the strongest indicator supporting their contention is the emergence from postpositivistic thinking of a different kind of consciousness. The second purpose was to showcase the functionality of the diverse postpositivistic methods of thinking as a critique of modernism and of each other. The importance of this purpose lies in the act of critique. New consciousness is not a naturally emergent phenomenon. New consciousness is a social construction that arises out of continuous and rigorous critique of oneself and society.

Finally, the question was raised as to the nature of the potential safeguards that could protect idealistic visions from developing uncritical essentializing metanarratives that merely replace the outdated modernistic metanarratives. Post-formal conversation is posed as a mechanism that can act as a safeguard. To explore the potential of post-formal conversation to function in this capacity, first post-formal conversation will be explained and then post-formal conversation will be examined as metaconversation.

3.1   The Foundations of Post-Formal Conversation

Post-formal conversation is grounded in the post-formal thinking proposed by Joe L. Kincheloe and Shirley R. Steinberg (1999a; 1999b). Post-formal thinking is centered on paradigms of justice and caring, provides tools to interrogate the social environment, offers a critical critique of modernistic and formalistic thinking structures, promotes the value of difference and diversity, and enhances egalitarian tendencies in the conservative dominant culture. Also, there is a degree of pragmatism in this thinking concerning the coexistence of elements of modernism and postmodernism. Kincheloe and Steinberg allude to this coexistence in the intent of their post-formal proposition. "We have sought a middle ground that attempts to hold onto the progressive and democratic features of modernism while drawing upon the insights postmodernism provides concerning the failure of reason, the tyranny of grand narratives, the limitations of science, and the repositioning of relationships between dominant and subordinate cultural groups" (1999a, p. 55).

Post-formal thinking is a critical critique and extension of formal thinking as personified by Jean Piaget's theories of cognition. Post-formal thinking politicizes and humanizes Piagetian formal cognition. Formal cognition is politicized by the recognition and inclusion of the ubiquity of power arrangements in all human affairs, and the imperative to promote critical skills that lead to this awareness. These skills then can be used to critique these arrangements, and then lead to self-empowering action. Formal cognition is humanized by the re-integration of reason and emotion that further reunites logic and intuition, which in turn facilitates deeper and more complex understandings about the ubiquity and pervasive inequity of many current socio-cultural and economic power arrangements.

Kincheloe and Steinberg (1999a) propose that post-formal thinkers operate at a meta-cognitive level, and are able to understand the way power shapes their lives (p. 81). They are able "to create situations that bring hidden situations to our attention and make the tacit visible" (Kincheloe & Steinberg, 1999a, p. 68). Post-formal thinkers develop the ability to engage in ideological disembedding, which is the act of recognizing and critiquing the values that are buried (embedded) in all of our social constructions (Kincheloe & Steinberg, 1999a, p. 64 & 83).

In relation to the human condition, in their description of a post-formal psychology Kincheloe and Steinberg describe the range of the post-formal critique. "In this context the new psychology emphasizes the impact of power on the 1) intrapersonal—the domain of consciousness; 2) interpersonal—the domain of relationships, social interactions; and 3) corporeality—the domain of the body and behavior, people's physical presence in the social world" (1999b, p. 36). This range is achieved by the inclusion of cultural studies as a post-formal critique of societal systems and structures. Cultural studies "asserts that a wide variety of expressions of cultural production should be studied in relation to other cultural dynamics and social and historical structures" (Kincheloe & Steinberg, 1999b, p. 27). The four-part structure of post-formal thinking allows the post-formal thinker to also understand how our understanding of situations is shaped without our conscious awareness by the discursive practices and stories that we tell about the world around us (Kincheloe & Steinberg, 1999b, p. 23). This structure includes etymology, pattern, process, and contextualization (Kincheloe & Steinberg, 1999a).

3.1.1   Etymology

Post-formal thinking requires an identification and critical critique of the origins of our knowledge. Kincheloe (1993) describes this etymological aspect of the post-formal process in this way. "Many descriptions of higher order thinking induce us to ask questions that analyze what we know, how we come to know it, why we believe it or reject it, and how we evaluate the credibility of the evidence. Post-formal thinking shares this characteristic of other descriptions of higher order thinking, but adds a critical hermeneutic and historical epistemological dimension to the idea. In order to transcend formality we must become critically initiated into our own tradition (and other traditions as well) in order to understand the etymology of the cultural forms embedded within us" (p. 158).

The inclusion of the process of on-going interpretation of what we know, in relation to the history of that knowledge, adds a broadening dynamic to our critical inquiry and practice. Kincheloe and Steinberg's post-formalism utilizes Foucault's notion of genealogy to facilitate the post-formal thinker's "struggle to become aware of their own ideological inheritance and its relationship to their own beliefs and value structures, interests, and questions about their professional lives" (1999b p. 62). A historical analysis of our bodies of knowledge, power arrangements, and forms of self-understanding strives to see if they make sense, if they are consistent. An etymological analysis of this kind is essential in critiquing the trustworthiness of our constructions of progress, improvement, development, the present and the future. A post-formal analysis of this kind demystifies the past and the present, and problematizes our socially constructed human experience. In relation to idealistic visions, tyranny and oppression can be part of the vision, masked by the use of symbols such as democracy, participation, holism, justice, and caring. The post-formal task is to unmask and understand how power is being manifested in these symbolic representations constructed by individuals and groups to further their own agendas. However, to go beyond Foucault's postmodern analysis, post-formal thinking adds a critical imperative to act against the tyranny and oppression.

3.1.2   Contextualization

The post-formal thinker realizes that to develop a more complex meaning about a situation requires attention to the circumstances and setting that surround and imbue the situation. Broadening the temporal and spatial aspects of a situation creates a more narrowly focused and also systemic view which results in greater understanding of the situation (Horn, 1999). Of course, context and etymology are mutually informing.

Moving from the limiting contexts provided by modernistic reductionism requires attention to the particular as well as the general. Kincheloe and Steinberg point out that "formal thinking often emphasizes the production of generalizations" (Kincheloe & Steinberg, 1999b, p. 79), and that attention must be paid to particulars such as the uniqueness of individuals and places. Once again this blending of different perspectives of context broadens our knowledge and critical consciousness about the social constructions that shape and often control our beliefs and actions.

An analysis of place (Kincheloe & Pinar, 1991) expands our attention to the setting and "brings the particular into focus". An analysis of place is imperative in light of the social construction of knowledge. This critical constructivist perspective recognizes that "our psychosocial disposition shapes how the world is perceived" and holds important implications for understanding how we construct knowledge (Kincheloe 1993, p. 108). "Because individuals are often unable to see the way their environment shapes their perceptions (that is, constructs their consciousness), the development of cognitive methods for exposing this process must become a central goal of the educational enterprise. This is where critical postmodern theory collides with constructivism–hence, the etymology of our term, 'critical constructivism'" (Kincheloe, 1993, p. 109). The psychoanalysis of place is a central cognitive method in this process because it transcends mere generalization or mere particularity, but instead "brings the particular into focus, but in a way that grounds it contextually in a larger understanding" of the psychological and social forces that shape it (Kincheloe, 1995, p. 224).

Through a critical exploration of etymology and context, patterns can be discerned–deep, hidden patterns that greatly affect our understandings about our individual and social reality. Going beyond the surface layer of our understanding to the critical depths requires a post-formal engagement with the etymology and context of our knowledge.

3.1.3 Patterns

Kincheloe and Steinberg state that formal thinking is unable to penetrate to the deeper hidden structures of reality, and can only deal with the simple patterns and characteristics of the explicate order of the world that repeat themselves in similar ways (Horn, 1999). Kincheloe and Steinberg propose "that continuous etymological questioning leads to the discernment of the deeper hidden patterns of the implicate order (Bohm & Edwards, 1991; Bohm & Peat, 1987)" (Horn, 1999, p. 28). David Bohm's "implicate order is a much deeper structure of reality. It is the level at which ostensible separateness vanishes and all things seem to become a part of a larger unified structure" (Kincheloe and Steinberg, 1996, p. 179). Kincheloe further observes that "when post-formal observers search for the deep structures which are there to be uncovered in any classroom, they discover a universe of hidden meanings constructed by a variety of sociopolitical forces that many times has little to do with the intended (explicate) meanings of the official curriculum" (Kincheloe, 1993, p. 149). Focusing on the detection of implicate patterns offsets the dominant culture's conversation which is formalistic and focused on the explicate order.

Pattern detection also employs metaphoric cognition to see the relationships between ostensibly different things (Kincheloe & Steinberg, 1999b, p. 69). This "involves the fusion of previously disparate concepts in unanticipated ways. The mutual interrelationships of the components of a metaphor, not the components themselves, are the most important aspects of a metaphor" (Kincheloe & Steinberg, 1999b, p. 69).

If patterns representing the explicate and implicate order of the world can be discerned through a post-formal analysis of the etymology and context of knowledge, what are the post-formal processes that comprise this analysis?

3.1.4 Process

In order to penetrate the surface reality to discover the implicate order requires a variety of research methods. To expand one's critical consciousness requires a bricolage of research methods (Denzin & Lincoln, 1994; Levi-Strauss, 1966). "Bricolage involves taking research strategies from a variety of disciplines and traditions as they are needed in the unfolding context of the research situation. Such a position is pragmatic and strategic, demanding a self-consciousness and an awareness of context from the researcher" (Kincheloe, 1998, p. 1200).

Integral to this bricolage are all the definitions of deconstruction ("as a method of reading, as an interpretive process, and as a philosophical strategy" [Kincheloe & Steinberg, 1999b, p. 73]). In addition, "critical theory, feminist theory, critical multiculturalism, cultural studies, ecological theory, postmodernist epistemologies, indigenous knowledges, situated cognition, and post-structuralist psychoanalysis all can provide insight" (Kincheloe & Steinberg, 1999b, p. 5). Post-formal thinking pragmatically utilizes all methods of inquiry in its critical inquiry into our knowledge and the patterned order of our knowledge.

Post-formality responds to the modernistic bifurcation of logic and emotion by reconnecting "logic and emotion, mind and body, individual and nature, and self and other" (Kincheloe & Steinberg, 1996, p. 185). Kincheloe looks to Afrocentric and Native American epistemologies, which have never divided reality into spiritual and material segments, as examples of unified thinking processes. Also, "feminist constructivists have maintained that emotional intensity precedes cognitive transformation to a new way of seeing. Knowing, they argue, involves emotional as well as cognitive states of mind"

(Kincheloe & Steinberg, 1996, p. 186). Recognition of the necessity to include emotion grounds cognition that allows "post-formal thinkers [to] tap into a passion for knowing that motivates, extends, and leads them to a union with all that is to be known" (Kincheloe & Steinberg, 1996, p. 186).

The post-formal process is related to the consciousness that we wish to attain. Post-formal thinking recognizes the connection between the processes employed and the consciousness attained. Kincheloe (1999) explains this connection. "The concept of negation, central to critical theory and to accommodation [in the Piagetian process of cognitive development], involves the continuous criticism and reconstruction of what one thinks she knows. For example, critical theorist Max Horkheimer argued that through negation we develop a critical consciousness that allows us to transcend old codified world views and incorporate our new understandings into a new reflective attitude" (Kincheloe, 1999, p. 14).

There is purpose behind the critical negation of one's personal and societal constructions of difference, power arrangements, knowledge base, and representational language. The purpose of this criticism is to create metacognitive leverage points that make personal and social constructions accessible to further critique through post-formal lenses. This post-formal process results in the construction of a post-formal container in which personal and collective consciousness are both critiqued and nurtured. As transcendental forms of consciousness (i. e., evolutionary consciousness) develop within this container, the post-formal process acts as a strange attractor in that the post-formal process pulls the developing consciousness into the pattern of emancipatory consciousness.

The post-formal process is a "dynamic dance." An example used by Goerner to describe the "dynamic dance" of self-organization is an apt analogy for the post-formal process. "A whirlpool, for example, is not a fixed lump of molecules like a chair. It is a *dynamic dance*, a whir of motion held together largely by the momentum of its own spin. The matter involved in this dance doesn't even stay constant. Molecules come in at the top and circle out through the bottom in an endless stream. Scientists call these kinds of organization 'dynamic structures'–because dynamics are crucial. Stop the momentum or break apart the forces, and the organization disappears as if it had never existed" (Goerner, 1999, p. 156). The dynamic nature of this example requires the continuation of the process, and the dynamic nature of the post-formal process requires continuous critical critique. Her example continues to be analogous to the post-formal process, especially in relation to describing the attractor effect of the process on the developing critical consciousness. "On the other hand, this gossamer invention is also durable. Once the dance is going, its momentum tends to resist deviation. Thus, if you stick your finger in a whirlpool, it will keep its form and rebuild when you remove your finger. In the lingo of the field, the system has *structural stability*. The system is resistant to change because its dynamics are self-reinforcing" (Goerner, 1999, p. 156). In relation to the post-formal process, structural stability refers to the permanence of the critical consciousness developed through the post-formal process.

Finally, a basic condition of the post-formal process is to continuously elicit and critique the emotions and cognition that arise from the post-formal process. Both emotion and cognition are the sources of energy for this dynamic dance. Despite the modernistic bifurcation of cognition and emotion, the interplay of these descriptions of being human is an ever present dynamic dance that demands awareness and critique from those who wish to deeply understand.

3.1.5   A Synergetic Process

To be correctly understood, these four structures must be viewed as a process in which all four are dynamically interrelated and integrated in a synergetic whole. One does not do these as singular, isolated activities. Origins, pattern, process and context are always intertwined as we critically question the construction of our reality. In this brief and limited presentation of post-formality, I must refocus on certain basic elements of post-formality that are directly related to the governing ideals of social justice and caring. Considerations about difference, power arrangements, language (including media representations), and knowledge are lenses that always focus this dynamic post-formal process on social justice and caring. The overt purpose of post-formal thinking is to contest oppressive structures, thoughts, and actions. Individuals who desire to critically promote justice and caring will critique the origin and context of their individual and collective knowledge and emotions through a diversity of processes to discern the deep and hidden patterns of our human experience.

3.2   Conversation

3.2.1   The Problem

The idealized visions being used as the context for this discussion are essentially about building global community. However, whether local or global, evolutionary community building requires a concomitant evolution in the type and nature of conversation utilized by the communities. Visions of ideal communities usually identify dialogic and generative conversation as the optimum conversational type, and position more combative and conflictual forms of conversation as antithetical to the realization of their ideals. This dichotomous assessment of perceived combative versus generative conversation usually results in the avoidance of human interaction that involves combative and conflictual conversation. The further outcome is an isolation of the proponents of idealized visions into small communities of individuals who are like-minded in their ideals and proficient in dialogical conversation. Unfortunately, the effect of their vision is then limited by their inability to engage the predominant form of community culture, which is characterized by the more combative and conflictual conversation.

The conversational challenge for those promoting an idealized vision is first how to utilize conversation to function productively in a conflictual arena, and second, how to develop dialogical capacity in all members of a community. Engaging in dialogue requires a reasonable capacity to, if not trust oneself and others, at least adopt a neutral disposition. Unfortunately, there are many individuals where reason is not sufficient justification as a starting point in the acceptance of others and the beliefs of others.

To foster widespread interest in an idealized vision requires a strategic and disciplined view of conversation. Conversation is ubiquitous in human activity systems. The type of conversation is an indicator of the type of community (i. e., democratic, authoritarian, oppressive, visionary) which we engage, and specifically the power arrangements and social hierarchy in that community. More important is the fact that knowing the dominant type(s) of conversation in the community provides an entry point for change. Conversation is a political site that can become a contested site within in a community. Knowledge of conversational types and the concomitant capacity to instrumentally engage the political landscape through these conversational types are essential components in the propagation of an idealized vision. However, as mentioned before, having the ability to function effectively within the conflictual types of conversation is only the prelude, the entry point to building collaborative and collegial conversational capacity in the participants.

Building capacity in community members to collegially and collaboratively converse is the determinant of the viability of the idealized vision. In a community, all types of conversation are evident. In most communities, collegial types of conversation are probably subordinate to conflictual conversation. To use the metaphor of a conversational container (the individual and collective assumptions and beliefs of a community), a community of this kind acts as a container that holds and shapes conversation. William Isaacs (1999) proposes that if there are no dialogue-friendly elements in the container, then dialogue cannot occur (p. 244). Issacs maintains that as people communicate, pressure builds and the container must hold the pressure. Therefore, as the conversation progresses, the people involved must continuously recreate and sustain the container. In the case of communities where conflictual conversation dominates, attempts at dialogue would be constrained and limited by a container of this nature. Isaacs reports that "the shape of our internal container guides our ability to hear what is being said. The shape of a collective container equally determines what can be said and heard (p. 248). Members of this community tacitly understand this and because of the constraints placed on individuals and groups by their dominating culture, accept the conversational boundaries of this container.

This conversational scenario reinforces the uncritical container and the individuals' acquiescence to conflictual conversation. Hence a sustainable and uncritical conversational environment is established and mutually reinforced by the greater majority of the community members.

This is the reality faced by proponents of idealized visions. Therefore, one of the major tasks is to attack this conversational container. Post-formal conversation, which includes the postpositivistic discourses, provides the means to attack this type of container and at the same time build a new container that includes collaborative and collegial types of conversation. Interrogation of the old container and capacity building for a new one are simultaneous activities. To Isaacs (1999) "containers that are capable of holding our experience in ever more rich and complex ways, [make] legitimate many approaches and styles" (p. 256).

There are critical implications attached to the previously described container. Where the purpose of conversation is to promote self interest and/or the interest on one's racial, ethnic, gender, economic, or political group, considerations of justice and caring (about humans and the earth) are sharply defined within the parameters allowed by the established container. The type of conversation and purpose of conversation becomes the promoter of reality as determined by the dominant culture. It is this reality and it's associated definitions of human activity that need to be post-formally interrogated. The dominant forms of conversation need to be appropriated for this interrogation and also need to be utilized to build capacity for more ideal and generative types of conversation. In this political endeavor to promote egalitarian and caring attitudes in this community and towards the world, conversation becomes the battleground–the essential and imperative mediating force between those who strive to promote egalitarian and caring change and those who are entrenched in the old oppressive culture.

3.2.2   Types of Conversation

Patrick M. Jenlink and Alison Carr (1996) identify four types of conversation: discussion, dialectical, dialogue, and design. Discussion and dialectical conversation are similar and the most frequently occurring types. They are characterized by disciplined, logical, and emotional, arguments used to promote ideologies and beliefs. Unfortunately, this type of conversation invariably results in a polarization or alienation of some people. People who engage in dialectical conversation "are threatened by anyone who thinks differently from them, and so regard it as their responsibility to convert others to their view" (Avers, Broadbent, Ferguson, Gabriele, Lawson, McCormick, & Wotruba, 1996, p., 32). Discussion and dialectical (also known as debate) are combative and conflictual types of conversation.

On the other hand, dialogue and design facilitate the development of a "oneness"—a shared culture sustained by morally committed people. In dialogue, people examine their personal assumptions and then suspend them; thus opening new spaces where new meanings can be constructed (Bohm, 1992; Horn & Carr-Chellman, 2000; Jenlink & Carr, 1996). Banathy (1996) maintains that if members of a group can suspend their mindsets, then they can generate a shared consciousness. Banathy (1996) continues by mentioning that "in the dialogue event people are able to be honest and straight with each other, they level with each other, and they share content freely. They develop a common mind, a shared mind, that can think together in a new and creative way. They awaken their collective intelligence and feelings of genuine participation, mutual trust, fellowship, and friendship. They can think and talk together. Shared meaning and understanding flow freely in the group" (p. 216). One caveat that Banathy issues is that if there is hierarchy or authority represented in the group, then none of this can happen.

Dialogue requires a respect for other views and recognition that the intended outcome is the development of community. The distinction between dialogue and design is that when engaged in design conversation, people focus on creating something new. When engaged in creating change through design conversation, the participants are committed "to change *of* the system rather than change *within* the system" Jenlink & Carr, 1996, p. 35). Design conversation would lead to something new; not just a reshuffling of parts resulting in the same outcomes. Dialogue and design are generative in that through critique newness and difference are welcomed. Discussion and dialectical conversation purposefully promote one position in opposition to other positions.

Banathy (1996) identifies two specific modes of dialogue as strategic and generative. Strategic dialogue "implies communication among designers that focuses on specific tasks of seeking solutions" (p. 215). Generative dialogue, attributed to David Bohm, is used to generate a common frame of thinking, shared meaning, and a collective worldview in a group (Banathy, 1996, p. 215). Banathy reports that generative and strategic dialogue function together to create design conversation.

Another important dimension of dialogue in a post-formal context is that to dialogue is to be human. The imperative of dialogue is to recognize and transcend difference without denigrating the humanity of those holding different views. Sidorkin (1999) sees this in the works of Bakhtin and Buber in that "what they did was to see the difference among groups and individual as not simply an important human condition, but as a central, defining condition of human existence" (p. 10). A post-formally contextualized dialogue expands the participants' exploration of their individual and collective humanity. In essence, dialogue of this type has the potential to facilitate the creation of a broader and deeper conscious awareness of one's self to others. Sidorkin asserts that "Buber and Bakhtin, like Copernicus, discovered the new center of the human universe, the *dialogical*" (p. 11). In a critique of Nicholas Burbules (1993), Sidorkin stresses that dialogue is not to be *used* in teaching, but is the very essence of teaching. "Dialogue is an end in itself, the very essence of human existence" (Sidorkin, 1999, p. 14). Sidorkin's position rings true with the activity of visionaries like Banathy, Goerner, and Hubbard in that the development of an evolutionary and ecological consciousness is contingent upon the creation of dialogical opportunities or "moments of being" between people" (p. 17).

3.2.3   Post-formal Conversation

Post-formal conversation values not only dialogue and design conversation but also discussion and dialectical/debate conversation. Non-dialogic types of conversation are pragmatically valued as conversational sites of leverage that can move conversants along in how they understand themselves, their environments, and the implications of their conversation. If change is to occur, the nature of our society requires those who desire change to utilize all types of conversation. The growing demographical diversity of our society will result in increased conflict and confrontation between these diverse groups. To move toward any idealized vision will require knowledge and skill in all forms of conversation, which can be imparted to these antagonistic groups. Community building efforts will require expertise in promoting dialogue and design conversation, and also in utilizing discussion and dialectical conversation to combat oppression and create opportunities for dialogue.

A working knowledge of non-dialogic types of conversation is also necessary because of the difficulty in sustaining dialogue. The fundamental act in dialogue is to suspend one's own mindset. The suspension of one's mindset contributes to the transitory nature of dialogue. At some point, if the dialogue is relevant and authentic to the participants, someone's basic assumptions and beliefs will be threatened to the point where the individual will have difficulty in continuing to suspend their own mindset. When the condition of suspension collapses, the person can only submit to the other view, disengage from the conversation, or engage in discussion and dialectical conversation to protect those basic beliefs. The act of suspending one's mindset is essentially a cognitive activity, and when cognition fails, emotion returns. This is the post-formal point when emotion must be honored and dealt with expeditiously but respectfully. The personal and social contexts of moments like these, need to be investigated to not only discover the deeper patterns that also need to be critiqued, but also to create a more just and caring condition of trust, which in turn leverages a stronger base for further dialogue.

Change agents employing post-formal conversation need to be conversant in non-dialogical types of conversation for another reason. In the postmodern age, conversation has been redefined to include computer-mediated conversation. Here the chat room and email messages are characterized by detachment because of the asynchronous nature of their communication. Asynchronous communication fosters detachment because of the narrower context of the communication moment. Detachment is created by the pressure for brevity, which is induced by the technology, and the narrowing of the human interchange with the loss of the context (i. e., body language, sensory stimuli) of personal contact. Without the personal, the interactive text constructed by the conversants becomes solely abstract, devoid of the enrichment provided by the demanding concreteness of the personal. This decontextualization exacerbates the negatives involved in the emotional component of impersonal human interaction. How does one dialogue over email? How sincere is the dialogue when mediated by an asynchronous computer interaction? What effects does this have on the promotion of community or idealized visions?

Another type of conversation that invites post-formal inquiry and conversation is media conversation. Once again detachment and isolation inform and mediate the human interaction represented by movies, videos, television shows, compact disks, books, and radio. Interestingly, recipients can only respond to themselves or to a third party; the interaction is distinctly a one-way communication. Also, there is more interpretive responsibility on the recipient. Recipients can only rely on their knowledge base and deconstructive and interpretive skills, and if those are minimal, then their interpretations will be less complex and more controlled by the sender. The predominance and power of media conversation requires the promotion of post-formal skills and the utilization of those skills to unmask the hidden agendas and deeper messages that seek to manipulate and oppress the viewer.

The previous expansion of conversation indicates that in a postmodern society conversation is a whole new ballgame. To play in this game requires expertise in post-formal conversation. Post-formal conversation can be used to critique a conversational system from the inside or outside; to interrogate and disrupt the tacit assumptions held by the participants in a conversation; to force a critique of the individual and collective consciousness propagated by the conversation; and to disrupt the integrity and structure of the group's conversational container. A post-formal process leads to a critical and therefore more authentic design process. In situations characterized by difference and inequitable power arrangements, post-formal conversation is not a harmonious process but a political project that reflects the emotions and beliefs associated with an on-going struggle for a just and caring community within the constraints imposed by conflicting personal agendas and economic scarcity. The aim of post-formal conversation is two-fold: to achieve an idealized community, and to achieve a critically pragmatic resolution of inequity in any community.

3.2.4 The Limits of Dialogue

The promotion of dialogue as a panacea for a plethora of societal ills is ubiquitous in utopian, educational, systems thinking, and business literature.

The support for the use of dialogue is undoubtedly based on personal intuition, observation, empirical study, and a desire to avoid the unpleasantness and inefficiency of non-dialogical conversational types. I am a proponent of dialogue, but I am also a proponent of the emancipatory outcomes resulting from postpositivistic inquiry. Therefore, through these lenses of inquiry I see the judicious use of dialogue as an essential component in our effort to facilitate the development of individuals who are concerned about justice and caring for themselves, others, and the Earth. However, my postpositivistic view requires me to view the promotion of dialogue as I would any other metanarrative, which means that dialogue as a construct and as a practice has to be post-formally interrogated. The imperative for this on-going interrogation is that like any other human construction, dialogue can be used inadvertently or covertly to mask oppressive practices and structures. A brief review of Daniel Yankelovitch's concept of dialogue will act as an example of my critical concern.

Yankelovich (1999) is a respected advisor to large corporations, government and professional organizations, therefore what he proposes is seriously entertained by many in these fields. However, a critical reading of his thoughts on dialogue showcases how the meaning of dialogue can differ from the idealized usage and how it can be used to mask oppression. In his understanding of dialogue, Yankelovitch uses all of the symbolic language encountered in literature about dialogue–trust, agreement, honestly, openness, respect, and transformation. In Yankelovitch's case, a post-formal reading of the context in which these are used indicates that they mask understandings that are quite different from other interpretations by those with different agendas.

For instance, on the same page that he refers to Martin Buber's idea of the "Thou", "treating the other as an equal in every respect" (Yankelovitch, 1999, p. 88), Yankelovitch explains that to facilitate mutual respect requires the conversation facilitator to confront misunderstandings that will arise. Yankelovitch states that "we have seen that misunderstandings arise from many sources: friction between subcultures, differences in interests, and, most complex of all, transference-driven distortions" (p. 88). When given a cursory reading, few would disagree with his conclusion; however, what is not mentioned becomes significant, especially in relation to the complete narrative as detailed in his book. In this narrative segment, Yankelovitch does not mention oppression perpetuated by those in power over others as an obstacle to the development of mutual respect. Can a lack of respect merely be the result of misunderstanding others, or can it be a purposeful act of resistance to those perceived as oppressors? In a post-formal inquiry, a reductionist analysis of one segment of a story is important but does not reveal any larger patterns of thought. To go deeper requires broadening the analysis.

Yankelovitch addresses the effectiveness of dialogue in hierarchical organizations. He disagrees with Bohm and Buber (1988, 1992) who he represents as believing that "dialogue among equals is impossible" in hierarchical organizations (p. 96). He supports his disagreement with their skepticism by citing his own experience and the similar thoughts of Peter Senge (1990), who is another proponent of using dialogue in the corporate workplace. Yankelovitch then suggests that focus groups can be used as a rudimentary form of planned dialogue in hierarchical organizations. These are groups of eight to twelve consumers, voters, or workers who are brought together for approximately two hours for the purpose of reacting to an issue, a candidate, a product, or a communication (Yankelovitch, 1999, pp. 96-97). Yankelovitch describes one such group comprised of African-Americans and whites that clearly expressed the problem between these groups as a lack of trust.

In his description, Yankelovitch (1999) concludes that after a rapport was established through dialogue, both sides believed "that merit should be the deciding factor" in resolving their disagreements (p. 98). However in this case, the result of the dialogic process was an inability to explore the reasons why one group (the African-Americans) would consistently lose out in situations mediated only by merit. Here the dialogic process did not allow the discernment of structural and systemic racism that prohibits many African-Americans to compete equitably in a "merit" situation.

His description continued with an anecdote about how trust was enhanced when an African-American woman reported her fear of being endangered in her African-American community. Yankelovitch reports that trust was developed because whites could agree with her about their own safety concerns in Black neighborhoods without appearing racist. The outcome was the mutual condemnation of the media for their "needless emphasis on the color of the criminals" (Yankelovitch, 1999, p. 99). Yankelovitch reports that "these statements helped create rapport with Black participants" (p. 99).

However, once again the deeper issue of systemic poverty fostered by racist economic and political policies were left unexplored by the participants. Yankelovitch (1999) concluded that "they still didn't agree with each other, but they had developed respect and sympathy for each other's viewpoints" (p. 99). He continued in that after two hours of dialogue, "as these stereotypes dissipate, they are replaced by glimmerings of respect and fragile bounds of community" (p. 100). But, the critical bottom line is that the racist structures, attitudes, and policies that perpetuate the symptoms of oppression went unchallenged. This type of superficial, decontextualized feel-good dialogue does nothing to facilitate the development of justice and caring in the participants' consciousness. Yankelovitch's statement, that "it is hardly an exaggeration to state that in focus groups where those holding contrary views have been demonized, each side makes the unexpected discovery that the other is human: a kindred soul who laughs at the same jokes and has similar worries" (p. 101), rings hollow in critical depth and substance.

Yankelovitch's (1999) fundamental beliefs that color his interpretation of dialogue become readily apparent in his identification of those who "will never do dialogue well" (p. 129). His conservative view becomes apparent in his conclusion that "anyone who has ever argued with a committed Marxist has experienced the frustration of banging one's head against a rigid barrier of thought. The same is true of certain religious fundamentalists, passionate free-market advocates, ideologically committed liberals, and so on" (Yankelovitch, 1999, p. 129). His interpretation and instrumental use of dialogue becomes more clear when he states that "the first principle is that dialogue participants must faithfully express the concerns and values of mainstream America" (p. 167). An interpretation of Yankelovitch's position is that dialogue requires those who oppose "mainstream American values" to suspend their own feelings and thoughts that are oppositional to those of the dominant culture. This attitude dooms any substantial resolution of significant societal problems by refusing to engage the real and perceived origins and context that created and maintains these problems.

In conclusion, Yankelovitch's (1999) use of dialogue as a manipulative tool of the culturally dominant is once again masked by his statement that "power is not an issue. The objective is not to get recalcitrant people to follow orders; it is to invite them to take ownership of a vision, a strategy, a set of values. Dialogue is ideally suited to this objective" (p. 173). This mask is again revealed in his comments on the fear experienced by the Elites when engaging in dialogue.

> The actual experience of dialogue helps enormously to allay fears of status and power loss. Elites who have had this experience come to realize that they do not relinquish power or status by empowering others to reason together with them as equals. In fact, they gain in authority and respect. The kind of 'power' involved in exchanging views in a dialogue setting is not the zero-sum type. In a dialogue, everyone wins. Opening oneself to the views of others through dialogue is an effective way of uniting people to advance shared goals. As we have seen, dialogue mutes conflict, creates a sense of community and goodwill, causes people to react sympathetically to one another as people rather than to negative stereotypes, and nudges people toward the same side of an issue rather than fixing them on opposite sides. (Yankelovitch, 1999, p. 173)

Unfortunately, the cost of this sense of community fostered by reasoning together is the inability to truly empower the Others to interrogate the deeper and well concealed oppressive structures and attitudes that are responsible for societal oppression and inequity. Basically, in Yankelovitch's employment of dialogue, the Others are empowered to dialogue within the constraints of the values and beliefs of those who dominant. In this case, dialogue is used to get "buy-in" from the disenfranchised and marginalized.

The Elites do not have to fear Yankelovitch's (1999) use of dialogue because "dialogue is a unique method for transforming people's views from raw, mushy, and unrealistic wishful thinking into the kind of thoughtful and considered judgment that should allay the legitimate concerns of elites" (p. 175). This brief deconstruction of Yankelovitch's use of dialogue shows the limits of dialogue. Like all human constructions, dialogue is not an essentialized or generic entity, but a process that needs to be post-formally interrogated and problematized.

Used as part of a post-formal process, dialogue is not an end-state but a temporary way station in the process. To continuously suspend your mindset is to disembed yourself from your emotional self and from the complete context of the social realities of your environment. Also, as any other conversational type, dialogue can be appropriated and utilized to promote a diversity of purposes. The singular use of dialogue or, its use in conjunction with other types, has limitations that need to be critically critiqued by the participants in the conversation.

3.3   A Metaconversation

Post-formal conversation has been proposed as a critically centered, methodological eclectic form of conversation. More accurately, post-formal conversation is a metaconversation, which contains these components:

1. Situational use of postpositivistic methods of inquiry.
2. A recognition and utilization of all other types of conversation.
3. The ability to recognize emotional and cognitive situations that can be used to leverage emancipatory change.
4. The reintegration of emotion and cognition as dynamic and interrelated phenomenon.
5. The metacognitive ability to critique the cognitive process, the outcomes of cognition, and the inclusion and integration of morality, ethics and spirituality in cognition.
6. The metaemotional ability to critique emotion, the outcomes of emotional activity, and the inclusion and integration of morality, ethics and spirituality in human interaction.

Developing a widespread ability in individuals to engage in a post-formal metaconversation must become a critical component in what is proposed by visionaries like Banathy, Hubbard, and Goerner. The failure of these evolutionary and holistic visions will not be from their lack of acceptance over time, but from their potential to become metanarratives that mask oppression which is perpetuated by agendas driven by self-interest and reciprocity, which is a level of moral decision making that is solely guided by an instrumental exchange of self-interest (Kohlberg, 1981).

As an example of this danger, Hubbard promotes David L. Cooperrider's idea of appreciative inquiry as one of the significant mechanisms that can facilitate the growth of conscious evolution. Cooperrider (1999) acknowledges that human beings create their own realities, and that, because of this individual and social construction of reality, conscious evolution of the future is a viable human option. Cooperrider, Sorensen, Whitney, and Yaeger (2000) propose a process of appreciative inquiry which is about "the co-evolutionary search for the best in people, their organizations, and the relevant world around them" (p. 5). This process is the "art and practice of asking questions that strengthen a system's capacity to apprehend, anticipate, and heighten positive potential" (Cooperrider et al., 2000, p. 5). In appreciative inquiry, "intervention gives way to the speed of imagination and innovation; instead of negation, criticism, and spiraling diagnosis, there is discovery, dream, and design" (p. 5). They describe this process as a way "to build a constructive union between a whole people and the massive entirety of what people talk about as past and present capacities: achievements, assets, unexplored potentials, innovations, strengths, elevated thoughts, opportunities, benchmarks, high point moments, lived values, traditions, strategic competencies, stories, expressions of wisdom, insights into the deeper corporate spirit or soul, and visions of valued and possible futures" (p. 5).

There is no doubt that appreciative inquiry can be a powerful force in moving humanity to a new level of consciousness. However, this process needs an on-going post-formal interrogation of the past and present capacities to challenge the entrenched oppressive structures and attitudes embedded within the history and current manifestation of these capacities. Each of the capacities, cited by Cooperrider et al., are complex social constructions that have explicate and implicate components. An achievement, asset or innovation may mask oppressive structures that not only marginalize individuals but also will be perpetuated and become part of the new metanarrative. A post-formal critique is not contradictory to the method and intent of appreciative inquiry, but creates metacognitive and metaemotional leverage points that will critically complement the affirmation of existing and evolving emancipatory practices.

In relation to the potential of appreciative inquiry in facilitating the establishment of a new essentializing metanarrative, Hubbard (1998) pursues her vision by explaining that "when a culture has a story everyone understands, it gives direction and meaning to that culture" (p. 23). In a statement like this, a post-formal red flag is raised by the phrase "a story everyone understands," and by her use of the words "direction" and "meaning." I do not disagree with her perceived need by humans for a culturally centering narrative. However, since the human activity represented by these words is socially constructed, the evolving center, which is an individual and collective consciousness, needs to be continuously interrogated and problematized. Without a post-formal analysis, questions go unanswered like: Who determines the meaning and direction? Who is marginalized by the story? What is the status of those who understand but challenge the story?

She reiterates the need for a socially constructed metanarrative in what she calls a "guided worldview called conscious evolution." She explains that this guided worldview "holds that through our unprecedented scientific, social, and spiritual capacities we can evolve consciously and cocreatively with nature and the deeper patterns of creation (traditionally called God), thus enabling us to manifest a future commensurate with our unlimited species and planetary potential" (Hubbard, 1998, p. 57). It is difficult to contest the idealism of this vision, but the etymological and contextual components of anything scientific, social, and spiritual demand a post-formal inquiry through post-formal conversation in order to realize the idealistic emancipatory potential of this kind of human activity.

In conclusion, a case has been made for post-formal conversation as a metaconversational process to function as a safeguard within idealistic visions, and to function as a conversation that contests the sites of oppression in human activity. One thing is for certain, current and future human activity will be contested by those who wish to move to a different level of awareness and activity, and also by those who wish to maintain the status quo. Post-formal conversation has the potential to facilitate just and caring change by critically critiquing, in a disciplined and rigorous way, the most basic of all human activities—conversation.

References

Avers, D., Broadbent, M., Ferguson, T., Gabriele, S., Lawson, T., McCormick, S., and Wotruba, D., 1996. Design conversation and systems design: Group report. *Proceedings of the Eighth International Conversation on Comprehensive Design of Social Systems, Pacific Grove, California*, pp. 1-42.

Banathy, B. H., 1996. *Designing Social Systems In a Changing World: A Journey Toward a Creating Society*. Plenum Press, New York.

Bohm, D., 1992. *Thought as a System*. Routledge, New York.

Bohm, D., and Edwards, M., 1991. *Changing Consciousness*. Harper, San Francisco.

Bohm, D., and Peat, F.D., 1987. *Science, order, and creativity*. Bantam Books, New York.

Botnik, J.W., and Maltiz, M., 1979. *No Limits to Learning*. Pergamon Press, Oxford, UK.

Buber, M., 1988. *Eclipse of God*. Humanities Press International, Inc., Atlantic Highlands, NJ.

Buber, M., 1992. *On Intersubjectivity and Cultural creativity*. The University of Chicago Press, Chicago.

Burbules, N.C., 1993. *Dialogue in Teaching: Theory and Practice*. Teachers College Press, New York.

Cahoone, L., (ed.), 1996. *From Modernism to Postmodernism: An Anthology*. Blackwell Publishers, Cambridge, MA.

Cherryholmes, C.H., 1988. *Power and Criticism: Poststructural Investigations in Education*. Teachers College Press, New York.

Cherryholmes, C., 1999. *Reading Pragmatism*. Teachers College Press, New York.

Cooperrider, D.L., and Whitney, D., 1999. *Appreciative Inquiry*. Berrett Koehler Communications, Inc., San Francisco.

Cooperrider, D.L., Sorensen, Jr., P.F., Whitney, D., and Yaeger, T.F., 2000. *Rethinking Human Organization Toward a Positive Theory of Change*. Stipes Publishing, Champaign, IL.

320 Raymond A. Horn, Jr.

Denzin, N.K., and Lincoln, Y.S., (eds.), 1994. *Handbook of Qualitative Research*. Sage, Thousand Oaks, CA.

Flax, J.. 1990. Postmodernism and gender relations in feminist theory. In L.J. Nicholson (ed.), *Feminism/Postmodernism*. Routledge, New York, pp. 39-62.

Fraser, N. and Nicholson, L.J., 1990. Social criticism without philosophy: An encounter between feminism and postmodernism. In L.J. Nicholson (ed.), *Feminism/Postmodernism*. Routledge, New York, pp. 19-38.

Goerner, S.J., 1999. *After the Clockwork Universe: The Emerging Science and Culture of Integral Society*. Floris Books, Edinburgh, UK.

Hinchey, P.H., 1998). *Finding Freedom in the Classroom: A Practical Introduction to Critical Theory*. Peter Lang Publishers, New York.

Horn, R.A., 1999. Joe L. Kincheloe: Teacher-as-researcher. *Educational Researcher*, 28(4): 27-31.

Horn, R.A., and Carr-Chellman, A.A., 2000. Providing systemic change for schools: Towards professional development through moral conversation. *Systems Research and Behavioral Science*, 45(3): 255-272.

Hubbard, B.M., 1998. *Conscious Evolution: Awakening the Power of Our Social Potential*. New World Library, Novato, CA.

Isaacs, W., 1999. *Dialogue and the Art of Thinking Together*. Currency, New York.

Jenlink, P., and Carr, A.A., 1996. Conversation as a medium for change in education. *Educational Technology*, 36 (1): 31-38.

Kincheloe, J.L., 1993. *Toward a Critical Politics of Teacher Thinking: Mapping the Postmodern*. Bergin & Garvey, Westport, Connecticut.

Kincheloe, J.L., 1995. *Toil and Trouble: Good Work, Smart Workers, and the Integration of Academic and Vocational Education*. Peter Lang, New York.

Kincheloe, J.L., 1998. Critical research in science education. In B. Fraser, and K. Tobin, (eds.), *International handbook of science education*. Kluwer Academic Publishers, Boston:, pp. 1191-1205.

Kincheloe, J.L., 1999. Trouble ahead, trouble behind: Grounding the post-formal critique of educational psychology. In J.L. Kincheloe, and S.R. Steinberg, (eds.), *The Post-formal Reader: Cognition and Education*. Falmer Press, New York, pp. 4-54.

Kincheloe, J.L, and Pinar, W.F. (eds.), 1991. *Curriculum as Social Psychoanalysis: The Significance of Place*. State University of New York Press, New York.

Kincheloe, J.L., and Steinberg, S.R., 1996. A tentative description of post-formal thinking: The critical confrontation with cognitive theory. In P. Leistyna, A. Woodrum, and S.A. Sherblom, (eds.), *Breaking Free: The Transformative Power of Critical Pedagogy*. Harvard Educational Review, Cambridge, Massachusetts, pp. 167-198.

Kincheloe, J.L., and Steinberg, S.R., 1999a. A tentative description of post-formal thinking: The critical confrontation with cognitive theory. In J.L. Kincheloe, and S.R. Steinberg, (eds.), *The Post-formal Reader: Cognition and Education*. Falmer Press, New York, pp. 55-90.

Kincheloe, J.L., and Steinberg, S.R., 1999b. The post-formal critique of educational psychology. In J.L. Kincheloe, and S.R. Steinberg, S. R. (eds.), *The Post-formal Reader: Cognition and Education*. Falmer Press, New York, pp. 4-54.

Kohlberg, L., 1981. *The Philosophy of Moral Development*. Harper Row, San Francisco.

Lather, P., 1991. *Getting Smart: Feminist Research and Pedagogy With/in the Postmodern*. Routledge, New York.

Levi-Strauss, C., 1966. *The Savage Mind*. The University of Chicago Press, Chicago.

Pinar, W., Reynolds, W., Slattery, P., and Taubman, P., 1995. *Understanding curriculum*. Peter Lang, New York.

Purpel, D.E., 1989. *The Moral and Spiritual Crisis in Education: A Curriculum for Justice and Compassion in Education*. Bergin & Garvey, New York.

Senge, P.M., 1990. *The Fifth Discipline: The Art and Practice of the Learning Organization*. Doubleday/Currency, New York.

Sidorkin, A.M., 1999. *Beyond discourse: Education, the Self, and Dialogue.* State University of New York Press, New York.

Willower, D.J., 1998. Fighting the fog: A criticism of postmodernism. *Journal of School Leadership*, **8** (5): 448-463.

Yankelovitch, D., 1999. *The Magic of Dialogue: Transforming conflict Into Cooperation.* Simon and Schuster, New York.

Chapter 15

FUTURE SEARCH CONVERSATION

KAREN E. NORUM
Gonzaga University

> And so it was that the people devised among themselves a way of asking each other questions whenever a decision was to be made on a New Place or a New Way. We sought to perceive the flow of energy through each new possibility and how much was enough and how much was too much.
>
> – Underwood, 1991, p. 38

1. INTRODUCTION

We can have any future we want. We just have to identify it and design it–purposefully. "Future Search," as popularized by Marvin Weisbord, provides a framework for creating a system's future. The purpose of a Future Search conference is for the system to identify and aim for an ideal future. Two primary goals are to a) help large, diverse groups discover common values, purposes, and projects and b) enable people to create together a desired future that can be implemented immediately (Weisbord & Janoff, 2001). No prior training or expertise is needed to participate meaningfully in a Future Search. In fact, there is evidence that when people "begin working on real tasks relevant to a shared purpose," the skills needed to participate in the Future Search process "appear naturally and effortlessly" (Emery & Purser, 1996, p. 16). The process has been used to address a variety of issues (health care, education, public transportation, water quality), in a variety of settings (schools, hospitals, publishers, churches, government, non-profit organizations), in a variety of locations (North and South America, Australia, Africa, Europe, South Asia).

2.   BACK TO THE FUTURE

As developed by Weisbord, Future Search is an integration of several approaches to cooperative planning. It borrows from the "leaderless group" principles developed by Wilford Bion and Eric Trist during WW II, which are now principles for self-managing teams (Weisbord, 1992b). It takes the idea of a global context setting (looking at the global context before the local) from the Search Conference model developed by Fred Emery and Eric Trist (Weisbord, 1992b). The democratic (vs. autocratic) leadership style was adapted from the work of Ronald Lippett and Kurt Lewin (Weisbord, 1992b). From Ronald Lippett and Eva Schindler-Rainman, Weisbord used images of potential explored by whole communities (Weisbord, 1992b). Because Weisbord was most heavily influenced by the Lippett and Schindler-Rainman's large-scale community futures conferences and Emery and Trist's Search Conference, he named his innovation "Future Search" (Weisbord & Janoff, 2000). The spin Weisbord provided was boxing all these elements together in one room: A Future Search Conference brings "into one room people who each have pieces of a complex puzzle" (Weisbord, 1992a, p. 10). Making the benefits of systems thinking and creating space and place for people to work under an umbrella of shared values and goals are two primary goals of a Future Search Conference (Weisbord & Janoff, 2000).

Typically, a Future Search involves 60-70 people. This allows for many perspectives while still keeping the group small enough that the full group can be in conversation throughout the process (Weisbord & Janoff, 2001). It lasts for two and one-half days, which allows for building trust and committing to actions (Weisbord & Janoff, 2001). The process is based on an assumption that "when groups share a common purpose or ideals about a more desirable future, they can learn to work together, respect each other, and cooperate toward the achievement of shared goals" (Emery & Purser, 1996, p. 16). The task is always to identify the future of the system by considering where the system has been, where it is now and present trends that affect the system, identifying "Prouds" and "Sorries", determining the ideal future, and staking out the widest common ground possible for action planning (Weisbord & Janoff, 2001).

3.   COREVALUES, ASSUMPTIONS AND CONDITIONS FOR FUTURE SEARCH CONFERENCES

Embedded in the Future Search model is certain core values, assumptions about learning, and conditions for success. Each of these will be described below.

3.1. Core values

Seven core values are at the foundation of the Future Search model. The first is epistemological: The real world is knowable to ordinary people; their knowledge can be collectively and meaningfully organized (Weisbord, 1992a). It would follow then that people can create their own future (Weisbord, 1992a). The third core value assumes that people look for opportunities to engage their head, hearts and hands. They want to be part of organizational decision-making and in fact, are extraordinary sources of information about what is happening in the organization (Weisbord, 1992a). The fourth core value follows-up on this idea: Everyone is an equal; planning should not be left to the elite of the organization (Weisbord, 1992a). Given the chance, people are more likely to cooperate rather than fight is the fifth core value (Weisbord, 1992a). The sixth core value reminds us that the process should empower people to feel more knowledgeable and certain about the future (Weisbord, 1992a). The last core value is about diversity: divergent views and opinions are to be welcomed, respected, and valued (Weisbord, 1992a). These core values send the message that the wisdom of ordinary people is not expendable (Norum, 1997); rather, it is essential to creating exciting organizational futures. These core values also provide clues regarding the assumptions about learning from which Weisbord operates.

3.2 Assumptions

Seven assumptions about how we learn are foundational to the Future Search Model (Weisbord & Janoff, 2000).

Assumption 1: Everyone has a unique learning style. To honor this belief, a variety of methods are used during a Future Search Conference.

Assumption 2: People learn at different rates. In the Future Search model, this means that some people may be confused or lost in the early stages if this is a very different style and model of learning for them. Thus, patience with one another is essential.

Assumption 3: Everyone learns different things from a common experience. We can all be in the same meeting and each come away with a different interpretation of what happened. The sharing of perceptions is part of the Future Search process along with accepting different interpretations and viewpoints as valid.

Assumption 4: We learn best from our own experiences and need to test new ideas and viewpoints against our own knowledge. The goal is to avoid falling into the trap that there is "one best way" and remain open to several options that will probably work.

Assumption 5: You will learn more in a single Future Search Conference than you will be able to apply. To avoid being overwhelmed, local action within a global context helps to focus what learning can be applied and how it is relevant.

Assumption 6: Everyone has the ability to teach others. Participation and drawing on each other's expertise is one way to help and teach others. This type of interaction is built into the process.

Assumption 7: We all benefit from trial and error if given the support and opportunity for success. The Future Search Conference provides a low-risk setting in which to try out new ideas.

These assumptions about how we learn along with the core values reveal a belief that Weisbord shares with many others: We do not need to rely on experts to design our social systems (Banathy, 1996; Carr, 1997; Owen, 1997; Weisbord, 1992a; Wheatley & Kellner-Rogers, 1996; Whitney, 2001). "Each person is born with sage-like wisdom waiting to be awakened" (Daft & Lengel, 1998, p. 72). Organizations are coming to realize that what its employees know "is at the heart of how an organization functions" (Davenport & Prusak, 1998, p. x). In fact, Davenport and Prusak suggest that many organizations are misdirected in seeking the expertise of consultants: "much of the knowledge they [need] already [exists] within their organizations" (1998, p. xii). The problem may be in accessing this knowledge. A Future Search Conference provides a way to access the knowledge already existing about the organization's future. Meeting certain conditions for success will ensure the knowledge that exists is accessed.

3.3   Conditions

From several years of experience creating Future Search Conferences, Weisbord and Janoff (2000) believe there are eight conditions for success. Three of these are the most critical. All will be described below.

Condition 1: Get the "whole system" in the room. The "whole system" is the "broadest temporary planning community feasible" (Emery & Weisbord, 1992, p. 66). A broad cross-section of stakeholders is needed for diverse perspectives. A variety of perspectives will allow for each snapshot view to contribute towards creating a new picture of the whole (Senge, 1990; Weisbord & Janoff, 2000). This also allows for new relationships to develop as well as the cross-pollination of visions and imaginations (Whyte, 1994). Weisbord and Janoff admit it may not be feasible to literally get the "whole system" in the room but insist on a diagonal slice of the system. They suggest a diagonal slice of 60-70 stakeholders provides for ample diversity as well as ensures face-to-face dialogue and a balance of small group and whole system time.

Condition 2: The "Whole Elephant" as context for local action. This condition refers to the Sufi story of the six blind men describing an elephant.

In order to pool individual experience to create a shared reality, the task of the group is considered in the context of society as a whole. Trends within and between the system and trends outside of the system are explored.

Condition 3: Explore current reality and common futures. The Future Search Conference is not meant to be a problem-solving or conflict-management experience. Thus, differences are acknowledged, but are not worked through during the conference. They are put on hold. Instead, the focus is on imagining and inventing new ideal futures. The widest common ground everyone can stand upon is identified and used for action planning purposes.

Condition 4: Work in self-managed and small groups. Everyone is responsible for sharing and interpreting information. Everyone participates in action planning. This reduces dependency, hierarchy, conflict, and task-avoidance. It increases the chances of people experiencing discovery, learning, and cooperation. Small groups determine how to delegate the tasks and are encouraged to rotate the roles group members play (discussion leader, recorder, reporter, time keeper, data manager).

Condition 5: Attend the whole meeting. People need to be there to act. A fully shared experience is the goal. This fully shared experience creates a common future and an understanding of how that common future was identified.

Condition 6: Meet under healthy conditions. People will be spending up to three days together; daylight and good food are conducive to a productive meeting.

Condition 7: Work across three days. Weisbord and Janoff contend that a 2 1/2 day process is critical to allow for "soak time" (2000, p. 55). The evening session commonly ends when people are working on important tasks to keep the learning alive overnight, while the creative process continues. The 2 1/2 day format also ensures that action planning will not come at a time when people are overloaded and too tired for it.

Condition 8: Take public responsibility for follow-up. At a Future Search Conference, people will be asked to publicly share what they will do next. The role each person will play when they go back to "work" is declared. Having public accountability increases the odds that each person will follow through on implementing the action plan.

Weisbord suggests that of these seven, three are "minimum critical specifications" (Emery & Weisbord, 1992 p. 66). These are *getting the whole system in the room* (Condition 1), *exploring the local context within the global* (Condition 2), and *working in small self-managed groups* (Condition 4). Weisbord asserts these three particular conditions interact to allow for a wide group of stakeholders working interdependently in a wide field of inquiry (Emery & Weisbord, 1992). This increases the likelihood of the conference going "beyond participation to the farther reaches of common ground, creativity, and committed action" (Emery & Weisbord, 1992, p. 66).

4.   THE FUTURE SEARCH PROCESS

Five key tasks make up the structure of a Future Search Conference. These tasks are accomplished by people working in small mixed groups–groups that reflect the diversity of the stakeholders. Their first task is to review the past to establish personal histories, identify key world events, and share milestones in the history of the organization. This past becomes prelude to the future (Cooperrider & Whitney, 1999) as each group develops and shares a picture of where the organization has been and how it got to the present moment.

The second task is to focus on the present by creating a mind map of trends that are currently affecting the organization. The trends are global and once the map has been created, each person identifies the trends they think are most critical to creating a new future. The entire group becomes engaged in producing a collective reality. The map is then reinterpreted by common rather than mixed stakeholder groups to allow peers to hear what each other is thinking. Each stakeholder group then reports how they believe these trends are affecting the system now. A common surprise is through this exercise, different stakeholders discover they share concerns, "worry about the same issues and want to live in the same kind of world" (Weisbord & Janoff, 2000).

The third task is to focus on "prouds" and "sorries": each stakeholder group is asked to share what they are doing presently that they feel proud of or sorry about, particularly in relation to creating the new ideal future. The purpose of this task is for people to take responsibility; not to do anything to make amends, etc. Weisbord and Janoff believe "our perceptions of our own behavior, good news and bad, need to be public for people to get beyond blaming and complaining" (2000, p. 96). While the mind-map is a descriptive exercise about the present, "Prouds and Sorries" is affective, getting at what the group feels about what they are doing (Weisbord & Janoff, 2000).

Groups are mixed again for the fourth task: creating a desired future. As people discover what they are ready, willing, and able to do, they start moving themselves toward their new ideal future. Groups imagine they are five, ten, or twenty years in the future and create a concrete image of the new organization. They also identify major barriers they had to overcome to get to this new future. The scenarios are presented to the large group and as they are presented, people make note of themes they hear that were present in their group's scenario as well as ideas, projects, innovations they like. Three lists are created: Common Future (what everyone agrees they want in the future organization), Potential Projects (proposals for how to get what everyone has agreed they want) and Not Agreed (differences and conflicts that still exist). Similar themes are grouped and a picture of a shared ideal future emerges.

Now it is time to act on creating the identified new desired future. In this fifth and last task, action planning is based on only what has been identified as the common ground. People take responsibility for what they intend to do to make the desired future a reality–next steps are decided upon, the work is divided up, goals are set, who else needs to be involved is determined. These commitments and timetables are made public so everyone is on the same page and knows what needs to happen when they return to the organization.

"We have created this world together and we now face it together, listening to each other, building on each other's perceptions" (Weisbord & Janoff, 2000 p. 93). Confusion, chaos, and contradictions are embedded in the Future Search process. Differences and disagreement are acknowledged as paradox but not reconciled. In order to stake out the widest common ground, conversation becomes strategy: if the knowledge sought already exists in the system, people are probably already engaged in a "collective search for meaning about the direction of the [system]" (Thomas & Roberts, 1999, p. 519).

5.   STAKING OUT THE WIDEST COMMON GROUND

Conversation is a powerful low-tech way to change entire systems (Wheatley & Kellner-Rogers, 1996b). In the Future Search process, it is the pathway to discovering common ground.

One of the key features of the Future Search model is that differences are acknowledged, but not dealt with at that point in time. Learning Assumptions Three and Four (described earlier) are central to this concept. Learning Assumption Three encourages the sharing of perceptions and accepting different interpretations and viewpoints as valid. Learning Assumption Four reminds us to challenge our assumptions. We all carry mental models, images of how we believe the world works, around with us (Senge, 1990). These mental models are deeply embedded in our memory banks (Ellinor & Gerard, 1998). They are reflected in our beliefs and ultimately, the actions taken based on those beliefs. Thus, challenging our mental models is critical to discovering common ground. Daft and Lengel (1998) state "mind potential is released when people open to new information and multiple perspectives" (p. 69). Seeing the limitations in our own perceptions (Daft & Lengel, 1998; Senge, 1990) allows us to "loosen our grip on our certainties" (Ellinor & Gerard, 1998, p. 68) and hold differences in paradox.

When we engage in the kind of conversation that allows us to challenge assumptions and recognize differences but not focus on them, different kinds of questions are asked. The questions asked illustrate the group is involved in mutual inquiry or exploration. The questions reflect an open-minded curiosity, a wide-eyed innocence rather than cynicism or a desire to impose an agenda. The questions are directed towards making me clear about what the other person is saying–questions that indicate a softening and opening up of the mind (Bohm, 1990). This is dialogic conversation, directed toward discovery and new understandings (Bohm, 1990; Burbules, 1993, Senge, 1990).

The radical approach to acknowledging conflicts but not working through them then and there means that people learn to hold their position instead of being held by their position (Senge, 1990). Conflict is put on hold while common ground takes center stage (Weisbord & Janoff, 2000). Fears are allayed as "commonalities take precedence and human diversity is appreciated" (Emery & Purser, p. 17). This creates space for each person to talk (Bohm, 1990; Burbules, 1993). In the process of sharing perspectives and having others respond, people learn about their own perspective by re-evaluating its viability, thus coming to understand it more fully (Dixon, 1996). "A dialogue not only gives voice to the other, but is an exchange based on the presumption that each participant has something meaningful to give" (Oliner & Oliner, 1995, p. 116). Wisdom emerges from this way of listening. Wisdom born of paying attention and responding to changes in our surroundings:

> Usually we think of wisdom in terms of lofty abstractions, not survival skills ... and yet, the central survival skill is surely the capacity to pay attention and respond to changing circumstances, to learn and adapt, to fit into new environments. (Bateson, 1990, p. 231)

Common ground is the product of listening deeply to one another. We listen deeply and actively when we invite others to talk consistently and frequently; listen naively, without intention to preach; give feedback; and ask "dumb" questions to understand the thinking behind the assumption (Oliner & Oliner, 1995). We are all capable of such conversation, but may need to develop skills as "strategic conversationalists" (Thomas & Roberts, 1999).

Thomas and Roberts (1999) suggest that engaging people in five key activities will develop their skills as strategic conversationalists. First, they must learn to continuously scan their "world." In the Future Search process, the scan takes place when working through the second task of identifying trends (local and global) that affect the system. The data received from scanning needs to be interpreted to determine how or if it is relevant to the organization. Determining relevancy means respecting different views of what is important. This key activity is also reflected in the Future Search process. Strategy involves making choices. Thomas and Roberts suggest that the key activity be a conversational process where options are considered in detail and the thinking behind them explored. Choices must also be made in light of the organization's desired future. This third key activity is embedded throughout the Future Search process and particularly in the "Prouds and Sorries" task. Strategic choices need to be operationalized and planning through open conversation is a key activity proposed by Thomas and Roberts. The Future Search process is ultimately an open conversation directed at planning the future of the system. "Intelligently executing" (Thomas & Roberts, 1999, p. 522) the action plan is the last key activity for strategic conversationalists. The Future Search Conference parallels this activity with the Action Planning task. Thomas and Roberts contend that the largest group of people in an organization is "strategically dormant": they can learn to be effective strategists but need to be involved in strategic conversations (2000, p. 523). This mirrors Weisbord's belief that all people are capable of creating the future of the organization, if given the opportunity.

When a diverse group of stakeholders is assembled in the same room for over two days, multitudinous and divergent perceptions are revealed as realities are shared with one another. In being quiet long enough to listen to what others deem significant, common ground emerges. Creating action plans only around what has been staked out as the widest common ground typically creates a momentum such that those at the Future Search conference may become "evangelists and warriors" (Daft & Lengel, 1998) for insuring the action plan does not collect dust. It may be that the paradox created by acknowledging but not focusing on differences "unifies a diverse group of complexity of cultures" (Banathy, 1996, p. 220) such that collaboration and fusion is achieved among diverse parts of the system (Daft & Lengel, 1998).

6.   FUTURE SEARCH AS DESIGN CONVERSATION

As described by Jenlink and Carr (1996), the focus of a design conversation is to create something new. The Future Search model can be considered to be a type of container (Banathy, 1996; Jenlink & Carr, 1996) that allows for conversation focused on designing a new future. This container "intentionally creates conversations where we can speak about what has importance and meaning for us," (Ellinor & Gerard, 1998, p. 96) particularly regarding the desired future of the organization. It creates what Apatow (1998) calls the ideal of "friendship": a state of unity such that we become absorbed in what we are doing. The container also allows for risk-taking. A diverse cross-section of stakeholders makes for "many tinkerers focused on figuring out what's possible" (Wheatley & Kellner-Rogers, 1996a, p. 25).

Designing the system's ideal future is the particular focus of the design conversation associated with Future Search. This does not need to be a one-time conversation. Part of the action planning process includes determining when the ideal future may need to be sought once again. In ever-changing environments, the future that made sense today may not make sense tomorrow. Using conversation as strategy means it will be used as a means to determine when the organization is off course or needs to change course.

The Future Search process is well suited for social systems design. Its foundations acknowledge that all systems are embedded in larger systems. The local context is used to explore the global context as it applies to the desired future of the system. The belief that design should not be the realm of the elite of the organization is reflected in Weisbord's "minimum critical specification" of getting the whole system in the room (or at least a diagonal cross-section of it) (Emery & Weisbord, 1992; Weisbord & Janoff, 2000). Further verification of the Future Search model's appropriateness for social systems design is found in the types of organizations that have used the model. Examples of the many and diverse organizations that have engaged in Future Search activities can be found in Weisbord's book, *Discovering Common Ground*, as well as at the Future Search Network website (http://www.futuresearch.net).

The Future Search model devises a way for people to ask questions when decisions are to be made on a New Place or a New Way (Underwood, 19991). The process of working in small self-managed groups over a long period of time creates the ideal of "friendship" (Apatow, 1998) and allows for a flow of energy through each new possibility to be evaluated (Underwood, 1991). These new possibilities create a "messy playfulness" that "creates relationships that make available...new capacities" (Wheatley & Kellner-Rogers, 1996a, p. 18). Through purposeful conversations, an ideal future emerges; a future that is attainable because it is the progeny of the engagement of diverse stakeholders' heads, hearts and hands.

REFERENCES

Apatow, R., 1998. *The Spiritual Art of Dialogue*. Inner Traditions International, Rochester, VT.
Banathy, B.H., 1996. *Designing Social systems In a Changing World*. Plenum Press, New York.
Bateson, M. C. (1990). *Composing a life*. NY: Plume.
Bohm, D., 1990. *On dialogue*. David Bohm Seminars, Ojai, CA.
Burbules, N.C., 1993. *Dialogue in Teaching: Theory and Practice*. Teachers College Press, New York.
Carr, A.A., 1997. User-Design in the creation of human learning systems. *Educational Technology Research and Development*, **45**(3): 5-22.
Cooperrider, D.L., and Whitney, D., 1999. *Appreciative Inquiry: A Constructive Approach to Organization Development and Social Change (A Workshop)*. Corporation for Positive Change, Taos, NM.
Daft, R.L., and Lengel, R.H., 1998. *Fusion Leadership*. Berrett-Koehler Publishers, Inc., San Francisco.
Davenport, T.H., and Prusak, L., 1998. *Working Knowledge: How Organizations Manage What They Know*. Harvard Business School Press, Boston, MA.
Dixon, N.M., 1996. *Perspectives on Dialogue: Making Talk Developmental for Individuals and Organizations*. Center for Creative Leadership, Greensboro, NC.

Ellinor, L., and Gerard, G., 1998*)*. *Dialogue: Rediscover the Transforming Power of Conversation.* John Wiley & Sons, Inc., New York.

Emery, F., and Weisbord, M.R., 1992. Conditions for success: An exchange between Fred Emery and Marvin R. Weisbord. In M.R. Weisbord (ed.), *Discovering Common Ground.* Berrett-Koehler Publishers, Inc., San Francisco, CA, pp. 55-70.

Emery, M., and Purser, R.E., 1996. *The Search Conference: A Powerful Method for Planning Organizational Change and Community Action.* Jossey-Bass Publishers, San Francisco.

Jenlink, P., and Carr, A.A., 1996. Conversation as a medium for change in education. *Educational Technology,* **36** (1): 31-38.

Norum, K.E., 1997. *Divergent Voices, Divergent Connections: Stories of Expendable Wisdom and the Challenge for Authentic Engagement.* Unpublished Dissertation, University of Colorado at Denver.

Oliner, P.M., and Oliner, S.P., 1995. *Toward a Caring Society: Ideas Into Action.* Praeger, Westport, CT.

Owen, H., 1997. *Open Space Technology: A User's Guide* (2nd ed.). Berrett-Koehler Publishers, Inc., San Francisco, CA.

Senge, P.M., 1990. *The Fifth Discipline: The Art and Practice of the Learning Organization.* Doubleday/Currency, New York.

Thomas, A., and Roberts, C., 1999. Strategy as conversation. In P. Senge, A. Kleiner, C. Roberts, R. Ross, G. Roth, and B. Smith (eds.), *The Dance of change.* Doubleday/Currency, New York, pp. 518-523.

Underwood, P., 1991. *Who Speaks for Wolf: A Native American Learning Story* (2nd ed.). A Tribe of Two Press, San Anselmo, CA.

Weisbord, M.R., 1992a. Applied common sense. In M.R. Weisbord (ed.), *Discovering Common Ground.* Berrett-Koehler Publishers, San Francisco, pp. 3-17.

Weisbord, M.R., 1992b. Parallel paths to community: Equifinality in action. In M.R. Weisbord (ed.), *Discovering Common Ground.* Berrett-Koehler Publishers, San Francisco, pp. 45-53.

Weisbord, M.R., and Janoff, S., 2000. *Future search: An Action Guide to Finding Common Ground in Organizations and Communities* (2nd ed.). Berrett-Koehler Publishers, Inc., San Francisco, CA.

Weisbord, M.R., and Janoff, S., 2001. *What is a Future Search?* Retrieved from the World Wide Web 11/25/01: http://www.futuresearch.net/fsis.htm.

Wheatley, M.J., and Kellner-Rogers, M., 1996a.. *An Evening Conversation With Margaret J. Wheatley and Myron Kellner-Rogers.* Sponsored by the Colorado Issues Network, Denver, CO.

Wheatley, M.J., and Kellner-Rogers, M., 1996b. *A simpler Way.* Berrett-Koehler Publishers, San Francisco, CA.

Whitney, D., 2001. Postmodern principles and practices for large scale organization change and global cooperation. In D.L. Cooperrider, P.F. Sorensen Jr., T.F. Yaeger, and D. Whitney (eds.), *Appreciative Inquiry: An Emerging Direction for Organization Development.* Stipes Publishing, Champaign, IL, pp. 397-412.

Whyte, D., 1994. *The Heart Aroused: Poetry and the Preservation of the Soul in Corporate America.* Currency/Doubleday, New York.

Chapter 16

CREATING NEW CONNECTIONS
Dialogue & Improv

GLENNA GERARD
Glenna Gerard Unlimited, Inc.[1]

1.   INTRODUCTION

This chapter is the distillation of my reflections on an exploration of the synergy between dialogue and improvisation theatre games in developing the capacity for creating more meaningful connections. This may manifest as deeper and more authentic connections between people. It may show up as an increased ability to discern important connections between ideas or parts of a system. I've attempted to outline the principles involved in consciously, and with intention, creating such connections and tapping into the new possibilities they offer. This is followed by a discussion of how the practices of both dialogue and improv support these principles, along with practical suggestions for how to explore bringing some of this synergy into your own personal and professional lives.

2.   CONNECTIONS: THE STUFF OF LIFE

Only connect. – E.M. Forrester

Two words and possibly one of the most powerful prescriptions for meaningful conversation, building trust-based relationships, tapping into the creative genius of people, perceiving whole systems, coherent strategic thinking, powerful decisions and aligned action.

By developing the ability to consciously and intentionally perceive and create connections we bring more aliveness, satisfaction and joy into all areas of our lives and the greater world we inhabit. Work and life become more creative, and we become more intelligent human beings as we access the collective wisdom available to us in partnership and collaboration.

Dialogue as a Means of Collective Communication, Edited by Banathy and Jenlink
Kluwer Academic/Plenum Publishers, New York 2005

3.   DIALOGUE & IMPROV

Two disciplines and a core set of principles that, when brought to life through specific practices and activities, heighten people's awareness of existing connections and open the door for discovering new ones. These connections may be intrapersonal, interpersonal and/or systemic (e.g.: within a community, organization, etc.). They may involve thoughts, feelings, physical structures, infrastructures, strategies, decisions, actions, and results produced.

What follows are two brief descriptive definitions of dialogue and improvisation. Since our focus here is not specifically on these two disciplines, but rather on what their interweaving may bring forth, we have chosen not to give any more detailed information.[2]

3.1   Dialogue

Dialogue comes from the Greek **dialogos**: **Logos** means 'the word', or 'meaning' and **dia** means 'through'. The image suggests a stream of meaning flowing among and through two or more, out of which will emerge some new understanding, something creative...When everybody is sensitive to all the nuances, and not merely to what is happening in one's own mind, there forms a meaning which is shared. And in that way we can talk together coherently and think together. It is this shared meaning that is the "glue" or "cement" that holds people and societies together.

– David Bohm

The following are phrases used by people who have engaged in dialogue in many different venues–schools, corporations, government, not-for-profits, communities, families:

- a level playing field with respect for all
- a chance to get all our cards up on the table and play with a full deck
- space and pace that allows for all to hear and be heard
- recognition and strengthening of relationships
- an exploration of our individual and group assumptions to reveal our thinking and generate new possibilities
- building shared understanding of differing points of view
- ability to hold the tensions of complexity and paradox and see systemic patterns

3.2.   Improv (improvisation)[3]

Improvisational theatre dates back to Prehistoric times when cave men and women enacted ritualized dances celebrating and incarnating the hunt, fertility, the forces of nature, the Gods. In medieval times improvisation took the form of mystery and miracle plays staged by trade guides and enacting Biblical stories. Most recently it has been performance based. Improv may also be used for personal growth. The aim is to enhance our connection with each other. It is not speed nor cleverness but relaxation, awareness and being in the moment that we seek. From this state of mind and body we are encouraged to co-create with each other.

– Lynne Kaufman

It is the focus on awareness and the ability to be fully present in the moment, opening to creative connections and possibilities that is of interest to us in these pages. Improv helps us to "embody" dialogue, to heighten our ability for inquiry, spontaneity, and creative connections built from the richness of multiple perspectives.

3.3   Unlikely Partners?

A brief story.   Some 4 years ago, I was teaching a 5-day program on dialogue at Esalen Institute with Linda Ellinor. On Wednesday evenings at Esalen there is always an "optional program", led by one of the visiting teachers. That week it was improvisation and theatre games. I decided to go. As the evening unfolded I became more and more intrigued. It seemed that every "game" we played was a perfect metaphor for some aspect of dialogue. The leader asked a woman named Lynne Kaufman to help him with some of the activities. He remarked that she had a lot of experience with improvisation. She was also attending our dialogue program that week. Over the coming months Lynne and I had many conversations about the apparent synergy between dialogue and improv. Bottom line? Lynne and I decided to offer a weekend at Esalen on Dialogue and Improv to try out our theories. At the conclusion of that program we both agreed - we were definitely on the right track and decided to offer a 5-day program the next year. As I write I have just returned from that program. Exciting, amazing, illuminating, intriguing, wonderful, curious, refreshing, all words that were used by the members of the group to describe that experience.

What follows are my reflections on our learnings and the continuing inquiry that have emerged from our exploration of dialogue and improv and the aliveness and creativity they bring to our connections, with one another and to our perceptions of our world.

4.   CONNECTIONS THAT ENLIVEN

"You can't live with 'em and you can't live without 'em."; words most often spoken in reference to some relationship that is a source of irritation in that moment. Whether we want them or not we exist within the relationships and connections of our lives.

How do we create connections that add to our sense of wellbeing, our ability to manifest our dreams, and create the results we want at home and work, in our communities and our world?

A primary way we connect with one another is conversation of all forms; written, verbal and non-verbal. We have conversations that are satisfying and ones that are anything but. There are many factors that contribute: "I didn't get what I wanted from him/her/them." "No one was listening to what I had to say." "She was so busy multi-tasking, I couldn't tell what her reaction was." "Everyone contributed and we collected some really great new ideas." "The conversation just flowed and we got a lot done in very little time."

In the next pages, I borrow a page from Appreciative Inquiry (David Cooperrider & Diana Whitney) and rather than attempting to "fix what doesn't work", I will put the spotlight on "what brings life" to our conversations.

5.   CORE PRINCIPLES

When Lynne and I first started to design a program, our focus was on how improv could be used to support dialogue. As time unfolded we began to understand that rather than a program where dialogue was the centerpiece and improv the support, or even a patchwork quilt of dialogue and improv pieces sewn together, there was some "third body" that was emerging from the dance between the two. At this point in time we see that "third body" as a set of principles for perceiving and creating connections. What dialogue and improv contribute are ways of being in conversation that empower the principles, resulting in enhanced awareness of existing connections as well as the ability to create openings for discovering new connections and possibilities.

The core principles we want to propose are three: "intend yes-and"; "attend to the focus of energy"; "allow transformation". Below are definitions of each principle and our thinking about how the specific practices from dialogue and improv can help you breathe life into them and enlarge your capacity to create meaningful connections.

5.1   Intend Yes-And

This is a basic principle of improv and an essential ingredient in seeing the whole system in dialogue:

> **Intend**: *to have in mind to accomplish or do; to have the purpose of...*

To **intend yes-and** is to have in mind, to have the purpose of, receiving whatever is offered to you by saying "yes", and then adding your contribution.

If you have watched good improvisation you know that one of the things that keeps the conversation or story alive is each person's ability to take what has come before and add to it. The story may be taken in some wholly unexpected direction. In fact, often this is what creates the humor, surprise and aliveness. Yet, always the person that follows builds on what has come before.

In creating connections with others, whether they are new beginnings or the discovery of new connections in ongoing relationships, saying **yes-and** to what is offered acknowledges the other and demonstrates a willingness to co-create. All too often we may feel that what we offer is not even heard; that the person has only been waiting for our mouths to stop moving so he can begin to tell us his story. Or, we are met with "yes-but", which means "okay you've had your turn, now let me tell you how it really is/works". **Yes-and** is a way of honoring the other, a first step to creating connection and shared creativity.

In dialogue, we seek to create shared meaning and a whole systems picture of how we are thinking/feeling about any given topic. **Yes-and** can be a way of saying "I see your perspective and I would like to offer one that is different". This **yes-and** is distinct from the "yes-but" of discussion where we are evaluating and comparing ideas to choose the best one. It is the **yes-and** of offering a diverse perspective so that a more complete picture of the system can be developed. In dialogue we seek, not only the areas where we agree, but to see the whole which makes sense of all perspectives, including those that differ significantly from ours. **Yes-and** is essential too creating the shift of mind that lifts us out of debate and either/or comparisons of parts of the whole to a level where we are looking at the entire landscape that has been laid out before us.

Yes-and enables us to focus on the relationships between the diverse aspects of ourselves, between individuals, departments in an organization and even groups within a community or nation. In a land that delineates, separates and chooses between alternatives, **yes-and** offers creative possibilities that depend on inclusion and collaboration.

But what about setting boundaries? Saying "No!". What if the offering is dangerous or abusive as in anger or some form of attack. First, we are assuming that most people who want to form connections come to the table with good will. However, there are always exceptions. And, conflicts do arise when differences are present and when people feel strongly about what they are talking about. In such cases, it is important to remember that "yes" is not meant to signify agreement. "Yes" means "I heard you and acknowledge your right to the way you see and experience this". In some cases this acknowledgement and a willingness to listen without defensiveness will diffuse the strong negative emotion and may even help bring clarity and new possibility to the situation. In other cases the appropriate response is "yes, I hear you and I choose to not participate or engage with you".

Yes-and is always an invitation. In receiving and passing it on you create connections that expand and deepen understanding and hold the potential for innovative ways of seeing and working with a person, an idea, a whole project.

6.   ATTEND TO THE FOCUS OF ENERGY

To "attend" is at the core of both dialogue and improv.

Attend: to wait upon, to sit well beside; to be present; give heed to

To attend is to listen deeply, to be fully present to your self, the other and to what is unfolding in the space between.

We've all been with people whose "lights are on but they're not home". No doubt we have even been those people from time to time. To create connections that enliven us personally and professionally requires presence, being present "here and now" rather than "there and then".

In improv presence is an absolute requirement for creativity. Each move, each statement, is generated out of what is occurring in the exact moment and space between those involved. This kind of listening and presence is what makes improv come alive. We can all tell the difference between a response that arises in the moment and one that is pulled up from memory or comes from thinking about "what would be good here". The latter may produce continuity, but it rarely creates the surprise and the freshness that improv relies on to hold our attention. The difference between improv that engages us and improv that bores us is a direct function of individuals' ability to 'attend to the focus of energy' in the present moment; listening to the other, to one's self and to the connections that emerge between.

A dialogue that generates new ways of thinking occurs only when people focus their attention and listen for what is present in the moment. We've all been in conversations where we "didn't hear anything new". If we are honest with ourselves we might even say that we didn't say anything new either. The same stories, the same questions, the same opinions. It is almost like playing a tape recording. Such conversations rarely produce new insights or new dimensions in the connections between the people. We've heard it all before. This is not to say that we don't enjoy tossing the same ideas around or retelling a story from time to time. In fact, this type of conversation may even develop into a sort of "ritual" for some groups. However, if your objective is generating new possibilities and fresh ideas, a different strategy is needed. Engaging with a willingness to listen for what might arise in the present moment, rather than from memory, is the key to creating an opening for fresh thinking and the possibility of a "rabbit hole into a whole new world".

Attending to the focus of energy in the present moment is essential to **yes-and** as well as a doorway to **allowing transformation**. In improv this attention enables the dance present in the connection to unfold. Where energy is focused is where interests intersect, where movement initiates, and where transformation can enter.

Here's a more practical example. Imagine that you and another person just met at a professional conference. You are engaged in conversation. Maybe you are just passing time, waiting for a friend or the next event. Perhaps your curiosity was peaked by the other. Either way, by practicing **yes-and** the connections you generate will yield more energy than the common fishing expedition of disconnected questions and comments. If you couple **yes-and with attending to the focus of energy** you may be surprised at the interest the conversation generates. You might discover and follow a single thread or find yourselves surprised by unanticipated links and leaps. Either way, it is almost guaranteed you will get to know a lot more about the other person and vice versa. The same phenomenon applies to two or more people on a work team exploring a problem or opportunity, such as designing a new product, making decisions about a new educational curriculum or resolving a recurring problem in a manufacturing process.

Yes-and will yield a fuller picture. **Attending to the focus of energy** will highlight key questions and challenges, tap creative interest and open the door for discovering new approaches.

6.1 Allow Transformation

Both dialogue and improv rely on this principle for their generative life. Change is a natural process. It lies at the very center of evolution. Nature is always both seeking to reinforce what works about a particular organism/organization and change it in ways that will create even more advantageous connections with the immediate environment.

Transformation happens by receiving what is offered with **yes-and**, **attending to the focus of energy**, and allowing that focus to move. Intentionally opening the doorway for transformation and for the emergence of new possibilities in how we think and relate to a question or another person requires a mindset of curiosity, of open-ended exploration.

Next time you are in a conversation try noticing when a particular theme or thread in the conversation really grabs peoples' attention and ask a question or two to learn more about "what is so compelling/interesting/important here?". Or, if you notice a perspective that triggers resistance or disagreement in you, experiment with "trying on that alternative way of thinking and see where it takes you". In both cases you will be **attending to a focus of energy**, saying **yes-and** and allowing an opening for something new and not previously experienced to emerge.

Allowing transformation requires courage, a willingness and confidence to step into the unknown. Heading for a specific outcome will not do. The opening for transformation will be too small. Preconceived notions of where we need to go, of what will work and won't work, leave little to no room for surprise.

New ways of seeing things, an expanded world of more options and possibilities, creativity, more satisfying relationships, breakthrough ideas–these are the fruits of intentionally creating new connections using the principles described.

7.   DIALOGUE AND IMPROV PRACTICES

Both dialogue and improvisation have rich histories. My purpose here is to briefly describe some of the practices from these disciplines that can breathe life into the principles I've outlined so far. It is also my intention to provide you with a few ideas you can try to enhance your own capacity for expanding and deepening current connections and creating new ones, whether in your personal relationships or in tackling a professional challenge.

7.1   Dialogue Practices

The capacities associated with the practice of dialogue and described below in connection with improvisation are Suspending Judgments; Checking Assumptions; Listening to Self, Other and In-Between; and, Inquiry and Reflection.

7.1.1   Suspending Judgments

Our normal way of thinking divides, organizes, and labels. Because our egos become identified with how we think things are, we often find ourselves defending our positions against those of others. This makes it difficult for us to stay open to new and alternative views of reality. It is hard to listen, and virtually impossible to practice **yes-and**, when we are engaged in evaluating every contribution as right or wrong.

To suspend judgment is not to do away with our judgements and opinions–this would be impossible. Rather, we learn to "hold our positions more lightly". By doing this we open the door to see others' points of view and to the possibilities of co-creating with them.

Suspending judgment is essential to building a climate of trust where all feel confident that their contributions will be met in the spirit of **yes-and**. Where there is a commitment to practice suspension of judgment the result is an environment that is more open and truthful, where we can all feel freer to express ourselves authentically.

A few experiments:

- Make a pact with yourself to notice your judgments and the impact they have on your listening in at least one conversation each day.
- Use your imagination to put your judgments to one side as you continue to listen. Each time a judgment arises, suspend it and continue to listen. Notice what happens as a result. This is a form of saying "**yes** I'm having this judgment **and** I choose to continue to listen.

7.1.2 Checking Assumptions

Assumptions are like the meat on the bones of our judgments. We judge something good or bad, right or wrong, because of assumptions. For example: "It would be a bad idea to say that to my boss." Why? Because my boss doesn't handle feedback well. To be aware of our assumptions is to understand what and how we think about our world and to be able to make more conscious choices.

Pretty powerful stuff, assumptions. Yet, often we overlook them when we seek to solve problems, resolve conflicts, or create synergy among diverse people. Why? David Bohm would say because our "assumptions are transparent to us". They are such a built-in part of our seeing apparatus that we do not even know they are there. We look at our world through them without even knowing it.

Assumptions have a powerful impact on our ability to create connections that are viable, alive and satisfying. Consider **yes-and**. Behind this strategy is the assumption that what others have to contribute has value and can enrich our experience. My assumptions can just as easily, and often do, limit what I am willing to receive. For example, I might have the following thought about a friend. "I can't talk to him about this problem; he doesn't understand anything about business". Or, I might cut someone off completely, deciding that she is dishonest and untrustworthy because "She said one thing last night and another this morning." I don't ask for clarification. I simply assume, judge and react.

Next time you want to connect with someone new or more deeply with someone you already know. Next time you want to see more of the relationships and the bigger picture where an issue or challenge at work is concerned. Take a few minutes to notice how your judgments and assumptions influence your ability to practice **yes-and**, to both create and perceive connections. Make a conscious choice to open your willingness to listen and co-create a connection by suspending a judgement or checking-out an assumption.[4]

7.1.3   Listening to Self, Other and In-Between

> *Dialogue is not just talking with one another. More* than speaking,
> it is a special way of listening to one another–listening without
> resistance... from a stand of being willing to be influenced.

> – Sarita Chawla

> Listen.
> The silence is not empty
> A universe rests within
> A symphony between the notes. – *Glenna Gerard*

Without the listening of our cells our bodies would die. Without listening people and ideas become disconnected and fragmented. Listening is essential to conversation, connections and life. And within the context of this chapter, listening is a key element for "yes-and", "attending to the focus of energy" and "allowing transformation".

When I listen to you I open myself to experience who you are. I say "yes, let me see and hear this person". If I choose to enter the connection that exists between us I say, "yes-and here is who I am". In order to add the "and" of self-revelation I have to know how to listen within myself as well. What is it that emerges in me in response to what you have offered?

If we continue the dance we will begin to listen to the space in between, to what is emerging between us in the conversation. What is the larger picture we are co-creating? Where is the energy focused? And, continuing to listen we open the door for transformation to enter in the form of new thinking, greater understanding and a stronger relationship between us.

Remembering to focus our listening at these three levels, we nurture the connections and possibilities among us. *We listen to one another.* This is a profound act of respect. We acknowledge the value of the other, his perspective and contribution. *We listen within ourselves.* We open the ears of our hearts and minds by quieting the many voices of our judgments and assumptions. We listen to discern what thinking and feeling arises within us that we would offer into the stew we are cooking. *We listen to what is emerging in the co-created space between* us. It is here we create shared meaning and perhaps even experience new ways of seeing and thinking that are the products of the **yes-and** dance.

7.1.4 Inquiry & Reflection

Thus, the task is not so much to see what no one yet has seen, but to think what nobody yet has thought about that which everybody sees.

– Schopenhauer

Learning is always an uneasy guest in the house of "I Know". The very lessons we are taught as children can become the greatest limits to us as adults when it comes to discovery and creativity. When learning is measured by our ability to come up with the right answer quickly our contributions are often valued based on what we know about something. Contrast this with historical stories that tell us it was often those who challenged what was the certain knowledge of their times that brought new insight into the world. In the 1500's Copernicus suggested it was the Sun not the Earth that was at the center of our Solar System. Columbus was convinced the world could not be flat. He didn't sail off the edge of the world and he didn't reach China but he did run into the Americas on his way.

A willingness to "think what nobody yet has thought about that which everybody sees" is the key that continues to unlock our minds and reveal whole new worlds to us. This is as true in relationships and connections among people as it is in physics and the world of semi-conductors. Often these insights emerge out of questions that have a different slant, have not been asked before, are "out of the box".

Questions create openings for new possibilities. They may be associated with challenges to the status quo and a willingness, even desire, to see things differently. Questions may be pure open-ended curiosity as in "why is the sky blue?".

Often powerful of questions ask about connections between two or more observations. Consider the story of Isaac Newton and the apple falling from the tree. Mr. Newton could have asked the simple question "why does the apple fall from the tree?" He could have, but he didn't. He asked the question: "If the apple falls from the tree (which it does) then why don't the stars fall from the sky?" This is a question of an entirely different sort. From this question was unfolded the theory of gravity.

Questions that ask about connections intrinsically support **yes-and**. In fact, you could say they are "yes-and-yes and" by their very nature. They acknowledge two or more contributions, connect them, and then ask "what might this connection mean and lead to? " Such questions generally require time–time to reflect on what one is observing. They are not first order, quick response questions like the simple "Why?". The inquirer must first draw in more data and speculate about possible connections.

Questions are wonderful. But questions alone do not lead to learning or insight. Attentive listening must follow inquiry. We listen for what emerges in response, to the other, within ourselves and in the space between. We reflect on what we hear. We attend to the focus of energy. We become curious. We offer another question. We listen and reflect on what we hear. And so on. Through cycles of inquiry and reflective listening we follow the energy and hold open our minds for something new to emerge.

The next time you want to open doors for innovative thinking or creating new connections with others, try being curious, listening and then being curious some more about the connections between what you are hearing and observing emerge in your conversation with the other. And remember to listen from a mindset of **yes-and**.

7.2   Improvisation Practices/Games

Below I describe a series of improv theatre games that Lynne and I work with in some detail. My hope is that the descriptions will help you form an image and create a feeling for what can emerge from such games. I also comment on the connections between these activities, the capacities of dialogue and the principles outlined in the first part of this chapter.

7.2.1   Mirroring

Most of us have played this game. Two people stand facing each other, perhaps a few feet apart. Both of you hold your hands up at about shoulder height, with palms facing out. Your palms will be 6 inches to a foot from each other's. You look ahead, with what we call "soft eyes", not really focusing on anything in particular, but aware of the person in front of you. Take a couple of breaths and relax into your body. Once you are both present and ready, move through the following steps. As you do, be aware of your experience. You are participating and witnessing simultaneously.

1.   One person begins as "leader", initiating movement. The other follows, mirroring each movement. It is important, in the beginning that the leader moves slowly so that the other person can track the movements with continuity and flow. The objective is for the two of you to move together in as near perfect unison as is possible. As leader, notice what you are listening to and for? What influences how you lead? As the follower, notice how you

attend, or listen, and what is involved in how you follow? Observe any feelings or thoughts that surface as you continue.

2. Switch the roles of leader and follower and repeat step 1.
3. When you have both taken a turn leading and following, pause and stand quietly facing one another. Take a few breaths and focus on the space in between your two sets of hands. During this third phase you are going to allow the movement to initiate and emerge from the space between the two of you. No one is the "leader" or the "follower". You are both responding to what is present between you. Notice your responses to listening and waiting for the movement to emerge from the space in between. What is the experience as the movement begins? Continues?

You have just been practicing listening at three different levels; to the other, within yourself and to what is emerging from the space in between. The next time you are in conversation with one or more people experiment with recalling this activity. See if you can bring the quality of listening and the shared dance into your speaking and listening with one another. What happens when you participate in the conversation as a shared co-creation?

7.2.2 Lemonade Joe

The group divides in two. The two halves stand about 20ft apart facing one another, behind or on their "safe/goal line". One sub-group is going to mime (movements without words) activities associated with a profession. The other group's challenge is to figure out what that profession is. The flow is outlined in the steps below.

1. Group #1 huddles and decides what profession they will mime. When they are ready the two groups face one another. Members of group #1 take one step forward saying "Here we come." Group #2 takes one step forward and replies "Where from?" Group #1 takes another step and says "New York." Group #2 advances one step and asks "What's your trade?" Group #1 replies "Lemonade" and begins to mime the activities associated with the profession they have chosen.
2. Group #2 focuses on what the members of Group #1 are doing and tries to discern what the profession is. When any member of Group #2 guesses correctly Group #1 says "yes". At that moment Group #2 members try to tag Group #1 members before they can get back behind their "safe line". Any members of Group #1 that are tagged become members of Group #2.
3. Groups #1 and #2 take turns switching back and forth until one group has acquired all the members on the floor, or a set amount of time has elapsed.

This game makes a good prelude for "Build a Room" (described next). It's objective is to focus our awareness on where the energy is in a particular mime activity and how that creates and defines a reality, in this case a profession. In "Build a Room" this is further developed into an experience of how we create shared meaning through focused and repetitive attention.

Lemonade Joe is also a clear reminder of how quickly we interpret and jump to conclusions and actions. We focus on a locus of energy (in this case a set of mimed movements), and immediately begin to interpret in order to create a picture or definition. Other things people may notice or that can be pointed out are: a) different people focus on different cues and make radically different interpretations.; and, b) some sets of movements carry the power to actually call to mind an entire cultural context or environment (e.g. miming the taking of an oath with a bible = courtroom).

When you are engaged with different groups of people and in conversations about different topics notice where the energy is focused for you. What is the scope of your attention and perception? How much of the picture do you naturally hold in your awareness at once? What words, questions, statements grab your attention? What triggers your interpretation circuits? Some of these "hot" spots may peak your interest and open you up, others may evoke a negative response and limit your listening and willingness to connect. The more you discover the more options you will have for consciously choosing how you engage.

The next time you want to explore connections with someone from another culture (whether that be a different department, community, family or nation) notice your own interpretations and be curious about how others see, interpret and make meaning. At the very least you will expand your view of the world. Who knows, you may even find that through curiosity, suspending your own assumptions and engaging in **yes-and**, you create a whole new set of connections and possibilities.

7.2.3   Build a Room

This is an energizing and fun theatre game that also has a lot to teach us about the role of focused attention and co-creation of meaning and reality. Here's how it goes.

The group sits facing an empty space at one end/side of the room. The empty space is the "stage". The group is given or decides on a room in a house or company that they are going to build together.

1. One member/player of the group gets up and approaches the "room". She will be the first to make contact with the room. She does this by miming some object that is part of that room. Often the first "addition" is a door through which the person enters the

room. The mime movement might be the motion of reaching for the doorknob, pulling or pushing the door open, entering and then either leaving the door open or closing it. Perhaps she then walks around the room, delineating the spatial dimensions, returns to the door and leaves the room.

2. The next member now approaches and enters the room. He will make contact and interact with each object that the person(s) before him placed in the room. Then he will add one more object to the room and leave. For example. If the first person added the door and the dimensions of the room, person # 2 will also need to enter through the door, remembering which way it opened. He would then move into the room and perhaps add a refrigerator by miming opening the door and taking something out of it and placing it on an imaginary surface (counter). When he is done, he then leaves the room, through the door. Now the next person will need to interact with the door and the refrigerator, before adding some other object to the room.

3. All members of the group repeat step 2 until everyone has entered the room, interacted with all objects previously placed there, added an object and then left the room.

Note: When subsequent members enter the room and interact with objects previously placed in the room they need not repeat the exact actions of previous players. For example. One person may interact with the stove by turning the burners on and off. Another may cook something. Another may clean up a "mess" left by the previous person, etc. What is important is that each player interacts with every object in the room before adding one and leaving.

It is fascinating to watch the room take on substance as subsequent members enter and interact with the "imaginary" objects. This is a wonderful experience of how when we focus our attention repeatedly on something that "something" becomes more and more real to us. In the case of this game the objects are all imaginary, yet no less real. We would not even think to "walk through the stove" in our room.

This simple and fun game is a metaphor for the way we co-create and sustain meanings in cultures. If we grow up in a particular culture there are certain behaviors and ways of thinking that all members enact that are based on repeatedly reinforced and shared thoughts about how the world works. By virtue of shared agreement and repeated focus all manner of groups (teams, families, communities) create and interact with psychological and emotional "virtual" realities. These realities are quite compelling and can be the source of judgments and assumptions that make listening from a posture of **yes-and** challenging. The degree to which we are willing to meet others and ourselves with a spirit of curiosity and **yes-and** will define the scope of possibilities we can create together.

7.2.4 Walk my Walk

If you've ever sat in a public place and noticed the different ways that people walk, you've played a short version of this game. Our objective here is to develop our ability to "attend to where the energy is focused" and to "allow transformation". Here's how it works.

1. One person walks back and forth across the room with his normal, average gate. He might imagine himself walking down the street, or from one room in his home to another. He continues for a few minutes during which the group is observing.
2. As a group member, you are looking for the focus of energy from which the movement of this person's walks originates. One person's walk may originate or "lead" from their chest, another from the hips, still another from the thighs, or the knees. Once you've located the focus of energy from which the walk originates, become aware of the rest of the body: how the shoulders are held, how the arms move, how the head is held. Now you have the overall "gestalt" of the walk.
3. As a group, begin to walk behind the person, allowing your bodies to move in the way the person is walking. The key here is to focus on the same location in your own body where the walk originates and then allow the movements of the other body parts to add in.
4. Repeat steps 1-3 for all groups members or until your allotted time is up.

Again, the first object in this game is to practice noticing where the energy is focused. In a conversation being aware of where energy coalesces provides the cues for openings for further exploration. Attending to where the energy is focused is also a first step in intentionally participating in "allowing transformation". The next two games illustrate the connection between our focus of attention and intentionally participating in transformation.

Walk my walk is also great practice for "walking in another's shoes", literally embodying a walk and approach to life and noticing what it feels like (for you). Next time you want to suspend your judgments and assumptions and experiment with "taking a walk on the other's side", recall this game. Not only will you add whole new vistas to your landscape you will be exploring your capacities for empathy and compassion at the same time.

7.2.5 Object Transformation

Depending on where we focus our attention, reality shifts. This game is about experiencing this phenomenon. It will also give you an opportunity to practice enlarging the scope of possibilities for connection and creativity you are able to generate in any given situation or conversation.

1. In the center of the group place a selection of objects. Examples: scissors, celery stick, computer disc, marker, twig, koosh ball, etc.
2. One person begins by looking at the objects and noticing which one seems to draw her attention. She then picks up that object and says what it is. E.g. Scissors.
3. Once she has spoken the name of the object she then continues to look at the object and allows her attention to be drawn to some aspect of the object. If the object has moving parts, she may move them. Again, she continues until some feature of the object draws her attention. She then focuses on that point and allows the object to be redefined by the new focus of attention. E.g. She is opening and closing the scissors. She notices her attention focused on the opening and closing blades. The scissors have become a shark moving through the water. She names the new object and passes it to the next person in the circle.
4. The next person receives the "new object", in this case "a shark moving through the water". Step 3 is repeated by each person until the "object" has made its way around the circle, being transformed and passed on by each person in turn.

The objective in this game is to **attend to the focus of attention** and **allow transformation** of the object in the present moment, i.e., when you receive it. This may be uncomfortable. Most of us don't often listen and focus our attention in the present. Rather we prepare, we think ahead to what we might see and say. See if any of these thoughts are familiar. "What if nothing shows up?" "Don't come to me with questions. Come with solutions/answers." "I may look dumb or incompetent if I'm not prepared." Such thinking may be useful in certain circumstances, such as when you have been asked to make a proposal for a new process at work. Yet, in other instances where you are seeking to see new connections, open the door to previously unimagined possibilities, such pre-thinking limits spontaneity. If you want to become aware of the shifting energies and openings for exploration in a group conversation, and you look only for familiar or expected patterns, you will miss any openings that fall outside your expectations.

You may see different objects as others are "transforming the object". Great. Take notice. And then let go of that vision. If you find yourself thinking about possible things you could see, breathe and let go of that thought as well. Practice observing, breathing and letting go, until you receive the object. Then breathe and allow your attention to show you a focus. Remember, the goal is to practice noticing where energy focuses *in the moment* and the moment only arrives when the object enters your hands.

7.2.6 Space Object Transformation

This is a slightly more engaging version of the last game for the simple reason that in some sense you are the object that is going to transform. In this activity you will actually embody the principles **yes-and, attend to the focus of energy** and **allow transformation**.

Space object refers to an "imaginary" object (recall build a room), that is defined by the movement made by the person who is playing. This object will be transformed through a change in the movement. The new movement will define a new object. In some sense, the movement transforms first and then we interpret the new movement to define the transformed object.

1. The first person begins to make a movement with his body. E.g. He is pulling a rope in a downward motion from above, like a "bell rope". The "space object" that this movement defines is a rope. People might say "he's ringing a bell". The focus is on the object rather than the movement, in this case a rope.
2. Once the object has been defined the person continues the movement. Now he focuses on where the energy is in the movement. Is it in his hands? His elbows? Once he has discovered the focus of the energy he begins to place all his attention there and to follow the movement. In nature, no movement will remain identical over time. It will begin to shift and mutate. That is the transformation that the player is going to allow and follow.
3. Without intentionally making any change in the movement the person continues, attending to the primary focus of energy. If no change begins to emerge he is allowed to make the movement smaller or larger. Often this helps increase the focus of attention and facilitates the transformation. Note: As in the last activity it is important to allow the change…rather than produce it. To those watching it is always obvious when a change has been "thought of" and "made" rather than emerging naturally. The first is always discontinuous; the second fluid. The trick here is to continue to focus and allow the change.
4. Once the change has occurred, the player continues the new movement until it becomes clear what object that movement is defining. When that happens he will name the object and pass it along, with the movement, to the next person. Note: It is possible that the person may not recognize the object defined by the new

movement. In that case, another player will often be able to see it easily.

5. Play continues until the object has been passed and transformed by each person.

This improv game is a great practice for all three of the core principles outlined in this chapter. And, it ups the stakes by fusing the observer and the object of transformation. You are both, the observer of the transformation and the object/movement that is transforming. You are quite literally the means and the end of connection and transformation. One of the corollaries, is that when we connect with another person or way of thinking we ourselves are transformed by that connection. There is no such thing as connection and objective witness, something that is well known by our scientific community. This reality may be disconcerting to many of us, depending on the circumstances, and we may be open to connecting and co-creating to different degrees, accordingly. And, yet, if your interest is to create more and richer connections in your life, it is a reality you will need to learn to embrace with open arms (and mind).

Earlier I noted that at times the player may be unable to identify the "new object" and that often the other players are able to do so. This is also a powerful reminder that when we are so intimately engaged in a process (or conversation) it is often difficult for us to see ourselves, our assumptions, and our behaviors. One of the great values others bring us is the vantagepoint and advantage of their perspectives. We may choose to accept them or not. Regardless, the potential for gaining clarity is worth listening for carefully.

Lynne and I often repeat this activity more than once or twice over time with a group because we find that it greatly enhances peoples' ability to attend to the shifting foci of energy in a conversation. By noticing these foci as they emerge and taking them as cues for further inquiry and reflection the conversation is more alive and new insights or learnings are more likely to unfold.

A final note: This is one activity where there is distinct value in having an experienced coach. It is easier for some people to trust and allow the transformation, while others will be more inclined to "create change" based on past patterns of movement they are familiar with. Of course, being aware of this, group members can help one another. The important thing is that people be supported, rather than critiqued.

8. IN CONCLUSION?

Though this chapter must end, it is but one small piece of an ongoing conversation, a conversation that I hope will continue on as an open exploration into how we as humans create connections–among ourselves, with our environment, within our multiple cultural and conceptual frameworks and worldviews.

We live in an infinite web of connections and we are creating more and more each moment. There is no way we can "manage the complexity" of this living connective tissue that is our world. The best we can hope for is to participate fully in those connections most immediate to us with an awareness that our creations ripple out (sometimes in tidal waves) to the farthest corners of our Earth, and farther. After all, if we believe the "heavens" influence us, why would we think that we do not influence the "heavens".

Why not create connections of respect that honor all people and life? We can. Why not create a world where freedom is a state of being and peace is? We can. Not in your lifetime, you say. We won't change the world. How about our homes, schools, organizations? And then, perhaps the world, in your children's lifetime, or their children's, or their children's.

We are told that Native Americans tribes made decisions looking seven generations into the future. Many people today bemoan our short-term focus. Well, this is one case in which I encourage you, even beg you, to take the short-term focus. Don't put off what you can do today because you can't see far enough down the road. Go ahead. Be selfish. I assure you this is one instance when focusing on the present is a plus. Exploring some of the ideas and games in this chapter to create living, growing connections and new possibilities for yourself will only water the seeds of freedom and peace and joy in your and your children's future gardens.

And, please, have fun!

9.   SUGGESTED READING

For those interested in learning more about dialogue and improvisation (particularly theatre games) the following books may be useful. And, a reminder, perhaps unneeded, that there is a wealth of additional information and thinking contained in the other chapters of this book.

9.1   Dialogue

Bohm, David, Nichols, Lee (ed.). *On Dialogue*. Routledge, London-NY. 1996. The text of a conversation where David Bohm speaks about dialogue. Includes other writings/transcriptions from David Bohm's work. If you want to read something from by the man responsible for bringing dialogue to our attention in the late twentieth century. Bohm's work is the foundation from which other people such as Glenna Gerard, William Isaacs, Peter Senge, and others have developed their individual bodies of work.

Dixon, Nancy. *Perspectives on Dialogue: Making Talk Developmental for Individuals and Organizations.* Greensboro, NC. Center for Creative Leadership, 1996. A simple, easy, straightforward book. A good overview of the field and how dialogue can be used as a means for leadership development.

Ellinor, Linda, & Gerard, Glenna. *DIALOGUE: Rediscover the Transforming Power of Conversation.* John Wiley & Sons, NY, 1998. A guide to the historical roots, the principles and skills of the practice of dialogue and its application in organizations. Contains many suggestions for developing self-awareness and competency in the foundational skill areas, as well as ways leaders can integrate dialogue into their organizations..

Flick, Deborah. *From Debate to Dialogue.* The work and model used by Deborah, developed through her work in diversity. Another interesting addition to the field.

Holman, Peggy, & Devane, Tom (eds.). *The change handbook: Group methods for shaping the future.* Berrett-Koehler, San Francisco, 1999. A guide to group technology for creating and sustaining organizational change. Contains chapters on Dialogue, Open Space, Appreciative Inquiry, Future Search, to name only a few. Gives a concise description of each technology as well as a grid comparing the various methodologies.

Huang-Nissen, Sally. *Dialogue Groups: A practical guide to facilitate diversity communication.* Medicine Bear Publishing, P.O. Box 1075, Blue Hill, ME 04614, 1999. Description of Sally's work within the specific application of dialogue diversity circles at Lawrence Livermore Labs and a few other organizations.

Isaacs, William. *Dialogue and the Art of Thinking Together. A pioneering approach to communicating in business and in life.* Currency-Doubleday, NY. 1999. This book is replete with models for how to think about (Part I) as well as practice dialogue (Parts II, III, IV). It is definitely for those who are serious practitioners. It is best read through and then re-read for specific sections.

Ross, Doug and Friends. *The Tao of Dialogue.* Medicine Bear Publishing, P.O. Box 1075, Blue Hill, ME 04614, 1998. A wonderful heartfelt collection of writings from different folks on dialogue.

Yankelovich, Daniel. *The Magic of Dialogue: Transforming conflict into cooperation.* Simon & Schuster, NY. 1999. This book makes a good case for the value of and need for dialogue, presents a simple set of "essential qualities & skills", and suggests strategies for dialogue. Part I makes the case, Part II speaks to the skills and strategies, Part III moves into considering the role of dialogue in the public arena.

9.2   Improvisation

Spolin, Viola. *Improvisation for the theater.* Northwestern University Press, 1999 (third edition).

NOTES

[1] Glenna can be reached by phone at 949-497-9757; glenna49@earthlink.net; www.thedialoguegrouponline.com

[2] For more information on both dialogue and improvisation please see the suggested reading list at the end of the chapter.

[3] I would like to acknowledge the invaluable contribution that Lynne Kaufman has made to this exploration and thank her for reviewing these pages. She is a nationally recognized short story writer and playwright whose plays have been produced at such theatres as The Magic Theatre, Theatreworks, and Actors Theatre of Louisville. She currently directs the Travel with Scholars Program at U.C. Berkeley Extension.

[4] If you are not sure when you may be operating from an assumption you want to reference the following: Ellinor, L., & Gerard, G. (1998). *Dialogue: Rediscover the transforming power of conversation.* New York: John Wiley & Sons.

Chapter 17

THE CONDITIONS FOR THRIVING CONVERSATIONS

KATHIA CASTRO LASZLO and ALEXANDER LASZLO
Syntony Quest and the Monterrey Institute of Technology (ITESM)

1.   INTRODUCTION

Our planet is in trouble as result of the conscious and unconscious collective choices of humanity that dominated the 20th century. Human conflict and environmental degradation are two of the complex interconnected global problems that challenge the way we think, interact, and live. New scientific understanding offers insight into the interconnected nature of our universe. This is the context of our inquiry. An inquiry into the meaning of being and becoming human; a quest toward sustainable and evolutionary ways of living in planet Earth.

Our work on conversation methodology, as a means for searching together–and co-creating–connections and meaning, emerges from the interest in "research methods that can deal with the kinds of 'data' that emerge out of the everyday world of human conversations and activities" (Salner, 1996, p. 6). We are particularly interested in purposeful conversations that go beyond social/interpersonal aspects to embrace an explicit learning and design inquiry. The competencies required for engaging in this kind of conversation overlap with the competencies required for designing more just and sustainable social systems.   By this we mean to indicate evolutionary competency–the understanding and capacity to participate in conscious evolution.

Conversation, in contrast with debate and other forms of antagonistic discourse, is collaborative. It demands from the conversants openness to changing views and perspectives–that is, it involves learning–and can foster coordinated action. This has been our experience in the Asilomar Conversation Community of the International Systems Institute (ISI). This Conversation Community meets annually in Pacific Grove, California, and

Dialogue as a Means of Collective Communication, Edited by Banathy and Jenlink
Kluwer Academic/Plenum Publishers, New York 2005

our reflections on thriving conversations are based primarily on our involvement with a group of colleagues with whom we have been exploring, since 1993, the notion of Evolutionary Learning Community as the means for facilitating the emergence of an evolutionary Design Culture.

2.   WHAT IS A THRIVING CONVERSATION?

We are living in a world that more and more demands the ability to work flexibly and loosely together in ways that combine rational thought, technical skill, creativity and intuition (Rowland, 1992). As a result, conversation is re-emerging as a method of inquiry and a form of creative and synergistic interaction. But not all conversations can be described as thriving conversations.

An improvisational jazz session is a good metaphor for a thriving conversation–both jazz and conversations can generate enough excitement and positive energy to keep going those involved. In a jam session, one can admire the fluidity and graciousness of the melodies generated as the players build on each other's contributions. The players are truly listening to each other, complementing and furthering each other's musical ideas. For jazz musicians to engage in a jam session, they need to have dedicated enormous amounts of time and energy in perfecting their skills as players of each of their instruments, and equally important, they must have learned to play together–to co-create. Thriving conversations, like improvisational jazz, are co-creative processes that involve competence, mutual support, and enrichment. Thriving conversations are challenging and fun.

Conversation, as a disciplined method of inquiry (Banathy, 1996), is an art form just as is improvisational jazz. There is no way one can predict or control a conversation in order to make it a thriving conversation. It is like a dance that is created and re-created, step by step, idea by idea, consciously and volitionally.

3.   REFLECTING ON CONVERSATIONS EXPERIENCES

In 1994, we participated in a weeklong conversation sponsored by the International Systems Institute, which exemplified a thriving conversation. It was the first time that the six participants in that conversation gathered as a team to explore how to facilitate the emergence of a design culture. Some members of the group had been part of the inquiry on design culture in previous ISI events. The understanding of the history of Group D, also known as the Design Culture group, was helpful in creating a common identity and a shared purpose (essential characteristics of authentic community (Laszlo &

Laszlo, 1997). The bonding of the conversation group members resulted in the evolution of their common identity:

> We began by revolutionizing the group: based on our continued quest and the sense of identity that all the members shared (even those joining the group for the first time), we decided we were no longer a group – we had evolved into a Gang! From now on, we would be Gang D, or better, D-Gang. (Castro, et. al , 1994, p. 57)

The reflections on our personal experiences working in this team, using conversation as our research methodology, are full of amazement at the energy level and the flowing and synergic dynamic of the group. Was this a thriving conversation? We think so, because:

- It integrated and balanced the generative (i.e., community building) and strategic (i.e., learning and design inquiry) aspects of design conversations;
- It honored and celebrated the contributions of all the members of the group, regardless of age, gender, ethnicity, education or nationality;
- It built on the different contributions to advance a collective understanding and to co-create new meaning;
- It was exhilarating and fun;
- It could have continued for months and years–and it did!

4. EXPLORING CONDITIONS FOR THRIVING CONVERSATIONS

When we ask ourselves what the conditions necessary for the replication of thriving conversations, such as the one described above, are we can identify aspects that fit four categories: context, past, present, and future.

By context we mean the physical environment where the conversation will take place. We believe that a relaxing and enjoyable environment will influence the quality of the conversation. Expressions such as "the container flavors the contained" and "where the sake hits the cedar" reveal the popular wisdom of preparing a comfortable and creative space for a thriving conversation. In Western capitalist societies we are all too often used to square rooms, artificial lighting, monotonous colors, and a complete disconnect from nature. These conditions are considered to provide acceptable and even productive spaces. And although many thriving conversations can happen in such "industrial" environments, we think that things like sunlight and wind, trees and flowers, fireplaces and art, can be central pieces in the creation of the creative space for a thriving conversation.

The other three categories–past, present, and future–make reference to the conditions prior, during and after the face-to-face conversation itself. A thriving conversation does not "happen" out of nothing. It usually is the result of a growing friendship, a collaborative inquiry, or a personal quest that began way before the actual conversation. In this sense, a thriving conversation may actually begin before it begins! The thread that pulls together past and present is often a key condition for the conversation to thrive. Another aspect related to the "past" is the level of preparedness of those who come together with the purpose of engaging in conversation. Past experience in other thriving conversations, a shared knowledge base or a common cognitive map to support the conversation, and basic design competence are examples of elements that can increase the possibility for thriving conversations.

But no matter how experienced and how prepared the members of the group are, it is important to recognize that a thriving conversation is a complex dynamic process that can never be predicted or controlled. In fact, there are no guaranties for its "success." Just as the ISI action-research team described above was able to move upwards in a spiral of mutual support and increased meaning, the opposite can also happen. There is one condition that over the years we have identified as a useful way of guiding a group through the dynamics that lead to thriving conversations. This guiding system is derived from an evolutionary consciousness, that is, an understanding of the dynamics of evolution grounded in the sciences of complexity (Laszlo, 1987). The particular aspect of this understanding that is useful is the appreciation of divergence and convergence, differentiation and integration, as movements of the evolutionary dynamic. A thriving conversation would most likely present a stochastic process that fits the general dynamic pattern of differentiation and integration. An example of group dynamics that follows this pattern is Weisboard's (1995, pp. 138-139) description of the process of community building in four stages: contentment, denial, confusion, and renewal. These stages can also be thought of as forming, storming, norming, and performing. Thriving conversations are not exempt from such stages–it often happens that an initial agreement (integration) is followed by disagreement and chaos (differentiation). However, a true thriving conversation transcends this stage of divergence and arrives at a new level of organization and meaning, or in Weisboard's terms, at a stage of renewal.

A thriving conversation tends to make waves into the future. Relationships become stronger, projects get planned, and new conversations emerge. The future thinking of those involved in a conversation, that is, their intention to continue the learning and design inquiry beyond the conversation encounter, can also affect the quality of the conversation itself.

In the categories past, present, and future conditions for thriving conversations, there is a constant factor that seems always to affect the quality of the conversation. This factor corresponds to the expectations conversants bring with them going into the conversation regarding both the way the conversation will go and where it will lead.

5.   WHAT DO YOU EXPECT FROM OUR CONVERSATION?

People come together to participate in a conversation with different aims, intentions and expectations in mind. What is the impact of these expectations on the quality and outcomes of the conversation? Reflecting on our experiences in thriving (and not-so-thriving) conversations, we have concluded that the purposes and dispositions of the individual participants are important to the success of the community and their conversation. In other words, not everyone can make a thriving conversation happen.

5.1   Proximate Life Passions and Ultimate Life Passions

The inquiry on design culture carried out by D-Gang evolved into an exploration of Evolutionary Learning Community (ELC) as the vehicle for creating such a culture. We describe one of our ELC conversations of ISI as "the year of angst." The experience was exactly the opposite of what we are calling thriving conversations. Although unpleasant and unproductive in the strategic sense, the experience of a not-so-thriving conversation helped us learn important lessons. After this experience, we reported on how "a review of the essential elements for effective group work reveals at least three non-productive 'tension sources' that arose during [the first] three days [of our conversation]" (Laszlo & Laszlo, et. al., 1995, p. 66). The first tension source was individual expectations that impeded the agreement on common goals for the conversation week. The second was problems with communication such as the absence of active and respectful listening, despite the fact that we had established communication ground rules. The third significant source of tension was due to the lack of well-defined decision taking procedures for consensus making. As a result, the creation of common ground was an elusive task.

Months later, Alexander (in Halstead, et. al., 1997) articulated the experience in a way that captured the deeper individual conditions for a thriving or non-thriving conversation:

> The composition of a group is critical to its success.... Perhaps the filter relates to "relative passion objectives:" if the passion objective is to live, learn, and understand from the process in order to enrich one's life, then the ELC will not transcend; if the passion objective is to live, learn, and understand from the process in order to enrich the world, then the ELC will transcend. In the former, the quest is for realization of the self, with contribution to and betterment of the world being secondary and a by-product. In the latter, the quest is for contribution to and betterment of the world, with realization of the self being

secondary and a by-product. ELCs cannot emerge from individuals with proximate life passions. They must seek and attract and embrace individuals with transcendent life passions. (p. 58)

Just as ELCs cannot emerge from individuals with proximate life passions, neither can thriving conversations. A thriving conversation is much more than the sum of individual interests. But for true synergy to take place, individuals need to put aside their personal agenda–as well as many of their assumptions–in order to transcend with the rest of the group and create new meaning.

The interesting thing about the distinction between proximate and ultimate life passions is that they do not present an "either/or" choice. The proximate life passion is an egocentric position that leaves issues pertaining to the larger environment and our collective long-term future out of the conversation. But the ultimate life passion, which is an ecocentric and evolutionary position, includes the proximate life passion as an integral part of inquiry. As a result, those individuals motivated by an ultimate life passion are also moved from within by an interest that touches their own life in a very personal and profound way.

6.   DEVELOPING CAPACITY FOR CONVERSATION THROUGH COMMUNITY BUILDING—AND BUILDING COMMUNITY THROUGH CONVERSATION

M. Scott Peck (1987) explains how "the rules of communication are best taught and only learned through the practice of community-making. Fundamentally, the rules of communication are the rules of community-making" (p. 325). He also advises: "community-building first, problem-solving second" (p. 104). The essence of his message is that there cannot be effective conversation if the basis of trust, friendship, mutual support and caring relationships are absent. Thriving conversations are interdependent with the quality of the communication of the group. In fact, it is the very sense of healthy and authentic community that creates a safe and nurturing environment for rich learning and design explorations.

Banathy (1996) defines design conversations as the combination of generic and strategic dialogue. The first refers to the parts of the conversation that build trust, create bonds, and strengthen the sense of community among the conversants. The second refers to the parts of the conversation that are focused on the task that brought the group together in the first place, that is, on the specific form of learning and design inquiry. There is no required sequence for these two types of dialogue in design conversations, but in our experience, it is helpful to begin with generative dialogue to get to know each other, to set the bases for the collaborative inquiry and to make explicit the values and guidelines to be honored during the conversation. Generative dialogue naturally leads to strategic issues. And as the strategic dialogue unfolds, there are always elements of generative dialogue that continue to infuse and hold the process.

6.1 Approaches for Generative Dialogue

When a conversation is a learning and design conversation, generative dialogue could appear to be less important than strategic dialogue. But more and more and in different contexts, we learn the importance of community building for the effectiveness and productivity of a group's interaction.

While there exist rigorous methodologies for strategic dialogue (e.g., social systems design (Banathy, 1996), soft systems methodology (Checkland, 1981), future search (Weisboard, 1995)), the generative part of the dialogue tends to be aided by less structured approaches. This does not mean that there are no generative approaches, however, they rarely are used in conjunction with strategic approaches. In fact, many of the approaches that seem clearly to aid community building are often presented as stand-alone strategic processes, instead (e.g., team Syntegration events, Psyche gaming activities, and Synergic Inquiry programs).

Synergic Inquiry (Tang, 1997) is an example of an approach that has great potential to aid the generative dialogue phase and to create conditions that propitiate thriving conversations. Similarly to Weisboard's description of the dynamics of community building, Synergic Inquiry follows the evolutionary pattern of differentiation and integration. The phases of this approach involve self-knowing, other-knowing, differences holding and differences transcending. It is this last stage that characterizes an authentic community–"a way of being together with both individual authenticity and interpersonal harmony so that people become able to function with a collective energy even greater than the sum of their individual energies" (Scott Peck in Banathy, 1996, p. 239).

Synergic Inquiry can be used in an explicit or implicit way. By explicit we mean its conscious use by a group in a way that applies exercises to move along the four phases of the process. An implicit use would involve a shared knowledge of the SI process and an unstructured unfolding of the generative and strategic conversation interspersed with guided reflection on where in the SI process they have been or need now to be.

Design conversations are always learning conversations. Design is a future creating inquiry that requires innovation and openness of evolutionary learners. As such, design conversations enhance both individual and collective development, which become the foundations of the co-creative design journey. Synergic Inquiry parallels the individual and collective development at the strategic level, where conversants learn and develop the shared knowledge base to support their inquiry, by guiding the differentiation and integration dynamics of the group along the path toward becoming a learning and designing community (see Figure 1).

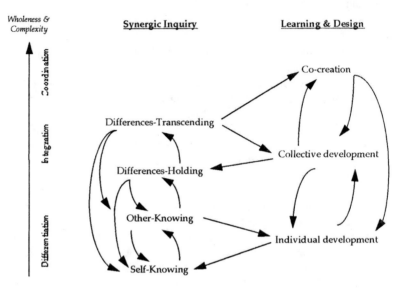

Figure 1. Interrelations between Synergic Inquiry and the process of Learning and Design Inquiry.

7.   FACILITATING THRIVING CONVERSATIONS

Can someone facilitate a conversation in which he or she does not participate? We will look at this questions from the perspective of thriving conversations by using a particular design heuristic: the five generations of designers.

7.1   Generations of Designers and Conversation Facilitators

A conversation facilitator is the person who guides and supports the interactive processes of the group. To *facilitate*, according to Webster's Dictionary, means, "to assist the progress of a person." It also defines it as "to make easier or less difficult." Both of these definitions are relevant when considering the role of a conversation facilitator. They indicate that the function of the facilitator is to help the group move toward common meaning and transcendence through the not-always-easy stages of differentiation and integration involved.

We draw the analogy between generations of designers and of conversation facilitators. In social systems design we differentiate among five generations of designers (Laszlo, 1992). The *first generation* designer is consider an expert and specialist in the design process. She studies the situation of the group and decides which is the best solution for them. The *second generation* designer is akin to the classical consultant who asks for information from the members of the group, and then analyses it and gives them a solution according to her perception of their needs. These two first generations design *for* others. In contrast, the last three generations of designers design *with* others. The *third generation* designer gets the group involved in the creation of alternative solutions, but at the end of the process, she nevertheless selects the best alternative for them. The *fourth generation* designer works to create an adequate group environment that facilitates the processes of generating alternatives and selecting solutions. The newest generation, the *fifth generation*, not only involves the group in the design process, but also helps the group to learn how to learn to facilitate. A group that does so can sustain the continued design process by themselves (Banathy, 1996.)

How are these designer generation roles related to the role of the conversation facilitator? We believe that a facilitator of a conversation cannot operate out of the values and assumptions derived from the first two generations. That is to say, there is no possibility for an authentic conversation facilitator to "design *for* others" or to assume a position of authority and control over the conversants. The conversation facilitator cannot be an external agent to the community but rather needs to be just another member of it. In fact, many thriving conversations are characterized by a shared facilitation process in which the role of the facilitator is not assumed by only one individual but rotates among the members of the community.

The facilitator of a conversation can function out of the framework of a third, fourth or fifth generation of designer. But facilitators of thriving conversations tends to work from the basis of the fifth generation—completely integrated into the group, sharing the facilitation functions and responsibilities, and helping the group to become more and more capable of facilitating their own process evolutionary change and transcendence.

Bela Banathy (1996) suggests a set of guardianship roles to share responsibility and accomplish the tasks of the group. These roles include:

- the guardian of participation
- the guardian of keeping the focus
- the guardian of selected group technique
- the guardian of documentation
- the guardian of accepting and honoring all contributions
- the guardian of values
- the guardian of "keeping the fire burning"
- the guardian of time and coordination

Each role is descriptive of the functions that a facilitator carries out, but in thriving conversations, they are not assumed by just one individual but shared by the community as a whole. As with SI, these guardianship roles can be used explicitly or implicitly. The thriving conversation in which Group D became D-Gang used these roles explicitly, and the members of that conversation community found them extremely useful for the success of their conversation. The group that participated in the year of angst, because they were familiar with these roles and responsibilities, decided not to assign or rotate the functions explicitly, and the group was unable to secure processes such as that of accepting and honoring all contributions or keeping a common focus. It takes time and practice for these functions to be embodied in a community in a way that does not need to be consciously taken care of.

8.   MANAGING PLACE AND SPACE

Conversation is a human activity that involves much more than language. Emotions, intentions, expectations, intuitions, and dreams as well as knowledge, imagination, interpretation, and experiences are intertwined elements that shape the quality and meaning of the conversation. Conversations are characteristically complex, because so are human interactions (as well as humans, themselves!).

While before it was only possible to have a conversation when two or more people were physically in the same place at the same time, with the emergence of communication technologies it is becoming more common to have conversations that transcend boundaries of time and space. The Internet has revolutionized the way we interact with each other and is making it possible to establish connections with people all around the world.

The design conversations that we have convened through the International Systems Institute are week-long face to face conversations. In these intense encounters we have had the opportunity to learn much about conversation methodology and ways in which we can facilitate thriving conversations. Our yearly weeklong conversations are supplemented with an on-line component in preparation and follow-up of our week together.

Thus far, on-line interaction has been limited to e-mail, listservs, telephone, and fax. The intensity of the on-line interaction with D-Gang has varied widely. While in some weeks the interaction is rich and focused, there have also been months during which there was no interaction at all and others when it was limited to administrative issues. One thing is for sure: access through email to the rest of the team members gives some sense of continuity from one intense week of face-to-face learning and designing to the next. But it is difficult to keep the fire of our conversation burning once we get back to "life as usual." The week at Asilomar remains as our main place for collaboration.

We have used Internet technologies, such as chat rooms and discussion lists, to facilitate conversations in other contexts outside of ISI. One example is our collaboration on a listserv that ended up creating a book with contributors from a variety of different countries (Miller, 2000). Our action-research has also benefited from other types of conversation over the Internet. For instance, we facilitated a community development project in Mexico in which the co-design and learning required for its implementation was accomplished through interactive chats and email exchanges (Laszlo, 2000). Much of our teaching at the doctoral and masters level has also been enriched by the opportunity for conversation beyond the classroom. With all but the experience on the collaborative book, our rich and thriving conversations that have been mediated by information technology have also been complemented by face-to-face encounters. In fact, we have found that in many cases the very success of on-line conversations depend on the effectiveness of the kind of generative dialogue–the bonding–that happens when we interact in person.

On-line conversations can certainly be strategic, and if well defined, can bring about very positive and concrete results. It is the generative part of thriving conversations that still seems to call for the high-touch aspects of face-to-face interaction. A combined use of on-site and on-line conversations offer many possibilities for ongoing community building, learning, and design.

9.   POSSIBILITIES EMERGING FROM THRIVING CONVERSATIONS

Thriving conversations involve trust and friendship, learning and transformation, democracy and participation, diversity and synergy, playfulness and enjoyment, connection and meaning.

Thriving conversations go beyond the social and community dimensions of many other forms of dialogue to embrace a collaborative learning and design purpose. In a world in distress, thriving conversations offer spaces for the joint creation of knowledge and meaning, for finding hope and energy to work together toward a better world, for learning and discovering new possibilities. Those communities that learn how to engage in thriving conversations experience what Csikszentmihalyi (1993) describes as "flow" or "optimal experience."

We have chosen the term "syntony" to describe the creative aligning and tuning to each other and to the greater environment that allows a community to engage in a thriving conversation. In other words, the ultimate thriving conversation is a *syntonious* conversation–one that is purposefully focus on developing evolutionary consciousness for conscious evolution. Creating such conversations is at once tremendously challenging, tremendously fun, and tremendously rewarding.

REFERENCES

Apatow, R., 1999. *El Arte del Diálogo: La comunicación para el crecimiento personal, las relaciones y la empresa.* EDAF, Madrid.

Castro, K., Laszlo, A., et.al., 1994. Design tools: Toward the concrete and conceptual heuristics of a design culture. Proceedings of the Sixth International Conversation on the Comprehensive Design of Social Systems. International Systems Institute, Pacific Grove, CA.

Checkland, P., 1981. *Systems Thinking, Systems Practice.* Wiley, New York.

Csikszentmihalyi, M., 1993. *The Evolving Self: A Psychology for the third Millennium.* Harper Collins, New York.

Halstead, Jack, Quiñones, M., et. al., 1997. Evolutionary learning community inquiry: Reflections on our conversation experience. Proceedings of the Ninth International Conversation on the Comprehensive Design of Social Systems. International Systems Institute, Pacific Grove, CA.

Laszlo, A., 1992. Fostering Design Competencies: Empathizing With and Enhancing Individual and Collective Self-Development Capacities. Unpublished Manuscript.

Laszlo, K., and Laszlo, A. 1997. Partners in Life: Syntony at work. Proceedings of the Ninth International Conversation on the Comprehensive Design of Social Systems. International Systems Institute, Pacific Grove, CA.

Laszlo, A., Laszlo, K., et.al., 1995. Building a design culture through evolutionary learning communities. Proceedings of the Seventh International Conversation on the Comprehensive Design of Social Systems. International Systems Institute, Pacific Grove, CA.

Laszlo, E., 1987. *Evolution: The Grand Synthesis.* New Science Library, Boston.

Laszlo, K.C., 2000. Co-creating learning communities in Mexico. In R. Miller (ed.), *Creating Learning Communities: Models, resources and new ways of thinking about teaching and learning.* Solomon Press, New York.

Miller, R., (ed.), 2000. *Creating Learning Communities: Models, Resources and New Ways of Thinking About Teaching and Learning.* Solomon Press, New York.

Peck, M.S., 1987. *The Different Drum: Community building and peace.* Simon and Schuster, New York.

Rowland, G., 1992. Do You Play Jazz? *Performance & Instruction.* **Nov./Dec.**: 19.

Salner, Marcia (1996). A new framework for human science. *Saybrook Perspectives.* San Francisco: Saybrook Institute.

Tang, Y., 1997. Fostering transformation through differences: The Synergic Inquiry (SI) framework. In *ReVision,* **20**(1).

Weisboard, M., 1995. Future searches. In K. Gozdz (ed.), *Community Building: Renewing Spirit and Learning in Business.* New Leaders Press, San Francisco:

SECTION IV

PRACTICAL APPLICATIONS
OF CONVERSATION

Chapter 18

A COMMUNITY ROUND TABLE
An Experiment with a Self-Organizing Conversation

JUDITH BACH
International Systems Institute

1.   INTRODUCTION

In 1994 I was a co-facilitator at an annual International Systems Institute Conversation. The purpose of the Conversation was to better understand the conditions that foster transcendence in a group context, specifically in relation to systems design. After the weeklong Conversation, I wrote:

> I'm wondering what it was about our group experience that led to the most interesting Conversation that I've encountered to date. Several things occur to me: The question what we addressed was: *How do we create the conditions that foster the experience of transcendence in a design system?* The creative tension that accompanied the dialogues moved us into a powerful experience of transcendence itself. Wrapping ourselves around the subject led us from talking about the path to creating the path as we walked. Once condition that may hold the key to what happened was the nature of intra-and inter-group interactions. There was a quality of "heart-centeredness" in the experience that, I suspect, enhanced the special quality that many of us felt. Not only did we, as a group, leap into (for us) uncharted territory in terms of ideas, but we also experienced a qualitative shift in our collective experience of trust and intimacy and, in at least one case, a spiritual epiphany.

Now, that conversation was defined by its purpose. I recalled that Jantsch (1980) had written that self-organization provides the context for a system to not only co-evolve with its environment, but to also transcend itself. Might a self-organized conversation with no particular stated intent or purpose lead to self-transcendence?

I decided to initiate a nine-month experiment of such conversations in my own community. The group would define its own core values. It would be self-organized in the sense that there would be no inherent structure or leadership and it would be open to anyone who was interested in becoming involved. This chapter is an account of that experience.

2.   TRANSCENDENCE AND SELF-ORGANIZATION

Transcendence, which means going beyond ordinary limits, is the ability to "leap out" of our so-called normal beliefs into an enlarged landscape of possibilities. This is not an arcane concept. Individually, we transcend all the time. Whenever we solve a problem, at that moment we have risen above the frustrations and shadowy obscurity of the issue to behold a grander context which holds other possibilities. Group transcendence follows the same principles, but, obviously, is more complex. I define it as a condition when a group moves beyond its usual functioning to either arrive at a new solution or acts in total harmony for a greater good.

Self-organization is the capacity of a system to evolve and transcend itself (Jantsch, 1976; 1980). Process and structure become linked in service of the system's evolutionary thrust. This evolutionary process runs through all systems levels, from the purely physical (atoms to galaxies) to the human domain (individuals to complex social systems). I believe that when a human system, such as a conversation group, is open, that is, when its structure and process co-create each other, learning occurs on both an individual and group level. Such learning can provide the conditions for the participants of a group to creatively help it evolve into new forms that are expressive of the combined will of its members (Bach, 1993).

3.   THE ROUND TABLE

I live in a town of about 800 people. Because of its small size and rich mix of people from all walks of life, the community lends itself to interventions such as the one I attempted. In an article I wrote for the town newspaper, I called for a meeting for the purpose of forming a "round table" which would meet regularly to talk about any issues on which the group decided. The conversation group would be completely open to everyone in the community.

Twenty-two people came to the first meeting. The group represented a cross-section of old and young, long-time residents and newcomers. There were also an almost equal number of and women. Many of the attendees did not know each other. Others were long-time acquaintances or friends.

After introductions, I asked the group if they would be interested in engaging in a process of defining core values for the conversation. My rationale for doing this was to, hopefully, "lift" the conversation from gossip and discussion to dialogue and conversation. Bohm (1990) points out the distinction between discussion and dialogue. Discussion is an analytical process

> where there may be many points of view, and where everybody is presenting a different one–analyzing and breaking up. That obviously has its values; but it is limited, and it will not get us very far beyond our various points of view. (p. 1)

In the presence of dialogue, we operate more intuitively, reaching for meaning. It is a more holistic process than discussion, which leads most often to each person trying to "win" his or her position. I like Parrakos' (1995) definition:

> Dialogue, as a concept, takes on a new and deeper meaning when it is perceived as a group's accessing a larger pool of common spirit through a distinctively spiritual connection between the members...Spirit flowing through the participants in dialogue leads to collective thinking which, in turn, facilitates common understanding thereby resulting in...'collective learning'. (pp. 322-23)

I would add that collective learning, spawned from experiences of unstructured conversation, could lead to collective action that expresses the core values of a group.

In order to define these values, I employed a "values hierarchy" (Bach, 1993), eliciting responses from the group to the question, "Why are you interested in the Round Table?" followed by "What is the value in that (response)? "They were asked to continue to ask themselves the latter question over and over, writing down the responses until they were satisfied they had expressed themselves as fully as they desired. For example, in response to "Why are you interested in the Round Table?" one person wrote "To try and find out what the people in town are collectively interested in." As she probed deeper as a result of asking herself "what is the value in that?" her responses were:

> To build a community spirit.
> *What is the value in that?*
> So people are interested in people.
> *What is the value in that?*
> So life and living may improve.
> *What is the value in that?*
> To remove self from self.

What is the value in that?
To rebuild ethics.

We then created the values hierarchy by assigning each response to either a Personal level, such as "To live longer through enjoying life", a Community Level, such as "To increase contact with neighbors", and a "Beyond Community Level", such as "Service." Some of the other responses on this more universal level were "Love and creativity; enlightenment, to enrich, to rebuild ethics." It is clear that the group began to move into a more transcendent space as they engaged in this process.

The final step was to create a statement that reflected and combined the three levels:

> The Round Table expresses love, creativity, service and ethics so as to enrich life and create harmony through building community spirit and working with others to determine what people are interested in and helping people get their needs met. These aims are accomplished through sharing ideas, discussing concerns, helping solve problems and utilizing the available resources of time, talent and finances in the community.
>
> Involvement in the Round Table brings to its members enjoyment of life, a sense of accomplishment, self esteem and a purposeful existence through participating together to improve the quality of life and creating a better place to live.

By this process we had created a guiding perspective (Banathy, 1991) that contained the group's needs and core values. Normally, such a guiding perspective functions as the content of a mission statement for a design process (Ackoff, 1981) or the "front end" of a systems-design process (Banathy, 1996). In this case, it was to guide our Conversation for the next nine months.

One event particularly stands out from that first meeting. After the initial preparation–the completion of the guiding perspective–I sat down and stated that it was now up to the group to decide what to do. I was "retiring" from any leadership role and wanted to be included as an equally involved member of the group.

One woman looked at me and asked, "Should we elect officers now?"
"It's up to you and everyone else," I replied.

I will never forget the expression on her face of puzzlement and excitement as she nearly jumped out of her chair.

"You mean we can do anything we want?"

It is moments like these that I consider markers of transcendence, which raise a group to a new level of understanding.

4.   THE CONVERSATION

We decided to meet once a month at a house volunteered by a member of the group. Because of many other commitments, conversations would be limited to 90 minutes, followed by coffee and snacks. The conversations would begin at 7:30 PM and end promptly at 9.

At our first conversation, there were 15 people, which became the norm throughout the experiment. Initially, people looked to me for an agenda or guidance. I pulled back, explaining it was up to all of us. People would come and go, but there was always a core of about 10 regulars at all of the meetings. As the group began to relax into letting go of an agenda, the new ones who showed up fell very naturally into the conversational rhythm that had become established. At the first few conversations I passed around copies of the Guiding Perspective, and then let it go. For the most part, the conversations ranged around the interests of group members, which were varied and interesting. Dialogue was consistently the modality—very rarely, discussion. Gossip was never an issue.

The ninth and final meeting—final because summer was upon us and we were all too busy to continue—was a powerful experience of group transcendence. At this meeting, a local artist came for the first time with a couple that lived across the road from his gallery. He had heard about us through the ever-efficient community grapevine. Inviting his friends to tell their story, he told us he hoped we might help them. They explained that they had recently purchased a Bed and Breakfast in town and had hoped to finance their business by the sale of their house in a neighboring state. Because the real estate market had gone sour, they realized very little from their house. They had tried to secure a loan from banks, but were turned down. Facing bankruptcy and overwhelmed by debt, they were in a desperate place. They looked drawn and unhappy.

The group immediately went into helping mode. No one knew these people, but their predicament became the centerpiece of the conversation. For 90 minutes we struggled with their problem. The atmosphere in the room was electric and the group was completely focused. Although we never came up with a concrete solution, something far more healing happened. As we were standing in the kitchen afterwards, talking, I overheard the woman say to someone in the group, "Now I feel that I have the strength to go on!"

When I heard these words I knew we had succeeded. Through the power of self-organizing conversation, we had as one body, in that final meeting, expressed the qualities of love and service, transcendent values of the guiding perspective. This act of caring was the catalyst that enabled the couple to transcend their own despair and feel empowered to fight on. It was only a month or two later that we learned they had retained a lawyer, returned to one of the banks and succeeded in obtaining a loan which helped them launch their business.

5.   THE CULTURE OF CONVERSATION

In any neighborhood or community conversation, unless one has grown up in a particular community, it is essential to learn that particular community's conversational culture. As a transplant from a large city to a small New England village, my own learning has been profound. Two years after my husband and I had moved to our town over 30 years ago, we were introduced to its conversational culture in a gentle and amusing fashion. At that stage in our lives, we were both in major work transition, struggling financially and trying to become active in the town. Long before any organized programs for senior citizens had been organized in this area, we were drawn to the idea of contacting the elder members of the community to meet together for the purpose of designing an activity together. The meeting was held at our house.

Seven women showed up between the ages of 60 and 80. In retrospect, I'm sure they came because they were avidly curious about us; the activity for elders was a minor consideration. And they were highly entertained. Before the meeting, I was nervously cleaning in preparation for our visitors. Our furniture was scuffed and old. I hurriedly threw a spread over our decrepit sofa. When our visitors arrived, I sat in our Great Dane, Boris' chair, which had become his special safe place. He looked at me in astonishment because no one ever sat in his chair. As the women arranged themselves in the living room, Boris climbed into the chair, settled down with a sigh and I was on the floor. Amidst the general hilarity, my husband mentioned that he had changed his name from Bernard to David. One of the women, on her way to the bathroom, tossed off, dryly, "Oh, that's nice. Bernard does have a bit of a doggy sound to it."

Thus we were launched. As the meeting was to last for only an hour, we presented our idea to the group and then, for exactly 55 minutes we mostly observed a conversation that, if it had been charted, would have resembled the streets of Boston which were constructed on old cow paths. The conversation, or, more precisely, sharing of town news, ended abruptly after 55 minutes. One of the women then suggested that it might be fun, and a service, to sing weekly for the residents of the local nursing home. Before we realized it, the plan was approved and one person offered the idea that we approach younger members of the town to see if they would like to join. And so our chorus was born–in the last five minutes of the meeting.

The lesson I learned from this meeting has always stayed with me. Here, in retrospect, was my first experience in self-organization. The quality of the conversation was what I consider "feminine", that is, totally circular. Conversation in a masculine mode tends to be purposeful and linear. It might be argued that the experience was not a conversation in the literal sense. I consider that it was, and that the first 55-minute exchange was the group's way of "warming up"–a prelude which led to the successful finale.

During the ensuring years I have observed that when new people from New York or Boston moved to town and attempted to organize projects, they would tend to be directive, linear and, yes, sometimes arrogant, often failing because they did not take the time to understand the local culture.

6.   SUMMARY

Self-organized conversation is a generative process that fosters creativity and deepens relationships, essential ingredients in community building. As individuals, we have the potential to evolve into more conscious and loving human beings, so do social systems, particularly when driven by spiritual, or transcendent values that are self-generated. These values sound a tone that resonates throughout the Conversation, helping to stabilize the experience so that it stays on the level of dialogue, and providing the context for experiences of individual and group transcendence

REFERENCES

Ackoff, R., 1981. *Creating the Corporate Future*. John Wiley & Sons, New York.

Bach, J., 1993. *Evolutionary Guidance System in the Redesign of a Professional Society*. Dissertation.

Banathy, B.H., 1991. *Systems Design of Education*. Educational Technology Publications, Englewood Cliffs, NJ.

Banathy, B.H., 1996. *Designing Social Systems in a Changing World*. Plenum Press, New York.

Bohm, D., 1990. *On Dialogue*. David Bohm Seminars, Ojai, CA.

Jantsch, E., 1976. Evolution: self-realization through self-transcendence. In E. Jantsch and C.H. Waddington (eds.), *Evolution and Consciousness*. Addison-Wesley, Reading, MA.

Jantsch, E., 1995. *The Self-Organizing Universe*. Oxford: Pergamon Press, 1980.

Pattakos, A. N. Searching for the soul in government. In B. DeFoore and J. Renesch, (eds.), *Rediscovering the Soul of Business*. New Leaders Press, San Francisco, CA.

Chapter 19

CORPORATE CONVERSATION

DIANE GAYESKI AND GORDON ROWLAND
Ithaca College, Ithaca, New York, USA

1.   INTRODUCTION

Communication in organizations involves a wide range of activities, processes, and events, and has moved from being considered an isolated function to an area of strategic importance. Corporations, for example, are seeing their ability to manage information and knowledge as key competitive factors (Fitz-enz, 2000; Gayeski, 2000; Gayeski, in press). As is the case elsewhere, communication behaviors in organizations are driven by underlying assumptions, beliefs, and values. They reflect what individuals see as their role in relation to others, for example. It is rare that such assumptions and beliefs are made explicit, so people continue to behave in established patterns. This may sometimes enhance efficiency, but it can also reinforce bureaucracy and stifle creativity. Our attempt here is to examine representative communication behaviors in corporate environments and demonstrate how shifting those behaviors toward conversation might enhance performance.

2.   CONVERSATION

As is described throughout this volume, conversation implies a type of human interaction with special characteristics. Yankelovich (1999) states that the key requirements of dialogue (which we will use as a synonym for conversation) are equality, empathic listening, and surfacing assumptions nonjudgmentally (p. 46). He cites the following fifteen strategies for successful dialogue:

1. Err on the side of including people who disagree
2. Initiate dialogue through a gesture of empathy

3. Check for equality, empathic listening, and surfacing assumptions nonjudgmentally
4. minimize the level of mistrust before pursuing practical objectives
5. Keep dialogue and decision making compartmentalized
6. Focus on common interests, not divisive ones
7. Clarify assumptions that are held by various subcultures of the group
8. Bring forth your own assumptions before speculating on those of others
9. Use specific cases to bring out issues
10. Focus on conflicts between value systems, not people
11. Where applicable, identify mistrust as the real source of misunderstandings
12. Expose old scripts to a reality check
13. Be sure trust exists before addressing transference distortions
14. Where appropriate, express the emotions that accompany strongly held values
15. Encourage relationships in order to humanize transactions.

(pp. 127-128)

These strategies capture our view of desired behaviors in conversation, while our view of underlying assumptions and values are consistent with Banathy (1996), Bohm (1990), Jenlink and Carr (1996), and other authors in this volume.

To be able to analyze cases and compare behaviors and assumptions to those implied by conversation we will adopt the following framework:

Process
- communication behavior: the ways we speak and listen, our goals and attitudes in doing so
- roles and relationships
- feelings toward one another, e.g., trust and respect
- initiation and organization of communication activities
- setting
Outcomes
- understanding and perspective
- alternatives (divergence)
- action (convergence)
- capacity

Table 1 is how we would fill out the framework for conversation.

Table 1. Conversation

Process	Conversation
- communication behavior	offer input as gift; express oneself without reserve; open up to, commit to process; listen & seek to understand; ask others to unpack their statements in order to access their assumptions
- roles and relationships	equal participants; mutual engagement; authentic participation; collaboration
- feelings toward one another	mutual trust and respect
- initiation and organization of comm activities	initiated with carefully selected trigger question; self-organizing thereafter
- setting	private group space; much time
Outcomes	
- understanding and perspective	view of the whole; assumptions made explicit; shared understanding & insight; collective worldview
- alternatives (divergence)	potential alternatives increased
- action (convergence)	coordinated action; plan(s) for addressing complex issue
- capacity	greater creative capacity; greater sense of community

---

We will use the framework for examining four typical communication activities in organizations and the characteristics of conversation for comparison. The four activities are: planning processes; employee supervision; leadership in change; and employee orientation. For each, we'll use "before" to represent a behavior that the first author has observed, "analysis" to consider underlying assumptions and causes of the behavior, and "alternative" to speculate on how a move toward conversation might alter the behavior and outcomes.

3. THE PLANNING PROCESS

3.1 Before

One organization for which I (first author) have done some consulting seems to structure most of its meetings in terms of a "pitch"–this is the term people continually use to describe their input for a meeting. Even when the topic is in a relatively preliminary state of exploration, proposers decide on what they feel is the best course of action, and present it to a constituency in terms of a sales pitch. For example, I worked with the manager of one of their prestigious executive leadership training programs, and she wanted to make some changes to better address the needs of the organizations that would be hiring these candidates. Although she had many possible approaches in mind, she told me that their company's expectation was that she would select what she thought was the optimal approach, and "pitch" it to the group in a short persuasive presentation supplemented by glitzy Powerpoint slides. It's considered a failure if the audience doesn't "buy into" the one approach that was selected, so a lot of time and effort goes into building a very persuasive argument.

3.2   Analysis

The company described is a Fortune 50 company with very diversified product lines and operations around the world. They are known for their speed of execution, and for being at the top of all their business sectors. I found their "pitch" approach to planning a bit disturbing. It seemed that there was little opportunity for brainstorming or for presenting a number of candidate solutions to a problem. Instead, one approach was chosen to be aired, to be given a "thumbs up" or "thumbs down" at the end of the meeting. Are potentially great ideas not being given exposure? Does a presenter think in terms of "winning" or "losing" the pitch rather than gaining valuable perspectives and criticism?

When I presented this picture to a friend who is CEO of a small company, he commented that my client was large and complex, and that probably speed of execution was more important than spending time finding the "one best" solution. His comment was that they hire smart people and that they probably would choose a good idea to "pitch"–and that getting fast buy-in to something workable was more important than waiting around to perfect an approach. Table 2 is how "the pitch" would be defined in terms of our framework.

3.3   Alternative

We suggest that a change toward conversation could have positive effects in two areas. First, suppose the manager was able to offer ideas (more than one), which may not be fully worked out, rather than or in addition to selling single answers. Others might listen, more with an attitude of contribution than criticism, and find ways to tailor a solution to problems that the idea's originator did not anticipate. The result might be a greater range of possibilities, with more than one person's perspective and effort involved, include alternatives that others build on to create a very powerful solution. Sharing in the idea's development could lead to greater commitment, also. This is likely a slower process, but with greater potential. It could be reserved for more important issues.

Table 2. "The Pitch"

Process	"The Pitch"
- communication behavior	sell answers; try to win; criticize others' ideas
- roles and relationships	salesperson and customer; play the game; compete
- feelings toward one another	suspicion
- initiation and organization of comm activities	convened meeting; personnel assigned; predetermined rules regarding roles and process
- setting	meeting room (with clear front); limited time
Outcomes	
- understanding and perspective	focus on parts; tacit assumptions; underlying perspectives unchanged
- alternatives (divergence)	eliminated by individual before meeting
- action (convergence)	agreement on direction/action/strategy
- capacity	creative capacity limited to individuals; group members buy in or out of each decision

Second, going beyond "the pitch" to examine the assumptions underlying recommendations could lead to better foresight of consequences, in particular, consequences at the level of the whole, not just parts. Actions could thus be better coordinated across various decisions and areas of the system and more clearly aligned with the organizational mission and goals. A more shared perspective and, again, greater commitment to the strategy could result. The individuals would co-own the strategy and its outcomes rather than just the decision that something "seems like the best option we can think of at the moment."

4.   SUPERVISOR AS COACH

4.1   Before

Stan, the owner of a 70-employee company that manufactures filters is known for his style of coaching... one might describe it as direct, Socratic, and perambulatory. Almost every day he walks around the plant just looking and talking; he says he basically has two questions: "Are you having fun?", and "Are we making money?". He lets the co-presidents of the firm manage (they set expectations and make decisions), but he's kind of the elder teacher.

One vignette describes his style. The supervisor of operations told him that one of their new sales guys, John, specified and sold an order to a customer without properly consulting the planning department and the head of the "bug" or "business unit group". They were upset with John and also said that they had to spend a lot of time in one of their weekly planning meetings trying to figure out if and how they could meet this order. Stan said he'd look into it. He didn't immediately confront John, but rather waited until he ran into him the next day. John walked up and complained to him that the planners and operations folks were being uncooperative and delaying his big order. He claimed he did look into capacity himself, and when he was called into the planning meeting just told them that he had studied it and no further discussion was necessary.

Here was Stan's response. He said "John, you're a smart kid and you've got a great future around here–if you just avoid stepping on your own d**k." John was a bit taken aback and asked what he meant. Stan went on to say that he did a great sales job to the outside customer but he failed to sell inside. He asked John what the operations and planning staff must have felt like when they just were told about the order instead of consulting them. John admitted that they mustn't have felt any ownership of the project, and that in fact, they could have gotten pretty excited about this great new order. Stan complimented him for his understanding of this, and reinforced John's ability as a salesman...he restated that selling inside was harder than selling outside, and that was his next challenge...to avoid that kind of d**k-stepping again. This conversation was held while walking around the plant.

4.2   Analysis

This might seem to some like a pretty crude conversation–but it has certain interesting assumptions. First, Stan assumes that everybody is trying hard and to improve his or her performance just needs a different way to look at the situation. When he coaches, he wants to get the person's attention, but he also wants to use the vernacular to be firm but funny. By asking questions instead of telling John what to do, he was able to get John to see how he could do better next time. And, by assuring John that he had the skill to do better, (he could sell outside, now he just needed to sell inside), he made success seem likely. Stan also says that he usually holds difficult conversations while walking around–sometimes outside. He says that this helps to dissipate energy and puts the conversation on 'neutral' territory–actually emphasizing the mutual territory of the plant operations rather than positioning the conversation in his office or that of the employee. Table 3 is how this case looks in our framework.

Table 3. Supervisor as Coach

Process	Supervisor as Coach
- communication behavior	give and get advice; coach assumes greater understanding and wisdom
- roles and relationships	coach-performer
- feelings toward one another	performer expected to respect "elder" coach
- initiation and organization of comm activities	problem identified, then coach solves and seeks opportunity to share solution
- setting	private; where and when coach finds opportunity
Outcomes	
- understanding and perspective	view of whole or parts depends highly on coach; performer's understanding and view expected to change
- alternatives (divergence)	alternatives may be explored by coach before meeting with performer
- action (convergence)	performer expected to comply
- capacity	depends on success of the interaction

4.3 Alternative

While the coaching seemed to be effective in this case, the practice it represents lends itself to making false assumptions, predetermining solutions without knowledge of details, reduced listening, even to potential accusations of harassment given the language employed. If the advice was not right on, then the performer may lose rather than gain confidence and may develop an attitude of resentment toward management that thinks it has all the answers without knowing situations fully, leading toward just "doing the job" (and seeking a position elsewhere). The mindset of "I have greater wisdom" without healthy skepticism/humility, and using crude language (like using humor when you don't really know the audience) is risky. We suggest that the coach assuming that s/he has an incomplete understanding of the situation, genuinely listening, and avoiding crude language would have a better chance of success over a wider range of instances

5.   LEADERSHIP IN CHANGE

5.1   Before

An agricultural research center at a top university was known for its brilliant
scientists and wonderful facilities, but it suffered from years of
mismanagement. Many grant opportunities were missed, budgets were sloppy
and not allocated fairly, and the researchers often got into petty arguments
with each other over facilities and support staff. Communication and
cooperation among the 5 different research labs throughout the State was
virtually nonexistent, morale was low, and they were losing their motivation
and "edge". The staff was worried that the decrease in funding would mean
that people would lose their jobs, or that some of the labs would be closed and
operations would be consolidated at the main university campus.

When the 7th Director in 8 years resigned in frustration, the scientists and
university administration decided to hire somebody who was more of a
business manager than a scientist. In her previous career, Linda, the 42-year-
old new director, held management positions in a pharmaceutical
manufacturing plant, a call center for a bank, and the claims processing group
in a big insurance company. Her skill, in a nutshell, was in bringing order to
chaos – in re-designing positions and reporting structures and adopting new
technologies to enhance productivity.

Linda approached the communication-planning department at the
university, and they developed a series of "Road Trips" for her. Linda
provided the communication department with reams of data about the genetics
research industry, predictions about how changes in federal and state funding
would impact them, and made sure that the overall message would be that
most people would retain their jobs, although their jobs or locations might
need to change.

Linda went out with the University President, and made presentations at
local offices–trying to hit the majority of the employees at each location by
repeating each presentation at different times to cover different shifts. They
used very slick electronic graphics to back up their presentation, and their
speeches were smooth–the result of lots of coaching and practice. They
presented a clear plan for re-structuring management in the labs, and an
outline for a new online budgeting and procurement system that would
expedite some of the day-to-day roadblocks that they'd been experiencing
when managing their grant monies. Clearly, they felt, they had demonstrated
their commitment to improving employee communication and morale by
investing significant money and time, not only Linda's but also that of the
President.

After the presentations, Linda hoped for the best... but what she heard from the regional directors was that employee comments had gone from merely dissatisfied to positively cynical and hostile. What happened here?

5.2 Analysis

To Linda, communication meant presenting information. She certainly did that, and the employees at the research sites "got the message. It wasn't a bad message overall, considering the uncertainty of the situation. But employees didn't want to be talked to, they wanted to be *listened to*. And they understood that even the most well-informed, honest predictions for the future were likely to be wrong in the end. While Linda and the President wanted to allay fears by acting all knowing, what they really did was to make themselves appear threatened, dishonest, and unapproachable. In terms of our framework, Table 4 illustrates the situation.

Table 4. Leadership in Change

Process	Leadership in Change
- communication behavior	leader presents information, sells messages, seeks no input
- roles and relationships	speaker-listener
- feelings toward one another	lack of respect; distrust; workers feel they are being coerced
- initiation and organization of comm activities	convened meetings; attendance required
- setting	formal meeting spaces
Outcomes	
- understanding and perspective	management has naive view of whole and tacit assumptions; perspectives further divided
- alternatives (divergence)	single answer
- action (convergence)	action either stalled or mandated
- capacity	weaker creative capacity; weaker ability to pursue common goals

5.3 Alternative

Here is how this situation might have played out very differently. Suppose that in her first week, Linda buried herself in the paperwork of the organization, learning everything she could about its current projects and operational processes. In her second week, she just walked around the research center talking and observing people. Finally, in her third week, she set up a meeting of all 70 of the staff–from the most senior researcher to the part-time cleaning crew.

Everybody expected that she'd outline her plans for re-structuring the center. People anticipated the meeting with a combination of hope and fear: would this just be another stupid plan made by somebody who didn't know the first thing about genetics research? Instead, the theme of her speech was "life energy". She shared with them what brings energy to her life, and how her approach to life changed dramatically when her 3-year-old son was tragically killed in an accident. She talked about her fascination with growing orchids, her hobby. And she exhorted them to bring energy to their jobs and to seek inspiration in novel places.

After the meeting, people were surprised. There were no plans announced. She didn't even talk about any of their projects. All they could remember was "life energy", that phrase she kept repeating. But somehow, they felt refreshed, even restored. What makes a "restoring word" and is inspiration a major work-product for leaders?

Nichols (1987) describes the convergence of research in therapeutic and religious communication with regard to the elements of message structures that lead to significant insight or inspiration. Across disciplines, the characteristics of powerfully inspirational messages are: optimally self-involving, ambiguous, and intense. These generally involve a powerfully meaningful narrative (often in the context of a personal, mundane story), a metaphoric process with tension between representation and embellishment, and the context of talking not about ordinary things but rather the "limit" or unusually powerful experiences of life.

The alternative strategy described here represents an initiation of conversation. The new director shares a message along with a personal narrative that gives listeners a rich understanding of the experiences that have led her to her views. She doesn't presume to know others' views and feelings, and doesn't act upon assumptions that have not been checked. We suggest that this type of initial move, not necessarily the particular message, but the choice to inspire rather than manage, could have more positive results in terms of subsequent relationships of management with employees and the restructuring process.

6.   THE ORIENTATION

6.1   Before

A global manufacturing company in the plastics industry has established a sophisticated program for recruiting and training those who they hope to be their future corporate leaders. Each year, they recruit about 50 of the most talented engineers from top universities, and enter them into their Technical Leaders Circle (TLC).

The program had originally been structured as an elaborate curriculum of 15 courses that the new recruits would take while they also rotated among three different job assignments in their first 18 months. After that time, they would be placed into their first permanent position, based on their performance in the courses, their preferences for work assignments, and the needs of the company. The company made what it felt to be Herculean efforts to orient the TLCers to the company; they had brochures on each division, set up meetings with presentations made by all the division chiefs and vice-presidents, and put them through rigorous courses on company policies and practices. The aim here was to retain these high-powered young engineers, and make their entry into the company as smooth as possible. However, after several years of doing this, they found that the turn-over was high–and typically, the engineers were leaving for jobs where the training and development systems were not nearly as sophisticated, the eventual opportunities not as good, the working conditions and budgets worse, and the salaries were often lower. What was happening here?

6.2   Analysis

Actually, the new recruits were being over-trained–and the perception turned out to be that the company was trying to mold them tightly into its culture and system of operation. They felt unchallenged. Table 5 reflects the situation within our framework.

6.3   Alternative

Here is how this case actually changed with a totally different approach. Instead of thinking of the recruits as "empty buckets" to be filled with knowledge, some new metaphors were suggested. An orientation system was built around the metaphors of the recruits being "fresh eyes" and "investigative reporters". They were presented with some actual business challenges facing the company and told to go out and provide a new perspective on them. Through interviews, examination of processes, and observations, the new recruits learned how the company was now set up–and what its policies and theories of operation were. But instead of being told to learn that system, the TLCers were asked to *challenge* the system–ask *why* things were being done the way they were, and suggest new alternatives, where appropriate. They were also asked to document interesting projects and approaches, and to share them in dialogue sessions with top management.

The result: greater satisfaction among the trainees, higher retention, and a lot of value by their participation in the program. Managers who used to feel that training and talking to TLCers was an obligation that had little direct value to them now were excited about a relationship where they could provide some mentoring, but also get some innovative new ideas. The TLCers became an important new mechanism for sharing knowledge within the organization, and the excitement of authentic communication and problem solving was readily apparent. Here behaviors based on the underlying values of conversation–mutual respect, equality, careful listening, valuing different perspectives, and examining assumptions–clearly enhanced performance.

Table 5. Orientation

Process	Orientation
- communication behavior	present information—lots of it; expect reception
- roles and relationships	trainer-trainee; indoctrination
- feelings toward one another	company provides for (in debt) employee and expects loyalty (payback)
- initiation and organization of comm activities	employees selected and assigned; formal program
- setting	formal meeting room(s)
Outcomes	
- understanding and perspective	molded to single view; individual attitudes and perspectives discouraged
- alternatives (divergence)	single view promoted
- action (convergence)	employees expected to buy into and act upon culture and system of operations
- capacity	individual and therefore collective creative capacity reduced; "cult-like" loyalty encouraged

7. CONCLUSIONS

Communication is a key strategic factor in organizational success and deserves careful attention. While formal conversation events may not be practical, small shifts in typical processes based on the underlying values of conversation can be made. We suggest that these have potential to contribute to company goals.

REFERENCES

Banathy, B.H., 1996. Conversation in social systems design. *Educational Technology,* **36**(1): 39-41.

Bohm, D., 1990. *On Dialogue.* David Bohm Seminars, Ojai, CA.

Fitz-enz, J., 2000. *The ROI of Human Capital: Measuring the Economic Value of Employee Performance.* AMACOM, New York.

Gayeski, D., 2000. *Managing the Communication Function: Capturing Mindshare for Organizational Performance.* San Francisco: International Association of Business Communicators.

Gayeski, D., in press. From communication audits to information system analytics. *Communication World.*

Jenlink, P., and Carr, A.A., 1996. Conversation as a medium for change in education. *Educational Technology,* **36**(1): 31-38.

Nichols, J.R., 1987. *The Restoring Word: Preaching as Pastoral Communication.* Harper & Row, San Francisco, CA.

Yankelovich, D., 1999. *The Magic of Dialogue: Transforming Conflict Into Cooperation.* Simon and Schuster, New York.

Chapter 20

Conversation and the Development of Learning Communities

KATHRYN KINNUCAN-WELSCH* and PATRICK M. JENLINK[#]* *
University of Dayton*; *Stephen F. Austin State University*[#] *and International Systems Institute***

1. INTRODUCTION

The process of designing social systems, including educational systems, is most likely to contribute to sustainable systems if the context for the design process is that of community. From a systems perspective, the people who serve the system and those who are served and affected by the system constitute the designing community (Banathy, 1996). The concept of design of professional learning communities for educators is particularly critical as we face the 21st century, given the historically dismal prospects for meaningful, substantive, professional development for teachers and other practitioners (Wilson & Berne, 1999). The purpose of this chapter is to examine the role and nature of conversation in designing professional development communities for teachers and other educators.

The context of our exploration is a two-year research/professional development initiative in Southeast Michigan where we (Kinnucan-Welsch and Jenlink) worked with a consortium of twenty-five school districts to design professional development activities related to creating and sustaining inquiry-based communities. Design conversations were an integral aspect of the process, and exploring the conversations themselves provides a unique lens through which to understand the evolution of system design.

For the purposes of this chapter, we will first explore conversation as a medium for designing professional learning communities as human activity systems. We then examine the concept of community from a variety of perspectives, including sociological, anthropological, and philosophical, and connect professional learning among educators with the notion of dialogic, inquiry, and design communities. We then draw from our experiences as participants in design conversation to construct a case study of professional learning community design. As a final note, we offer our reflections on the connections between a designing community and a

Dialogue as a Means of Collective Communication, Edited by Banathy and Jenlink
Kluwer Academic/Plenum Publishers, New York 2005

community for professional learning as we experienced in the professional development initiative described in this chapter.

2.   CONVERSATION AS DESIGN MEDIUM

Social systems design, as Banathy (1996) explains, "is a process that carries a stream of shared meaning by a free flow of discourse among the stakeholders who seek to create a new system" (p. 213). In order to understand the communicative nature and mediational importance of the design conversation, "various modes of social discourse are explored to search for the mode that is the most appropriate to systems design" (p. 213). As such, these different modes of social discourse serve as a medium for various design activities within the design community. Examples of the different modes of discourse include inquiry discourse (Banathy, 1996; Burbules, 1993; Isaacs, 1996), critical discourse (Burbles, 1993; Carr, 1997; Giroux & McLaren, 1986; Lambert, 1995), sustaining discourse (Hollingsworth, 1994; Lambert, 1995), debriefing conversations (Jenlink, Reigeluth, Carr, & Nelson, 1996), conversations with contexts (Banathy, 1996; Jenlink, 1995) and dialogue conversation which serves as a medium for emotional and cultural change (de Mare, 1991).

The root of the word conversation means, "to turn together." Conversation, then, is people speaking together, engaged in reflection and deliberation. This reflection and deliberation enables participants to "consciously and unconsciously weigh out different views, finding some with which they agree, and others that they dislike" (Isaacs, 1993, p. 35). As Berger and Luckman (1966) suggest, people engage in conversation for the purpose of coordinating their separate interpretations of experience to establish shared meanings, therefore

> the most important vehicle of reality-maintenance is conversation....At the same time that the conversational apparatus ongoingly maintains reality, it ongoingly *modifies* it....Thus the fundamental reality-maintaining fact is the continuing use of the same language to objectify unfolding biographical experience. In the widest sense, all who employ this same language are reality-maintaining others. (pp. 172-173)

Conversation, by its very nature, is relational. Whether it is dialogue, discussion, debate, or design discourse (Banathy, 1996; Jenlink & Carr, 1996), it embodies relationships as a foundation of the interaction between one individual and another. In this sense, relation is the foundation of conversation. Likewise, relation is the foundation of an ethic of care. An ethic of care "is fundamentally concerned with how human beings meet and treat one another. It is not unconcerned with individual rights, the common good, or community traditions, but it de-emphasizes these concepts and recasts them in terms of relations" (Noddings, 1993, p. 45).

Martin Buber (1970) in his explication of the "principle of relatedness" acknowledged two modes of encountering or relating to other entities. He identified these as the I-Thou mode, which is the way of relation, and the I-It mode in which we observe others or listen to what they have to say by assimilating it to prestructures, or preselected ways of interpreting and understanding the phenomena we experience. The I-It mode is instrumental in the sense that as we encounter, through conversation and experience, events and phenomena, we appropriate materials and ideas to be used for our purposes. However, the I-thou mode is both ethical and spiritual, acknowledging the value of relation between "self" and others, thereby acknowledging the ethical responsibility one has for helping another and for the betterment of the human conditions of others. The "principle of relatedness" gives way to "betweenness" that exists in and through the I-Thou mode of interacting or meeting other entities.

"Betweenness," by its nature and caring orientation, is a form of social discourse that connects one's self with others, the I-Thou, and enables the building and sustaining of communities that serve to transform the conditions in which individuals live and work. These communities are characterized by a caring relation that serves as a foundation for the social structure of the community, and by the nature of the social discourse that pervades and gives substance to the relatedness of individuals comprising the community. Caring, like "betweenness" is a form of social discourse. As such, it is concerned with "affirming and encouraging the best in others" (Noddings, 1992, p. 25) and involves an "orientation of deep concern that carries us out of ourselves and into the lives, despairs, struggles, and hopes of others" (Noddings, 1994, p. ix-x).

Other types of social discourse, such as discussion, debate, dialogue, and design discourse, may be critically examined and the nature or purpose of the discourse discerned by the type of relation that is present and supported. Where an ethic of care is applied as in "care as a moral orientation" then the social discourse can be said to be a moral discourse. Social discourse, such as dialogue or design conversation, when guided by caring helps to establish conditions in which participants seek to address issues of social justice, equity, and inequalities, and wherein participants recognize "deep and perhaps irremovable differences–differences which counsel against sweeping solutions that affect people's lives directly and preclude their effective use of self-chosen strategies" (Noddings, 1999, p. 19).

2.1   Conversation as Medium

Conversation as design medium arises from an understanding that dialogue and design conversations give form to the reciprocal processes of systems design that make up the patterns of collective consciousness, of community. "The conversations serve as the medium for the reciprocal processes that enable [participants] to construct meanings toward a common purpose" (Lambert, 1995, p. 83). As a medium for design, the primary benefit of conversation "is in creating and maintaining the conditions for more conversation" (Burbules, 1993, p. 127). Relatedly, conversation serves as a medium through which participants connect to create a collective consciousness that enables a "community of mind" to form.

Conversation, as a medium, also contributes to the building of community. In this sense, community-building discourse is one of reciprocally engaging participants in "...mutual and dynamic interaction and exchange of ideas and concerns," seeking to create maturity in the community that usually "emerges from opportunities for meaning-making in sustainable communities over time" (Lambert, 1995, p. 95). Community building discourse provides a forum for exploring individual and collective concerns, examining common experiences, developing shared meaning, identifying core ideals, values, beliefs—what is *sacred*, constructing a change community language, and creating "community of mind" essential to a design community (Jenlink, 1996). Dialogue is essential to the collaborative process of community building. In a sense, design community is a discourse community, and the power of conversation is in its ability to weave "webs of relationships" among all stakeholders in an intersubjective fabric of cultural creativity.

2.2   Design Conversation

Design conversation is a system of discourses giving rise to a meta-conversation process. One definition of design conversation is provided by Banathy (1996) who suggests that design conversation "combines two specific modes of dialogue, namely, "generative" and strategic," as the most appropriate modes of social discourse in design inquiry" (Banathy, 1996, p. 214). Generative dialogue is viewed as that discourse which generates a collective worldview. Stakeholders engage in constructing shared meaning and understanding. Strategic dialogue is different in that it focuses on specific tasks and is applied in finding specific solutions in social design settings.

Jones (1984) offers the following in way of understanding design conversation when he explains the design process as

> unlearning what we know of what exists, of what we call the "status quo," to the point where we are able to lose our preconceptions sufficiently to understand the life, and the lives, for which we design, and where we are aware of the ways in which new things added to the world, can change the ways we see it. (p. 172)

Design conversation acknowledges the need for a "users language" which implies paying attention to actual users, that is people "in situ," people in the here and now, each with his or her own history, and his or her own peculiarities. Such peculiarities have to be transformed into resources for action. User languages will emphasize differences between actors, in terms of intended use" (de Zeeuw, 1993, p. 13). "The term "user" means the users of the enculturation learning systems, those who want to become competent in design and eventually will become designers in designing their own systems" (Banathy, 1996, pp. 245-246). Systems design language–the words, concepts, meanings informed by the philosophy, theory, and practical experiences of systems–provides the user with a language for communicating within and through the design conversation, and change process.

Returning to the conversational nature of design conversation, it is important to recognize that the systems design process requires multiple forms of conversation which enable the participants to access as many dimensions of the design process as is possible. This may include such types of conversation as dialogue, community building, sustaining, inquiring, and conversations with *self* and *context*.

Incorporating different types of conversation, design conversation is an ongoing discourse that moves through different phases of communicative interaction. Participants are "caught up" in the ongoing flow of interchange. At various times this flow and interchange can change its tone, its purpose, and its direction through choices of its participants. Recognizing how new and varied "moves" are "appropriate at some points, and not at others, is an important part of how one can remain within the spirit of dialogical relation while being flexible about just what that entails from moment to moment" (Burbules, 1993, p. 129). Key characteristics of design conversation include authenticity, sustainability, uniqueness, personal and collective learning, and ethics of design.

2.2.1   Authenticity

Design conversation is authentic if it is "...carried out by the stakeholders of the system. An authentic design has to build on the individual and collective values, aspirations, and ideas of those who serve the system and who are served and affected by it" (Banathy, 1996, p. 228).

2.2.2   Sustainability

A design conversation is sustainable only if it "...is accomplished and put in place by the creative, collective, and unconstrained participation and contribution by all people in the system" (Banathy, 1996, p. 229). When stakeholders make these types of contributions, the participation enables people to understand their system as well as their role and relationship to the system. This in turn enables the creation of like-mindedness or a *community of mind* that generates genuine respect for each other as the process develops fellowship. Participation and contribution by stakeholders which enables sustainability takes place at a deep level of commitment which gives way to a conscious or "deep" community, a consciousness essential to designing a new social system and which represents the stakeholders individual and collective values, ideas and decisions (Banathy, 1996).

2.2.3   Uniqueness

Design conversation must convey a rich uniqueness that is sensitive to certain conditions. If we aspire to create viable systems, the conversational process must understand the uniqueness of the human activity systems which includes the systemic context, the nature of the system to be designed, the individual and collective readiness and capability of the people involved, the resources available, the design situation, the values and world views of the designing community, and time, space, and complexity factors (Banathy, 1996).

2.2.4   Personal and Collective Development and Learning

Design conversation, as the medium for systems, must provide opportunity for and contribute to personal and collective development, capacity building, and learning. By engaging in design, the stakeholders, as individual and collective, have benefit of the design community as forum and context for collective involvement as a learning community. Engaging in systems design enables stakeholders to participate in double-loop and triple-loop learning (Banathy, 1996; Isaacs, 1993).

2.2.5   Ethics

Banathy (1996) suggests that the design conversation can

> be termed to be ethical only if it enables the self-determination of the stakeholders and respects their autonomy and uniqueness. Design should be self-guided and self-directed by the users of the system...The ethical and liberating involvement...is based on the understanding that we have the right and responsibility for the design of our lives and for the design of the systems in which we live. (p. 230)

The ethical nature of conversation figures largely into both the path that conversation follows as well as whether the conversation takes the participants on a journey that conjoins them into common purpose and enables them toward the creation of something new.

3. PROFESSIONAL LEARNING WITHIN THE CONTEXT OF COMMUNITY

3.1 Community as a Concept

The notion of community has captured the attention of philosophers (Buber, 1965; Dewey, 1916/1966; Ladd, 1998a, 1998b; Noddings, 1996), sociologists (Cohen, 1985/1995), and anthropologists (Geertz, 1973). It is our intent in this chapter to explore community through these lenses so that the connections we make between community in general and design community can enhance the understanding of how design communities and the design process for professional development are related. Ladd (1998a), speaking from an ethical perspective, reminds us of the difficulty in capturing the essence of community, from even a singular perspective: "Community is truly an anomalous concept" (p. 5). The elusive nature associated with construct of community has been noted by Hamilton (1985/1995), who, in his opening comments to Cohen's sociological treatise on community, commented: "The concept of community has been one of the most compelling and attractive themes in modern social science, and at the same time one of the most elusive to define" (p. 7). Despite these caveats, some attempts to describe characteristics of community may be useful in our discussion of design conversation and professional development within the contest of community.

Cohen (1985/1995) set the stage for his argument that community is symbolically constructed as follows:

> A reasonable interpretation of the word's [community] use would seem to imply two related suggestions: that the members of a group of people (a) have something in common with each other, which (b) distinguishes them in a significant way from the members of other putative groups. 'Community' thus seems to imply simultaneously both similarity and difference. The word thus expresses a relational idea: the opposition of one community to others or to other social entities. (p. 12)

It is in learning the culture of a community, and the social ways of being, that members become socialized into a community. Dewey (1916/1966) recognized the importance of communication, experience, and education in this process, particularly in the development of communities based upon democratic ideals of responsibility.

Noddings (1996), however, reminds us that the essence of what defines a community, how and why the members relate to one another, can also result in the dark side of community, "its tendencies toward parochialism, conformity, exclusion, assimilation, distrust (or hatred) of outsiders, and coercion" (p. 258). This dark side can be seen in the pressure to conform to the norms of the community, such as the world saw in the rise of fascism in the 1930s. Noddings reminds us that we can learn from those communities grounded in relation and an understanding of the Other. She comments, " I still do things–*must* do things–but my moral agency is in a deep sense subject to the Other" (p. 262).

It is within the context of the relation with Other that perhaps we find a conceptualization of community that encompasses a multitude of perspectives. Buber (1965) developed the notion of I-Thou relational dynamic in contrast to I-It. As Maurice Friedman commented in the introduction to Buber's work:

> I-Thou is a relationship of openness, directness, mutuality, and presence. It may be between man and man, but it may also take place with a tree, a cat, a fragment of mica, a work of art—and through all of these with God, the "eternal Thou" in whom the parallel lines of relations meet. I-It, in contrast, is the typical subject-object relationship in which one knows and uses other persons or things without knowing them to exist for itself in their uniqueness. (p. xiv)

It is the I-Thou relationship that characterizes community from Buber's point of view. Buber contrasts community; a binding together based in relationships and confirmation of life lived towards one another, with collectivity, a bundling together of organized atrophy of personal existence (p. 31).

When we conceive of community as the essence of the I-Thou relationships characteristic of members, then the concerns about the dark side of community and the questions of whether or not community can be embraced as an ethical concept become irrelevant. It is in the deep binding of individuals who see themselves in relation to Other that the meaning of community becomes crystallized. Ford Slack (1995) refers to the importance of *communities of difference*, and that communities of difference are relationship-centered, grounded in the interdependence of one community with another.

We now turn to examples of how educators engage in professional learning in community, dialogic communities, inquiry communities, and design communities. Benne (1990) offers a description of learning within community in which those persons involved "view learning and relearning not primarily as cultural transmission, but as a future-oriented process of personal and cultural renewal" (p. 68). We examine professional learning in these communities through the lens of personal renewal.

3.2   Learning within Dialogic Communities

Dialogue as a form of discourse is at the heart of community. It is, from Buber's perspective, the essence of the I-Thou relationship. But it is also useful to turn to others for a description of dialogue, and the nature of learning within dialogic communities. David Bohm (1996) has offered to the world one of the foremost and often-cited articulations of dialogue as an entity. He suggested "The picture or image... is of a *stream of meaning* flowing among and through us and between us. This will make possible a flow of meaning in the whole group. Out of which may emerge some new understanding. It's something new, which may not have been in the starting point at all" (p. 6).

It is this stream of meaning contributing to a new understanding that is the essence of a dialogic community. As Jenlink (2000) has noted, "dialogue is crucial to bringing the participants to a level of collective and transformational consciousness" (p. 7). Isaacs (1999) in applying the principles of dialogue to business communities identified four practices that support the evolution of a dialogic community: 1) suspending taken-for-granted ways of operating, 2) respecting the ecology of relationships that develop in and around the organization, 3) listening, and 4) paying attention to the central voice or story of the group or organization (p. 340).

Some researchers have explored the notion of dialogic communities in educational settings. Practitioner inquiry community is one example, and will be examined in the next section of the chapter. Dialogue is seen by many as one type of conversation (Jenlink & Carr, 1996), and Hollingsworth (1994) notes the importance of conversation in learning communities: "collaborative and sustained conversation became the exchange and the reformulation of ideas, intimate talk, and reconstructive questions" (p. 6).

Classrooms as dialogic communities are particularly intriguing, given the historically teacher-dominated nature of discourse in classrooms. Pourdavood and Fleener (1997) found in their research that "opportunities to share ideas, take risks, articulate and challenge beliefs, and examine classroom practices are necessary for teacher change and are facilitated by dialogic teacher communities" (p. 416).

It is in the spirit of the possibility of creating something new that we now turn to an exploration of learning within inquiry communities.

3.3. Learning within Inquiry Communities

Design is disciplined inquiry. Relatedly, communities of professional learners engage in inquiry, thus creating inquiry communities. The concept of inquiry community has received some attention in the literature for the past four decades. The principles and processes embedded within inquiry communities have been articulated for different contexts in which educators find themselves: as administrators (Lambert, et al., 1995; Sergiovanni, 1994), as teachers (Cochran-Smith & Lytle, 1999; Wilson & Berne, 1999), as teacher and administrator educators (Jenlink, 1997; Kinnucan-Welsch, Seery, Adams, Bowman, & Joseph, 2000; Lieberman,

1992). The focus in this chapter will be on teacher inquiry communities, although we believe that the profession of education would be enhanced if the multiple stakeholders of educational communities would engage in sustained design conversation. As Jenlink, Kinnucan-Welsch, and Odell (1996) have noted,

> Given that the traditional state of professional development is one of fragmentation, we are suggesting, as Benne (1990) has, that we must move beyond the bundling of practitioners as collectives to a new level of consciousness wherein those educators who touch the lives of children are connected in meaningful relationships of responsible action to form community. (pp. 79-80)

Cochran-Smith and Lytle (1999) have developed the construct *inquiry-as-stance* to engage educators in understanding the professional development of teachers within the complex and ill-structured domains of teaching, teacher knowledge, and practice. As they note, "Teachers and student teachers who take an inquiry stance work within inquiry communities to generate local knowledge, envision and theorize their practice, and interpret and interrogate the theory and research of others (p. 289). Discourse is one of the salient elements of inquiry communities from this perspective as teachers and student teachers "engage in joint construction of knowledge through conversation and other forms of analysis an interpretation" (p. 294). Shared inquiry into practice within the context of community, then, is a powerful and enduring element of professional development. Many others have noted how transforming inquiry within a community can be.

Craig (1995) described knowledge communities as places where educators can feel safe, where their voices are heard, and where the personal practical knowledge (Clandinin & Connelly, 1996) jointly constructed by educators can serve to inform the profession as a whole. Kinnucan-Welsch and Jenlink (1998) described professional learning within communities where the professional learning was focused on principles of constructivist pedagogy.

Inquiry communities offer educators an opportunity to engage in sustained conversation and dialogue in an exploration of "what might be" in our educational systems. It is in the focused dialogue of a future state that design communities offer what Parker Palmer calls pockets of possibilities.

Many educators have come to recognize that disciplined inquiry and sustained conversation, i.e. dialogue, within communities of inquiry are essential to an educational system that is responsive, regenerative and guided by design. In communities of inquiry, the inquiry takes on a dialogic relationship between participants, and the dialogic relationship enables the inquiry to be guided by a common purpose and collective voice. It is to the nature of design communities that we now turn our attention.

3.4   Learning within Design Communities

Systems design is a disciplined inquiry approach to creating a new f(
(Banathy, 1996). Design conversation is a medium in which participants
learn through their active and authentic engagement in the discourse.
Systems design of human activity systems, like professional learning
communities, is recognized as a type of learning–design learning. Design
learning is a function of a designing community, that is, a community that
engages in designing, through inquiry-oriented processes, its own learning
activities. As Banathy (1996) noted, of the designing community, it is a
"social structure of unique individuals who play specific roles by which
they contribute to the overall design" (p. 236). The design of learning
activities by the community members brings the community together in
conversation and disciplined inquiry, focusing the energy and intention of
the community inward on its own growth, development, and sustaining
actions.

The challenge of a design community, much the same as the challenge
of a professional learning community is to learn. However, with the
challenge to learn comes the realization that design learning is a journey
"laden with risk" and often results in "the consequence of introducing
disequilibrium" into the community by the pursuit of design.

Designing learning for the community requires a stance of authenticity
as a community. The challenge then, as Banathy (1996) suggested, is "to
learn to become an authentic community of scholarly practitioners and
practicing scholars, to apply what we learn in all aspects of our lives, and
help others to learn to develop their own authentic community" (p. 239).
Learning within the design community is about an ethic of design that
recognizes the importance and responsibility of the community to enable
the active participation of members, therefore the design of learning
activities must always consider the unique nature and needs of each
individual as it undertakes design.

Learning within design communities occurs at many levels. Learning
occurs when the community self-critically examines its own needs,
determining what practices need to change or need to be acquired. Learning
occurs when the community, acting on its needs, engages in a disciplined
inquiry to design the activity systems that are responsive to these needs.
Learning occurs when the community members take part in the activity
systems, which it has designed, such as professional development activities
like study groups and or inquiry communities. One might reflect that
learning in the design community is really design, and that design is really
learning. There is a reciprocal nature to design and learning, so that as
participants conjoin to design through disciplined inquiry and dialogue,
individual and collective learning occur as the design process cognitively
connects individuals in fostering new understandings and construct new
knowledge.

4. ONE CASE STUDY OF PROFESSIONAL LEARNING COMMUNITY DESIGN

In this section, we now turn to a case study of our experiences over a two-year period as participants in designing a professional learning community. The context for our design conversations was a professional development initiative for teachers entitled *Staff Development 2000* (SD 2000), an eighteen-month professional development experience funded by the Michigan Department of Education under the US Department of Education Goals 2000 authorization. The funds were awarded to the Wayne County Alliance for Math and Science, a consortium of twenty-five districts in an urban area of Southeast Michigan, USA.

A design team comprised of a project director (Cherie Cornick), process facilitation and study group facilitator (Jenlink), and an evaluator (Kinnucan-Welsch) facilitated the SD 2000 initiative. The role of the design team was to design the professional development experiences, which focused on study group method as an alternative approach to professional development and process facilitation of study groups. Also integral to the SD 2000 initiative was the integration of technology, both as a focus topic for study groups and as a communications infrastructure for the overall initiative.

Participants in the SD 2000 initiative included a group of teachers and administrators interested in learning about how study groups and facilitation of study groups could offer a new approach to professional development and teacher learning. The educators who took an active part in the initiative formed three tiers of participants. Each group, or tier, is described below.

The first tier included the design team members (Cornick, Jenlink, and Kinnucan-Welsch) who provided facilitated assistance to all participants throughout the initiative. The design team members wrote the grant funding the eighteen-month initiative and collaboratively designed the learning activities supporting the evolution of facilitation as a part of study group method. The design team members were active participants in the initiative from the initial conceptualization of the grant through dissemination activities.

The second tier of participants included the design team plus those individuals invited to study and learn how to facilitate teacher professional development through study groups. This group was comprised of twelve educators. Included were six classroom teachers, two lead teachers responsible for supporting professional development in their own district, two technology consultants, one administrator, and one intermediate school district professional development consultant. The invitation to participate was advertised by a flier distributed through the math and science alliance of which Cherie is director. In reality, most of the participants had experienced previous contact with Cherie through other professional development venues. The second tier met for the first time as a group during a retreat, which served as an initial immersion into the initiative on August 17-18, 1997. The second tier of participants was active from the retreat in August 1997 through the writing retreat in June 1998.

In order to learn about study groups and facilitation, the second tier participants were formed into a study group, or a professional learning community, focusing on facilitation as it related to study groups. It was the design of the development of this learning community that is the focus of this case study. During the course of the initiative, this core group became known as the Thursday Night Study Group (because they met on alternating Thursdays) or Facilitation Study Group. The exploration of facilitation by this group followed a path of inquiry and study guided by questions like "What is facilitation?", "What is a study group?", "What is the role of facilitation in study groups?", and "How do study groups contribute to professional development?" This inquiry was in preparation for the facilitation of study groups for a third tier of participants.

The third tier of participants included educators who formed nine study groups, each convened and facilitated by members of the second-tier study group. These newly convened study groups ranged in size from five to fourteen members and focused on a variety of topics. The nine study groups met regularly from February until June 1998, with the exception of one group, which began in January. The second tier study group members who were facilitating these groups continued to meet as their own study group to engage in dialogue, reflection, and examination of the facilitation and study group processes from a perspective of their own experiences.

It is the design of Staff Development 2000 as a professional learning community that is the substance of this case study. We will structure the case study in alignment with the spirals of the design of a professional development activity system (Banathy, 1996; Jenlink, Kinnucan-Welsch, & Odell, 1996).

As members of the design team, Cherie, Pat and Katie engaged in design discourse throughout the life of the SD 2000 initiative. Most of our conversation occurred in face-to-face meetings, but given that each member of the design team lived some distance from each other, we often engaged in phone conversations as well as electronic mail exchanges. The design of SD 2000 emerged from our purposeful conversations to incorporate all elements of educational systems design: core ideals and values, specifications, functions, enabling systems, and contexts. Core ideals and values represent the very essence of the system.

As Banathy (1996) commented, the core ideals and values represent what the system is about and what purposes and shared commitment are held among the stakeholders of the system. The specifications give clarification and guidance to the evolution of the system. The functions refer to those aspects that enable the system to attain the core purpose and mission of the system. The enabling system gives support to the functions.

4.1   Core Ideals and Values

The purpose of SD 2000 was to create a professional learning community based upon principles of inquiry and practitioner self study. This learning community was developed around several study groups, which were designed to build capacity for extending professional development opportunities throughout the consortium districts. Furthermore, we were committed to inquiry-based professional development for teachers that offered members of the learning community an opportunity to develop personal practical knowledge embedded within their own practice. In following these principles, we were challenging the assumptions about the current structures and practices in schools that alienate teachers from their own craft knowledge. Core to all of this was the facilitation of the second tier study group, the Thursday Night Group, and the third tier groups that would form during the second half of the project. The vision of these study groups was clear from the beginning conversations:

C: Even the technology part of it is, is secondary to the facilitation and ultimately developing small study groups.

K: Plus the other aspect of this is that teachers do form study groups around those things about which they do want to know more...So, for example, we'll have groups of teachers getting together to talk about reading or writing. Or you'll have groups of teachers to get together to talk about how to bring art into the classroom. Or whatever, where those resources are readily available and teachers feel comfortable in going out and seeking those resources on their own. My sense is, is that there is a barrier.

C: The other thing though, that I guess hit me when we were first talking about study groups, we've got find a way of at least helping them see that this does go beyond just talking about it. I mean, there's some aspect of the things that you talked about Pat, about what they're doing and exposing themselves to each other and creating and, and, what's involved when you really do risk by showing other people what you're doing. And ask for some feedback on it. I want, I'm hoping with at least some of the groups will be able to get to that point. Because I don't want folks to just leave the idea that a study group is just a group of people that just sits and talks about very, very, surface things.

P: Two or three things are kind of popping up in my mind right now. I'm thinking about the need to begin to understand facilitation. Begin to understand process facilitation as a critical part of study groups. As a critical part really of overall process, the grant implementation. Part of what we want to understand, is what is the life of a facilitator like? And what is it, what does it require for this person to have this kind of facilitative capacity. Or the term I use sometimes is the facilitative self. What do we do to help the person to develop the facilitative self? So what we're really suggesting is a way of studying what we do to operationalize this grant and to bring these folks along as facilitators within many different kinds of contexts. And those, to some degree, are defined; those contexts are defined by the type of content that the facilitator will be working with practitioners to address. And we want to, to understand or study ourselves. The three of us and others that will come into that kind of set of people that are a part of this grant. Ultimately at some point we want to look at the transferring of all of this into the classroom. Vis-à-vis, skill or capacity that the teacher brings to the learning environment and what has that done to change or shape some of those? So study group, in and of itself, becomes part of what we want to learn about. And I think it's about the philosophy and practice of study groups, its about facilitating study groups. (design conversation 3/28/97)

The conversation of 3/28/97 was the first design conversation related to the SD 2000 initiative. Pat and Cherie had previously talked about study groups and the potential for professional development in previous contexts, but the grant had been funded, and now we were about designing a human activity system for professional development grounded in study groups and process facilitation. Several core ideals are voiced in this initial conversation.

First, study groups grounded in practitioner inquiry are a viable and valuable context for professional learning. They offer teachers a safe context connected to their own practice within which to learn and grow professionally. The topics of the groups when they formed would be of their choice and, therefore, embedded in their own practice and craft knowledge. As Pat noted, transferring to the classroom was the ultimate goal. Second, facilitation is an important aspect of the success of learning in study groups. The study of facilitation was essential to this initiative, and the questions related to facilitation drove the inquiry and self-study from the beginning.

Related to the importance of study groups and facilitation was the ideal of self-study that was infused throughout the initiative. SD 2000 was designed to be generative process, building on the study of facilitation, the study of professional learning, and the study of practice. Pat referred to the change in mindset about teacher learning that would occur. As he commented during that first conversation: "What we're really looking at is how are we going to learning about ourselves?" Phrases like critical self-examination, deep introspection, reflective processing were common throughout our conversations.

Finally, a core ideal and value grounding the initiative was the hope that SD 2000 would, in some way, improve the conditions of professional learning not just for those involved, but across the districts in the consortium. As Cherie noted on 3/26/97, "I hope that we're able to take from this some things that will help the school districts or that will help other groups who are wanting to do some small group things." Pat extended this thought when he commented on our goal "to scale up the capacity of these 25 districts." Katie took this notion a step further: "So, you're really talking about proactive professional development at all levels. How can we as facilitators learn more about how to facilitate people at being better at their jobs? Let's provide a facilitative context for that. How can school districts and administrators provide that context and then how can teachers be proactive about that?' We all agreed that long-term commitment to professional learning community through study groups was a value embedded within the design.

4.2   Specifications

Two of the specifications of the ideal state of SD 2000 that emerged throughout the design conversation were that, first, the activity system be inquiry driven and, second, be community based. The very foundation of the design was inquiry; inquiry related to how document the personal and professional growth of members within a learning community, inquiry focused on the processes of facilitation, and inquiry into the structures and processes necessary to support community. Pat commented:

> P: I think what self study also connotes, and it ought to carry forward very strongly, is I have to engage in acquiring new knowledge or understanding the knowledge I had differently. But there are elements of facilitation technology that these people will not have, and there's a level of self-assessment. And there's a level of ego, of self-perception you know, that says I've done all that. Been there, done that. And I don't need to learn that again. What we're going to be asking them to do some reading and engaging in dialogue about that reading. We're going to immerse them in ongoing kinds of activities in the sense of facilitators of self-study groups. Keeping a personal or reflective journal. Providing some kind of feedback for the facilitation self study. So that we are all engaged in a public conversation about our experience as facilitators. (design conversation 3/27/97)

As a design team we struggled with how to structure the inquiry into how teachers learn. We knew that keeping a journal throughout the project was important, not only for our documentation purposes, but also as a way for the participants to reflect on their own growth. In our design conversation of 9/9/97, which was a phone conversation due to complex schedules, we talked about how important keeping a journal was to the reflective and inquiry driven nature of SD 2000, and decided to spend part of the Facilitator's meeting on 9/11/97 talking about journals. The meeting of 9/11 was the first meeting for the second tier participants, the Thursday Night Group, after the initial retreat which was held in August. The discussion of the topic of journals during the 9/11 meeting did not go well, and this was reflected in the design phone conversation of 9/23/97: We opened our conversation with a reflection on the meeting:

C: We hadn't really asked the facilitators to reflect on the process itself. What we do teach and what we don't teach. What are some things that make it work. For example, reflect on the rationale for keeping journals. Why do we keep journals in the first place?

P: We might want to consider having the facilitators be involved in a feedback process where we ask them to reflect on where they are. Written reflections on the sessions themselves. These could be half-sheets where they reflect on their experience in the facilitator meeting. Concerns, meaningful learning, notes on facilitation. What kinds of questions do you have related to facilitation after today's meeting? What questions about facilitation were generated in this session? What is the role of facilitation in study groups?

K: We can type these up and either bring them to the next meeting or mail them to the participants before.

P: I think it would be a good idea of they had them before the meeting

C: Everybody is online and we can email the feedback sheets to them

K: That is a great way to use the technology and remain connected, but there might be a problem receiving attachments.

P: Then we could incorporate it right in the body of the email.

C: Try it a number of ways.

P: The two questions could go on the same sheet Reflections of facilitation for one and questions that were generated. A third possibility could be related to professional growth and learning: what did you find meaningful. Maybe do that question every two times.

C: I agree about being specific.

P: Use the responses as a pool or base to generate an assessment tool or evaluation questions.

K: Perhaps focus group questions?

P: They would be great focus group questions.

C: Should the participants identify themselves on these?

P: No. We can also use this process in the context of the study group. What questions are emerging around your role as facilitator? Have them help us generate questions; in effect, they are creating their own evaluation.

The generative nature of our design conversation is illustrated in the above excerpt. We began by exploring the dilemma we faced at the voiced resistance of many of our participants about keeping a journal. This was something we had not expected. Our conversation soon moved in ways, however, that acknowledged what was, and how we could use that information to feedback into the design. We moved from wondering how to encourage the participants to keep reflective journals to designing a feedback system that supported the reflective processing and inquiry of each meeting as well as serve as part of the evaluation, one of the critical enabling systems of the SD 200 design. That feedback system became embedded in each meeting routine.

The other specification that was evident in the design process was that the professional learning context of SD 2000 was community based, and therefore, contextually sensitive. Our goal was that SD 2000 would become a learning community in its own right, and sensitive to the needs of the participants. One of the aspects of professional development that has historically plagued teacher learning is that persons removed from the life in classrooms set the agenda. Our design conversations frequently turned to the need for SD 2000 to be grounded in the needs of the teachers as learners in a community. As Katie commented on 5/19/97 at a design meeting with potential members of the Thursday Night Group, "It's really important that the teachers who are the participants in the study group feel that this is really coming out of their needs. That they have a sense of ownership. That this is driven by their needs rather than the district needs or whatever." Cherie followed this comment at a later point in the conversation emphasizing the need for a sense of community to pervade the group: "This kind of process is so dependent on the group. And if this group does not commit to each other, and to their own growth, then it just doesn't work."

As the group matured, the growing sense of community was evident in the Thursday Night Meetings, in their e-mail messages to their fellow group members, and in our design team conversations. The design of the Thursday Night Meetings was intentional in supporting the development of community. Each meeting was held from 4:30-8:30 p.m., and followed a similar routine. First, the study group members opened with a period of reconnecting and chatting. Participants valued the story telling, sharing their personal experiences, as well as reconnecting with conversations from the previous study group meeting. After the introductory chatting, we distributed the feedback sheets that had been written the meeting before. This provided a context to continue to think and reflect from each previous conversation. We then discussed readings that had been distributed the previous meeting, making connections through dialogue from the reading to evolving conceptions of facilitation and study group process. Dinner was catered about midway through the evening. We closed the meetings with a ten-minute period of written reflection, which was typed and used as feedback to open the next meeting.

In our design conversations we explored how to support the emerging sense of community beyond the Thursday Night meeting conversations. The facilitators always were engaged in lively conversation, but the dilemma the design team faced was how to structure the conversations to focus on developing the knowledge about and processes of study group facilitation. The following excerpt from an e-mail design conversation demonstrates how we designed learning activities to support their continuing professional development. We were planning to meet as a group at the MACUL (acronym for Michigan Association for Computer-Related Technology Users in Learning) conference in Grand Rapids, MI in March.

> Fri, 27 Feb 1998
>
> Hi Pat and Cherie,
>
> Pat, to bring you up to speed—Cherie and I had a conversation 2/26/ before we played with our computers about how we might structure the time with the facilitators in Grand Rapids.
>
> Here is a recap of some ideas.
>
> It is important that we structure a focused discussion, or we might have a free-for-all from which it would be difficult to capture key learnings. Two possibilities for structuring the discussion:
>
> 1. Have each facilitator come with a written reflection for the following prompt that would have been sent out prior to the meeting: Describe an event during your study group in which

you observed something happening, and then felt compelled as facilitator to act in a purposeful and intentional way based on your judgment.

Each person would come prepared to share those. We would then share in dyads, and have the person who is listening practice deep listening and be prepared to ask clarifying questions. After the first person shares, the pair would physically switch seats and roles; reverse the sharing and deep listening/questioning process.

2.   After the facilitators have shared in dyads, we will ask them to come together in groups of four. Have them reflect on their discussions from the dyads (making sure they don't repeat sharing events with the new dyads joining them) and write on newsprint "What have we learned about facilitation?"

Katie will bring copies of the feedback from the same questions from 11/13, and as Katie, Pat, and Cherie move around the room, we can decide whether or not we want to pass out the feedback sheets from that session as a discussion point.

Cherie—can you add or clarify?

Katie

Fri, 27 Feb 1998

Dear Katie and Pat,

I agree the two step structure of reflecting on the study group meetings is what we discussed. I would add to it that the three of us would make a decision about whether to pass out the summary of lessons learned at the November meeting based on what we see in the current lessons learned. My thought is that if the lessons learned seem to be the same as the November summary, then there might be little use in doing so. If, on the other hand, the lessons are significantly and hopefully more specific and deeper, then we might want to hand out the previous one to show folks their growth and maybe even ask then to reflect on what the difference is between their two levels of learning. It doesn't seem to be in the description, but I remember that we wanted folks to bring their reflections in writing so that we could use it as an artifact and so that they would have reflected before the session.

Cherie

Tues, 03 Mar 1998

Dear Cherie and Katie,

The lessons learned, November and subsequent, seem to be good points for evaluation and conversation to determine how folks are changing/evolving with respect to "What is facilitation?" I think we need to begin to examine, reflexively, with the facilitators how the experience is changing them and what the implications of their role as facilitator has for constructing and reconstructing their "self" as lens through which much of this process is being examined, carried out, etc.

Pat

Building community was a priority for the design team. The key goal of the retreat, the initiating event of the SD 2000 project, was to build community. We extended this goal through the structure of the Thursday Night meetings. The Thursday Night meetings were in a comfortable meeting space and included a catered meal. Time for sharing and knowing each member on both personal and professional planes was valued. Laughter and humor was the norm, as each member of the group became more comfortable within the group.

Another key aspect of building community was embedding a common purpose in all that we did: an examination of the role of facilitation in study groups. The excerpts of the e-mail design conversation indicated the importance of connecting the facilitators' current understanding of facilitation, with where they had been in their thinking at the beginning of the project in November. Our design for the learning activity when the group gathered in Grand Rapids at MACUL was to focus the conversation on the issue at hand: "What is facilitation?" The tension for us as design team members was to balance the need for the informal conversation that contributes to those shared experiences that are the very foundation of community with the purposeful dialogue that extends the understanding of the concepts around which the group is organized. We struggled with that need for balance on a regular basis.

Not only did we realize the importance of maintaining a sense of community among the Thursday Night group, but also that we as design team maintain a strong sense of connection across time and space. We were all engaged in busy lives outside of SD 2000, and how to communicate for design during those times between meetings was a challenge. We had decided we would create an electronic distribution list, or list-serve, for the Thursday Night Group. We needed to think about how we were going to regularly communicate as well. An excerpt from the design team meeting of 6/17/97 foreshadows that dilemma:

C: Here's something else that we need to talk a little more about. Communication, dialogue by e-mail. You know that idea of the listserv, cause I really think that's something that at least at the retreat we want to make sure that we can help people think about and be ready for.

P: What about ourselves? We would use e-mail and write that way versus a formal listserv?

C: I think so. If we were both on the other listserv, which we would be, we would still be involved in that dialogue. And then, at least that's worked well for me

K: I also like the way we're doing it, in terms of sending an attachment of a reflective journal. And that way we have that archived in a separate word file. And it's not locked in the body of an e-mail address on a listserv. It's easier for me when it comes as a document that way. So if I have a journal response as part of the conversation, I'll just send it as an attachment.

P: Well, it depends on how you use it. I mean you can just use it for more formal or professional communication. But I think you can also create dialogue there. It's different than reflective journals. Those attachments seem to me to be separate from what I would see as the evolving dialogue we would have. Rather threads of the dialogue. But I wouldn't see that as being the dialogue. That's my observation.

K: I think it's working well for us to communicate with each other the way we are. And then you can also be on the other 2 listservs. The one for facilitators and the one for advisory council. And then still have a webpage for the project as a whole that people can access. I think right now, those ideas that we've talked about seem to be a good starting place. And then I think others will, I'm sure, evolve. But I think that seems manageable at this point in time.

4.3   Functions

The functions of a human activity system bring to the system a level of conscious awareness of structure and order. The functions enable the system to attain the mission and meet the specifications. By design, the SD 2000 design incorporated functions that supported the mission of enhancing understanding of professional development that was inquiry driven through self study. Facilitating was, by nature, a key function of the system. The core mission of self study and inquiry was focused on the nature and role of facilitation while facilitation was one of the functions of the system. SD 2000 engaged members of the system in learning about facilitation while immersed in that function.

A function that supported that immersion in facilitation was dialogue. SD 2000 was an example of a dialogic community. Each learning event for the community represented the opportunity for a stream of meaning to flow through the community, thereby enhancing the collective and individual understanding of all. The initiating retreat held August 17-18/97 was the first opportunity for the second tier participants to be immersed into the core beliefs and values of SD 2000. Dialogue as a function of the grant was introduced during the retreat. An excerpt from the agenda design follows:

Agenda
8/14/97

12:00 Lunch

1:00 Introductions
The activity for introduction will involve having each participant divide their life into quartiles and share a story. They may either share a story from each quartile or share a story from one they choose.

Conversation about dialogue
Pat will facilitate a conversation about dialogue and how dialogue is different from discussion. The goal is to create a safe environment for conversations. It is intended that out of these conversations will come shared meaning and understanding.

Reflections: After each activity, we will reflect on that activity from a facilitation perspective, both from reflection - in - action and a reflection - on - action. What was purpose? What did you experience during that activity? What does a facilitator have to keep in mind during that activity? What are the implications for group dynamics? What concerns might be felt by participants as they engage in the activity? How does a facilitator facilitate self/others/group?

Following the retreat, opportunities for dialogue were woven throughout the Thursday Night Meetings and beyond. The medium for the dialogic exchanges outside of the Thursday Night Meetings was e-mail. The following e-mail exchange represents how we incorporated a sense of community through dialogue:

Fri, 17 Oct 1997

Dear study group:

What a good discussion last night. I'm sorry I missed part of it but I will see the tape. Thanks for everyone's contributions. Let's keep thinking about this idea of facilitation, our roles, and ways to help teachers see possible uses for technology. As I see the limitations of CUSee Me with modems and phone lines, I thought of Edison when he was looking for the right material to use for the incandescent light bulb. He said, "Well, now I know 112 things that don't work." The key was that he kept looking for what would work.

Let's see if we can have a discussion here regarding dialogue and constructivism since we really didn't get a discussion of that topic last night. As I sit here I'm reminded of how difficult it is to pose a question that will get others to really think about an issue. Well, here goes. Also remember that raising additional questions on your part is how we can keep the dialogue going–I think.

How is it or why is it that dialogue might be more conducive to helping staff construct their own understanding of issues in education rather than other forms of staff development in which we have all participated?

Cherie

Following Cherie's posting, Katie entered the electronic conversation:

Fri, 24 Oct 1997

Dear fellow facilitators—

I think Cherie really talked about two issues in her comments related to the question:
How or why is it that dialogue might be more conducive to helping staff construct their own understanding of issues in education rather than other forms of staff development in which we have all participated?

For me, that question really becomes why is it important for us to talk as professionals?

We have all been constructing our own understandings of what are possibilities of communicating through dialogue in our times together. For right now, we have hit some obstacles in terms of hi tech communication, but I think we have all learned, or constructed meaning, about technology and communication in the process. Even though we may not be able to use CUSee Me over modem lines, I think we should continue to explore sites where we may be able to. Pat is directly connected to the Internet at SFA I'm directly connected here at UD, Patty–you are the ace in the hole here–you have the coveted T1 lines. So, I think we move forward with what we have. And I know this is more about problem solving than it is about dialogue, but what we are about is trying to see how we can effectively dialogue with one another across time and space.

So, for me, the first issue is to see how we can dialogue using available technology. The second issue, then, is more closely related to Cherie's question–why is dialogue so important to our professional growth?

I keep going back to our conversation right before dinner last time together–I came away with a richer perspective about facilitation after that conversation/dialogue. What are some of the responsibilities of a facilitator? What differentiates a facilitator from the rest of group membership? How does a facilitator support dialogue in a group conversation? In our group, is each member taking on that responsibility?

Looking forward to future comments.

Katie

One of the members of the Thursday Night Group joined this conversation from her own experience.

Wed, 29 Oct 1997

Hi all.
Yes, I do have the magic T-1 line and it will cost you dearly. Aruba ticket or Mexico during February will do.

Now to the question. Why it is important to talk? So we know where we are in our own heads to get more info and then mull that over and add or delete to what we already know. But this doesn't occur because we are segregated into little rooms and we have a life after school, which requires us to change hats so often.

Our present manner in receiving info is a 3-hour inservice which is usually so structured that little dialogue happens. Even though we as a staff have agreed on a school improvement plan, the inservice doesn't match most of the time. We are still confined into everyone must be on the same page in most districts. Constructing knowledge depends upon your background knowledge and beliefs.

Everyone comes at different stages in that knowledge and belief and we don't always construct at the same rate and stage. Until some construct the knowledge, that dialogue is invaluable.

Pattee

It is evident from this exchange that our intentional design to include dialogue as a function was embracing the members as the design team had hoped. Not all Thursday Night Group facilitators were regular contributors to the electronic dialogue, but at least the opportunity to think and reflect between meetings was available.

4.4   Enabling Systems

Enabling systems give support to the functions of a system. The enabling system of SD 2000 included design communication as described in this chapter, as well as those supportive structures and processes that sustained the initiative. Key to this support was technology, the learning activities designed by the design team, and the third tier study groups providing the context for the second tier group to deepen their understanding of facilitation and inquiry.

The role of technology has been explored throughout this chapter. Suffice it to say, the design team engaged in much of our design conversation through the supportive medium of technology. The Thursday Night Group members also maintained their communication and sense of community through e-mail communication. One of the planned components of SD 2000, the use of CUSee ME, an interactive visual and voice communication system, did not work due to he lack of supporting infrastructure (i.e., high-speed T1 lines). Technology was also the subject of some of the third tier study groups, and was thus the medium for community and communication for the people in those groups.

The design of the learning activities through which the second tier members explored professional development, inquiry, study groups, and facilitation captured much of the conversation among the design team members. The first set of learning activities was encompassed in the initial retreat held on August 17-18, 1997 The guiding principles supporting the design of the retreat activities were explored in an e-mail design conversation prior to the retreat:

Thu, 10 Jul 1997

Hi Cherie and Katie

I'm working through a number of work items for the day and would like to see if we could focus on activities for the retreat set for

August 17-18. A rough draft will be ready for forwarding to you first of next week.

One idea I have is to use a series of mini-case studies on facilitation that are developed from field-notes, video data, and other sources and which reflect situations within the different types of or skills or knowledge or capacities that process facilitators need to develop. . .
.

Another idea which we initially discussed our last time together was an opening activity where we would unpack our conceptual bag so to speak with respect to what everyone believes facilitation to be and how that differs from consultation....This could be accomplished in a small group setting with each group beginning the activity by using a process of first, individually writing their own thoughts about what facilitation is and then sharing this within their small group. We would then debrief within the larger "whole" and share the conversations. This could then be built on by having each group brainstorm the type of skills and knowledge or capacities required for process facilitation, using flipcharts to record these and share out again. This activity could be used to introduce an overview of facilitation and some connections to the Staff Development 2000 responsibilities they will have.

We might want to consider exploring over the course of the two days: a) questioning skills, b) conversation and communication skills, c) groups process and dynamics, d) issues of technology such as "see-you-see-me" as well as electronic mail and how these are integral to the overall project, e) others....Since we have a limited amount of time over the two days, and part of that time should be marked for reflective journaling and/or dialogue, the number of activities will be limited. Minding what Alfred North Whitehead wrote once about process: "the how an actual entity becomes constitutes what the actual entity is; so that the two descriptions of an actual entity are not independent. Its 'being' is constituted by its 'becoming.' This is the 'principle of process.'"

Cherie built on Pat's thoughts in her response of 7/11/97:

Sat, 12 Jul 1997

Dear Pat and Katie,

I'm leaving tomorrow for a workshop, so I'd like to spend a few moments responding to some of your thoughts about the retreat right now.

I think that the quote on process from Whitehead is a good principle to keep in mind and to work from. It is essential that we model the facilitation that we want folks to work toward. For that reason, it is also important that we keep the agenda open enough or flexible enough to allow us to respond to the needs of the group. It is also essential to keep up front the difference between these groups and the ones working to complete a product. . . .

So, anyway, I think the most important things that we can do in the two days we have is to start talking and getting to know the people in the group....The communication skills and questioning are really important and so are group dynamics. These are things I'd like to see explored after we have at least had a chance to be involved in the exploration of some topic and then reflect on some of the group dynamics that occurred and the communication that went on.

Well, I'll keep checking my e-mail. Keep thinking.

Cherie

Katie contributed to the evolving electronic design conversation

Tue, 15 July 1997

Cherie and Pat--

Here are my thoughts on the retreat. I'll stack my thoughts into Pat's message and incorporate Cherie's responses as well.

In general I agree with Cherie that the key goal for the two days is to let people to know one another–begin to develop that sense of community among ourselves. And flexibility of agenda is crucial, but I also think starting with an agenda is a key aspect of facilitation. Actually, this e-mail dialogue might be an interesting case study–the issue of how much a facilitator plans and how directed the activities are might be an interesting place to start.

Like Cherie, I like the idea of exploring the above in the context of our group's process, questioning, etc. in the exploration of some topic. But I think it will have to be a topic with which they are somewhat familiar so the participants are comfortable enough to contribute and then move from the discussion of a topic to a discussion of process.

Katie

The learning activities the design team developed were based on principles of immersion and distancing (Lester & Onore, 1990). Immersion refers to the engagement in some activity, whether it is reading an article, viewing a video, teaching a lesson, or facilitating a group. Distancing refers to the act of stepping back from the activity itself and reflecting on the learning opportunities that the immersion offered. Individuals can be engaged in distancing when they read an article or book that is particularly meaningful to them and then reflect on that in a personal journal. For example, the design team asked the facilitators group to read a short reading. After immersion into the reading, we distanced from our own response to the reading and reflected as individuals and as a community of learners.

Learning activities supported the SD 2000 system throughout the project, and much of our design conversation was devoted to the construction of these activities.

4.5   Contexts

As Jenlink, Kinnucan-Welsch, and Odell (1996) have suggested, "The dynamic and embedded nature of the design within various professional development contexts helps the user-designer to see the emerging relationships, interactions, exchanges between professional development, the educational system, and its environments" (p. 75). The scope of SD 2000 as a professional development activity system touched many contexts beyond the Thursday Night Group. Through those connections, the project has lived beyond the bounded funding cycle.

Many of the second tier study groups continue to meet. The learning opportunities that were the design of this system have sustained beyond the initial system structure and design. The Thursday Night Facilitators have extended their own thinking about professional development and have influenced how professional development is structured in their own contexts. Two projects funded by the Michigan Department of Education have built on the learning and design of SD 2000. The work and design continues.

5.   REFLECTION AND CONCLUSION

Staff Development 2000 was, by design, a professional development system, which supported users of the systems in their growth as facilitators and members of study groups. As the learning community that was SD 2000 evolved over the course of two years, the core beliefs and values of the system were evident through the design conversation as well as the artifacts and processes of the design.

Although the conversations have been captured here as text frozen in time, the reality is that as these conversations are read and pondered, the intertextual possibilities across time and space serve to influence other conversations and other designs. Such is the nature of organic systems.

The landscape of professional development for educators is often barren. It is our hope that the principles of design and the process of design conversation can benefit those who hold the professional development opportunities for so many. Professional development learning communities, as sustainable inquiry-driven educational systems, have the potential to renew the stagnate systems of school and schooling that are so often suffocating to the adults and children within them. Engaging in meaningful and substantive design conversation, holds promise for those who dare to challenge the stagnation.

REFERENCES

Banathy, B.H., 1996. *Designing Social Systems in a Changing World.* Plenum, New York.
Benne, K.D., 1990. *The Task of Post-contemporary Education.* Teachers College Press, New York.
Berger, P.L., and Luckman, T., 1966. *The Social Construction of Reality: A Treatise in the Sociology of Knowledge.* Doubleday, New York.
Bohm, D., 1996. *On Dialogue.* (ed. by L. Nichol). Routledge, New York.
Buber, M., 1965. *Between Man and Man* (R. G. Smith, trans.). Macmillan, New York.
Buber, M., 1970. *I and Thou* (W. Kaufman, trans.). Charles Scribner & Sons, New York.
Burbules, N.C., 1993. *Dialogue in Teaching.* Teacher College Press, New York.
Carr, A.A., 1997. User-design in the creation of human learning systems. *ETR&D,* 45(3): 5-22.
Clandinin, D.J., and Connelly, F.M., 1996. Rhythms in teaching: The narrative study of studying teachers' personal practical knowledge in classrooms. *Teaching and Teacher Education,* 12: 377-387.
Cochran-Smith, M., and Lytle, S.L., 1999. Relationships of knowledge and practice: Teacher learning in communities. In A. Iran-Nejad and P. D. Pearson (eds.), *Review of Research in Education.* Washington, DC: American Educational Research Association, Washington, DC, (v. 24, pp. 249-305.
Cohen, A.P., 1985/1995. *The Symbolic Construction of Community.* Routledge, London.
Craig, C., 1995. Safe places on the professional knowledge landscape: Knowledge communities. In D. J. Clandinin and F. M. Connelly (eds.), *Teachers' Professional Knowledge Landscapes.* Teachers College Press, New York, pp. 137-141.
de Mare, P., Piper, R., and Thompson, S., 1991. *Koinonia: From Hate, Through dialogue, to Culture in the Large Group.* Karnac Books, New York.
de Zeeuw, G., 1993. The actor as a perfect citizen. In F. Stowell, D. West, and J. de Zeeuw (eds.), *Systems science.* Plenum, London, pp. 11-18.
Dewey, J., 1916/1966. *Democracy and Education.* The Free Press, New York.
Ford Slack, P.J., 1995. Reflections on community: Understanding the familiar in the heart of the stranger. In L. Lambert, D. Walker, D.O. Zimmerman, J.E. Cooper, M.D. Lambert, M.E. Gardner, and P.J. Ford-Slack (eds.), *The Constructivist Leader.* Teachers College Press, New York, pp. 159-170.
Friedman, M., 1965. Introduction. In M. Buber, *Between Man and Man* (R. G. Smith, trans.). Macmillan, New York.
Geertz, C., 1973. *The Interpretation of Cultures.* HarperCollins, New York.
Giroux, H.A., and McLaren, P., 1986. Teacher education and the politics of engagement: The case for democratic schooling. *Harvard Educational Review,* 56: 213-238.
Hamilton, P., 1985/1995. Editor's forward. In A.P. Cohen, *The Symbolic Construction of Community.* Routledge, London, pp. 7-9.

Hollingsworth, S., 1994. Sustained conversation: An alternative approach to the study and process of learning to teach. In S. Hollingsworth (ed.), *Teacher Research & Urban Literacy Education: Lessons & Conversations in a Feminist Key.* Teachers College Press, New York, pp.3-16.

Isaacs, W.N., 1993. Dialogue, collective thinking, and organizational learning. *Organizational Dynamics,* 22(2): 24-39.

Isaacs, W.N., 1996. The process and potential of dialogue in social change. *Educational Technology,* 35(1): 20-30.

Isaacs, W.N., 1999. *Dialogue and the Art of Thinking Together: A Pioneering Approach to Communicating in Business and in Life.* Currency, New York.

Jenlink, P.M., (ed.), 1995. *Systemic change: Touchstones for the Future School.* IRI/Skylight Training and Publishing, Inc., Palatine, IL.

Jenlink, P.M. (1996, February). *The power of dialogue in systemic change: Discovering our mental pathways.* Paper presented at the American Educational Communication and Technology National Convention, Indianapolis, Indiana.

Jenlink, P.M., Reigeluth, C.M., Carr, A.A., and Nelson, L.M. (1996). An expedition for change: Facilitating the systemic change process in school districts. *Tech Trends,* 41 (1): 21-30.

Jenlink, P.M., 1997, August. *New Directions in Preparation: Creating and Sustaining Professional Learning Communities.* Paper presented at the 51st Annual Conference of the National Council for Professors if Educational Administration, Vail, CO.

Jenlink, P.M., 2000, July. *Activity Theory and the Design of Educational Systems: Examining the Mediational Importance of conversation.* Paper presented at the ISSS 2000 Conference, Toronto, CA.

Jenlink, P.M., and Carr, A.A., 1996. Conversation as a medium for change in education. *Educational Technology,* 36(1): 31-38.

Jenlink, P.M., Kinnucan-Welsch, K., and Odell, S.J., 1996. Designing professional development learning communities. In D.J. McIntyre and D.M. Byrd (eds.), *Preparing Tomorrow's Teachers: The Field Experience.* Corwin Press, Thousand Oaks, CA, pp. 63-86.

Jenlink, P.J., & Kinnucan-Welsch, K. (1999). Learning ways of caring, learning ways of knowing through communities of professional development. *Journal for a Just and Caring Education,* 5, 367-385.

Jones, C.J., 1984. *Essays in Design.* Wiley, New York.

Kinnucan-Welsch, K., and Jenlink, P.M., 1998. Challenging assumptions about teaching and learning: Three case studies in constructivist pedagogy. *Teaching and Teacher Education,* 14: 413-427.

Kinnucan-Welsch, K., Seery. M.E., Adams, S.M., Bowman, C.L., and Joseph, L.M., 2000. Write(ing)(er's) support group: Stories of facing "publish or perish." *Teacher Education Quarterly.* 27(2): 105-118,

Ladd, J., 1998a. The idea of community, an ethical exploration, Part I: The search for an elusive concept. *The Journal of Value Inquiry,* 32: 5-24.

Ladd, J., 1998b. The idea of community, an ethical exploration, Part II: Community as a system of social and moral relationships. *The Journal of Value Inquiry,* 32: 153-174.

Lambert, L., 1995. Leading the conversation. In L. Lambert, D. Walker, D.O. Zimmerman, J.E. Cooper, M.D. Lambert, M.E. Gardner, and P.J. Ford-Slack (eds.), *The Constructivist Leader.* Teachers College Press, New York, pp. 83-103.

Lambert, L., Walker, D., Zimmerman, D. P., Cooper, J. E., Lambert, M. D., Gardner, M. E., and Ford Slack, P. J. (1995). *The Constructivist Leader.* Teachers College Press, New York.

Lester, N.B., and Onore, C.S., 1990. *Learning Change.* Boynton/Cook, Portsmouth, NH.

Lieberman, A., 1992). The meaning of scholarly activity and the building of community. *Educational Researcher,* 21(6): 5-12.

Noddings, N., 1992. *The Challenge to Care in Schools: An Alternative Approach to Education.* Teachers College Press, New York.

Kathryn Kinnucan-Welsch and Patrick M. Jenlink

Noddings, N., 1993. Caring: A feminist perspective. In K.A. Strike and P. L. Ternasky (eds.), *Ethics for Professionals in Education: Perspectives for Preparation and Practice.* Teachers College Press, New York, pp. 43-53.

Noddings, N., 1994). Foreword. In L.G. Beck (ed.), *Reclaiming educational Administration as a Caring Profession* Teachers College Press, New York, pp. ix-x.

Noddings, N., 1996. On community. *Educational Theory,* **46**: 245-267.

Noddings, N., 1999. Care, justice, and equity. In M. S. Katz, N. Noddings, and K. A. Strike (eds.), *Justice and Caring: The Search for Common Ground in Education.* Teacher College Press, New York, pp. 7-20.

Pourdavood, R.G., and Fleener, M.J., 1997. Impact of a dialogic community on the development of classroom sociocultural norms. *Journal for a Just and Caring Education,* **3**: 399-417.

Sergiovanni, T.J., 1994. Organizations or communities: Changing the metaphor changes the theory. *Educational Administration Quarterly,* **30**: 214-226.

Wilson, S. M., and Berne, J., 1999. Teacher learning and the acquisition of professional knowledge: An examination of research on contemporary professional development. In A. Iran-Nejad and P. D. Pearson (eds.), *Review of Research in Education.* American Educational Research Association, Washington, DC, v. 24, pp. 173-209.

SECTION V

REFLECTIONS ON SEARCHING
TOGETHER FOR THE FUTURE

Chapter 21

DIALOGUE IN SOCIO-CULTURAL EVOLUTION
Past, Present, Future

BELA H. BANATHY*[#] and PATRICK M. JENLINK[#]**
Saybrook Graduate School*, International Systems Institute[#], Stephen F. Austin University**

1. INTRODUCTION

In this closing chapter, first, we briefly review the purpose of this work and highlight the learning experience offered in the chapters of this compendium. Then, we follow the path of the unfolding evolution and explore the function of dialogue conversation in the history of human and societal evolution. This path leads up to the present. Today, we face a critical evolutionary predicament, as well as, the first opportunity in the life journey of *Homo Sapiens Sapiens*, to enter into the evolutionary design space, create evolutionary design communities, and use the power of dialogue in engaging in the deign of our future.

2. A REVIEW OF THE LEARNING JORNEY

Developing this Compendium, we have aimed to serve a two-pronged *purpose*. Our first purpose was to introduce the learner to dialogue conversation as the means of collective communication. The second purpose was to demonstrate–and develop an appreciation for–the empowering and liberating power of dialogue as a means of communication for cultural creativity, social change, and future creation.

In the course of the *learning journey*, we started out by exploring the historical perspectives of dialogue as means of collective conversation. This exploration created a foundational base for a grounded examination of the emergent and developing characteristics of disciplined conversation. In the main body of the text, we explored the philosophical and theoretical perspectives that are sources of methodological ideas and practices of dialogue. We examined different modalities of applications in a variety of settings, and provided examples of dialogue events. We also provided ideas and programs that serve capacity building that enable individuals, groups, and communities to initiate, engage in, and guide the disciplined inquiry of dialogue.

3.   THE ROLE OF DIALOGUE IN CULTURAL EVOLUTION: THE PAST

The evolutionary journey of our species is marked by three crucial events (Banathy, 2000). The first was the **appearance** *of the first humanoid* on the evolutionary scene some seven million years ago. The journey of the biological evolution of our humanoid and Homo ancestors lasted well over six million years, when–some 50 to 40 thousand years ago --the second crucial event, the *human revolution brought* forth *Homo Sapiens Sapiens*, modern man, who started our socio-cultural evolution that has led us up today. We are now entering the third crucial event, the *revolution of conscious evolution,* when, it becomes our opportunity to enter into the evolutionary design space and take responsibility for the design of our future.

We cannot account for the use of conversation during the first six million year of the evolutionary journey of our species. During their journey, their communication practice was limited to sign and body language. It is only when speech became possible by the development of the complexity of our brain and our vocal organs and the emergence of when self-reflective consciousness suddenly emerged that cultural evolution transcended biological evolution and collective communication became a key marker of the "human revolution."

In the evolution of *Homo Sapiens Sapiens* we can identify three Evolutionary Generations. The First Generation we label the *Cro-Magnon,* the second the *first Farmers* of the Agricultural Revolution, and the third the generation of the *scientific/industrial revolution.*

3.1   The Cro-Magnon

The Cro-Magnon emerged from the systemic interaction of self-reflective, sensory magical consciousness, coupled with symbolic speech, with the ability to learn, their aesthetic expression of art, their advanced technology of tool making and habitat building, and their social organization of creating a tribal society. Language ability and self-reflective consciousness were the dominant means that enabled the Cro-Magnon to engage in two kinds of communication activities. The first kind created a shared set of beliefs, values, and a collective world-view. Cro-Magnon tribes sitting around the campfires talked over the events of the day, as well as they passed on stories of the past. As time went on, the richer and longer these stories became. Telling these stories placed more and more pressure on language development as their life-events and social interactions became more and more complex. The refinement of their language skills resulted from the need to build mental models that stood for their construction of their reality, as they collectively perceived it.

The communication method of this first type of conversation was what we call today "consensus building *generative dialogue*." Conversing in an egalitarian social climate they were able to write their own "story" to live by, and generated a shared worldview and rules to serve a shared common good.

The second type of communication focused on a large array of issues and events that became the action agenda of their lives. This communication was in the nature of short-term planning and technology design. Such as: planning for next day hunting expeditions; shelter building; gathering food the next day; the design, the making, and evaluating of tools and hunting instruments; ceremonies for burying their dead; visiting neighboring tribes; trading journeys; and the like. We would call this type of conversation today *strategic dialogue*.

Using symbolic communication, the Cro-Magnon built the first culture of our species, and using generative and strategic dialogue as methods of collective communication, they created the first human society. Next we visit the agricultural village and explore their use of dialogue as their mode of collective communication.

3.2   The First Farmers

We can put the emergence of the agricultural revolution of the Second Generation somewhere around ten to twelve thousand years ago, when the "first farmers" established their agricultural villages. The second generation created its evolutionary systems from the systemic interaction of emotional/mythical consciousness, writing as a new mode of communication, a new agricultural and engineering technology, and new forms of social organizations. The agricultural age of the Second Generation had gone through several stages. The first, the life cycle of the agricultural villages lasted some seven thousand years. During that period of time, our ancestors began to organize their lives so that they were able to exploit food sources through agricultural practices to such extent that they could establish permanent home bases. This led them to full-scale food production in addition to hunting and gathering. This, then, brought to the end the nomadic lifestyle of our ancestors. It was a monumental leap in the evolution of our species.

Life in the agricultural villages was a peaceful egalitarian cooperation. Everyone was working hard for the benefit of the village. For them, there was clearly something that we call today "the common good." These farmers were the first long-range planners and the first collective social designers. They were the first future-oriented humans. The driving force of cultural evolution is *creativity*. The first Farmers were very creative.

They were planning for next year's crop, they were designing and building settlements, they were fashioning ever more effective tools for planting, cultivating, harvesting, storing, and transporting. They planned excursions to visit trading partners. They were designing rituals to ask for the help of the Great (Earth) Mother. They were pleading to her for fertility, for rain, for good-yield of the crop. They established a society, governed by ethical and moral precepts. Life in the agricultural villages was harmonious and well balanced. It was the quantum advancement of symbolic communication in the egalitarian society of the agricultural villages that made the emergence of the Agricultural Revolution possible. The accomplishments of all the tasks I described above depended on the ability of people in the agricultural villages to engage in intentional consensus building dialogue conversation. As was with the Cro-Magnon, the egalitarian society of the first farmers practiced two kinds of consensus building dialogue. Generative Dialogue was the means of establishing a shared worldview, and collective value and belief systems. In all their task-oriented conversations they used Strategic Dialogue, which became the communication mode of choice for all their planning, design, and their technology applications for creating agricultural means and methods and building their habitat.

The first six to seven thousand years of the agricultural period of the village communities was a peaceful period–"a lull before the storm." The storm came at the beginning of the second phase in the life cycle of the Second Generation of HSS. The harmonious life in the agricultural villages was drastically changed when the large cities of the Ancient Agricultural Surplus-based Based Civilizations emerged with their autocratic hierarchical social order. These Civilizations not only relied upon, but also brutally exploited the surplus production of the agricultural villages. Cultural evolution had to wait another two thousand years for the return of dialogue as the means of collective communication.

3.3   Dialogue in the Greek City States

The period of the classical Greeks was the third (brief) phase in the life cycle of the Second Generation. The citizens of the "City States" used dialogue as means of collective decision making. The Agoras of classical Greece were the places of assembly for the citizens of the City States. The Agoras were usually located at the city's central plaza. It was during the sixth to the fourth centuries B.C, during the highlight of the Greek classical period, when democracy was established and flourished in the City State of the Athenians. For their collective decision making, they practiced dialogue in the "public sphere" of the Agora, a place of about 26 acres, declared as an open public space. The Athenian citizens held forty statutory Assemblies a year at the Agora, and held others when need arose. These meetings provided the citizenry the opportunity to take part in deliberations and make collective decisions about issues that affected their lives and the life of their community.

3.4   Dialogue in the Third Generation of HSS

The Third Generation of HSS is defined as the scientific/industrial age in societal evolution. It emerged from the systemic interaction of mental consciousness, coupled with print as a new mode of communication, with the intellectual reign of modern science, with the new organizational arrangement of the nation state, and the introduction of industrial technology. The autocratic ruling class of nation states and the Church were not hospitable to egalitarian dialogic conversation as a mode of collective decision making and governing. In some isolated instances, however, collective dialogue survived.

The most notable use of dialogue as a means of collective decision-making in the American experience was the New England town meetings and the decision making practice of the Religious Society of Friends–the Quakers. Dialogue was practiced in the New England towns from the days of the early settlements as the means of collective decision making and governance. The town meeting was an assembly at which every citizen of the town was entitled to participate. As practiced in New England towns, it applied the theory of pure democracy more effectively than in any other political arrangement. (It is comparable to the decision making process in the Forest Cantons of Switzerland.) But Town Meetings were never established in their full sense outside of New England. Even in New England Town Meetings have survived only in the smallest of communities.

One of the purest examples of consensus building dialogue is the practice of the Quakers. At their monthly, quarterly, and yearly meetings they seek consensus on the issues considered to be important to their community. They don't take votes. After intensive conversation they take a sense of an emerging consensus. In case they cannot arrive at a shared decision, action is postponed.

4.   THE EVOLUTIONARY PREDICAMENT: THE PRESENT

Now, at the beginning of the twenty-first century, we are faced with an evolutionary predicament, marked by the accelerating decay and decomposition of the industrial machine age–The Third Generation of HSS. At the same time, we stand at the threshold of the emergence of the Forth Generation.

4.1   The Life Cycles of Evolutionary Generations

We have learned from a study of the various evolutionary generations of HSS that these generations have their own life cycles. They suddenly emerge and rise, fueled by a creative surge. Then, they attain maturity as they develop and establish themselves in a "standardized state" of habitual orders of customs, laws, and institutions. In time, these characteristics become rigid and inflexible. Change is rejected even in the face of newly emerging realities. Defending and sticking to "what IS," creativity becomes "out-of -order." The loss of creativity means not only stagnation but also the onset of decay and eventual destruction. In a twisted and paradoxical way, creativity is used to reject the creation of novelty and is mobilized to defend the status quo. In the course of our evolutionary journey, we have seen stagnation, decay, destruction in the life of the ancient civilizations, in the Hellenic, and the Byzantine and Roman civilizations, and during the scientific-industrial era.

Toynbee (1947) suggests that civilizations, after they experience maturity and success, are vulnerable to disintegration. It is difficult for them to let go of their ways of life and their institutions that have worked so well in the past. They become inflexible and deny the need to change. They invest much effort to maintain the status quo. Elgin (1993), characterizing the declining state of the industrial era, states that "the scientific-industrial era generated unprecedented social dynamism, moral relativism, intellectual absolutism, nation-state egotism, and technological gigantism" (p. 113). Living in the industrial society people became isolated in vast urban regions and alienated from nature and from others. The sense of community became lost. Life seemed to have little meaning beyond ever more consumption, ever more accumulation of material goods. But the gravest injury and destruction were inflicted on nature by the excesses of runaway technology.

Today we witness large-scale and desperate attempts of many–at all levels of the society–to hang on to the dysfunctional and outdated institutions and the destructive ways and means of the declining Third Generation. Most of us are cursed with *trained incapacities* (Margulis, 1999) to embrace change. It gives us security to stick to old ways of thinking and acting. It is easier to cling to the familiar and to be comforted by the conformities of the past. If it becomes a choice to change or not to change, people find all the reasons and arguments why we should not change. If we are pressed for change, at best we try to "fix" our systems that are grounded in the dying industrial machine age, systems that are totally out-of-sync with new realities.

4.2   The Challenge of Transcending the Present

Standing at the threshold of the Fourth Generation, one of our most important and most difficult initial tasks is *to transcend and leave behind* all manifestations of the machine age thinking of the Third Generation, so that we can engage in the collective creation of new ways of thinking and new consciousness of the Fourth Generation.

Evolutionary forces, operating in the evolutionary design space brought about past transformations. They were not created by the purposeful actions of people in the various generations of HSS. Those generations did not yet have evolutionary consciousness. But today we have attained it and having attained evolutionary consciousness–*it becomes our task, our responsibility, our burden and privilege to chose and create our evolutionary future.* This has again far-reaching implications for conscious evolution. The most salient implication–and greatest challenge our species ever faced–is that *we have to enter into the evolutionary design space and with purposeful creative surge give birth to the life-of the Fourth Generation of HSS.*

5. THE FUTURE ROLE OF DIALOGUE IN CONSCIOUS EVOLUTION

Evolutionary design is a creating activity, which brings forth a potential-driven, intended novel socio-cultural system in the *evolutionary design space.* In this space, alternative design ideas are proposed and tested for their viability and for their *"goodness of fit"* with their environment, which becomes their life-space. Evolutionary design is also a process that carries a stream of shared meaning by a free flow of conversation among members of an evolutionary designing community, who seek to create their own Evolutionary Guidance System (EGS) (*Banathy,* 2000). An EGS guides an evolutionary design community toward its envisioned ideal future system. A combination of generative dialogue and strategic dialogue comprises a comprehensive method of intentional social communication in an evolutionary designing community. (The root meaning of conversation is "to turn to one another.") Members of an evolutionary designing community turn to one another without reserve and in truth and openness, accepting and honoring each other. Before the design community engages in the substantive task of evolutionary design, it involves itself in generative dialogue. This involvement will lead to the creation of a "common ground" as the community focuses on the harmonizing of ideas, values and world views of its members and creates a flow of shared meaning, shared perceptions, a shared world view, in a social milieu of friendship and fellowship. At this point the community is prepared to move on and engage in the strategic dialogue of evolutionary design inquiry.

Recently, the idea of Conscious Evolution has gained wide-ranging acceptance through the works of Banathy (2000), Chaisson (1987), Csanyi (1989), Csikszentmihalyi (1993), (Elgin (1993), Hubbard (1998), Laszlo (1987), ad Salk (1983). We can attain Evolutionary Consciousness as we learn to understand: how evolution itself has evolved, how evolution has worked in the evolutionary design space, what are the necessary conditions of the emergence of a new evolutionary system, what are the rules of evolution, and what systemic organizational arrangements can generate the emergence of a new evolutionary system. The attainment of evolutionary consciousness is one of the prerequisites of engaging in Conscious Evolution. Others include: (1) the acquisition of evolutionary *competence* by *evolutionary learning* (2) the attainment of competence in social *systems design.* (3) the *willingness to engage* in *Conscious Evolution,* and (5) most significantly, the *mastery of consensus-building dialogue..*

How does Evolutionary Design Work? Let us assume that we are working in an evolutionary designing community; be it our family, our neighborhood, a system that we live in and work as a community. We also assume that we have developed evolutionary competence. The first question we ask is: What kind of society do we wish to have? Now we envision that society by creating an ideal image of it. That ideal image becomes a magnet that pulls us and guides us toward our evolutionary future. The second question we ask is: given, that ideal societal image, what system can we design as our evolutionary system that can make a contribution toward creating the envisioned society? We now create an image of our intended evolutionary guidance system. The image we create should define all the key dimensions of the human experience; including the social-action and social-justice dimensions; the moral/ethical dimension; the wellness dimension: including the spiritual, the emotional, the cognitive, and physical/health; the economic; the aesthetic; the learning and human development dimension, the scientific and technological dimensions, the communication dimension, the societal/polity dimension, and the relationship with nature. And there is the integrative dimension, which integrates all the above dimensions and, thus, creates the wholeness of the human experience. These dimensions are built on explicitly stated and collectively defined values and beliefs shared by an evolutionary design community. The dimensions defined become the key markers around which our evolutionary guidance system is created. The mode of communication in developing all the above dimensions is design conversation, an integration of generative and strategic dialogue.

6.   A CLOSING COMMENT

We often say that necessity is the mother of invention. In the life journey of our species there never has been more need for creative invention that it is today, when it becomes our responsibility to enter into the evolutionary design space and create our own future. This necessity has brought forth well-formulated design theories, models, principles, and methods that we can now engage in the service of evolutionary design. This necessity has also brought fourth rich and comprehensive resources produced by dialogue research and scholarship; such as: dialogue approaches, methods and tools; which we can now learn and employ as the means of collective, consensus building evolutionary design. The editors and authors of this Compendium are pleased to offer their contribution to the advancement of the dialogue movement.

REFERENCES

Banathy, B.H., 1996. *Designing Social Systems in a Changing World.* Kluwer Academic/Plenum Publishers, New York.

Banathy, B.H., 2000. *Guided Evolution of Society: A Systems View.* Kluwer Academic/Plenum Publishers, New York.

Banathy, B.H., and Jenlink, P.M. (2003), *Dialogue as a Means of Collective Communication.* Kluwer Academic/Plenum Publishers, New York.

Bohm, D., and Peat, F.D., 1987. *Science, Order, Creativity.* Bantam Books, New York.

Chaisson, E., 1988. *The Life Area.* The Atlantic Monthly Press, New York.

Csanyi, V., 1989. *Evolutionary Systems ad Society.* Duke University Press, Northern Carolina.

Csikszentmihalyi, M., 1993. *The Evolving Self; A Psychology for the Third Millennium.* Harper Perennial, New York.

Elgin, D., 1993. *Awakening Earth.* Crown, New York.

Hubbard, B.M., 1998. *Conscious Evolution: Awakening the Power of Our Social Potential.* New World Library, Novato, CA.

Margulis, L., 1999. *Symbiotic Planet; A New Look at Evolution.* Basic Books, New York.

Martin, D., 1999. *The Spirit of Dialogue.* International Communication for the Renewal on Earth, New York.

Toynbee. A., 1947.. *A Study of History.* Oxford University Press, New York.

Index